For anyone concerned about passing along an inheritance without the long delays and penalizing costs usually involved in settling an estate, *The Living Trust* is an essential reference and guide.

In clear, direct language stripped of legal jargon, Henry W. Abts III, a licensed/registered investment adviser, explains what probate is, why you will want to avoid it, and how to do so with a Living Trust. Based on his experience in creating more than two thousand Living Trusts and the questions most frequently raised in his many seminars, *The Living Trust* provides explanations, illustrations, and detailed answers. The result is a complete course that answers every question in language you can understand:

- Why and how a Living Trust works, with illustrative examples for every size and type of estate

- Provisions to look for in a good Living Trust, with advice to help you screen out attorneys writing worthless documents from those who can create a personalized, ideally designed Living Trust

- Which special provisions to consider in specific circumstances: the Living Will (Right to Die), Durable Power of Attorney, Transfer of Personal Property, Appointment of Guardian, and others

- Plus information about tax-saving provisions like the Insurance Trust, Spousal Gift, Children's Trust, and the Generation-Skipping Trust

Not a "do it yourself" substitute for proper legal advice, *The Living Trust* is designed to provide the information you need in order to work with a qualified attorney in creating a legally proper and specifically designed Living Trust.

"For most people, the available materials on estate planning and probate are frustrating and incomprehensible. Even for the lawyer with interest in this field, the search for reliable information can be tedious and time-consuming. Now, at long last, *The Living Trust* presents in clear, concise, and readable language what every person needs to know. I heartily recommend *The Living Trust* as required reading for every caring husband, wife, parent—all those with an estate to pass along to their heirs."

—Byron Countryman, Esq.
Countryman and McDaniel
Attorneys at Law
Los Angeles

THE
LIVING TRUST

THE LIVING TRUST

The Fail-Proof Way to Pass Along Your Estate to Your Heirs Without Lawyers, Courts, or the Probate System

Henry W. Abts III

CB

CONTEMPORARY
BOOKS

CHICAGO · NEW YORK

Library of Congress Cataloging-in-Publication Data

Abts, Henry W.
   The living trust / Henry W. Abts III.
      p.   cm.
   ISBN 0-8092-4416-0 : $25.00
   1. Living trusts—United States.   I. Title.
KF734.A93   1989
346.7305'9—dc20
[347.30659]   89-33184
                                        CIP

Unless indicated otherwise, all Figures and Tables © 1989 by The Estate Plan.

Published by Contemporary Books, Inc.
180 North Michigan Avenue, Chicago, Illinois 60601
Manufactured in the United States of America
Library of Congress Catalog Card Number: 89-33184
International Standard Book Number: 0-8092-4416-0

Published simultaneously in Canada by Beaverbooks, Ltd.
195 Allstate Parkway, Valleywood Business Park
Markham, Ontario L3R 4T8 Canada

This book is dedicated to my four children:
Henry W. Abts IV,
Christopher Kendall Abts,
Laurel Ashley Abts,
and Jeremy Stephen Preston Abts.
Now you know what Dad does.

Contents

Acknowledgments

This book did not just happen; it took blood, sweat, and tears. Even though the book is the result of almost twenty years of experience and four years of writing, it never would have come to fruition without the dedication of many people. I would like to take this opportunity to thank those special individuals who breathed life into *The Living Trust.*

My sincere appreciation goes to Michael and Martha Desch for their magnificent job of editing. They took my language and converted it to readable form. Their probing questions and attention to detail ensured that the complex subject matter was adequately covered in an easy-to-understand form.

I would also like to thank Karen Schenkenfelder for the outstanding job she did of organizing the text and Kathy Willhoite, managing editor of Contemporary Books, for her patience and diligence in coordinating the project.

My heartfelt gratitude goes to my sons Skip and Chris. Skip (a.k.a. Henry W. Abts IV) was responsible for creating the myriad illustrations as well as entering this book into the computer and then making numerous changes and reorganizations. Chris worked tirelessly and sacrificed much to provide necessary support

and assistance to make this work possible.

Words alone cannot express enough gratitude to Kathi Russell, who spent untold patient hours typing many changes over many months. Thanks also go to her husband, Jim, for his patience while Kathi spent long hours away from home.

I want to thank Peter Fleming, who encouraged me to write this book and kept after me to finish it.

I also thank the thousands of clients, and prospective clients, who have met with me to learn more about the Living Trust. The innumerable questions asked by these interested people, and my opportunity to answer the questions to their satisfaction and in terms they understand, are the basis for this book. These people, through their desire to learn about the many advantages of the Living Trust, have made this book possible.

And last, but definitely not least, my most sincere gratitude belongs to my very special wife and companion, Bonnie Jean, who continually provided the encouragement, strength, and support needed to complete this overwhelming project.

Introduction

Many people ask, "Why should I have a Living Trust?" As you will see, there are several reasons why a Living Trust can be beneficial to your estate planning. A Living Trust eliminates the need for your heirs or surviving spouse to be subjected to the agony and unnecessary cost of probate; a Living Trust provides the entity to ensure that you either pay no estate and inheritance taxes or at least minimize those onerous taxes. In addition, a Living Trust provides a means for your assets to receive full "stepped-up valuation"—a most important tax benefit that provides the major means of avoiding unnecessary taxation of capital gains.

Many people, with honest sincerity, say, "I have a Will, and therefore my estate will not go through probate." Unfortunately, that statement reflects one of the most common misconceptions of people in all walks of life. The words *Will* and *probate* are synonymous, and the cost of probate can be very expensive, even to the smallest estates.

Another common misconception heard all too frequently is that people will avoid probate by having their assets in joint tenancy. You will learn later in this book that having your assets in joint tenancy only *postpones* the agony of probate. Yes, probate is avoided when the first spouse dies, but probate is inevitable—and when the second spouse dies, the *entire* estate must then go through probate.

This book is the result of almost twenty years of experience with the Living Trust and four years of writing. Having met with thousands of clients and prospective clients, I have seen that once they have been introduced to the concept of the Living Trust, they want to learn more about it. My intent, throughout this book, is to communicate to you, in simple and easy-to-understand language, three major topics related to a Living Trust:

- Why you should have a Living Trust
- How a Living Trust works
- How you can distinguish a good Living Trust from a bad one

Understanding the advantages of having a Living Trust and deciding that you (or you and your spouse) desire to get your own Living Trust is not enough. Unless you understand how a Living Trust works, along with the particular advantages it can bestow on your personal financial and estate-planning goals, the Trust cannot work for you to its best advantage.

Even more importantly, once you decide to get your own Living Trust, you must be able to distinguish a good Trust from a bad one. As the popularity of the Living Trust increases, more and more attorneys are offering to draw up Living Trust documents, but few of these attorneys are knowledgeable about Living Trusts. Without the proper knowledge on your part, it is just too easy for you to pay too much money for a poorly drawn Trust—which can often be worse than having no Trust at all. When you finish reading this book, you will not be at the mercy of the legal fraternity; you will know what provisions you should have in your Living Trust, and why.

I am deeply concerned about the increasing proliferation of Living Trusts being thrust on the public today, with a resultant dramatic reduction in the quality of these documents. My intent is not to condemn the legal profession but rather to raise its standards in drawing quality documents that contain the provisions most appropriate for each client's individual circumstances. Although everyone should have a Living Trust today, I would like to think that because of this book a client can now be assured that his or her Living Trust will meet his or her needs and will also be of the highest quality.

After years of assisting thousands of clients in creating Living Trusts and hundreds of clients in settling their estates upon the death of a spouse or parent, I have yet to find a single disadvantage to a properly drawn and funded Living Trust. Furthermore, the advantages of having a Living Trust are limitless.

I also have yet to see a client, having once understood the Trust, complete his or her Trust and then walk away without a feeling of absolute relief—and peace. The Living Trust is the finest gift that one spouse can give the other, or that parents can give their children.

I have never worked with any other document that is as versatile and that allows you to do with your assets whatever your heart most desires. Whether married or single, young or old, owner of a small estate or a large one, every person has the same need for a Living Trust.

To acquaint people with the many advantages of a well-drawn Living Trust, I have presented hundreds of seminars on the Living Trust. The question most commonly asked at the seminars is, "Why doesn't everyone have a Living Trust?" The reason is simple: the people either have not heard of the Living Trust or do not yet fully understand its benefits.

The questions most frequently asked are categorized and answered for you (along with the chapter reference to where the subject is covered in more detail) in Appendix G: "Everything You Always Wanted to Know About the Living Trust—but Were Afraid to Ask."

The intent of this book is to impart a clear understanding of the Living Trust, as well as to make you aware of the importance a Living Trust plays in sound estate planning.

Experience with thousands of clients has shown that, before you can fully understand the advantages that can be yours with a Living Trust, you need to be fully aware of the pitfalls that await your heirs and the adverse tax consequences that can accrue to your estate.

Once you have been made aware of the various consequences of not having a Living Trust, you will be introduced to what a Living Trust is all about. A well-written Trust contains a wealth of provisions that provide you with a means to handle almost every contingency that may arise during your lifetime, as well as to ensure that your heirs receive the maximum amount of your estate.

Each Living Trust should be *individually* tailored to the needs and desires of the person or couple on whose behalf the Trust is created. *You* decide what is best for your particular situation, and you decide who is to get what and when. With a Living Trust, you are in full control of your assets.

Many examples are used throughout the book to illustrate various points in explaining how a Living Trust works for everyone—in all situations. All of the examples in the book are actual situations encountered by my clients. However, even though real-life situations are used, the names in the examples are fictitious to preserve the privacy of the individuals involved.

After many years of estate planning, I believe that I have an important message to share with people everywhere:

Everyone needs a *good* Living Trust.

Having a Living Trust provides a host of benefits. Most notably, because the Living Trust universally eliminates the need for probate and unnecessary estate taxation, it provides peace of mind.

Thus, the answer to sound estate planning and peace of mind for you and your heirs is very simple: a Living Trust (instead of the typical Will) and an organized estate (instead of a guessing game). The Living Trust becomes, in effect, your Will—and it specifically spells out to whom, and when, your assets are to be distributed. Most individuals do not plan to fail; they just fail to plan. Why not start planning now? Establishment of a Living Trust is a key step in planning for the future.

THE
LIVING TRUST

1

The Agony of Probate

When most people die, their estates are settled via the frustrating and agonizing process of probate—a costly legal procedure that usually consumes at least a year or more. However, with proper estate planning, estates *can* be settled in less than an hour at little or no cost!

The question "Why should I have a Living Trust?" can best be answered first by showing you what can happen to your estate—the agony through which your heirs must suffer and the monetary consequences that can befall even the most meager estates—if you do *not* have a Living Trust. Then it will be much easier for you to understand the many tangible advantages that can accrue to your estate if you have a Living Trust. Later chapters will introduce you to several additional advantages a Living Trust can provide for your peace of mind. A well-written Trust will handle many contingencies that may occur during your lifetime. A Living Trust is just that—a Trust that is a living document providing many advantages to you while you are living as well as after you pass away.

THE MOST IMPORTANT ADVANTAGE OF A LIVING TRUST

The single most important reason for having a Living Trust is to *avoid probate*. Some years ago, the American Bar Association (ABA) strongly recommended that every state revise its probate code because these codes had become bureaucratic and abusive. A few states gave only lip service to the ABA's admonishment, and the rest of the states simply rejected outright the association's recommendation.

In the United States today, probate is one of the most agonizing and expensive experiences in which an individual can participate. To name someone as the executor of your Will (which means that the individual will eventually take part in the probate process) is to place an incredibly painful burden upon that individual. I would not wish that experience on my worst enemy.

The single most important reason to have a Living Trust is to avoid the cost and agony of probate.

Upon the death of a spouse or a parent, the surviving spouse and/or children, in effect, have to leave the past and start their lives anew.

1

However, those people enduring the eighteen months to two years of probate remain suspended in the never-never land of their past. Only after the probate process is complete can the survivors really make a fresh start.

In contrast, the estates of clients who have established Living Trusts are settled within less than an hour. Within a week to ten days following the death of a spouse or parent, these people can stop mourning and realize that they can return to an active, productive way of life. Typically, the surviving spouse or children return to our office some four or five months after the estate is settled to reposition their assets (for example, change their stock portfolio from growth stocks to income stocks). By this time, the survivors' lives are usually back in order.

Our clients contrast sharply with people going through probate with their lives on hold—which is part of the agony of probate. Avoiding the probate process is the most important reason why the Living Trust is the best way to hold assets.

THE OLD WAY VS. THE NEW
In days gone by, almost everyone thought it was a good idea to have a Will, but now more and more people are becoming aware of the advantages of having a Living Trust rather than a Will. The following examples illustrate some startling differences between having a Will and having a Living Trust:

Laura Haines left an estate of $130,000 in cash. A year and a half later, the estate was finally settled and funds were released. Settlement of the estate cost $8,500. Howard Murphy, a grown man, broke down in tears over the sheer frustration of administering his father's estate of $600,000. Robert Courtland had to leave medical school while the administrators haggled over his father's estate of $8 million, which included funds for Robert's tuition.

In contrast, Mary Carson's estate of $180,000, Donald Scott's estate of $350,000, and Jim Boswell's estate of $1.4 million were each settled in less than an hour—and cost nothing to settle.

The estates in the second group were no less complex than the estates in the first group. The difference between the sets of examples is that each of the people in the second group had his or her assets in a Living Trust—and each estate was organized.

Most people spend their lifetimes putting assets together, but these people give little thought to how, upon their death, their assets will be transferred to their heirs. People assume that all of their personal assets, personal effects, business assets, insurance, and government benefits will go to their heirs. However, this presumption is not so, according to a study by the Estate Research Institute, an organization well known for its extensive research and professional publications in the area of estate planning. As shown in Figure 1-1, this study indicates that 10 percent to 70 percent of a deceased person's assets will be siphoned off by probate fees, federal estate taxes, state inheritance taxes, and other costs!

Unfortunately, the topic of probate results in more misinformation, myths, and just plain old wives' tales than any other subject I know. In fact, most people do not even have Wills, and most who do have outdated ones.

Everyone should know that the process of settling an estate can be incredibly costly, time-consuming, and frustrating. I have watched grown men cry over the sheer frustration of probate. I have watched stock values deteriorate while the legal process moved forward with laborious and painful slowness. I have watched valuable businesses, built through years of hard work, falter and die in the probate process. I have watched small estates be almost entirely consumed by legal fees. The tragedy is that none of this frustrating process is necessary—with proper estate planning.

The time and expense of preplanning—that is, creating a Living Trust—are minuscule in relation to the results of no planning. For example, having a Living Trust drawn up properly usually costs anywhere from $750 to $1,000, and occasionally as much as $3,500. However, the probate cost of settling an estate even as small as $100,000 for a married couple would typically be $12,000 ($4,000 on the first person to die and $8,000 on the second person to die). These figures assume a probate cost of 8 percent, which is reasonably conservative. The probate cost for larger estates would be proportionately greater. Yet, regardless of the amount of money involved in setting up a Trust, it is *insignificant* in relation to the human trauma of going through the probate process.

By 1974, I had been through enough probate with my own family and clients that I swore I never wanted my wife and children to suffer that same fate. Consequently, our family cre-ated a Living Trust and organized our estate.

The loss of a loved one can be a shattering experience. Why make it even more so by re-quiring the intervention of attorneys and ac-countants (in using the probate process), when none is needed (with a Living Trust)?

Most importantly, a revocable Living Trust

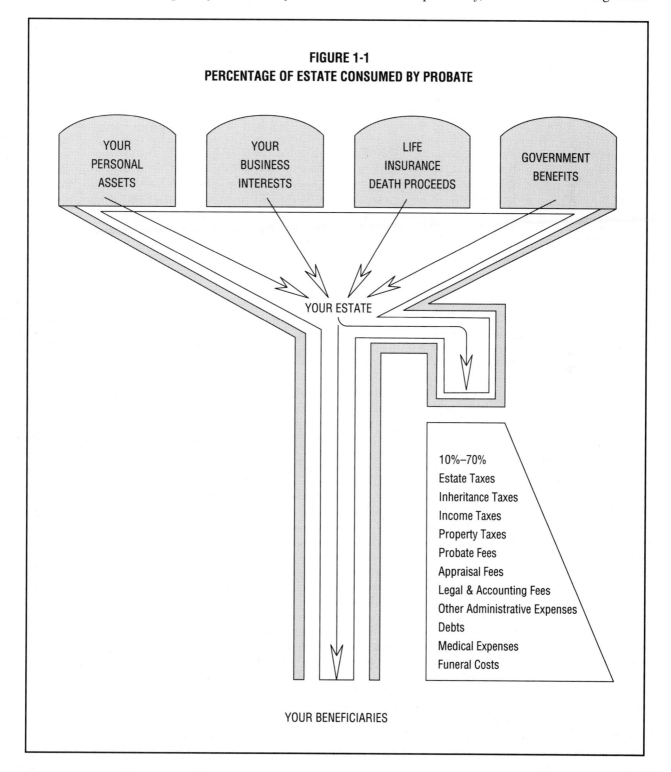

FIGURE 1-1
PERCENTAGE OF ESTATE CONSUMED BY PROBATE

YOUR PERSONAL ASSETS

YOUR BUSINESS INTERESTS

LIFE INSURANCE DEATH PROCEEDS

GOVERNMENT BENEFITS

YOUR ESTATE

10%–70%
Estate Taxes
Inheritance Taxes
Income Taxes
Property Taxes
Probate Fees
Appraisal Fees
Legal & Accounting Fees
Other Administrative Expenses
Debts
Medical Expenses
Funeral Costs

YOUR BENEFICIARIES

eliminates the need to seek legal help, unless the survivor or trustee(s) feels better by doing so. In fact, there is no need to have anyone get involved during this very personal and trying time, except those people whom the deceased would have wanted to be there.

THE PURPOSE OF PROBATE

The purpose of probate is to establish clear title to, or ownership of, an asset. Typically, when people buy homes, they also buy "title insurance," which promises to pay them if their land is lost to an unknown, but rightful claimant. Before issuing such an insurance policy, the title insurance company conducts a title search to assure that there are no other claimants— and that the title can clearly pass to the new owners.

Upon your death, before title to your assets can pass to your heirs, all claimants to those assets must be eliminated. The process of eliminating all claimants is called probate, a process that can be costly, time-consuming, and agonizing.

If you have a Will, your estate does not go directly to your heirs but must pass through probate.

Used as a protective process for creditors, the probate process is an overkill. You may say, "I have no debts." However, whether an estate has any debts or not, each estate goes through the same probate process—to determine whether unknown claims could exist against the estate.

THE PROCESS OF PROBATE

The size of an estate determines whether an estate must be probated. For most states, if real estate holdings exceed $10,000 or if the total estate, including personal effects, exceeds $30,000 to $60,000, the estate will go through probate. Because most people have assets that exceed the minimum limits, few people are spared the probate process.

The tremendously complex probate process is well illustrated by the Estate Research Insti-

tute's chart shown in Figure 1-2. Probate is not only incredibly complex, but it is also psychologically destructive at a time when people are least prepared for the mental stress.

THE HISTORY OF PROBATE

The probate process came to the United States from English law, which is the basis for all constitutional law in this country. Unfortunately, the founding fathers adopted the most complex of the English probate systems. In medieval England, land was probated in the king's courts, called "common law courts." Proceedings were complex, time-consuming, and costly. The system was vastly improved with the establishment of "ecclesiastical courts" to handle personal property simply and expeditiously. "Equity courts" were later established to expedite title transfer of fiduciary property, such as stocks and bank accounts. England eventually modernized its entire probate system.

Instead of adopting England's three-court system (common law, ecclesiastical, and equity courts), the American founding fathers heaped the entire process together into the more complex, time-consuming, and costly common law system and called it the "probate court." Unfortunately, the passage of time has complicated, rather than simplified, the probate process.

Recent efforts to modernize the probate system through adoption of the so-called Uniform Probate Code were conceived as joint projects of the American Bar Association and the National Conference of Commissioners on Uniform State Laws. The project attempted to bring some order to a system that was so archaic and complex that few, if any, of the country's scholars of jurisprudence could find any redeeming value in it at all.

Unfortunately, the Uniform Probate Code ran into such universal opposition that it was either rejected outright or, where adopted by certain states, watered down to such an extent that one legal scholar said, "One wonders whether the original writers of the model code would recognize their own work."

THE COST OF PROBATE

As one legal scholar expressed it so well, "The cost of probate expands to consume the money available." Although said with tongue in cheek,

FIGURE 1-2
ESTATE EXECUTOR'S DUTIES DURING THE PROBATE PROCESS

READS YOUR WILL
Expedites your burial instructions.

Meets members of your family and other interested parties who desire aid and information; confers with your attorney who drew the Will and persons familiar with your financial affairs.

SAFEGUARDS YOUR ASSETS
Takes such immediate protective measures as are desirable prior to appointment as executor.

Looks to insurance and protection of both real and personal property.

Secure knowledge of your going business interests.

Examines all your books and files.

Gives notice of your death to banks, safe deposit companies and others.

PETITIONS THE COURT FOR PROBATE OF YOUR WILL
Obtains proof of heirship; locates witnesses; through attorney for estate, petitions for probate of Will and, from time to time, applies for all necessary court orders in administration of estate; an appointment as executor, files oath of office.

ASSEMBLES AND INVENTORIES ALL OF YOUR ASSETS

Takes proper steps to collect policies of life insurance.
Secures tax waivers and collects all cash.

Inventories and appraises household goods and effects, removing valuables to vault.

Presses all claims for amounts due, locates evidence and witnesses on contested claims.

Arranges proper supervision and management for your going business interests.

Obtains custody of securities. Collects all interest and dividends.

Inspects condition, leases, taxes and mortgages of real estate, and arranges for management.

PROCURES APPRAISAL OF ALL YOUR ASSETS
Gathers complete and satisfactory evidence of the value of all assets at the date of your death.

ADMINISTERS YOUR ESTATE
Governed by the wishes expressed in your Will, the requirements of your estate, and the local probate law.

Gives special study to valuable collections; determines method and time of sale for articles not bequeathed; makes a careful estimate of amount of cash to be raised for payment of taxes, legacies and expenses of administration and of probable net estate for distribution.

Gives exhaustive study to your business interests and determines policy of continuance, liquidation or sale with due regard to expressions in your Will. Carries out or adjust incompleted contracts.

Makes comprehensive review of market conditions for each security to decide which should be sold first, if necessary to meet taxes, expenses, claims and specific bequests.

Investigates all real estate from standpoint of earnings, market, and desirability in case circumstances require its sale.

MAKES ALL YOUR TAX RETURNS
An intricate and involved procedure in which particular forms of information and return must be prepared and filed with each taxing body.

Pays Your Income Taxes

Pays Your Inheritance and Estate Taxes.

Attends to Income Tax for part of year prior to your death.

Files return and pays tax for part of year after your death.

Ascertains and pays inheritance tax in state of residence; obtains waivers for transfer of securities.

Arranges for necessary proceedings to release securities or property located in other states.

Makes careful survey of all possible tax claims to see that no further liability exists upon review by the government.

SETTLES ALL PROPER CLAIMS
Publishes notice to creditors; obtains all available evidence regarding propriety of each claim filed; resists all improper claims; pays out of estate funds all approved and allowed claims.

Files preliminary notice, prepares return and pays both State Inheritance and Federal Estate Tax.

DISTRIBUTES YOUR PROBATE ESTATE
Prepares data for final account showing in detail all receipts and disbursements; notifies interested persons of hearing on account; after settlement of account by court, distributes remaining property of your estate as directed by court.

OBTAINS FINAL DISCHARGE
After final payment and distribution to legatees and devisees, secures final discharge as executor.

TABLE 1-1
PROBATE AND ADMINISTRATIVE COSTS

Gross Estate	Probate and Administrative Expenses
$ 50,000	8.6 %
100,000	8.2
200,000	7.7
300,000	7.4
400,000	7.2
500,000	7.0
600,000	6.8
700,000	6.7
800,000	6.6
900,000	6.5
1,000,000	6.4
1,500,000	6.1
2,000,000	6.0
2,500,000	5.9
5,000,000	5.8
10,000,000	5.7

the remark was also an attempt to encourage the legal profession to reform a system that has become scandalously consumptive.

The most recent nationwide survey of probate and administrative costs was published in 1977 by the Estate Research Institute. Table 1-1 shows the relative consistency of the probate cost—as a *percentage* of the estate. Note that the fees are based on the *gross* estate, before any debts owed by the estate to other parties are deducted.

One of the leading county bar associations surveyed its membership of more than 23,000 attorneys about probate costs. The association, which published the survey results in its own journal, found that the cost of probate ranged from 8 percent to 10 percent of the gross estate.

Components of the Probate Fee
There are two parts to the probate fee: *statutory fees* and *extraordinary fees*. Statutory fees are those fees established by the state legislature and readily referred to when someone asks an attorney about probate costs. Extraordinary fees are those fees charged for additional services—and approved by the probate court. It is common practice for attorneys to charge both statutory and extraordinary fees, and it is

equally common for attorneys to receive approval, without question from the court, for these often outlandish fees. In legal jargon, the combination of these two types of fees is called *reasonable fees.* One scholar of the system reported that, in his fifteen years of active participation with the probate courts, he witnessed the reduction of only *one* extraordinary fee considered to be excessive—and that fee was reduced by only 25 percent!

All too often an attorney will downplay the cost of probate to a client. The attorney will show the client the statutory fees established by the state legislature and imply that these fees are the "maximum" fees. In actual practice, however, these statutory fees tend to serve as the "minimum" fees charged—with the unmentioned extraordinary fees added on to the total probate cost.

In addition, if a person happens to have a Testamentary Trust with a financial institution named as executor, the statutory fees apply both to the financial institution as executor *and* to the attorney who drew the Trust. In other words, the person gets to pay twice!

Basis for Computing Probate Cost
Actual costs of probate run from 8 percent to 10 percent of the *gross* estate before any liabilities (such as mortgage or other debts) are subtracted. This cost of probate is substantiated by two nationwide studies, as well as interviews with numerous estate planners, probate attorneys, and trust officials. As a rule of thumb, many organizations simply use a flat fee of 5 percent of the estate. In calculating probate expenses, however, most authorities consider the 5 percent figure to be too conservative. Whether the probate fee is 5 percent, 8 percent, or 10 percent of the *gross* estate, such a probate cost is excessive.

The value of a gross estate and a net estate can differ significantly. Let me illustrate the difference between the two values.

Some years ago I did an estate analysis for the treasurer of a large corporation. As an executive benefit, the company provided investment opportunities for its key employees. The following example shows this particular individual's estate:

Gross Estate	$ 5,000,000
Less: Loans outstanding	(4,500,000)
Net estate	$ 500,000

The income from the individual's investments would pay off the notes for the loans outstanding in five years—when his "net" estate would be worth $5 million. However, if the individual died before the loans were paid, a 10 percent probate fee would wipe out his entire estate ($5 million × 10 percent = $500,000)!

Unfortunately, during the estate-planning process it was discovered that the individual had a previously unknown serious heart disease. A Living Trust was quickly established to eliminate the necessity of probate—a process that could have left this successful businessman's family destitute.

Enormity of Probate Fees

A California court recently found that $23 million was *not* an excessive probate fee! The heirs challenged the fee as excessive; however, the court ruled that it could find no "intent of malice towards the heirs" and let the probate fee stand. (Even though the estate was $1.4 billion, I still wonder how $23 million of legal expenses can possibly be justified.) Many people would believe the often-heard comment that the cost of probate expands to consume the funds available.

LENGTH OF PROBATE

Probate is time-consuming. Although this complex process usually takes at least one and a half to two years to complete, many cases take as long as three or four years and more. Most people assume that their individual estates are simple and therefore will pass through probate quickly. This assumption is simply false.

Some time ago an attorney and friend who had heard my frequent complaints about the probate system called to illustrate a typical case. The attorney had just left the courtroom where he had settled a widow's very simple estate worth $110,000. The estate consisted entirely of cash instruments such as savings accounts, but settling the estate had taken eigh-

teen months, and the attorney's fee was $8,500—8 percent of the estate.

Remember that, regardless of how simple an estate appears to be, it is almost *impossible* to close an estate through the probate system in less than a year. Even though I occasionally do hear of an estate where probate closed in less than a year, far more often I hear of probates extending well beyond two years.

The main reason probate takes so long is that it is such a complex process. Summarizing the steps shown in Figure 1-3, the process can be broken down into the following sequence:

- Gathering material and filing petition
- Publishing notice to creditors
- Inventorying assets and obtaining appraisals
- Preparing accounting of assets and expenditures and filing petition for distribution and accounting
- Filing closing petition

Figure 1-3 indicates minimum and typical time periods required to accomplish each step in this sequence.

There are two other major reasons for the lengthy probate delays. First, attorneys have a natural inclination to procrastinate—put off until tomorrow what need not be done today. Many a client calls his or her attorney for a probate progress report only to hear that "it's moving along"—knowing full well that the attorney has set the case aside and is not actively working on it.

The second reason for delays in completing the probate process is more common than people would like to believe: the dishonesty of attorneys.

Following a television appearance, a desperate woman called me seeking any means to terminate her father's probate. The woman's father had died six years earlier, leaving her an estate of several million dollars. Sadly, the woman had yet to receive even a penny! The first attorney whom the woman had engaged had charged enormous fees, paid from the estate, but had come nowhere close to settling the estate. The woman replaced the first attor-

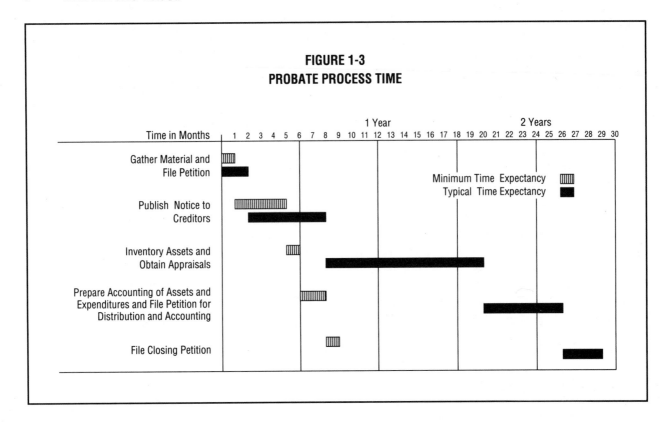

FIGURE 1-3
PROBATE PROCESS TIME

ney with another attorney, who proceeded to sue the first attorney for charging excessive fees. Six years had passed, the estate was no closer to settlement, and the woman was so frustrated with the whole process that she claimed she would gladly give up her inheritance—if only she could just extract herself from the probate process.

In this same vein, at one of my seminars a retired FBI officer told me that he had spent two years as a federal referee, investigating estates that were being exhausted of their assets by attorneys. By the time the investigations were completed, the estates were stripped bare—with nothing left for the heirs. The FBI agent saw the Living Trust as the legal means to prevent estates from being similarly drained in the future.

OTHER PROBLEMS ASSOCIATED WITH PROBATE

Besides being cumbersome and time-consuming, the entire process of probate causes other, related problems for individuals who must endure it.

Probate Cannot Be Stopped Once Begun

Once the probate process has started, there is no turning back. The process churns on with seemingly no end in sight. Similar to a Rube Goldberg invention, probate is a system that has grown topsy-turvy, makes little logical sense, creates work for many in the profession, and drones on without end.

Time and again I have been asked—in that special tone of anguish now so readily recognizable—whether there is any way that an individual can be extracted from the probate process. Can probate be shortened or even terminated? At seminar after seminar, I have asked hundreds of people who have gone through probate whether they would be willing to do so again, and I have always received an adamant "no!"

Probate Causes Discord

The probate process engenders contention among the family members involved in it. The longer the probate period continues, the greater is the stress on the surviving spouse. In addition, as probate drags on relentlessly, the greater is the chance of developing sibling rivalry—often resulting in irreparable wounds to the surviving family members.

Probate Results in Loss of Privacy

Most people religiously guard their right to be free from invasion of their privacy—whether it be protection from someone entering their homes uninvited or from someone looking at their financial documents. How much a person earns or the size of a person's estate is personal information and is considered sacrosanct. Yet, each individual sits on a time bomb set to go off upon his or her death or the death of his or her spouse—because part of the probate process is to make the estate known to the public. Anyone may go down to the local hall of records and review the assets of a deceased person's estate. Examples of typical public notices of probate are shown in Figure 1-4.

The estates of celebrities receive extensive news coverage. For example, the death in 1952 of Dixie Lee Crosby, Bing Crosby's first wife, resulted in the public knowing about the estate. Everyone learned the size of the estate, the debts, and the cash available—as well as the cost to settle the estate. The public also learned that Bing had to sell his interest in the Del Mar race track, as well as his horses, in order to settle the estate and pay all of the resultant costs.

However, Mr. Crosby had learned a valuable lesson from his experience with the probate process: within a few days of Bing's death, his legal firm in Beverly Hills announced that he had a Living Trust and that there would be no further comment. Consequently, no details of his estate have ever been made public. As a result of his Living Trust—which avoided probate—the public will never know the size of Bing Crosby's estate or who received what. Bing had learned how to preserve his privacy.

Probate Must Be Conducted in Every Jurisdiction Where You Own Real Estate

Another area of potential frustration arises from owning real estate in more than one state. If you have property in more than one state or country, recognize that an *independent* probate will be conducted in each state or country on the portion of your estate that is located in that jurisdiction. If probate is costly, complex, and agonizing in your resident state, imagine what it can be like in one or more absentee states or countries!

FIGURE 1-4
PUBLIC NOTICES OF PROBATE

NOTICE OF DEATH OF FRANCES L. HURLEY AND OF PETITION TO ADMINISTER ESTATE Case No. P64967
To all heirs, beneficiaries, creditors and contingent creditors of FRANCES L. HURLEY and persons who may be otherwise interested in the will and/or estate:
A petition has been filed by Cheryl W. Graham in the Superior Court of Ventura County requesting that Cheryl W. Graham be appointed as personal representative(s) to administer the estate of FRANCES L. HURLEY.
The petition requests authority to administer the estate under the Independent Administration of Estates Act with limited authority.
The petition is set for hearing in Dept. No. 42 at 800 S. Victoria Ave., Ventura, CA 93009 on June 6, 1988, at 10:00.
IF YOU OBJECT to the granting of the petition, you should either appear at the hearing and state your objections or file written objections with the court before the hearing. Your appearance may be in person or by your attorney.
IF YOU ARE A CREDITOR or a contingent creditor of the deceased, you must file your claim with the court or present it to the personal representative appointed by the court within four months from the date of first issuance of letters as provided in Section 700 of the Probate Code of California. The time for filing claims will not expire prior to four months from the date of the hearing noticed above.
YOU MAY EXAMINE the file kept by the court. If you are interested in the estate, you may serve upon the executor or administrator, or upon the attorney for the executor or administrator, and file with the court with proof of service, a written request stating that you desire special notice of the filing of an inventory and appraisement of estate assets or of the petitions or accounts mentioned in sections 1200 and 1200.5 of the California Probate Code.
Cheryl W. Graham, Petitioner(s)
IRWIN D. GOLDRING, Esq.
Attorney(s) for Petitioner(s)
1888 Century Park East, #350
Los Angeles, CA 90067
81367
PUBLISH: May 27, 28, June 2, 1988
DVI-376476-0-9

SUPERIOR COURT OF CALIFORNIA, COUNTY OF VENTURA
In re the Estate of JOYCE D. DOBBIN, Deceased,
Case No. P 64394
NOTICE OF SALE OF REAL PRROPERTY
NOTICE IS HEREBY GIVEN that RANDY MILLER DOBBIN, as the personal representative of the estate of JOYCE D. DOBBIN, Deceased, will sell at private sale to the highest and best bidder, under the terms and conditions herein mentioned, and subject to confirmation by the Superior Court, on June 6, 1988, at 10 AM, in Courtroom 42, of the Ventura County Superior Court located at 800 S. Victoria Ave., Ventura, CA 93009, all the right, title, interest and estate of the Estate of Joyce D. Dobbin, deceased, in and to the following described real property: 626 Kendale Lane, Thousand Oaks, California.
The terms and conditions of sale are: cash, in lawful money of the United States of America. Ten percent of the amount bid to accompany the offer and the balance to be paid on confirmation of sale by the court.
Bids or offers are invited for this property and must be in writing and will be received at the office of Pamela M. Hanover, attorney for the personal representative, at 141 Duesenberg Dr., #6, Westlake Village, CA 91362, or may be filed with the clerk of the Superior Court, at any time after first publication of this notice and before making the sale.
For further information and bid forms apply at the office of said attorney for the personal representative.
The first is reserved to reject any and all bids.
DATED: May 19, 1988.
/s/ Randy Miller Dobbin, Personal Representative of the Estate of Joyce D. Dobbin, Deceased
/s/ Pamela M. Hanover, Attorney for Personal Representative
141 Duesenberg Dr., #6
Westlake Village, CA 91362
PUBLISH: May 25, 29, June 1, 1988
DVI-376198-0-6

THE AGONY OF PROBATE

After seeing our audiovisual seminar on the Living Trust, an attorney said, in a manner of criticism, that he objected to the continual use of the phrase *the agony of probate*. In contrast, another attorney who participated in one of our seminars came away so moved by the intense anger expressed by so many people who had gone through probate that he summarized his feelings on paper and asked that he be given the opportunity to continue participating in the seminars. Even though the attorney professionally handled many probate cases, his attendance at the seminar was the first occasion where he had experienced being on the other side and had witnessed the sheer frustration and anger of so many people.

I have seen once-thriving businesses shrivel up and die as they were held in limbo by the probate process. I have watched large stock portfolios disintegrate to the point of being almost worthless. I have seen savings accounts remain locked in at 4 percent interest when the market rate (in 1979) was 16 percent to 20 percent. I have witnessed homes literally being given away in distress sales after standing unattended for two or more years. I have observed liquid assets being drained away by legal fees. Everything stands still—nothing can be sold—as the process of probate drones slowly on toward establishing clear title.

I watched as a widow was required to pay $6,000 for a bond in order to act as executor of her (and her deceased husband's) jewelry business. I watched as a son, a sole heir, almost had apoplexy as the court required him to purchase a bond in order to act as executor of his parents' estate.

Unfortunately, all of the mental trauma associated with probate happens during the worst period of an individual's life—the loss of a beloved companion or parent.

For example, I remember a mother of seven young children who had recently lost her spouse. She not only had to be both mother and father, but she also had to return to college in order to complete her education, so that she could provide for her family. By day's end, the young woman was exhausted, lonely, and very frustrated over the legal paperwork of probate and over delay after frustrating delay. Too often, I found the young mother in tears. As if the loss of the woman's beloved companion were not enough, she continuously had to try to cope with an unreasonable legal system.

THE MYTH OF AVOIDING PROBATE

Even though probate is essentially unavoidable unless a person has a Living Trust, people are constantly relating stories about acquaintances who have avoided probate. However, such purported occurrences are almost always false. Probate *can* be delayed, but the process is inevitable.

Some Estates Avoid Probate

Occasionally, someone will mention that a parent or spouse died and the survivors did not have to go through probate. This circumstance usually means either that the estate was small—under $30,000 to $60,000, depending on the particular state—or that the assets were held in joint tenancy. However, even when the assets are held in joint tenancy, the estate will inevitably go through probate upon the death of the survivor. The next chapter will discuss the pitfalls of trying to use joint tenancy as a way to avoid probate.

Probate Is Not Required—
Until an Asset Is to Be Sold

I am often asked whether there is a "Big Brother" standing over people to ensure that an estate goes through probate. The answer is no. No one *has* to go through probate—as long as the person does not want (or need) to sell an asset.

Many a widow or widower has come into our office to say that she or he has never gone through probate.

A widower once told me that his wife had died seven years earlier, and he had never gone through probate. The man went on to say, "My attorney said that I didn't have to do anything." Then he asked, "Why does my tax bill still arrive with my wife's name on it?" (Obviously, his wife's name is still on the deed.)

All too often, the survivor does not realize that title to the assets still must be transferred into his or her name—until the survivor attempts to sell an asset. He or she will then quickly discover that the sale must remain on hold until completion of the lengthy process of probate—the steps of clearing title, clearing creditors, and transferring the cleared title in the name of the new owner.

MISGUIDED ADVICE

Our clients invariably ask, "Why didn't my attorney tell me about the Living Trust?" I used to believe that the reason was that the attorney would not get his or her probate fee. Attorneys talk among themselves about their "accumulated Wills," much as you and I would speak about retirement plans. The attorneys will comment to each other with pride, "I've got ten drawers of Wills," or "I've got seventeen drawers of Wills," or "I've got twenty-three drawers of Wills." Such Wills are an attorney's "retirement plan"!

However, after having given numerous three-day workshops on the Living Trust to attorneys, I have watched them become ecstatic by the third day, as they recognize the tremendous potential of the Living Trust. Most of the attorneys then admit that they had never been taught about the Living Trust in law school. Unlike the typical legal courses, which include Wills and torts, the Living Trust is included only in the extracurricular courses taught for attorneys who wish to specialize in estate planning. Consequently, even though human greed is a predominant reason why many attorneys do not steer clients away from probate, lack of knowledge or familiarity with the Living Trust can also be a major factor.

Occasionally, a client will turn to his or her certified public accountant (CPA) for confirmation about the advisability of having a Living Trust. Invariably, the CPA will respond that, since the client's estate is under $600,000, the client does not need a Living Trust. However, the CPA is talking about federal estate taxes, *not* about the probate process. Recognize also that a CPA's function is to account for the estate *after* death. In almost twenty years of practice, I have found very few CPAs who either were knowledgeable of or participated in estate planning—which is the function of reducing estate taxes and probate costs in the future. To be fair to the CPAs, however, I acknowledge that estate planning is not a normal function of a CPA.

Please remember this word of advice: if your attorney or CPA tells you that your estate will not have to go through probate or gives you a specific probate cost, ask him or her to put the statement in writing.

THE GOOD NEWS

After reading about some of the many people who suffer so much, you can understand why I refer to the lengthy time delays, mental frustration, and costly process of establishing clear title to assets as "the agony of probate." However, the key message I wish to convey is that:

Probate is unnecessary!

With a Living Trust, upon the death of a spouse or loved one, the process of settling an estate is so simple that it may easily be done by the heirs without the intervention of attorneys or CPAs.

Every experienced estate-planning attorney I have ever met recommends the revocable Living Trust as the solution to avoiding the probate process. The following examples illustrate this point:

- George Turner, in his book *Revocable Trusts*, written for attorneys and published by McGraw-Hill, states, "[T]he most viable alternative presently available is the use of the revocable living trust."
- William Seligman wrote in the *Los Angeles Times*, "In most estates, the only one justification for not having a [living] trust is because the attorney will not get his probate fee."
- Max B. Lewis wrote in the *Reader's Digest*, "The living trust is the finest gift a husband can give his wife."
- One highly experienced estate-planning attorney feels quite strongly that attorneys who draw Wills for clients, and thus subject them to probate, should be sued for malpractice.

With these endorsements of the Living Trust in mind, I can only leave to your imagination the motivations of some of the attorneys I have encountered.

A young attorney practicing in Arizona who had seen our audiovisual seminar on the Living Trust said that the Living Trust did not apply in Arizona, because the state had the Uniform Probate Code. I asked him how much he would charge to probate a $200,000 estate. He said that instead of charging 8 percent to 10 percent of the estate, he would charge an hourly fee, totaling $3,000 to $4,000. I asked him whether he remembered the typical cost of a Living Trust—$750 to $1,000. When the young attorney concurred, I asked him how long it would take in Arizona to probate an estate. The attorney admitted to the typical inclination to procrastinate on settling an estate, and he mentioned a time period of about eighteen months. I asked the attorney whether he recalled the typical time to settle an organized estate in a Living Trust of this size. The attorney admitted that settling an estate in a Living Trust reportedly took about an hour.

However, the young man remained adamant that probate was the best way to handle an estate. I departed, shaking my head—not knowing how to argue with such stubborn logic.

2

Joint Tenancy: A Poor Alternative

All too often, individuals try to avoid probate by holding assets in joint tenancy. However, the use of joint tenancy has serious potential disadvantages:

- *Joint tenancy with children can be dangerous.* If you hold an asset in joint tenancy with one or more of your children, you could *lose* your asset. For example, if your child has an automobile accident that results in a lawsuit, the asset is subject to being lost as the result of a legal judgment, since the asset is a part of the child's estate.

- *Joint tenancy loses "stepped-up valuation."* When property is held in joint tenancy rather than as community property, half of the potential stepped-up valuation is lost. The loss of stepped-up valuation can result in very costly tax consequences.

- *Not all assets are held in joint tenancy.* Most estates fail to have the title to all of the assets in joint tenancy. Items that are not held in joint tenancy must go through probate.

- *Under joint tenancy, the survivor takes all.* When one of the joint tenants dies, the surviving joint tenant then owns the entire asset.

Such a result may conflict with the desires of a person's Will, yet joint tenancy will always take precedence over a Will.

- *Joint tenancy does not eliminate cost.* Although joint tenancy can avoid the time and frustration of probate, it does not avoid legal costs. Most survivors will turn to an attorney to transfer the assets into the name of the survivor—at an exorbitant cost.

- *Joint tenancy does not eliminate probate.* With joint tenancy, probate is inevitable. Even though joint tenancy can avoid probate on the first spouse to die, the entire estate must go through probate upon the death of the survivor.

- *Gifted property forfeits stepped-up valuation.* When an individual gives his or her children a share of a jointly owned asset, the children forfeit the benefit of stepped-up valuation upon the parent's death. The children may also be subject to gift taxes and penalties.

JOINT TENANCY WITH CHILDREN CAN BE DANGEROUS

People should be cautious when they try to avoid probate by sharing ownership with their children as joint tenants. Entering into joint tenancy with your children will not avoid taxes that were originally due, because the practice is so common that this situation is one of the first areas looked at by the Internal Revenue Service. Entering into joint tenancy with children to avoid probate creates an additional set of problems.

- The children's share of the property becomes subject to the children's creditors—including people who win lawsuits and legal judgments against them.
- The children have an equal right to the enjoyment of the property. They may move in or create such untenable conditions that the parents are forced to move out or sell the property.

If one of the children were unable to pay his or her debts or were involved in an accident, for example, and had a lawsuit or judgment rendered against him or her, the parents' assets held in joint tenancy with the child would be subject to the child's creditors. Therefore, the parents could well lose their home (or other assets) in order to satisfy their child's creditors or judgment.

Last year, two clients of my legal associate lost their homes because they decided to go into joint tenancy to avoid probate. In both instances, the clients named their children as joint tenants. In one instance, a child had a serious automobile accident, and the child's interest in the home was considered to be a part of the child's assets. The family home had to be sold in order to satisfy a legal judgment against the child!

When people hold property in joint tenancy with one or more of their children, the children have an *equal* right to the enjoyment of the property.

In one particular incident, the children added on to the home, reportedly to move into the home; however, then the children decided that they would sell the home. Obviously, the mother and father refused, yet the children moved into the house and made life so miserable that the parents eventually had no alternative but to sell their home and move. For their efforts, the disil-

lusioned parents ended up with only their share of ownership interest—one-half of the home—after the sale!

JOINT TENANCY LOSES STEPPED-UP VALUATION

Holding property in joint tenancy—instead of as community property, for example—can be very costly to the survivor from a tax standpoint. Property held in joint tenancy loses *half* of the stepped-up valuation.

Property held in joint tenancy loses half of the stepped-up valuation otherwise available.

Stepped-Up Valuation

The concept of stepped-up valuation is almost totally unknown to most people, but it is one of the most important concepts that should be understood by all people who wish to preserve as much of their estates as possible for their heirs. Stepped-up valuation is one of the key reasons why a well-drawn Living Trust can minimize and, in most cases, eliminate capital gains taxes on the eventual sale of highly appreciated assets (such as the family home).

The term *stepped-up valuation* means that, upon the death of the owner of an asset, the cost basis of the asset (the price at which the asset was originally bought) is automatically "stepped up" to the market value of the asset (the price at which the asset could be sold today).

Stepped-up valuation is a key way in which a Living Trust can minimize or eliminate capital gains taxes upon the sale of assets.

Receiving full stepped-up valuation can have significant tax advantages by shrinking the size of capital gains. On the other hand, not receiving stepped-up valuation can mean that a large capital gain is realized upon the sale of an asset whose market value is much larger than its cost basis. If an asset is jointly owned, for example, by a husband and wife, stepped-up valuation can be realized when one of the spouses dies. Depending on how the couple held title to the property, the amount of stepped-up valuation attributed to the asset can be nothing, can be half the current market value, or can be all of the current market value.

NOT ALL ASSETS ARE HELD IN JOINT TENANCY

Even where clients decide that they are going to use the joint tenancy method to avoid probate, they never quite seem to get all of their assets into joint tenancy. As a result, even the best-intentioned people eventually have to take some of their assets through the frustrating probate process.

UNDER JOINT TENANCY THE SURVIVOR TAKES ALL

Another important aspect of joint tenancy is the concept of "the survivor takes all." This concept may be fine when the joint tenants are husband and wife. However, let's look at the situation where two brothers and their wives decide to pool their resources to buy a mountain cabin. The two families decide to hold title to the cabin in joint tenancy. The effect of this action is that, if one husband and wife die, the surviving couple will take all. However, this division of property certainly was not the real intention of the families. In such situations, it is usually the intention that each couple has the right to pass their share on to their children. Thus, in the case of two couples purchasing a cabin together, it would be most appropriate for them to hold title to the cabin as tenants in common, which allows each individual owner to "will" his or her interest in the property to whomever he or she desires. A Living Trust would accomplish the same thing.

JOINT TENANCY DOES NOT ELIMINATE COST

Joint tenancy does not necessarily avoid the high cost of settling an estate. The cost of probate can often be exorbitant, but so can the cost of transferring title under joint tenancy. *Estate Planning and Taxation Coordinator*, one of the authoritative publications of the estate-planning industry, makes the following observation:

While overall estate administration costs may be reduced through joint ownership, attorneys' fees, fiduciary commissions and other costs relating specifically to jointly owned property may be incurred after a co-owner's death. Such costs could include fees for contesting inclusion of jointly owned property in the deceased co-owner's gross estate, determining death taxes apportioned against jointly owned property and collecting taxes from survivors, costs of securing tax waivers to permit transfer of jointly owned assets to the survivor, fees for reregistering jointly owned property in the sole name of the surviving joint tenant, recording fees, legal fees for establishing rights to joint bank account funds, etc.*

The abbreviation *etc.* at the end of the statement means that the attorney will obtain his or her fee one way or another.

A typical example of the onerous costs that can be charged for relatively simple actions associated with settling an estate was cited in an article that appeared on August 30, 1984, in the *Los Angeles Times*.

In the article, the staff writer stated that she was dumbfounded when she was charged $850 for transferring her deed from joint tenancy into her name (a transaction that should have cost only about $50). The writer said that she did ask about the fee, but was never told what it would be. When the woman filed a complaint against the attorney, the complaint was dismissed on the basis that, since she had engaged an attorney, there need be no limit to his or her "fee for professional services." The attorney need only state that his fee was for "professional services," and therefore the fee must be paid!

JOINT TENANCY DOES NOT ELIMINATE PROBATE

Joint tenancy does not entirely eliminate the process of probate. Even though joint tenancy can avoid probate on the first spouse to die, the entire estate must go through probate upon the death of the survivor.

Estate Planning and Taxation Coordinator (Paragraph 27, 105) (New York: Research Institute of America, 1988). Reprinted with permission.

Joint tenancy avoids probate only on the first spouse to die; upon the death of the survivor, the entire estate must go through probate.

All too often, I hear attorneys say to a married couple, "You don't need a Living Trust; you can avoid probate by putting your assets into joint tenancy." However, I then have to pose the question, "What happens upon the death of the second spouse?" Later, after the death of one of the individuals, I hear these same attorneys say to the surviving spouse, "You don't need a Living Trust, because, since you are single, you now can't have an A-B Trust." What hypocrites! Too many unknowing people are swept up by this "logic," which is actually illogical. What a shame!

Having the entire estate go through probate upon the death of the second spouse is one of the strongest arguments against joint tenancy. At best, joint tenancy simply delays the inevitable probate cost on the second to die. It seems logical that, if probate is eventually certain (when the assets are held in joint tenancy) and if there is a better way to avoid probate entirely—and there definitely *is* a better way—then the time to act is now.

GIFTED PROPERTY FORFEITS STEPPED-UP VALUATION

Another reason for parents not going into joint tenancy with one or more of their children is that they effectively *gift* to them that share of the parents' asset (or assets). When the child receives the parents' share of the asset as a gift, the value of the share is received at the parents' original cost basis (thus losing the tax benefit of stepped-up valuation).

For a brief clarification of this point, let's look at an example that, unfortunately, is fairly typical.

If you owned a home worth $200,000 (with a cost basis of $50,000) and decided to go into joint tenancy with one of your children, the child would end up with *half* a home worth $100,000 and a cost basis of only $25,000. Upon your death, your child would receive a $200,000 house but would retain the original cost basis

(i.e., he or she would have a $200,000 house with a cost basis of only $50,000)—thus forfeiting stepped-up valuation. If the child had, instead, inherited the house after your death, the asset would have received stepped-up valuation, and the child then would have received the house with a new cost basis of $200,000.

In addition, be aware that, if the gift exceeds $600,000 for a single person or $1.2 million for a married couple with an A-B Trust (explained later), a gift tax is imposed on the estate. Any taxes not paid at the date of gift are eventually due, with appropriate penalties.

METHODS OF HOLDING TITLE TO ASSETS

To understand why joint tenancy is a poor alternative to the Living Trust, you need to be familiar with some basic concepts concerning methods of holding title to your assets. There are several common ways of holding title to assets:

- Joint tenancy
- Tenancy in common
- Tenancy by the entirety
- Community property
- Separate property
- Living Trust

Joint tenancy is the most commonly used form of ownership throughout the United States. Until only a few years ago, most people were not even aware that alternative forms of ownership were available. Depending on your individual circumstances, however, the particular form of ownership by which you hold title to your assets can have very different effects on your estate when you die.

Co-Ownership

People who share ownership of an asset may choose joint tenancy, tenancy in common, or tenancy by the entirety. Under the joint tenancy form of ownership, two or more individuals jointly own an asset (such as a house). When one of the joint tenants dies, ownership of the property passes to the surviving joint tenant(s). The property will eventually pass to the last surviving party. Joint tenancy takes precedence over any existing Will or Trust.

Tenancy by the entirety is essentially the same as joint tenancy, except that tenancy by the entirety must involve a husband and wife and may be terminated only by the *joint* action of both owners during their lives, whereas joint tenancy may be terminated by either one of the parties. Tenancy by the entirety is commonly used as a joint form of ownership in separate property states, which will be discussed later.

A third form of co-ownership, tenancy in common, differs in terms of what happens to the property upon the death of an owner. If a tenant in common dies, that person's share of the property passes—through probate—to the heirs of the decedent, who may or may not be the other owners of the property.

Note that, in all of these cases, the share of ownership in the property that is inherited is not a specific physical part of the property. When an asset such as real estate has more than one owner, each person's interest in the property is usually considered to be an undivided interest. "Undivided" means that one owner cannot try to divide up the property and sell "his" or "her" share of it. The property is treated as an indivisible unit. For example, in the situation of the two couples who bought a cabin, the ownership of the property could be recorded in all the owners' names, and the brothers and sisters-in-law would each be part owners of the whole property. Each owner's interest in that property is known as an undivided interest.

From a tax standpoint, the Economic Recovery Tax Act of 1981 specifies that tenancy in common and tenancy by the entirety will be treated in the same manner as joint tenancy in separate property states.

Community Property and Separate Property

Ownership of assets by a married couple may be affected by whether those assets are legally considered community property or separate property. Under the community property form of ownership, all property attained prior to marriage and property that one spouse receives by gift or inheritance during the marriage is separate property. All other property acquired during marriage is community property and is attributed equally—one-half to each spouse. Regardless of whether one or both spouses are wage earners, each is considered to own half of these assets. In states that recognize community property, the community property form of ownership can yield significant tax advantages over joint tenancy, from the viewpoint of settling an estate.

The term *separate property* can easily be confused, because it can mean two entirely different things. In states that do not recognize community property, separate property usually refers to the property of a husband and wife, and all property acquired by a married couple is considered to have one owner (typically the husband, depending on the law of the state).

Transferring your undivided interest in property into your Trust has no effect on the other holders of undivided interests in the property.

The term *separate property* is also used, in community property states and particularly with Living Trusts, to denote property that was acquired by a spouse before marriage or property gifted to or inherited by one spouse. Such property is uniquely specified to be separate property (by using a Separate Property Agreement), and the other spouse has no claim to it.

Living Trust

With a Living Trust, property is owned by the Trust but is under the complete control of the trustees.

Clients who want Living Trusts often ask what they should do when real estate is held by more than one party. Let's return to the example of the two couples who purchased a cabin together. If one of the families had a Living Trust, a deed would be written that would transfer title of the family's one-half "undivided" interest into the name of the Living Trust.

Writing a deed to transfer an undivided interest into a Trust has no practical effect on the other real estate holders. If, for example, the other brother decides not to hold his share of the asset in a Trust, but chooses instead to leave title in joint tenancy with his wife, he may do so. If you place your interest in real estate in the name of your Living Trust, you sever the joint tenancy and create a tenancy in common. Therefore, you have the right to *will* your interest in the property as you desire and, at the same time, avoid probate for your heirs.

The most advantageous form of ownership is to hold assets in the name of your Living Trust and, wherever possible, to hold assets as community property—in order to get maximum stepped-up valuation upon the death of a spouse.

Community Property States vs. Separate Property States

It is easiest to arrange the most advantageous way to hold title to your property (as community property in a revocable Living Trust) if you live in a community property state. Community property states originate from Spanish or French law and provide certain tax advantages—especially the opportunity to attain full stepped-up valuation. There are eight original community property states: Arizona, California, Idaho, Louisiana, Nevada, New Mexico, Texas, and Washington.

Because of the particular tax advantages available to community property states, many state legislatures are in the process of declaring their states to be community property states. The Wisconsin legislature was the first to pass such a statute. All other states are separate property states and assume that the husband holds *sole* title to all property.

An understanding of community property has far greater application than one might think throughout the United States, because many people today move from state to state. Although community property states are few, the United States populace is transient, so people will often move to a community property state, if only for a short period of time. While residing in a community property state, people should take advantage of their right—*with the Living Trust*—to transfer their assets from separate property to quasi community property (effectively community property). Thereafter, those assets will have the community property benefit of stepped-up valuation and will also retain the community property characteristic, even if the individuals owning those assets move back to a separate property state.

If the individuals execute their Living Trusts in a community property state, all of their assets (except those assets specifically identified in the Trust as separate property in Separate Property Agreements) are considered to be community property.

COMMUNITY PROPERTY VS. JOINT TENANCY

Community property is not treated as community property if the characteristic of that property is modified by changing its title to joint tenancy, which takes precedence over the principles governing community property. Although the surviving spouse retains his or her rightful share of community property under state law, the surviving spouse will lose stepped-up valuation under Internal Revenue Service rules.

The tax implications of holding property in joint tenancy versus community property can thus be very different. The following examples illustrate the different tax implications affecting an estate when property is held as community property instead of in joint tenancy. The same tax implications apply to assets held in tenancy in common and tenancy by the entirety.

Let's assume that you are married and own a home that you purchased for $50,000. Let's further assume that it is many years later, and your home is worth $200,000—which is not unusual in many of today's housing markets.

	Husband and Wife	
Market value	$200,000	
Cost basis	50,000	OURS

Home Owned in Joint Tenancy

Let's see what happens under the assumption that you own your home in joint tenancy. If you do, the Internal Revenue Service says (for some unknown reason) it can effectively draw a line straight through the center of your home (for taxation purposes). This ruling means that you do not own a whole home; each spouse owns half a house worth $100,000, and each of you has a cost basis of $25,000 for your half of the house.

	Husband	Wife	
Market value	$100,000	$100,000	HIS HERS
Cost basis	25,000	25,000	

Now, let's illustrate what would happen from a tax standpoint if the husband were the first to die. The husband's cost basis (on only *his* half of the house) would receive stepped-up valuation—simply meaning that his cost basis *becomes market value at date of death.* However, the same is *not* true for the wife's half of the house. The wife would inherit a home worth $200,000 (the current market value); however, she would also inherit her husband's *new* cost basis of $100,000 (whether she wants to or not), while still retaining her original cost basis of $25,000. Therefore, the wife would end up with a total cost basis of $125,000. If the wife were to sell the home, she would realize a taxable gain of $75,000!

	Husband	Wife	Survivor	
Market value	$100,000	$100,000	$200,000	HERS
Cost basis		25,000	(25,000)	
Stepped-up valuation	100,000		(100,000)	HIS
Taxable gain			$ 75,000	

Home Owned as Community Property
In contrast, let's assume that you and your spouse own the same house as community property. With community property, for some unknown reason, the IRS says that it *cannot* draw a line through the center of the house. Therefore, upon the death of one spouse, the entire cost basis (the original cost of $50,000) receives that special tax benefit called stepped-up valuation—meaning that cost basis ($50,000) becomes market value ($200,000) at the date of death. Under these circumstances, the surviving spouse would inherit a home

worth $200,000, as well as the *new* cost basis of $200,000. If the surviving spouse were to sell the home, he or she would have a taxable gain of zero! Realize that nothing has changed, except the manner in which the title to the home is held.

	Husband and Wife	Survivor	
Market value	$200,000	$200,000	
Cost basis	50,000	25,000	OURS
Stepped-up valuation		(200,000)	
Taxable gain		-0-	

Even though the principle of stepped-up valuation has been described with regard to a home, the principle also applies to everything a person owns: stocks, bonds, mutual funds, Ginnie Maes, real estate, trust deeds, interest in a business, and so on.

Being able to receive full stepped-up valuation is almost a necessity when a person owns a privately held business. Typically, the cost basis is close to zero; yet, if the business owner is successful, the privately held business can become quite valuable. In this situation, being able to receive full stepped-up valuation (upon the death of a spouse) can be extremely valuable.

If, for some reason, you decide to share ownership of your business as joint tenants with your children, be aware that your children will receive the business at your *original* cost basis. Your children lose the opportunity of gaining stepped-up valuation (for those assets in which they are joint tenants) upon the death of their parent or parents.

PRESERVING YOUR ESTATE THROUGH STEPPED-UP VALUATION
Interestingly, there have been many cases where individuals whose assets are held in joint tenancy with their spouses have lost their spouses and then have elected to go through the probate process—specifically to *revoke* the joint tenancy and thus have the assets become

community property (which can then receive the benefit of full stepped-up valuation).

Such an example is the case of Marian Trumble, who, many years ago with her husband, bought a small home in the Hollywood hills for $20,000. The husband and wife owned the home in joint tenancy. Many years later, the Trumbles' house was worth $500,000. Since the home was owned in joint tenancy, this situation meant that Mr. and Mrs. Trumble each owned half a house worth $250,000 (and each had a cost basis of $10,000).

	Husband	Wife
Current value of home	$250,000	$250,000
Original cost basis	10,000	10,000

When Mr. Trumble died, the cost basis for his half of the house received stepped-up valuation. However, because the house was held in joint tenancy, Mrs. Trumble's cost basis remained at the original $10,000. Mrs. Trumble inherited her husband's half of the house worth $250,000, along with her husband's *new* cost basis of $250,000; when Mrs. Trumble's original cost basis of $10,000 was added, she had a total cost basis of $260,000 (for a home worth $500,000).

	Husband	Wife	Survivor
Current value of home	$250,000	$250,000	$500,000
Cost basis		10,000	(260,000)
Stepped-up valuation	250,000		
Taxable gain			$240,000

When Mrs. Trumble decided that she needed to sell the family home (in order to have sufficient funds to live on in the future), she had a taxable capital gain of $240,000. Since Mrs. Trumble was over the age of fifty-five, she could use her once-in-a-lifetime exemption of $125,000; however, she would still have a $115,000 taxable gain!

	Survivor
Current value of home	$500,000
Cost basis	(260,000)
Gain	$240,000
Less: Once-in-a-lifetime exemption	(125,000)
Taxable gain	$115,000

In contrast, it would have been to Mrs. Trumble's financial benefit to elect to go through the agonizing and costly probate process in order to *revoke* the joint tenancy with her late husband. After the joint tenancy ownership was severed, Mrs. Trumble would have inherited the home and also would have gained *full* stepped-up valuation—thus inheriting a home with a new cost basis of $500,000. Then, when the family home was sold, the taxable gain would have been zero!

	Survivor
Current value of home	$500,000
Cost basis	(500,000)
Taxable gain	-0-
Tax on gain	-0-

Why, you may then ask, have most people been told to hold their assets in joint tenancy even though, in most cases, this advice is now outdated? The answer is that in the earlier days of our country, holding property in joint tenancy was a good recommendation because then, as now, few people had Wills, and joint tenancy, in effect, created a Will for that piece of property. Joint tenancy takes precedence over all other Wills and legally specifies that the survivor will be the recipient of the entire asset. Now, however, most real estate brokers and stockbrokers will no longer recommend joint tenancy. In 1978, stepped-up valuation was reinstated by the tax code, but it took the legal fraternity at least a year or two to recognize the value of stepped-up valuation. By 1984, most stockbrokers and real estate brokers had been specifically directed *not* to advise clients to place assets in joint tenancy.

When you now buy stocks or real estate, the broker usually asks you, "How would you like to hold title?" Unfortunately, most people today are so conditioned to placing their assets in joint tenancy that they simply respond, "Why, the same way we have always done it—in joint tenancy."

Joint Tenancy—An Example of the Consequences

At this point, let me illustrate another true story. Sometimes it helps to learn from another's sad experience.

Years ago, two clients, a husband and wife, built a home near Malibu, California, in an area called Big Rock, which was situated on a bluff overlooking the ocean. The clients built the house themselves, so their only cost was the materials—which amounted to $20,000. As the years passed, that location overlooking the ocean became more and more valuable, and the home was eventually worth $500,000. The home was held in joint tenancy when the wife died almost eight years ago.

When the wife died, only her half of the house received stepped-up valuation. The husband's cost basis of $10,000 remained the same. Therefore, the husband ended up inheriting a home worth $500,000, but with a cost basis of only $260,000.

After Wife's Death—Joint Tenancy			
	Husband	Wife	Survivor
Market value	$250,000	$250,000	$500,000
Cost basis	10,000	250,000	260,000

Some years later, the bluff overlooking the ocean began to slowly slide toward the ocean. It seems that far too many homes had been built on the mesa, and the irrigation and water flow from all of the homes percolated down into the rock, causing the bluff to begin slipping. With the use of submersible pumps embedded deeply into the bluff, the movement of the mesa has been slowed. However, even though the families are still living in their homes, the houses may *not* be sold!

As a result of the moratorium on the sale of the houses, the value of the client's $500,000 home has dropped to zero. Consequently, the client was able to write off his cost basis in the house as a loss against his taxable income. Unfortunately, because he held the home in joint tenancy, he could write off only $260,000.

If, instead, the clients had held their home as community property, upon the death of the wife, the entire cost basis would have received stepped-up valuation. The husband would have inherited a home worth $500,000 with a corresponding cost basis of $500,000. He could have then taken a tax loss against his income for the full $500,000. What a costly error!

A Living Trust—An Example of the Advantages

Now, let's look at a true-life example where the Living Trust allowed a surviving widow not only to avoid the frustrating probate process, but also to avoid having to pay excessive taxes for capital gains.

In 1976, a woman came to me for help. She told me her husband was dying of cancer. The couple desired to have a Living Trust, so the woman and I went to the hospital where her husband was confined. A Living Trust for the couple was executed, and then all of the couple's assets were transferred into the Trust. The husband died only six weeks after the Trust was created.

Several weeks after the husband's death, I met with the widow in her home; within an hour, the estate of her husband had been settled. There were no estate taxes to pay.

About six months later, the widow went home to Indiana for a visit. While back home, the woman met her former high-school sweetheart. The man was now a widower; before the woman left to return to California, her former beau asked her to marry him. When the woman returned, she called me—all excited—and advised me that she was going to sell her assets, move to Indiana, and start her life anew. I was delighted for her.

However, only two days later, the woman called in tears and told me that her CPA had advised her that she could not sell her rather substantial real estate holdings—because the capital gains tax would be prohibitive. The woman owned two apartment buildings and a home in Los Angeles, as well as a home in a nearby community where she and her deceased husband had planned to retire.

It was obvious to me that the woman's CPA did not understand how a Living Trust had allowed all of the assets to receive full stepped-up valuation at the time of the husband's death. I told the now-distraught woman to have her CPA call me, and that I would "read him chapter and verse." When the CPA called me, I carefully explained the tax consequences of the woman's Living Trust.

Because all of the assets had been transferred into the couple's Living Trust, all of the assets received full stepped-up valuation when the husband died. Therefore *no* capital gain would be realized when the real estate was sold! Shortly thereafter, the woman sold all of her real estate holdings and paid *no* capital gains tax.

JOINT TENANCY VS. SEPARATE PROPERTY

Although the usual means of ownership in the past was for a husband and wife to hold assets in joint tenancy, people living in community property states have a substantial advantage— *if* the assets are held as community property instead of in joint tenancy. However, since most of the states are still separate property states, you also need to be aware of what happens to separate property when a spouse dies.

Between Husband and Wife

You have already seen the tax consequences of owning an asset in joint tenancy. If, in contrast, all of the property were held as separate property in the name of either the husband or the wife, very different tax consequences would occur, depending on which person were the first to die. Assume, for purposes of the following example, that the property is held as separate property in the name of the husband. If the husband were the first to die, his cost basis would receive stepped-up valuation. Since the wife legally had no ownership in the house, the market value and cost basis attributable to the wife would both be zero.

In this situation, the wife would benefit by

receiving a home worth $200,000, along with her husband's new stepped-up cost basis of $200,000. If the wife were to sell the home, she would have a taxable gain of zero (since the $200,000 market value would be offset by the $200,000 cost basis).

	Husband	Wife as Survivor	
Market value	$200,000	$200,000	
Cost basis			
Stepped-up valuation	200,000	(200,000)	
Gain		-0-	

However, let's now see what happens if the wife were to be the first to die. The results are *very* different! If the wife were the first to die, since she legally did not own any of the house (remember, the house is separate property held in her husband's name), the market value of the wife's share would be zero, and her cost basis would also be zero. Therefore, the surviving husband retains the home with a market value of $200,000 and retains the original cost basis of $50,000.

If the surviving husband were to sell the house, he would recognize a taxable gain of $150,000! The husband would receive no stepped-up valuation, since the home was held as separate property in the name of the surviving spouse.

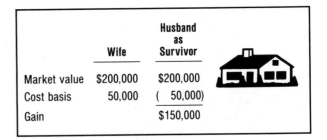

	Wife	Husband as Survivor	
Market value	$200,000	$200,000	
Cost basis	50,000	(50,000)	
Gain		$150,000	

Between Parent and Child

In a manner similar to the previous example of husband and wife, joint tenancy of an asset held by a parent and child deprives the child of stepped-up valuation. From a tax-saving viewpoint, it is much better if the child receives the asset (after your death) as a distribution from your estate.

For example, assume that a parent had purchased a home for $50,000 (the cost basis) and that years later the home is worth $200,000. If the parent decides to avoid probate by gifting one-half interest in the house to a child, the child would receive the parent's cost basis. The parent and child each would own a one-half interest in the house.

	Parent	Child	
Market value	$100,000	$100,000	
Cost basis	25,000	25,000	

Upon the death of the parent, only the parent's half of the home would get the benefit of stepped-up valuation. The child would inherit a home worth $200,000 with the parent's stepped-up valuation of $100,000. The child would retain his or her original gifted cost basis of $25,000, which would yield a new cost basis for the entire house of $125,000. If the child were to decide to sell the home, he or she would realize a taxable gain of $75,000.

	Parent	Child	Child as Survivor	
Market value	$100,000	$100,000	$200,000	
Cost basis		25,000	(25,000)	
Stepped-up valuation	$100,000		(100,000)	
Gain			$ 75,000	

Now, let's review the same situation, but assume that the home is held as separate property instead of in joint tenancy. Instead of gifting one-half interest in the home to the child, the parent retains the entire home as separate property. Upon the death of the parent, the entire cost basis of the home would receive the benefit of stepped-up valuation. The child would inherit a home worth $200,000 and a cost basis of $200,000. If the child were to decide to sell the home, he or she would recognize a taxable gain of zero.

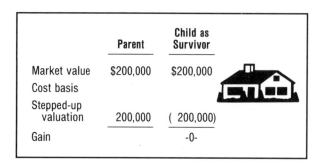

	Parent	Child as Survivor	
Market value	$200,000	$200,000	
Cost basis			
Stepped-up valuation	200,000	(200,000)	
Gain		-0-	

BETTER ALTERNATIVES

This chapter has introduced some very important concepts that help to set the stage for later, by showing you the many advantages of a Living Trust. One of the key contributions to minimizing unnecessary estate taxation is the special tax benefit of stepped-up valuation.

Remember that the concept of stepped-up valuation applies to more than just your home. This principle applies to everything you own: other real estate, stocks, bonds, mutual funds, Ginnie Maes, trust deeds, interest in a business, and so on.

You can see that joint tenancy can avoid probate, in certain instances, on the first to die; however, by holding property in joint tenancy, the owners lose the benefits of stepped-up valuation. Many years of experience have repeatedly proven that joint tenancy can be an incredibly costly means of avoiding probate.

Community property allows for assets to receive full stepped-up valuation but does *not* avoid probate. Separate property, on the other hand, may gain full stepped-up valuation *if* the property is held by the decedent (the person who died), but the asset is subject to probate. However, if an asset were not held by the decedent, then there would be *no* tax benefit because of stepped-up valuation.

In contrast, a Living Trust with the assets held in community property, or as separate property when single, is the best of both worlds, because a Living Trust avoids probate, and community property (or separate property where appropriate) gains full stepped-up valuation. Putting your assets in the name of a Living Trust is so much simpler, affords greater security, and provides a much better solution to proper estate planning.

3

Estate and Inheritance Taxes

People assume that their estates will pass, intact, to their heirs—but such an occurrence seldom happens. Upon your death, estate and inheritance taxes can destroy your estate, which you have worked so diligently all your life to create. Few people are aware of these two most unpleasant taxes, which can, in effect, take away almost *half* of some estates. Typically, the last person to learn about these taxes is the surviving spouse (or children), who is ill prepared to handle the tax aspects of settling an estate. As you will see as you progress through this book, however, payment of unnecessary estate taxes—an area that is so important to preserving your estate—can be reduced or eliminated altogether with a Living Trust.

The difference between federal estate tax and state inheritance tax is often misunderstood (and many people erroneously use the terms interchangeably). Estate tax is a federal tax levied upon an estate when the owner dies. In effect, when a person begins life, Uncle Sam says that he joins with that person in business; when the person dies, Uncle Sam wants out with his share of that person's estate—right away. If there is a tax to pay, the accounting must be completed within six months after the date of death, and any payment due must be made within three months thereafter.

Inheritance tax is a state tax upon the right to inherit. Typically, each state imposes an inheritance tax on any property located within that state. This tax is not paid by the heirs, but is instead paid by the estate *before* any assets are distributed to the heirs.

Until recently, estate and inheritance taxes were largely confiscatory and often took from the surviving spouse the very funds that were necessary for survival. One typical example of confiscatory taxes, repeated over and over again through many decades, will show you just how bad the tax situation had become (until the Economic Recovery Tax Act of 1981).

A retired couple, who had been farmers in Iowa, owned a 600-acre farm, part of which the husband and wife had purchased for a small sum in 1929, with the balance being inherited. Too old to work the farm, the couple leased it out to others. The couple's annual income was around $17,000—from the farm lease, a small pension, and social security benefits. The re-

25

tired pair considered themselves poor, and both were in ill health.

Unfortunately for them, since they weren't interested in selling their farm—they just wanted to survive—the value of their land had dramatically increased since they had acquired it. Farmland was now worth $1,000 per acre, and their 600 acres were therefore worth $600,000. The couple knew that when one of them died, the survivor would face estate taxes on half of the estate ($300,000).

Let's assume that the federal estate taxes and state inheritance taxes would be $80,000. How is the survivor supposed to pay $80,000 in taxes when the only asset in the estate is the farmland? Unfortunately, the farmer could not just sell the back forty acres. In this case, as was true of so many farmers, it would be necessary to sell the *entire* farm in order to pay the estate taxes when the husband or wife died. Thus, the survivor would lose his or her home of a lifetime, friends, and surroundings—and must find a new way of survival. Sadly, this story was being repeated daily.

THE ECONOMIC RECOVERY TAX ACT OF 1981

It has been my experience that Americans have not changed that much from their predecessors—who, when eventually pressed too far by the crown's taxes, dumped the tea in Boston Harbor. Similarly, when the estate tax ultimately became too overwhelmingly confiscatory, the ire of the American public was stirred up, and Congress was forced to react. (Unfortunately, Congress seldom acts; it only reacts.)

In 1981, Americans finally received long-overdue estate tax reforms—with the Economic Recovery Tax Act of 1981. The most significant estate tax reforms in the 1981 tax code were the *Maximum Marital Deduction*, a larger and more meaningful *Unified Credit*, and a ceiling on the *maximum federal estate tax rate.*

Unlimited Marital Deduction

The Unlimited Marital Deduction (sometimes called the Maximum Marital Deduction) enables a spouse to pass his or her entire estate to the other spouse free of any gift or estate taxes. Thus, the surviving spouse would no longer be required to liquidate hard-earned lifetime assets in order to pay the estate taxes due. Many states soon followed with similar legislation for state inheritance tax.

Some caution is advised, however, because the Unlimited Marital Deduction, even though a great benefit to the surviving spouse, can be a very deceptive benefit. By using the Unlimited Marital Deduction, people end up losing one of their federal estate tax equivalent exemptions. (The federal estate tax equivalent exemption will be explained and illustrated later in the book.)

Unfortunately, congressional legislation is often affectionately referred to by some people as the "Attorneys' Retirement Act," which means that, although Congress may pass legislation for the people's benefit, the advantage is lost unless the people seek the services of legal counsel to incorporate these benefits into their particular financial plan. The Unlimited Marital Deduction is an excellent example of this principle. Although Congress has given the American people a major benefit, unless the people incorporate it into their Wills or estate planning, the benefit will be lost (that is, it will go unused). Enacting this new benefit provision also meant, however, that all previously written Wills and estate plans needed to be modified in order to incorporate this new legislation—or its benefit would go unused.

One notable estate-planning attorney recently stated that, if a Will was written before 1981 and has not been appropriately updated since then, the Will is basically *worthless* as an estate-planning vehicle. Consequently, if you are married and have an out-of-date Will, your estate may be subject to federal estate taxes upon the death of the first spouse.

Unified Credit

The Unified Credit tax reform effectively exempts certain-sized estates from federal estate tax. The Unified Credit is a dollar-for-dollar credit against federal estate taxes; the credit is $192,800, which is the amount of estate tax that would be owed on an estate valued at $600,000.

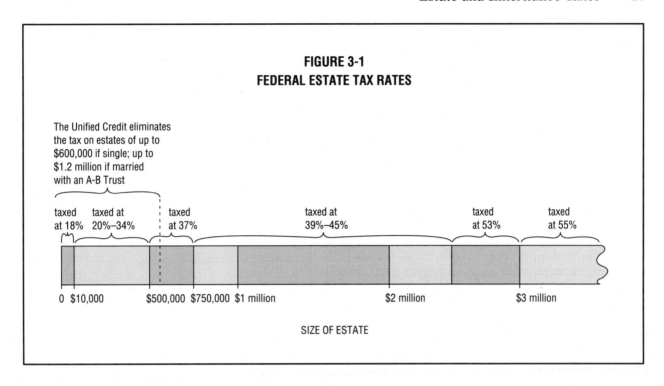

FIGURE 3-1
FEDERAL ESTATE TAX RATES

The Unified Credit eliminates the tax on estates of up to $600,000 if single; up to $1.2 million if married with an A-B Trust

taxed at 18%   taxed at 20%–34%   taxed at 37%   taxed at 39%–45%   taxed at 53%   taxed at 55%

0   $10,000 $500,000 $750,000 $1 million $2 million $3 million

SIZE OF ESTATE

Every person receives a Unified Credit of $192,800, which is the amount of estate tax that would be due on a $600,000 estate; this is also known as the federal estate tax equivalent exemption.

Many people think of federal estate taxes as beginning when the federal estate tax equivalent exemption is exceeded. However, Congress has not been so benevolent. The federal estate taxes actually begin with the first dollar, rise to 37 percent for estates valued at $600,000, and then culminate at 55 percent for estates valued at $3 million or more, as shown in Figure 3-1.

The best way to understand the concept of the Unified Credit is to look at a $600,000 estate and a $601,000 estate.

Net value of estate	$ 600,000	$ 601,000
Federal estate tax	192,800	193,170
Less: Unified credit	(192,800)	(192,800)
Tax due	-0-	$ 370
		(37% of $1,000)

Thanks to the Unified Credit, a $600,000 estate is exempt from federal estate taxes, but each dollar over $600,000 is taxed *beginning* at 37 percent. Each person has this Unified Credit of $192,800, which is more commonly referred to as a "federal estate tax equivalent exemption" of $600,000. For a married couple, each spouse has an equivalent exemption of $600,000; therefore, the total exemption for a married couple is $1.2 million. Unfortunately, however, most people lose this dual exemption because of poor estate planning (or a total lack thereof). Congress gave people a boon, but unless people recognize it and act properly, they lose it. (There's that "Attorneys' Retirement Act" again.)

The total exemption for a married couple is $1.2 million, but most people lose some of this benefit to poor estate planning.

Maximum Federal Estate Taxes
The federal estate tax graduates upward as an estate increases in size. The 1981 tax code gradually reduced the *maximum* tax from 70 per-

cent to today's 55 percent. The maximum tax level is scheduled to be reduced to 50 percent on January 1, 1992. However, if Congress follows its usual pattern, people can comfortably assume that the maximum estate and gift tax bracket will remain at 55 percent.

Few, if any, estate planners, who understand the history of the nation's confiscatory estate taxes and how Congress was eventually forced to react, can foresee Congress returning to its former position of imposing such a confiscatory tax. The pendulum of change swings back and forth. Therefore, when inflation so erodes the present federal estate tax equivalent exemption to where the estate tax is again confiscatory, the pendulum will swing back, and Congress will again be forced to react. Until then, I foresee little change from the present.

Many people tend to look at the federal estate tax equivalent exemption of $600,000 and do nothing, because they think that their $300,000 estate will never exceed the exemption limit. However, you are advised *not* to be complacent! Since Congress reacts rather than acts, it may be many years before these equivalent exemptions are again raised. In the meantime, inflation will reduce the real benefit of the equivalent exemption by making its worth less relative to the size of a person's estate.

For example, inflation can double, triple, and quadruple an estate fairly quickly, as shown in Table 3-1. With an inflation rate of 7 percent per year, a $300,000 estate would be worth $600,000 in just ten years and would increase to a value of $1.2 million in twenty years. The tax bite from such an estate would be painful.

A "do-nothing" approach can be very costly to your heirs. Inflation causes estates to increase in value over the years. Therefore, you should do some realistic estate planning now.

STATE INHERITANCE TAX REFORMS

The state inheritance tax has also been confiscatory in many states, but, as in the federal government, state tax reform has also been going on in many states. California is an excellent example of state tax reform. Following on the heels of California's now-famous Proposition 13 property tax reform, the voters adopted Proposition A, a significant inheritance tax reform measure.

TABLE 3-1
EFFECTS OF INFLATION ON AN ESTATE'S VALUE

Inflation Rate	Years to Double	Years to Quadruple
5%	14	28
6	12	24
7	10	20
8	9	18
9	8	16
10	7	14
11	6½	13
12	6	12

Prior to the adoption of Proposition A, the state inheritance tax on a $300,000 estate could be as high as $80,000. Unlike income taxes, federal laws disregarded the actual state inheritance tax paid and permitted only a nominal deduction against the estate for the state inheritance taxes that were paid. The allowable federal deduction was taken from a table titled "Maximum Credit for State Death Taxes."

Enacting California's Proposition A created two major reforms relating to the way the state handled inheritance taxes:

1. No state inheritance tax is due unless a federal estate tax is due.
2. If federal estate tax is due, the state inheritance tax will be the same as that allowed under the maximum credit for state death taxes (that is, the state tax will not be greater than the deduction allowed by the IRS).

With proper estate planning, no estate or inheritance taxes need be due when the first spouse dies.

Many states have followed California's lead and have enacted similar tax-reform measures.

The key to state inheritance tax reform is that, with proper estate planning (such as with an appropriate Living Trust), no federal estate taxes and, in many states, no inheritance taxes will be due when the first spouse dies. In addition, for the majority of estates, no federal estate or state inheritance taxes will be due when the second spouse dies—meaning that no "death taxes" need be paid.

MINIMIZING TAXES WITH PROPER ESTATE PLANNING

Few people are really aware of how proper estate planning can minimize the bite that federal estate taxes and state inheritance taxes take from their estates. Everyone should be reasonably knowledgeable of the federal estate tax and state inheritance tax; people need to know how to minimize these taxes and, where appropriate, how to eliminate these taxes altogether. In addition, people should be aware of when their estates will be subject to estate and inheritance taxes and how much of their estates will be affected. Estate planning should then provide an appropriate means of having the needed liquidity to pay those taxes without selling major assets. Each of these important issues will be addressed in subsequent chapters of this book.

4

The Living Trust vs. Other Forms of Wills

Unfortunately, the word *Will* is synonymous with the process of probate. In my experience, over 50 percent of the people who have Wills fervently believe that, because they have Wills, they will avoid probate. Not so! The good news, however, is that the Living Trust is an exception; it provides an alternative to the shortcomings of a Will.

The history of Wills is fraught with abuse. Thus, the laws pertaining to Wills are extremely rigid and vary widely from state to state. In fact, a person who moves to another state should have his or her Will reviewed for compliance with the new state's law and, in many cases, rewritten to bring it into conformance.

In early times, Wills were typically deathbed statements to the priest. Coincidentally, the church seemed to be receiving an inordinate amount of the estates. Eventually, two witnesses were required to be present for the deathbed statement. With the passage of time and further apparent abuse, it became customary for an individual to place in writing his or her last Will and testament, which was then witnessed by two or three people.

Even today, with all of the legal requirements necessary to adequately satisfy a Will, at least one-third of all written Wills are successfully contested by heirs. Why? After a person writes a Will, he or she typically places it in a safe-deposit box—seldom to be looked at again. As time passes, events occur in the person's life that "might" have caused the Will to be written differently. Thus, the contention is that, if the author of the Will could somehow be brought back to life in order to review the events that have taken place since the Will was written, he or she would change the contents of the Will.

At least one-third of all written Wills are successfully contested by heirs.

Each person who does write a Will typically changes it about four times during his or her lifetime. A change to a Will is called a "codicil"; however, instead of writing a codicil, most attorneys find it easier to write an entirely *new* Will. This practice is not only more costly to the individual, but it is also more profitable to the attorney.

INHERITANCE WITHOUT A WILL

Unfortunately, most people do not have written Wills, and, for those people who do have Wills, their Wills are usually neither current nor appropriate for their present estates. The results can be particularly tragic in second marriages following the death of a spouse.

Far too many people today have no written Will. However, never fear. The state has one for you—only far more complex and not necessarily written according to your desires.

Separate Property States

In separate property states, if two people are married and have children (and have no written Will), the results could be disastrous. If a married couple has one child, the surviving spouse typically will receive half the estate, and the child will receive the other half. If the married couple has two or more children, however, the surviving spouse could receive substantially less. Unfortunately, the surviving spouse's share usually is entirely inadequate for his or her future security and well-being.

If the children are minors (younger than age eighteen), the court must create a Trust to handle the children's portion of the estate, and the surviving spouse is subject to court supervision in order to use the children's funds. Once the child attains legal age (eighteen years old), his or her share is distributed outright (handed over in one lump sum), *regardless* of the child's experience or judgment. The child's age, needs, and degree of competency are ignored by the court.

If you don't have a written Will, the state has one for you—but it might not be the one you want.

Community Property States

In community property states, if a married couple have children and leave no written Will, the community property will pass entirely to the surviving spouse. However, separate property will be treated as indicated above for separate property states.

INHERITANCE WITH A WILL

With a properly written Will, *you* make the decisions. You decide not only who gets what, but when the heirs will get their allocations. You control what happens to the assets in your estate.

The following sections will acquaint you with the four types of written Wills:

• Holographic Will
• Loving (or Attested) Will
• Testamentary Trust
• Living Trust

Holographic Will

A Holographic Will is a handwritten Will that is signed and dated by the person writing it. This type of Will is *not* witnessed by anyone else.

Until recently, a Holographic Will had to be on *plain* paper with no other printing. There is an actual case of an unbalanced individual who rented a hotel room, sat down at the desk in his hotel room, and wrote out his Will on hotel stationery. After completing his Will, the individual then jumped out the window. The Will was successfully contested, because it was written on hotel stationery with the hotel name and address at the top of the page.

Many states have since eliminated the restriction about a Holographic Will needing to be on plain paper. However, if you decide to write a Holographic Will, you should still use plain paper until you are sure of the requirements in your own state.

In a few specific situations, I have recommended Holographic Wills as a temporary expedient to young people who have minimal estates and who are just getting started with their careers and building their estates. I have also suggested this form of Will to young newlyweds. Yet, in every case, I have ardently admonished the young people to do formal estate planning with a Living Trust when they decide to start their families—regardless of the size of their estates.

Loving Will

A Loving Will (also known as an Attested Will) is the typical Will drawn up by an attorney and attested (that is, witnessed). I refer to this Will as a "Loving Will" because it usually leaves everything to the surviving spouse or children.

Testamentary Trust

The Testamentary Trust is a step in the right direction—but only a half step, because "testamentary" means that a person must *die* before the Trust goes into effect. Since the Trust is not in effect during a person's lifetime, none of his or her assets are in the Trust. Therefore, this situation means that, upon your death, your assets must go through probate *before* they can be placed in the Trust.

The Testamentary Trust is the best of both worlds for the attorney, who collects a substantial fee for drawing up the Trust now and a probate fee later.

Even though the Testamentary Trust does not avoid probate, it *will* avoid unnecessary estate taxes on the death of the second spouse. Unfortunately, I have yet to find a Testamentary Trust for an estate in excess of $1 million that contains the C Trust. The C Trust, also known as the Q-Tip Trust, is a legal device created by Congress in 1981 to permit avoidance of estate taxes on the estate of the first spouse to die. (A more detailed explanation of the Q-Tip Trust is presented in Chapter 5.)

The Testamentary Trust also suffers from the same potential challenge as a Will, since the Testamentary Trust, like a Will, is usually drawn up, placed in a safe-deposit box, and seldom reviewed again. Events that inevitably occur during a person's life after drawing a Testamentary Trust will permit the person's heirs to successfully contest his or her Trust for the same reason that the heirs are so frequently able to contest a Will.

The best solution is the Living Trust.

The Testamentary Trust is, in effect, the best of all worlds for members of the legal profession. The attorney not only receives a substantial fee for drawing up the Testamentary Trust

but also will eventually have the opportunity to collect the probate fee.

Living Trust

The knowledgeable family or individual will choose the Living Trust as the best solution to holding assets. Besides the benefits you have read about so far, the Living Trust is, as you will learn in the next chapter, an excellent way to provide for the support and education of minor children. In addition, unlike other forms of written estate plans, a properly funded Living Trust is basically unchallengeable, because the Trust is "living" (that is, in existence) today and includes *all* of a person's assets. Unlike the Will, which has been badly abused, the Living Trust may be easily changed at any time by simply striking out or adding a section and initialing it.

It is a good idea to always keep an executed copy of your Living Trust at home, where you can make changes to the Trust whenever desired or whenever special circumstances dictate.

If a person makes any changes, it is strongly recommended that he or she have legal counsel eventually formalize them as an amendment (to ensure that a change is consistent throughout the document). However, such a simple change, without the formality of a legal amendment, *will* stand up in court. Since a person can easily and readily change his or her Living Trust document right up to the hour of death, the document is basically unchallengeable.

NO GREATER GIFT

I know of no greater gift one spouse can give the other, or parents can give their children, than a Living Trust. You need to go through probate only once to appreciate this statement.

The Living Trust has dramatic economic advantages over the Loving Will. To fully appreciate how a Living Trust can have a *significant* influence on preserving most, or all, of your estate for your heirs, you need to compare the economic differences between a Living Trust and a Loving Will.

The single most important reason for having a Living Trust is to avoid the cost and agony of probate. Attorneys and accountants often advise a client that he or she does not need a

Living Trust if the person's estate is less than $600,000. However, the professionals are confusing the federal estate tax equivalent exemption with the probate process, which is entirely separate. Most states require probate for an estate with real estate holdings that exceed $10,000 *or* total net assets, including personal effects, that exceed $30,000 to $60,000.

A second important reason for having a Living Trust is to avoid paying unnecessary estate taxes. Even though an estate of less than $600,000 is not subject to the tax, few people seem to realize that an estate of only $300,000 will typically *double* in value in the next ten to twelve years, by inflation alone. In the past six months, I have reviewed numerous estates that were worth only $200,000 to $300,000 six to seven years ago when the first spouse died. Today, these estates exceed $600,000. Such an estate can avoid estate taxation if it is in a form of Living Trust called an A-B Trust. However, an A-B Trust can be created only while both spouses are living.

The different types of Living Trust will be more fully explained in a later chapter. However, for now you need only know that there are three forms of a Living Trust, which will be referred to throughout this chapter: A Trust, A-B Trust, and A-B-C Trust. The only other bit of knowledge you need at this point is to understand that a Trust is a legal entity that "owns" (holds title to) your assets, but since you are the trustee of the Trust, you maintain full control over your assets.

THE SIZE OF YOUR ESTATE

The size of an estate is of great importance in determining the type of Living Trust that is best for each individual or married couple. All too often, I have seen Living Trusts drawn by attorneys who may have understood the Trust, but who failed to sufficiently understand the client's financial estate and therefore recommended the wrong type of Trust. Such a situation is similar to going into a shoe store, buying a beautiful pair of shoes, and then getting home and finding that the shoes do not fit.

The gross value of an estate and its net value are both important. Probate fees are calculated on the *gross* value of an estate, whereas estate taxes are calculated on the *net* value of the estate. A net estate is the result of subtracting the liabilities from the assets of the estate. A gross estate is the assets without the liabilities being removed. The example in Figure 4-1 indicates the difference between a gross estate and a net estate.

Note that life insurance on both spouses has been included in Figure 4-1. The reason is that life insurance is included in your estate for estate tax purposes. For estates that contain large amounts of insurance, Chapter 10 will show how the insurance can be insulated from the estate by using an Insurance Trust.

FIGURE 4-1
GROSS ESTATE AND NET ESTATE

Gross Estate

Checking and savings accounts	$ 10,000
Stocks and bonds	50,000
Home	200,000
Other real estate	100,000
Total gross estate	$ 360,000

Net Estate

Checking and savings accounts		$ 10,000
Stocks and bonds		50,000
Home	$ 200,000	
Less: Mortgage	(120,000)	
Net value of home	$ 80,000	80,000
Other real estate	$ 100,000	
Less: Mortgage	(60,000)	
Net value of real estate	$ 40,000	40,000
Total net estate		$ 180,000
Plus: Life insurance on both spouses		100,000
Net estate plus life insurance		$ 280,000

Before proceeding further, take a few moments to calculate the gross and net values of your estate. Several examples will be presented for various sizes of estates to illustrate the financial advantages of a Living Trust, and the examples will be much more meaningful when you can relate the most appropriate example to your own personal estate. If your own estate is larger than the value used in the most appropriate illustration, the beneficial effect of having a Living Trust will be the same—only proportionately greater.

The importance of a Living Trust can best be illustrated by showing how a Living Trust minimizes (and usually eliminates) the adverse financial impact of taxes on a person's estate. The balance of this chapter is devoted to examples comparing the Living Trust to the Loving Will and to the Testamentary Trust. The Living Trust is compared to a Loving Will for the following types of estates:

- Single person with estate under $600,000
- Single person with estate over $600,000
- Married couple with estate under $600,000
- Married couple with estate over $600,000
- Married couple with estate over $1.2 million

The Living Trust is also compared to a Testamentary Trust for the following types of estates:

- Single person with estate under $600,000
- Married couple with estate under $1.2 million
- Married couple with estate over $1.2 million

For simplicity in reading, select the examples that best illustrate your estate. You can read those examples and ignore the others. Once you see how the examples work, you may want to turn to Appendixes A through F, which provide comparisons for estates of varying sizes, to find a situation that more closely matches your own. The examples in the Appendixes are computed in the same way as the examples in this chapter.

Please note that "arithmetic license" has been taken with all of the examples and illustrations; the figures have been rounded off to make the illustration easier to read. In many examples, a calculator will probably not come up with exactly the same numbers! In addition, although probate fees are calculated on the gross estate and federal estate taxes on the net estate, for simplicity of arithmetic calculations, all of the following examples use the specified value of the estate in calculating *both* the probate fee and any estate taxes. For the probate fee, all of the examples use a conservative 8 percent of the gross estate.

THE LOVING WILL VS. THE LIVING TRUST

Since most people are accustomed to thinking of a Will as an estate-planning instrument, it is logical to first compare a Loving Will with a Living Trust. As pointed out earlier, everyone has a Will, whether it is written or not; if an individual does not have a written Will, the state mandates one for the person.

Single Person with Estate Under $600,000

The following example illustrates the financial difference between a Loving Will and a Living Trust for a single person's estate valued at less than $600,000—in this case, an estate worth $100,000. The probate cost would be 8 percent of $100,000—which is $8,000. Subtracting the probate cost from the original value of the estate leaves only $92,000 for the heirs, as shown on the left of Figure 4-2. (In addition, the probate process may have taken as long as two years!) Because the value of the estate is less than $600,000, no federal estate tax would be due.

In contrast, if the same individual had a Living Trust, there would be no probate and no cost of probate. Therefore, the full $100,000 value of the estate would come down (that is, be passed on) to the heirs, as shown on the right of Figure 4-2. The Living Trust therefore provides an $8,000 gain for the heirs. However, the amount of money saved is inconsequential compared to the fact that the heirs have been spared the lengthy time period and sheer frustration of the probate process.

Appendix A applies these same principles to an estate of a single person having the following values:

- $100,000
- $200,000
- $300,000
- $400,000
- $500,000
- $600,000
- $800,000
- $1 million
- $1.2 million
- $1.5 million
- $2 million

Single Person with Estate Exceeding $600,000

The following example illustrates the financial difference between a Loving Will and a Living Trust for a single person's estate valued at more than $600,000. Assume that a single person (unmarried or widowed) has an estate worth $800,000. An 8 percent probate cost would be $64,000.

In addition to the probate cost, the estate would also owe federal estate tax, because the value of the estate exceeds the $600,000 federal estate tax equivalent exemption for a single person. The federal estate tax on this estate would be $51,000. (When calculating the federal estate tax in a real-life situation, keep in mind that the cost of probate is first subtracted from the value of the estate, so the federal estate tax in this example would be computed on an estate value of $736,000. A comparison of the estate tax computations for a Loving Will and a Living Trust is shown at the end of this example.)

The cost of probate and the expense of the estate tax would yield an estimated death cost of $115,000! After the $115,000 is subtracted from the original estate value of $800,000, only $685,000 would remain for the heirs, as shown on the left of Figure 4-3.

If the same person has a Living Trust, there would be no cost of probate. However, federal estate tax would again be due. There are no probate fees to deduct from the value of the estate; consequently, the federal estate tax would be based on the entire estate value of $800,000. As shown on the right of Figure 4-3, when the federal estate tax expense of $74,000 is deducted from the original $800,000 value of

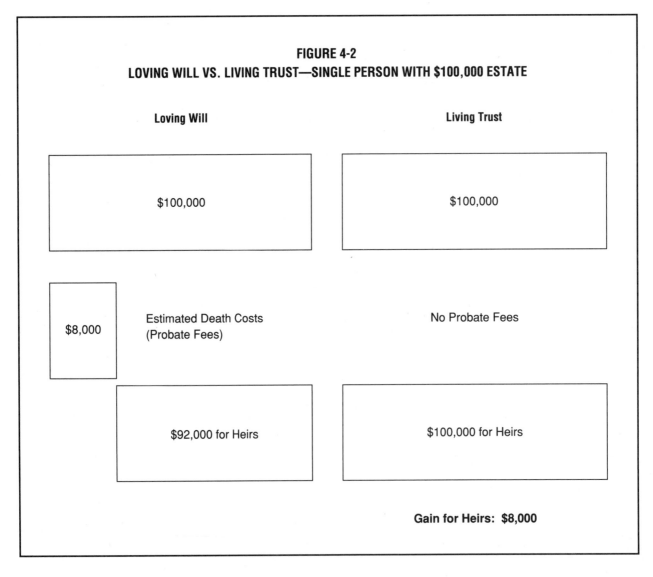

FIGURE 4-2
LOVING WILL VS. LIVING TRUST—SINGLE PERSON WITH $100,000 ESTATE

Loving Will

Living Trust

$100,000

$100,000

$8,000

Estimated Death Costs
(Probate Fees)

No Probate Fees

$92,000 for Heirs

$100,000 for Heirs

Gain for Heirs: $8,000

the estate, the heirs would be left with $726,000.

As a result, even though the federal estate taxes were higher with a Living Trust, the *total* death costs would be greater with a Will. The Living Trust would provide roughly an extra $41,000 for the heirs, as shown at the bottom of Figure 4-3.

Whether an estate is valued at $100,000 or $1 million, the impact of the Living Trust on a single person will follow this pattern. The savings for the heirs simply increases proportionately with the size of the estate.

Computation of Estate Taxes

In computing estate taxes for an estate having a Will, recognize that the attorney gets his or her share first. The probate fee is deducted from the value of the estate before the federal estate tax is calculated. An example of the calculation for an $800,000 estate is shown in Figure 4-4.

Married Couple with Estate Under $600,000

The following example illustrates the monetary difference between a Loving Will and a Living Trust for a married couple's estate valued at $100,000. No federal estate taxes will be due, since the estate is valued at less than $600,000. For simplicity, assume that, upon the death of one spouse, the $100,000 estate is to be divided equally between both spouses.

Upon the death of the first spouse, the estate would be divided in half—with $50,000 being attributed to the spouse who died and $50,000 attributed to the surviving spouse. With a Loving Will, the surviving spouse's $50,000 share of the estate would automatically pass to him

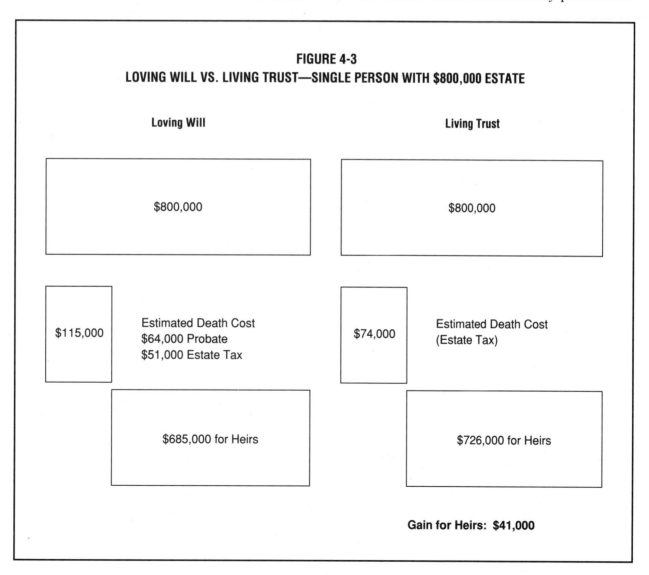

FIGURE 4-3
LOVING WILL VS. LIVING TRUST—SINGLE PERSON WITH $800,000 ESTATE

Loving Will

$800,000

$115,000 — Estimated Death Cost
$64,000 Probate
$51,000 Estate Tax

$685,000 for Heirs

Living Trust

$800,000

$74,000 — Estimated Death Cost
(Estate Tax)

$726,000 for Heirs

Gain for Heirs: $41,000

FIGURE 4-4
COMPARISON OF ESTATE TAX CALCULATIONS

Single Person with $800,000 Estate

	With a Will	With a Living Trust
Value of estate	$ 800,000	$ 800,000
Probate cost (8%)	(64,000)	-0-
Taxable estate	$ 736,000	$ 800,000
Federal estate tax equivalent exemption	(600,000)	(600,000)
Net taxable estate	$ 136,000	$ 200,000
Federal estate tax (37%)	$ 51,000	$ 74,000
Total cost to estate (Probate fees and estate tax)	$ 115,000	$ 74,000
Net Estate	**$ 685,000**	**$ 726,000**

or her without probate. However, the decedent's $50,000 share of the estate would be subject to probate. At 8 percent of $50,000, the cost of probate would be $4,000. If this probate cost were subtracted from the decedent's $50,000 share, as shown on the left of Figure 4-5, a net estate of $46,000 would be left. Thus, the surviving spouse eventually would receive $96,000—his or her own $50,000 share of the original $100,000 estate and $46,000 remaining from the decedent's share of the original estate.

Upon the death of the surviving spouse, the entire $96,000 estate would then be subject to probate, as shown in the lower left-hand corner of Figure 4-5. The probate fee on this estate would be $8,000 (figure rounded off for clarity). When the $8,000 probate cost is subtracted from $96,000, only $88,000 of the original $100,000 estate would be left to be distributed to the heirs.

In contrast, if the married couple had a Living Trust (in this example, it is assumed that the couple has an A Trust, defined later), the financial outcome would be decidedly better. The estate would also be divided equally upon the death of one spouse; however, since the entire estate is in trust, there would be no probate and, therefore, no cost of probate. As a result,

the entire $100,000 would come down to the surviving spouse in the Survivor's A Trust, as shown on the right side of Figure 4-5.

Upon the death of the surviving spouse, since the entire estate is in trust, there *again* would be no probate. Since there were no probate costs to reduce the value of the estate on either the first or second to die, the entire $100,000 would be available to be distributed to the heirs as shown in the lower right-hand corner of Figure 4-5. The heirs received approximately $12,000 more than they would have received with a Will. With a Living Trust, *all* of the assets of the estate have been preserved in the Trust to be used, for example, for the support and education of minor children or grandchildren.

The same principles used in the examples above are applied in Appendix B, comparing a Loving Will and an A Trust for married couples with estates of the following sizes:

- $100,000
- $200,000
- $300,000
- $400,000
- $500,000
- $600,000

Married Couple with Estate Exceeding $600,000

The following example illustrates a much more significant difference between a Loving Will and a Living Trust for a married couple's estate of $800,000. This example will show why it is important for any married couple with an estate exceeding $600,000 to utilize an A-B Trust.

With a Loving Will

With a Loving Will, upon the death of a spouse, the estate would effectively be divided in half, as shown at the top of Figure 4-6. The decedent's half of the estate must pass through probate before being distributed. An 8 percent cost of probate on $400,000 would cause an unnecessary expense of $32,000! Since the decedent's half of the estate is valued at $400,000, and the federal estate tax equivalent exemption is $600,000, no federal estate taxes would be due, and, in most states, no inheritance tax would be paid. When the $32,000 probate cost is sub-

FIGURE 4-5
LOVING WILL VS. LIVING TRUST—MARRIED COUPLE WITH $100,000 ESTATE

Loving Will

Living Trust (A Trust)

$50,000 First Spouse	$50,000 Second Spouse

$50,000 First Spouse	$50,000 Second Spouse

$4,000

Estimated Death Costs
(Probate Fees)

No Probate Fees

$46,000 $50,000
$96,000
Surviving
Spouse

$50,000 $50,000
$100,000
Surviving Spouse
Trust A

Estimated Death Costs
(Probate Fees)

$8,000

No Probate Fees

$88,000
for Heirs

$100,000
for Heirs

Gain for Heirs: $12,000

tracted from the original $400,000 estate, only $368,000 would be left to pass to the surviving spouse. At the completion of the probate process, the surviving spouse would have an estate of $768,000—$400,000 from the surviving spouse's half of the original estate plus $368,000 from the decedent's half of the estate.

Upon the death of the surviving spouse, the entire remaining estate of $768,000 would be subject to probate, as shown in Figure 4-6. Pro-

bate fees of 8 percent would amount to $61,000. The surviving spouse also has a federal estate tax equivalent exemption of $600,000. However, when the $600,000 equivalent exemption is deducted from the $768,000 value of the estate (less the cost of probate), the balance of the estate ($107,000) would be subject to federal estate tax beginning at 37 percent. Therefore, the federal estate tax due would be approximately $40,000.

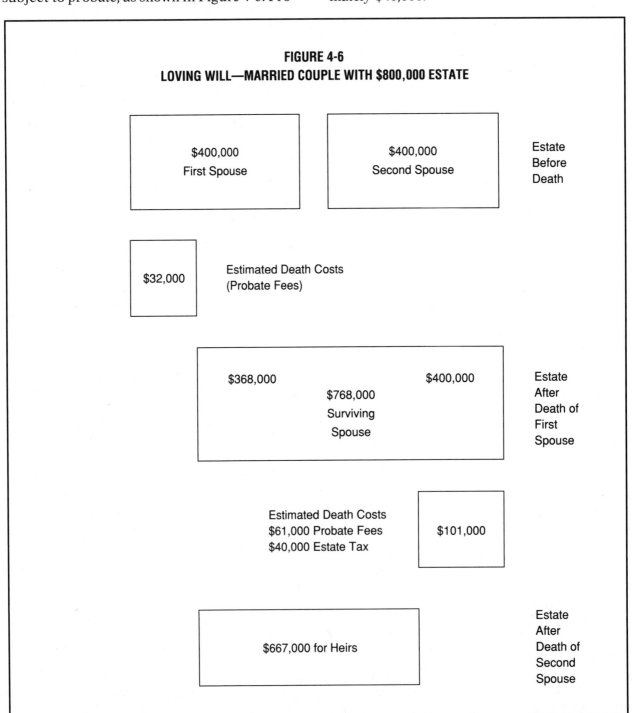

FIGURE 4-6
LOVING WILL—MARRIED COUPLE WITH $800,000 ESTATE

$400,000
First Spouse

$400,000
Second Spouse

Estate Before Death

$32,000

Estimated Death Costs (Probate Fees)

$368,000 $400,000
$768,000
Surviving
Spouse

Estate After Death of First Spouse

Estimated Death Costs
$61,000 Probate Fees
$40,000 Estate Tax

$101,000

$667,000 for Heirs

Estate After Death of Second Spouse

Surviving spouse's estate	$ 768,000
Less: Probate fee	(61,000)
Net taxable estate	$ 707,000
Less: Federal estate tax equivalent exemption	(600,000)
Taxable value of estate	$ 107,000
Approximate estate tax (at 37%)	$ 40,000

Thus, the estimated death cost would be $61,000 of probate cost plus an additional $40,000 for federal estate taxes—a total cost of $101,000! When this hefty sum is deducted from the estate of $768,000, only $667,000 would remain for the heirs from the original $800,000 estate.

With a Living Trust

If the same estate were held in a Living Trust, the estate would still be divided in half. However, since the entire estate is in trust, there would be no cost of probate, as shown in Figure 4-7. Since the surviving spouse has only one federal estate tax equivalent exemption of $600,000, when he or she dies, $200,000 of the estate will be subject to federal estate tax. The federal estate tax would be $74,000, leaving only $726,000 for the heirs. With only an A Trust, the federal estate tax equivalent exemp-

FIGURE 4-7
LIVING TRUST (ESTATE WITH AN A TRUST)—MARRIED COUPLE WITH $800,000 ESTATE

$400,000
First Spouse

$400,000
Second Spouse

Estate Before Death

$400,000 $400,000
$800,000
Surviving Spouse
Trust A

Estate After Death of First Spouse

$74,000

Estimated Death Costs (Estate Tax)

$726,000 for Heirs

Estate After Death of Second Spouse

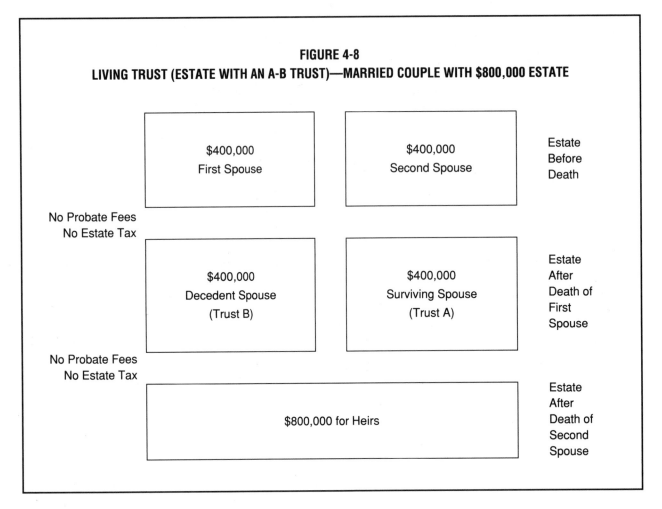

FIGURE 4-8
LIVING TRUST (ESTATE WITH AN A-B TRUST)—MARRIED COUPLE WITH $800,000 ESTATE

$400,000 First Spouse	$400,000 Second Spouse	Estate Before Death

No Probate Fees
No Estate Tax

$400,000 Decedent Spouse (Trust B)	$400,000 Surviving Spouse (Trust A)	Estate After Death of First Spouse

No Probate Fees
No Estate Tax

$800,000 for Heirs — Estate After Death of Second Spouse

tion of the first spouse would go unused (effectively *thrown away*).

The couple could benefit even more from a Living Trust if their assets were placed into an A-B Trust, a form of Trust in which each spouse's share of the assets comes down into a separate division of the same Trust, preserving both federal estate tax equivalent exemptions.

As shown in Figure 4-8, the entire $800,000 would come down to the surviving spouse in the following manner: The surviving spouse's half of the estate, $400,000, would come down to the surviving spouse in Trust A (the survivor's Trust). The other half of the estate, attributed to the spouse who died, would come down in Trust B (the decedent's Trust). The decedent's federal estate tax equivalent exemption of $600,000 would be deducted from the deceased spouse's half of the estate, yielding an estate tax of zero; in most states, there also would be no state inheritance tax to pay.

The assets in the Decedent's B Trust have

thus been insulated from any further estate taxation, regardless of the value to which they may grow. Trust B can therefore be an excellent estate-planning tool for sheltering growth items. (The use of the B Trust to shelter appreciating assets from unnecessary taxation will be discussed more fully in Chapter 13.)

Since the entire estate is still in trust, there would be no probate cost upon the death of the surviving spouse. Once the surviving spouse has died, the assets in the Survivor's A Trust would then be subject to estate tax. However, because the second spouse to die also has a federal estate tax equivalent exemption of $600,000, the $400,000 in Trust A escapes estate taxation and, in most states, no state inheritance tax would be due. As Figure 4-8 shows, the entire $800,000 estate has been passed to the heirs.

Another way to compare the A Trust and A-B Trust is to say that, by passing the *entire* estate to the surviving spouse, the A Trust "throws away" the first spouse's federal estate tax equivalent exemption of $600,000. For estates valued in excess of $600,000, this action would be a very costly mistake. In contrast, the A-B Trust preserves the exemption by putting the decedent's $400,000 into Trust B (the Decedent's B Trust), where that share of the estate would be insulated from further estate taxes (since, in effect, it has already been subjected to federal estate tax).

"Throwing away" the decedent's federal estate tax equivalent exemption means that if the decedent's share of the estate were simply passed to the surviving spouse (rather than put it in the Decedent's B Trust), the value of the surviving spouse's share of the estate would then *increase* in value. In most cases, the surviving spouse's estate would then be valued at more than the $600,000 federal estate tax equivalent exemption. When the surviving spouse dies, federal estate tax would be due on the estate. The share of the estate originally attributed to the first to die would have then been subjected to federal estate tax on *two* occasions!

Trusts A and B are not separate Trusts, but merely divisions of the same Trust.

Note that Trusts A and B are not really separate Trusts. Although it is common practice to speak of a Living Trust as being an A Trust, a B Trust, or an A-B Trust, the terms are not really referring to separate Trusts, but merely to two divisions of the same Trust. The next chapter will give you a better understanding of the different forms of a Living Trust.

Comparison of Loving Will and Living Trust
What has the A-B Living Trust accomplished? Compare the amounts that Figure 4-9 shows are left for the heirs. The result is an additional $133,000 for the heirs!

The A-B form of the Living Trust has avoided $32,000 of probate costs on the first estate and $61,000 of probate costs on the second estate. The A-B form of the Living Trust has also

avoided $40,000 of *unnecessary* federal estate taxes on the second estate. In addition, although $133,000 is a substantial sum of money, it is inconsequential when compared to what has really been avoided—the agony of probate on the first to die and again on the second to die.

Appendix C presents similar comparisons for estates of the following sizes:

- $100,000
- $200,000
- $300,000
- $400,000
- $500,000
- $600,000
- $800,000
- $1 million
- $1.2 million

Married Couple with Estate Exceeding $1.2 Million
The following example illustrates a significant difference between a Loving Will and a Living Trust for a married couple's estate that exceeds $1.2 million. These examples illustrate how an A-B-C Trust can be used to good advantage for an estate of $1.5 million. It is important to note that any married couple with an estate exceeding $1.2 million should have an A-B-C Trust to avoid estate tax upon the death of the *first* spouse.

With a Loving Will
When the first spouse dies (leaving only a Loving Will), the half of the estate attributable to the decedent would be subject to probate, as shown in Figure 4-10. The cost of probate would be 8 percent of $750,000 or $60,000! When the $600,000 federal estate tax equivalent exemption is deducted from the $750,000 estate being probated, a taxable estate of $150,000 would still exist (if the Will did not contain an Unlimited Marital Deduction provision).

However, let us further assume that this couple had a current Will that included the Unlimited Marital Deduction (described in Chapter 3). Therefore, the estate would pay no federal estate tax and, presumably, no state inheritance tax on the death of the *first* spouse. The net estate would be $690,000—the original estate

FIGURE 4-9
LOVING WILL VS. LIVING TRUST—MARRIED COUPLE WITH $800,000 ESTATE

Loving Will   **Living Trust (A-B)**

| $400,000 | $400,000 | | $400,000 | $400,000 |

| $32,000 | Estimated Death Costs (Probate Fees)

| $768,000 Surviving Spouse | | $400,000 (Trust B) | $400,000 Surviving Spouse (Trust A) |

Estimated Death Costs
$61,000 Probate Fees | $101,000 |
$40,000 Estate Tax

| $667,000 for Heirs | | $800,000 for Heirs |

Gain for Heirs: $133,000

of $750,000 minus the $60,000 of probate cost. This remaining estate would come down to the surviving spouse and, when added to the surviving spouse's $750,000 half of the original estate, would give the surviving spouse an estate valued at $1,440,000.

Upon the death of the surviving spouse, the entire remaining estate of $1,440,000 would be subject to probate, as shown next in Figure 4-10. At 8 percent, the cost of probate would be $115,000. Every penny beyond the surviving spouse's $600,000 federal estate tax equivalent exemption would be taxed beginning at 37 percent. (Remember that passing the decedent's share of the estate to the surviving spouse effectively wastes the decedent's federal estate tax equivalent exemption.) The estate tax on the balance of the estate ($840,000) would be

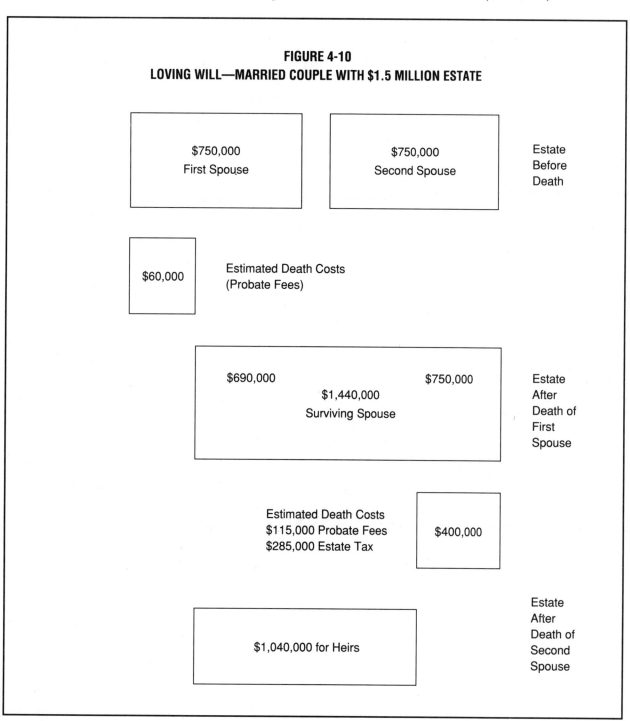

FIGURE 4-10
LOVING WILL—MARRIED COUPLE WITH $1.5 MILLION ESTATE

$750,000
First Spouse

$750,000
Second Spouse

Estate Before Death

$60,000

Estimated Death Costs
(Probate Fees)

$690,000 $750,000
$1,440,000
Surviving Spouse

Estate After Death of First Spouse

Estimated Death Costs
$115,000 Probate Fees
$285,000 Estate Tax

$400,000

$1,040,000 for Heirs

Estate After Death of Second Spouse

$285,000, which would result in an estimated death cost (probate costs plus estate taxes) of $400,000! When this amount is deducted from the surviving spouse's estate of $1,440,000, only $1,040,000 of the original $1.5 million estate would be left for the heirs.

Decedent's excess estate	$ 150,000
Less: Federal estate tax (40%)	60,000
Balance of Estate	$ 90,000

With a Living Trust

If the same married couple had an A-B Living Trust, the estate would again be divided in half upon the death of the first spouse. However, because the estate is in trust, there would be no cost of probate, as shown in Figure 4-11. The surviving spouse's half of the estate ($750,000) would pass down to Trust A (the survivor's Trust), and the other $750,000 would flow into Trust B (the decedent's Trust).

Because the amount in Trust B exceeds the $600,000 equivalent exemption, estate tax would be due on the excess amount. The estate tax on the excess $150,000 in the decedent's estate would be computed as follows:

The balance of the excess estate, after taxation, would flow into Trust B and would thereafter be sheltered from any further taxation, as shown in Figure 4-11. Trust B can be an excellent estate-planning tool, because whatever is in Trust B is insulated from further estate taxes.

If the couple have established an A-B-C Trust, the estate can defer paying estate taxes until the death of the surviving spouse. In 1981, Congress provided the C Trust. Under this arrangement, because the decedent has a federal estate tax equivalent exemption of $600,000, only $600,000 of the decedent's estate should be brought down into Trust B (to avoid payment of unnecessary estate taxes). The portion of the

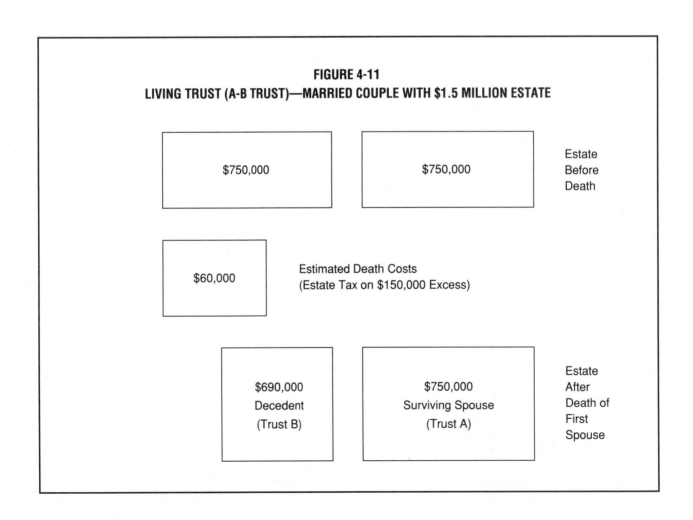

FIGURE 4-11
LIVING TRUST (A-B TRUST)—MARRIED COUPLE WITH $1.5 MILLION ESTATE

$750,000	$750,000	Estate Before Death
$60,000	Estimated Death Costs (Estate Tax on $150,000 Excess)	
$690,000 Decedent (Trust B)	$750,000 Surviving Spouse (Trust A)	Estate After Death of First Spouse

decedent's estate in the B Trust would then be insulated from further estate taxes.

Trust B is similar to a cup that holds only eight ounces; when you try to pour a quart of water into that eight-ounce cup, the balance will overflow. The overflow (any amount greater than $600,000) would be subject to federal estate tax. With an A-B-C Trust, the overflow goes into the C Trust.

In this particular example, after deducting the $600,000 federal estate tax equivalent exemption from the decedent's $750,000 share of the estate, $150,000 would still remain. If the excess $150,000 is placed in a C Trust, as shown in Figure 4-12, no federal estate tax would be due—until the death of the second spouse.

Upon the death of the surviving spouse, there would be no probate, since all of the assets are in trust. Any estate tax would be computed on the assets *remaining* in Trust C *and* in Trust A. The tax is based not on what went into the Trust, but what is *left* in the Trust, upon the death of the surviving spouse. The tax is not a deferred tax, but is simply a tax upon the assets remaining in Trust A and Trust C.

If the combined value of the assets in Trust A and Trust C were less than $600,000, then no federal estate taxes would be due. In the illustration of the $1.5 million estate previously shown in Figure 4-12, Trust C contains $150,000, and Trust A contains $750,000, yielding a total taxable estate of $900,000. When the

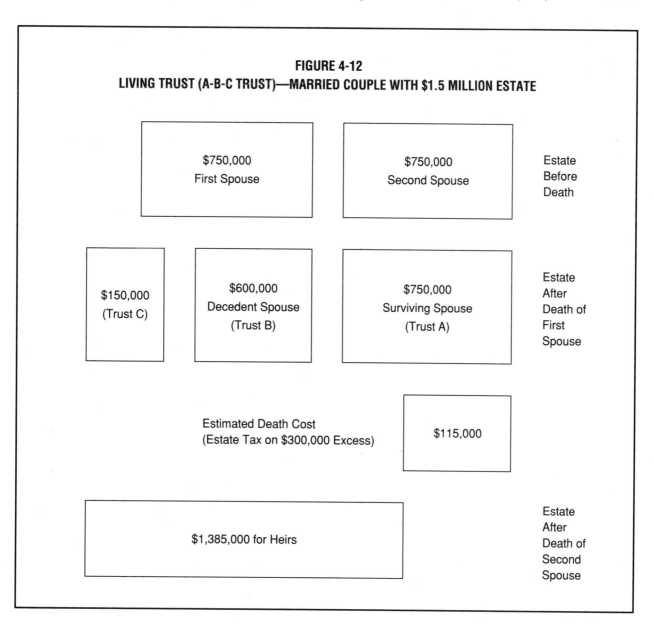

FIGURE 4-12
LIVING TRUST (A-B-C TRUST)—MARRIED COUPLE WITH $1.5 MILLION ESTATE

| $750,000 First Spouse | $750,000 Second Spouse | Estate Before Death |

| $150,000 (Trust C) | $600,000 Decedent Spouse (Trust B) | $750,000 Surviving Spouse (Trust A) | Estate After Death of First Spouse |

Estimated Death Cost (Estate Tax on $300,000 Excess) $115,000

$1,385,000 for Heirs   Estate After Death of Second Spouse

FIGURE 4-13
LOVING WILL VS. A-B-C TRUST—MARRIED COUPLE WITH $1.5 MILLION ESTATE

Loving Will

Living Trust

$750,000

$750,000

$750,000

$750,000

$60,000

Estimated Death Costs
(Probate Fees)

$1,440,000
Surviving Spouse

$150,000
(Trust C)

$600,000
(Trust B)

$750,000
Surviving Spouse
(Trust A)

Estimated Death Costs
$115,000 Probate Fees
$285,000 Estate Tax

$400,000

Estimated Death Costs
(Estate Tax)

$115,000

$1,040,000
for Heirs

$1,385,000
for Heirs

Gain for Heirs: $345,000

$600,000 equivalent exemption is subtracted from the $900,000 taxable portion of the estate, $300,000 would be subject to federal estate tax (which is 39 percent at the $900,000 level). The federal estate tax would therefore be $115,000. Deducting these taxes from the original estate of $1.5 million would leave $1,385,000 for the heirs.

By comparing the amounts left to the heirs in Figure 4-13, you can see that the heirs gain $345,000 from the use of an A-B-C Living Trust. The Living Trust has avoided $60,000 of probate cost on the first to die, has avoided $115,000 of probate cost on the second to die, and has reduced the bite of estate taxes by $170,000. In addition, the agony of probate has been avoided twice—on the first and second spouses to die. Do not forget that the cost and length of the probate process are proportionate to the size of the estate.

Refer to Appendix D to see similar comparisons of estates of the following sizes:

- $1.5 million
- $2 million
- $2.5 million
- $3 million
- $4 million
- $5 million

COMPARISON OF A TESTAMENTARY TRUST TO A LIVING TRUST

The Testamentary Trust is a Trust created *within a Will*—and takes effect only upon death. This type of Trust is only a half-step in the right direction, because it is created upon death and only after the assets have been subject to probate. The following examples show the different effects on an estate having a Testamentary Trust and an estate having a Living

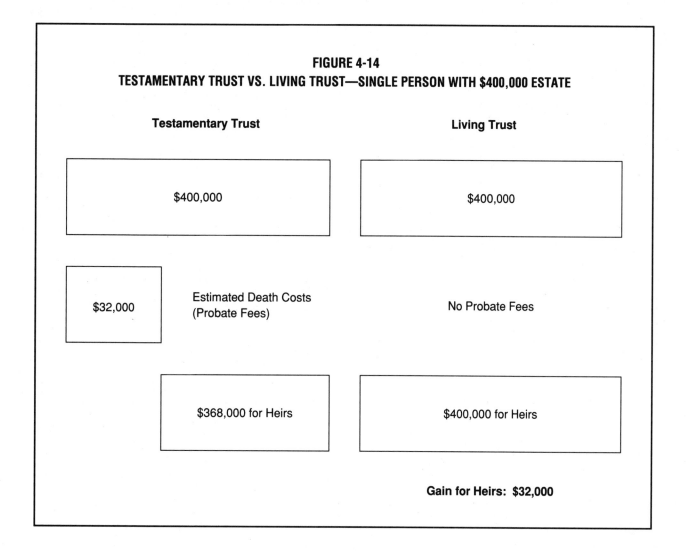

FIGURE 4-14

TESTAMENTARY TRUST VS. LIVING TRUST—SINGLE PERSON WITH $400,000 ESTATE

Testamentary Trust

Living Trust

$400,000

$400,000

$32,000

Estimated Death Costs (Probate Fees)

No Probate Fees

$368,000 for Heirs

$400,000 for Heirs

Gain for Heirs: $32,000

Trust. As in the examples of Loving Wills, an 8 percent probate cost is assumed.

Single Person with Estate Under $600,000

The following example illustrates the financial difference between a Testamentary Trust and a Living Trust for a single person's estate valued at less than $600,000.

Upon the death of the individual, the entire $400,000 estate must go through probate, as shown on the left of Figure 4-14. Eight percent of the $400,000 estate would be consumed by probate—a cost to the estate of $32,000. When the cost of probate is deducted from the original estate, only $368,000 would remain to come down into the Testamentary Trust.

In contrast, with a Living Trust the estate is already in trust, so there would be no probate.

FIGURE 4-15
TESTAMENTARY TRUST—MARRIED COUPLE WITH $400,000 ESTATE

$200,000 First Spouse	$200,000 Second Spouse	Estate Before Death
$16,000	Estimated Death Costs (Probate Fees)	
$184,000 Decedent (Trust B)	$200,000 Surviving Spouse (Trust A)	Estate After Death of First Spouse
Estimated Death Costs (Probate Fees)	$16,000	
$368,000 for Heirs		Estate After Death of Second Spouse

As shown on the right of Figure 4-14, the entire $400,000 estate would come down in trust for the heirs.

What has a Living Trust done that a Testamentary Trust could not have done? By avoiding the cost of probate, the Living Trust has provided a $32,000 gain for the heirs. As you can see, from a financial viewpoint, a Testamentary Trust for a single person has exactly the same effect on the estate of the deceased person as a Loving Will.

Married Couple with Estate Under $1.2 Million

The following pair of examples illustrates the difference between a Testamentary Trust and a Living Trust for a married couple with an estate valued at less than $1.2 million. These examples will illustrate an estate of $400,000.

With a Testamentary Trust

If the couple has a Testamentary Trust, upon the death of the first spouse, the surviving spouse's half of the estate ($200,000) would come down directly to the surviving spouse (not in trust), as shown at the top of Figure 4-15.

The decedent's share of the estate would be subject to probate. An 8 percent probate fee on the $200,000 share of the estate would yield a probate cost of $16,000. After the probate cost is deducted from the original estate, $184,000 remains, which would then come down into the Testamentary Trust B. These funds are now insulated from further estate taxes, but the agony of probate was *not* avoided. The surviving spouse would end up with an overall estate of $384,000—the survivor's $200,000 original share of the estate and the $184,000 in Trust B.

Upon the death of the surviving spouse, the first decedent's half of the estate (the $184,000 in Trust B) would not be subject to probate or estate taxes; however, the surviving spouse's half of the estate would be subject to probate. The probate cost on the surviving spouse's

FIGURE 4-16
LIVING TRUST—MARRIED COUPLE WITH $400,000 ESTATE

$200,000 estate would be $16,000. When this amount is deducted from the surviving spouse's estate and the remaining estate is combined with the $184,000 from the Decedent's Trust B, only $368,000 would be left for the heirs from the original $400,000 estate.

With a Living Trust

In contrast, with a Living Trust there would be no probate upon the death of a spouse, as shown in Figure 4-16, since the estate is already in trust. When the first spouse dies, the estate would be divided in half, and the surviving spouse's half of the estate ($200,000) would come down to the surviving spouse in Trust A. The decedent's half of the estate would come down to the Decedent's Trust B (without going through probate), where it would be insulated from further estate taxes.

Upon the death of the surviving spouse, since the entire estate is in trust, there would again be no probate. The entire $400,000 estate would come down in trust to the heirs.

Thus, a Living Trust avoids a $16,000 probate cost on the first to die and a $16,000 probate cost on the second to die—a total gain for the heirs of $32,000.

Appendix E contains additional comparative illustrations that examine the similarities and the differences of a Testamentary Trust and a Living Trust for married couples with A-B Trusts. The illustrations present comparisons for estates of the following sizes:

- $400,000
- $500,000
- $600,000
- $800,000
- $1 million
- $1.2 million

Married Couple with Estate Exceeding $1.2 Million

The final examples in this chapter illustrate the difference between a Testamentary Trust and a Living Trust for a married couple with an estate valued at more than $1.2 million. Specifically, this example illustrates an estate of $1.5 million.

With a Testamentary Trust

If the couple's assets are held in a Testamentary Trust, upon the death of the first spouse, the surviving spouse's half of the estate ($750,000) would come down directly to the surviving spouse without going through probate, as shown in the upper portion of Figure 4-17. The decedent's half of the estate, however, would be subject to probate. An 8 percent probate fee for the decedent's $750,000 share of the estate would produce a probate cost of $60,000. After the probate cost is deducted from the original estate, $690,000 would be left to come down into trust.

When the decedent's federal estate tax equivalent exemption of $600,000 is deducted from the $690,000 remaining after probate, $90,000 of the estate would still be subject to federal estate tax. The excess $90,000 would be subject to a federal estate tax of almost $35,000! Together, the cost of probate and the estate tax reduce the estate by $95,000. From the original $750,000 estate, only $655,000 would remain to be put in the Decedent's Trust B; the surviving spouse would have $95,000 *less* on which to live.

Upon the death of the surviving spouse, the decedent's half of the estate (the $655,000 in Trust B) would not be subject to probate or estate taxes; however, the surviving spouse's half of the estate would be subject to probate, as shown in Figure 4-17. The probate cost on the $750,000 estate of the second spouse to die would also be $60,000. After the probate cost is deducted from the original value of the estate, only $690,000 would be left—and some of that would be subject to federal estate tax. Deducting the surviving spouse's $600,000 federal estate tax equivalent exemption from the remaining value of the estate leaves a balance of $90,000 subject to federal estate tax beginning at 37 percent. The estate tax on the $90,000 excess would be $35,000. Thus, the probate fees and the estate tax on the second spouse's estate would further reduce the estate by $95,000. From the original $1.5 million estate, only $1,310,000 would be left to come down to the heirs—a loss of $190,000.

With a Living Trust

In contrast, with the Living Trust, since the estate is already in trust, there would be no probate when either spouse dies. As Figure 4-18 shows, when the first spouse dies, the estate would be divided in half, and the surviving spouse's $750,000 half of the estate would come down to the surviving spouse in Trust A. To avoid unnecessary estate taxation, only $600,000 of the decedent's estate would be placed in the B Trust; the $150,000 excess would be placed in the C Trust.

The $600,000 part of the decedent's estate in Trust B would be insulated from further estate taxes, because it would be offset by the

$600,000 equivalent exemption. Trust B not only preserved the decedent's federal estate tax equivalent exemption, but also insulated the assets in Trust B from any further estate taxes.

Upon the death of the surviving spouse, since everything is in trust, there would be no probate. Estate taxes would be due on the total value of whatever assets remain in Trust C and in Trust A. In Figure 4-18, the $150,000 in Trust C and $750,000 in Trust A yield a total taxable estate of $900,000. Deducting the $600,000 federal estate tax equivalent exemption of the sur-

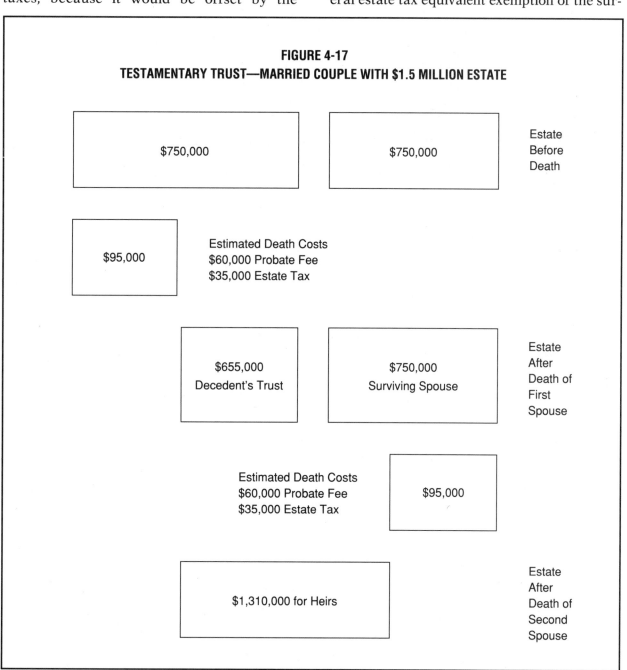

FIGURE 4-17
TESTAMENTARY TRUST—MARRIED COUPLE WITH $1.5 MILLION ESTATE

viving spouse leaves $300,000 subject to federal estate tax. The estate tax on $300,000 would be $115,000. When the $115,000 of estate taxes is deducted from the original estate of $1.5 million, a total estate of $1,385,000 would be left for the heirs.

What has been done with the Living Trust that could not be done with a Testamentary Trust? Figure 4-19 summarizes the differences between the two types of Trusts. The Living Trust has avoided probate costs of $60,000 on the first to die, as well as payment of $35,000 of unnecessary estate taxes. A probate cost of $60,000 has also been avoided on the second to die. Comparing the two different estates left to the heirs shows that the Living Trust provides the heirs with a total gain of $75,000.

In addition, with the A-B-C form of the Living Trust, the entire estate has been preserved for the surviving spouse—an essential advantage. The Testamentary Trust rarely, if ever, contains a C Trust. For estates in excess of $1.2 million, this lack of a C Trust means that estate taxes must be paid on the first to die—and such taxation is *entirely unnecessary*!

Appendix F contains additional comparative illustrations that examine the similarities and the differences of a Testamentary Trust and a Living Trust for married couples with A-B-C Trusts. The illustrations present comparisons for estates of the following sizes:

- $1.5 million
- $2 million

FIGURE 4-18
LIVING TRUST—MARRIED COUPLE WITH $1.5 MILLION ESTATE

If you are astute enough to realize that estate planning is important to you and your heirs, recognize that what you really should have is a Living Trust, *not* a Testamentary Trust. The Testamentary Trust is rightfully referred to as the "Attorneys' Retirement Plan." The attorney gets his or her fee for writing the Trust, and then he or she gets a probate fee on top of it. If you are going to have a Trust, have a Living Trust. The economics speak for themselves.

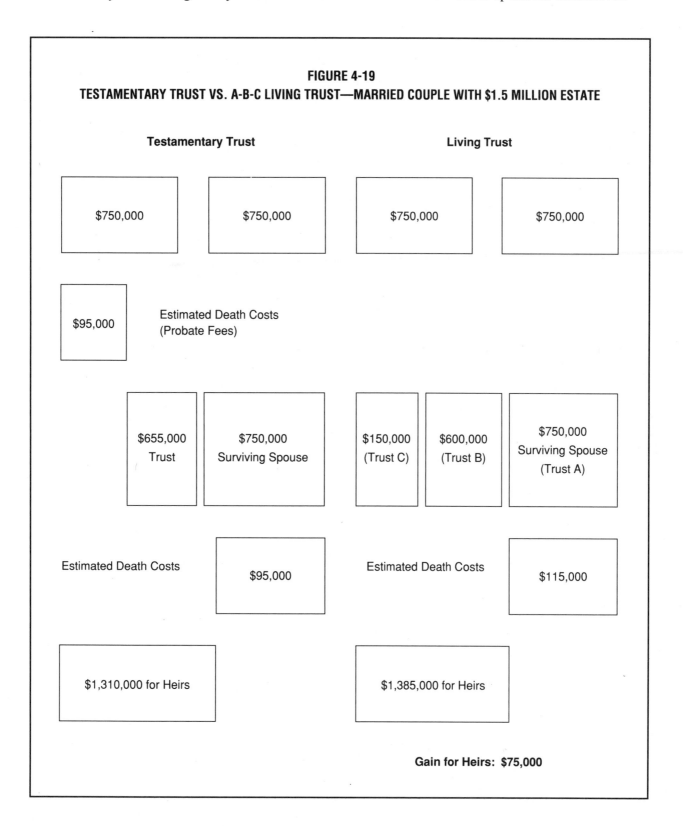

FIGURE 4-19
TESTAMENTARY TRUST VS. A-B-C LIVING TRUST—MARRIED COUPLE WITH $1.5 MILLION ESTATE

Testamentary Trust

Living Trust

$750,000

$750,000

$750,000

$750,000

$95,000

Estimated Death Costs (Probate Fees)

$655,000
Trust

$750,000
Surviving Spouse

$150,000
(Trust C)

$600,000
(Trust B)

$750,000
Surviving Spouse
(Trust A)

Estimated Death Costs

$95,000

Estimated Death Costs

$115,000

$1,310,000 for Heirs

$1,385,000 for Heirs

Gain for Heirs: $75,000

5

Understanding the Living Trust

By now, you should be well aware of several important reasons for putting your estate in a Living Trust. Yet two common misconceptions about the Living Trust tend to become stumbling blocks for people learning about it and turn into exaggerated fears that prevent people from taking the necessary steps to create their own Living Trusts. People fear that they will lose control of their assets (after the assets are placed in the Trust) and that the surviving spouse will lose control over the assets in the Decedent's Trust B.

Even though the Living Trust is unknown to most people, the Trust does not need to be difficult to understand or use. This chapter illustrates the various advantages of Living Trusts and describes how each advantage would best apply to your particular situation. When you complete this chapter, you should be comfortable with the concept of the Living Trust and recognize that it is an outstanding solution for almost all estate-planning situations.

A BETTER WAY TO HOLD ASSETS
If you are like most people, you have done a reasonable job of putting your assets together

and building your estate. You most likely own a home, some stocks and bonds, a savings account, and life insurance, and you probably participate in a pension plan. The problem is that, upon your death (whether you are married or single), your assets must go through probate, which is both costly and time-consuming. Fortunately, there is a better way—and that is for both husband and wife (if you are married) or just you (if you are single) to create and fund a Living Trust in which you are the trustee or trustees of your own Trust. (The roles of the trustee, surviving trustee, and successor trustee as well as the trustor, settlor, and beneficiary will be explained in Chapter 6.)

How the Living Trust Works
What, you may ask, does a Living Trust do for me? From the legal viewpoint of settling an estate, having a Living Trust means that you do not hold title to anything; since your assets are inside the Trust, the Trust holds title to everything. However, even though you have relinquished *ownership* of your assets, you still retain *control* of those same assets. As the trustee of your Trust, you continue to have the same

power to buy, sell, transfer, borrow, and do whatever you wish with "your" assets. Your control of those assets is no different on the day after you put them into the Trust than on the day before you put them into the Trust.

Even though you relinquish ownership of your assets when you transfer them into your Trust, you still retain total control over those assets.

The significance of your not "owning" anything becomes very important when you ultimately die. Upon your death, since you have nothing in title in your own name (because your assets are in the Trust), there is nothing to probate. If you are married, the surviving spouse typically becomes the surviving trustee and, as such, continues to have the same power to buy, sell, transfer, or do whatever is desired with those assets.

Upon the death of the surviving spouse, the same situation applies as before. Since no assets were in the name of the deceased, there is nothing to probate. In the Trust document, you would identify whom you want to act as the successor trustee or successor trustees. The successor trustee is the person who will take charge of the Trust upon the death of the original trustee(s). It is recommended that you stipulate one or more of your adult children, close family members, or close friends as successor trustees. That person, or persons, will immediately step in, upon the death of the surviving trustee, and have the same power to buy, sell, or transfer those assets and, more importantly, to use them and to distribute them as you would have wanted them used or distributed.

The Living Trust is just as important for a single person as for a married couple.

Even though our firm has prepared a few Living Trusts where the parents and a child or children are the joint creators and administrators, this situation is rare. Usually parents and children have entirely different objectives, and therefore the parents and children should each have their own separate Trusts.

The Trust works in the same manner for a single person as for a married couple. A Living Trust is meaningful for *all* individuals, regardless of whether they are single, widowed, married, or even two single persons living together. The Living Trust has just as much importance for a single person as it does for a married person.

All Assets Must Be in the Trust

For a Trust to be effective in avoiding probate and minimizing taxation, *all* of the estate's assets must be placed in the Trust, as symbolized in Figure 5-1. Unfortunately, all too often today, Living Trusts are drawn up but not funded with the assets (the assets have not been placed in the Trust, as shown in Figure 5-2). In such cases, the Living Trust acts as a Testamentary Trust; since there are no assets in the Trust, the estate must go through the probate process upon the death of the first spouse before the assets can pour into the Trust.

Another important point to remember is that, as in a Testamentary Trust or a Loving Will, an unfunded Trust is readily challengeable. If you created a Trust and then did not transfer title to your assets into the Trust, your heirs could someday claim that circumstances have changed since the Trust's creation and that, if you were now present, you would wish to change the distribution of your Trust.

For a Living Trust to be effective in avoiding probate, all of your assets must be placed in the Trust.

ADDITIONAL ADVANTAGES OF THE LIVING TRUST

Besides the advantages discussed so far, other benefits of the Living Trust are important to consider when creating Living Trusts:

- Providing for minor children or grandchildren, or handicapped children of any age
- Assuring privacy of the estate
- Being able to use an A-B Trust for a small estate

FIGURE 5-1
ALL ASSETS IN THE TRUST

INDIVIDUALS

TRUSTEES

Home

STOCK

Stocks and Bonds

INSURANCE

Insurance

Savings

Pension Fund

Real Estate

FIGURE 5-2
UNFUNDED TRUST (WITHOUT ASSETS)

INDIVIDUALS

TRUSTEES

Home

STOCK

Stocks and Bonds

INSURANCE

Insurance

Savings

Pension Fund

Real Estate

Trust

Providing for Minor or Handicapped Children

A Living Trust is essential for providing for minor children or handicapped children of any age, in the event that the parents die prematurely. Small estates too often just seem to disappear—to be consumed somehow by administrative fees. The measurement used by most states to avoid probate is either an estate ranging in worth from $30,000 to $60,000 or *any* estate with real property. Nevertheless, anyone with children or planning to have children should have a Living Trust, regardless of the size of his or her estate. Remember, parents with children need to name a guardian of *their* choice and then provide for the children's welfare through a Trust, just in case something were to happen to the parent or parents.

If you do not have a Living Trust and were to die, and, because of your untimely demise, you left minor children or handicapped children of any age, the court would be required to set up a Trust to hold the assets until the minor children become adults or for the continuing care of the handicapped individuals. By necessity, such a Trust must be very restrictive, with the trustee required to report regularly to the court. Since the court would probably appoint as trustee an attorney unknown to you, you would want these restrictions to protect your assets. However, it would be much better to create your own Trust to provide for your children or grandchildren in the manner you would want and to name a trustee you know and trust.

If you have a Living Trust, you have already created that entity—and, more importantly, you have spelled out how you want your funds used. No court in the land can truly guess your particular personal desires for the care and upbringing of your children or grandchildren.

Assuring Privacy of the Estate

The Living Trust is not registered anywhere and is a confidential document. The only people who have a right to see the Trust document are the trustee(s) and, eventually, the successor trustee(s). Not even the beneficiaries have a right to see the document! This confidentiality is much in contrast to the way a Will is handled. Privacy, consequently, is one of the key advantages of a Living Trust.

Occasionally an adult child of a decedent calls me with the concern that his or her stepmother or stepfather is misusing the decedent's share of the funds. I will point out to this individual that the sole recourse available is to hire an attorney, who will then appeal to the probate court (the court that has jurisdiction over Trusts) and ask that the court review the trustee's use of the funds. The judge can then ask to see the Trust, review what that particular spouse has done with the decedent's funds, and, being satisfied or dissatisfied, so advise the child. Neither the child nor the child's attorney has the right to see the Trust. Furthermore, my experience has been that abuse of a Trust is negligible, and my advice to most individuals is that to pursue such a course of legal action is a waste of time and energy. As of this writing, our clients have never done so.

Using an A-B Trust for a Small Estate

Another important advantage of having a Living Trust is that the A-B Trust form may be used for a small estate. Although most CPAs think of an A-B Trust as applying only when an estate exceeds $600,000, there are three sound reasons for using an A-B Trust for a small estate:

- The Decedent's Trust B becomes irrevocable upon death.
- A "Catastrophic Illness Provision" can be included.
- No estate tax is due if the estate is eventually valued at more than $600,000.

Each reason has varying degrees of importance, depending on the individual circumstances of the estate.

Irrevocability of Decedent's Trust B

One of the primary reasons for using an A-B Trust for a small estate (one valued at less than $600,000) is to ensure that the assets attributed to the first to die eventually flow down to the decedent's heirs. Upon the death of a spouse with an A-B Trust, one-half of the estate becomes irrevocable. Thus, each spouse can be assured that at least "his or her half" of the assets will go to his or her heirs as desired.

Upon the death of a spouse, his or her share of the estate will flow down into the Decedent's Trust B. Typically, the assets in Trust B are there for the use of the surviving spouse for as long as he or she lives; however, upon the death of the surviving spouse, those assets will go to the individuals specified by the original spouse. Although the surviving spouse has the right to use those funds, the one limitation specified in the Trust is that the surviving spouse *may not change* the beneficiaries of the B Trust.

Catastrophic Illness Provision

The second reason—and probably one of the most significant reasons today—that a married couple with a small estate should seriously consider utilizing an A-B Trust is that a Catastrophic Illness Provision can be part of an A-B Trust. Unfortunately, since an A Trust cannot be divided, the Catastrophic Illness Provision cannot be included in an A Trust.

A catastrophic illness is an illness that is expensive in relation to the size of the estate. Not only may the illness take its toll on a person's health (and even eventually be terminal), the financial effects of the person's illness may be devastating to his or her estate. For example, if one spouse were to become afflicted with Alzheimer's disease, the medical care required for the stricken person could eventually become so costly that it would be necessary to turn to government aid for assistance. Unfortunately, in order for the ill person to qualify for such financial assistance, practically all the assets in the estate must first be exhausted! In most states, the value of the estate must be reduced to *less than $2,500* before any state or federal assistance will be granted. Unfortunately, as shown in Figure 5-3, such a paltry sum leaves the surviving spouse a pauper.

However, when a Catastrophic Illness Provision is part of an A-B Trust, the financial outlook is much brighter. Upon the onset of a catastrophic illness, one-half of the assets are immediately *preserved* for the benefit of the other spouse. Therefore, only the assets that form the share of the estate belonging to the spouse with the catastrophic illness need to be consumed, as shown in Figure 5-4. Once the afflicted person's half of the estate is exhausted, that person can then receive government medical assistance—without reducing the other spouse's half of the estate.

The Catastrophic Illness Provision is especially meaningful for small estates. Large estates can usually afford the cost of a cata-

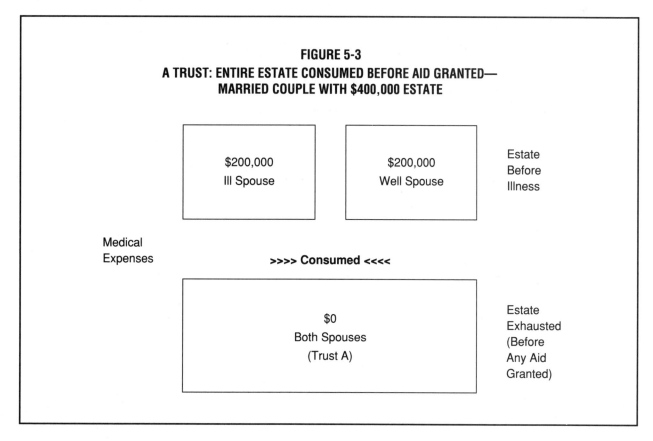

FIGURE 5-3
A TRUST: ENTIRE ESTATE CONSUMED BEFORE AID GRANTED—
MARRIED COUPLE WITH $400,000 ESTATE

$200,000
Ill Spouse

$200,000
Well Spouse

Estate
Before
Illness

Medical
Expenses

>>>> Consumed <<<<

$0
Both Spouses
(Trust A)

Estate
Exhausted
(Before
Any Aid
Granted)

strophic illness without causing the financial ruin of the estate. In contrast, small estates can be totally consumed by the financial effects of a catastrophic illness. For example, a medical bill of $400,000 may not be catastrophic to a $1 million estate, but it would be *absolutely devastating* to a $400,000 estate. Even though Congress has adopted a bill to provide for medical costs generated by catastrophic illnesses, there is *no* current provision for nursing home care. This cost can be very expensive and can drag on seemingly endlessly.

Preservation of Both Estate Tax Equivalent Exemptions

The third reason for using an A-B Trust for a small estate is to preserve the federal estate tax equivalent exemptions of both spouses. As an estate grows in value, an A-B Trust ensures that, as long as the value of the estate remains below $1.2 million (two federal estate tax equivalent exemptions), no estate tax will be due.

For example, as shown in Figure 5-5, a $500,000 estate in an A Trust would pay no estate tax upon the death of the first spouse. However, as the $500,000 estate grows, if only

by inflation, its value could exceed the $600,000 federal estate tax equivalent exemption. Every dollar thereafter will be taxed beginning at 37 percent! For the surviving spouse's estate of $500,000, 5 percent growth would increase the estate to a value greater than $600,000 in only four years, as shown at the bottom of Figure 5-5. Then, when the surviving spouse dies, the estate would be subject to federal estate taxes.

The A-B Trust can prevent these unnecessary taxes. If the surviving spouse had an A-B Trust already in place, there would be substantial room for growth in the surviving spouse's A Trust (from $250,000 to $600,000). Furthermore, the assets expected to appreciate in value (such as a house or stock) could be placed in the B Trust to insulate the growth from future taxation. Whatever is in the B Trust is sheltered from future estate taxes, as shown in Figure 5-6. How to use a Decedent's Trust B as an estate-planning tool to shelter growing assets will be discussed further in Chapter 12.

As these examples show, a couple with an estate valued at less than $600,000 would most likely want to use an A-B Trust instead of a simple A Trust.

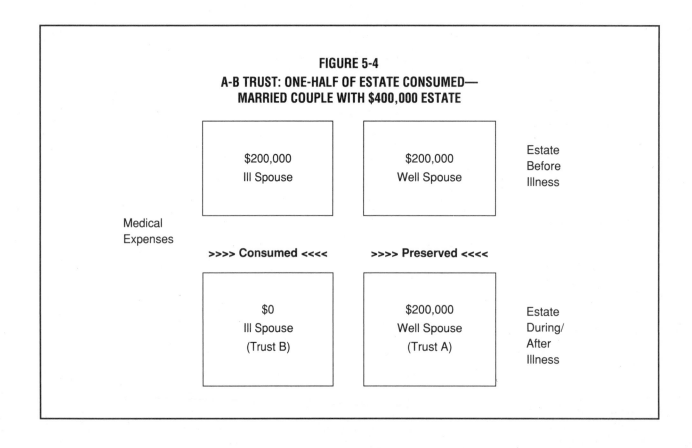

FIGURE 5-4
A-B TRUST: ONE-HALF OF ESTATE CONSUMED—
MARRIED COUPLE WITH $400,000 ESTATE

$200,000 Ill Spouse	$200,000 Well Spouse	Estate Before Illness
Medical Expenses		
>>>> Consumed <<<<	>>>> Preserved <<<<	
$0 Ill Spouse (Trust B)	$200,000 Well Spouse (Trust A)	Estate During/ After Illness

RIGHTS OF THE SURVIVING SPOUSE

One of the greatest fears of a married couple considering an A-B Living Trust is that the surviving spouse will somehow lose control of the assets in the Decedent's Trust B. I wish to dispel those fears. The rights of the surviving spouse to Trust B may, for good reasons, be restricted. However, most A-B Trusts for married couples name the surviving spouse as both surviving trustee and beneficiary of the Decedent's Trust B. Thus, the surviving spouse is granted full rights to the assets in the Decedent's Trust B.

If the surviving spouse is named as surviving trustee, he or she maintains full control of the assets in the Decedent's B Trust.

Rights as Surviving Trustee

As the surviving trustee, the surviving spouse continues to retain the same power to buy, sell, transfer, and borrow against the assets in Trusts A and B in exactly the same manner as before the demise of his or her spouse. How can the trustee's right to buy, sell, and transfer the assets in the Decedent's B Trust be reconciled with the trustee's fiduciary responsibility to the heirs of Trust B? Let's consider an example.

Assume that the decedent's half of the estate ($400,000) is in the B Trust. Today, the assets include a house worth $100,000, stock valued at $100,000, bonds worth $50,000, certificates of deposit with a value of $100,000, and savings of $50,000, as shown in the left-hand column of Table 5-1.

During the next year, the trustee decides that it is more appropriate to sell the house. Of the $100,000 proceeds from the sale of the house, $50,000 is added to the stock, and the other

FIGURE 5-5
ESTATE WITH AN A TRUST—MARRIED COUPLE WITH $500,000 ESTATE (INITIALLY)

$250,000
First Spouse

$250,000
Second Spouse

Estate
Before
Death

$500,000
Surviving Spouse
(Trust A)

Estate
After
Death of
First
Spouse

$607,000
Surviving Spouse
(Trust A)

Estate
Four
Years
Later

TABLE 5-1
MANAGEMENT OF ASSETS IN DECEDENT'S TRUST B—$400,000 ESTATE

Today		Next Year	
House	$ 100,000	House	-0-
Stocks	100,000	Stocks	$ 150,000
Bonds	50,000	Bonds	50,000
CDs	100,000	CDs	50,000
Savings	50,000	Savings	150,000
TOTAL	$ 400,000	TOTAL	$ 400,000

$50,000 is added to savings. The trustee further decides to transfer $50,000 from CDs to savings. Assuming no growth, the B Trust will then have $150,000 of stock, $50,000 in bonds, $50,000 in CDs, and $150,000 in savings—for a total amount in Trust B of $400,000.

Notice that the total value of the assets in Trust B did not materially change; only the form of the assets changed. This change in form of the assets in the Decedent's B Trust is in keeping with the fiduciary responsibility of the surviving trustee. The trustee has the right to buy, sell, and transfer these assets without restriction, as long as the investments are considered "prudent."

Beneficial Rights of Surviving Spouse
In most Living Trusts, the surviving spouse is named as the beneficiary of Trust B and, as such, has three beneficial rights:

• The right to all of the income of Trust B.
• The right to use any or all of the principal in Trust B as is necessary to maintain the same standard of living, including any medical needs.
• The right to spend, each year, $5,000 or 5 percent of the assets in Trust B, whichever is greater, for any reason, regardless of how frivolous. This right is not cumulative; the right must be used during the year, or it is lost.

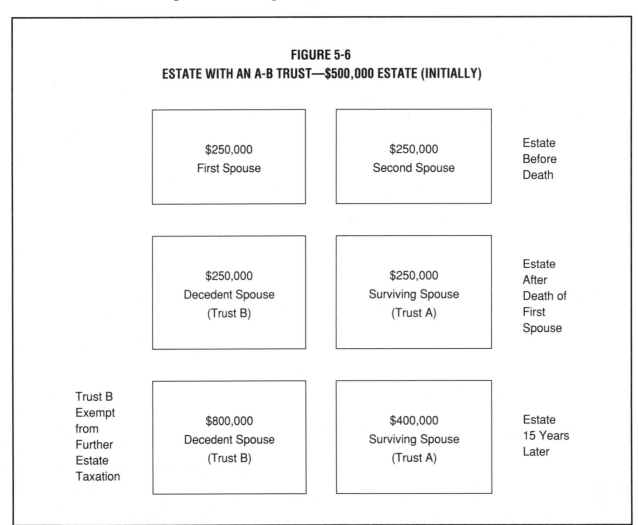

FIGURE 5-6
ESTATE WITH AN A-B TRUST—$500,000 ESTATE (INITIALLY)

$250,000 First Spouse	$250,000 Second Spouse	Estate Before Death
$250,000 Decedent Spouse (Trust B)	$250,000 Surviving Spouse (Trust A)	Estate After Death of First Spouse
Trust B Exempt from Further Estate Taxation — $800,000 Decedent Spouse (Trust B)	$400,000 Surviving Spouse (Trust A)	Estate 15 Years Later

These three rights, in effect, give the surviving spouse the right to use the funds in Trust B without restriction.

In effect, the surviving spouse has the right to use the funds in Trust B effectively without restriction.

The rights of the surviving spouse over the assets in Trust B are probably one of the greatest areas of confusion. The specific wording in the Living Trust document is used to satisfy the Internal Revenue Service Code in order to insulate the assets in the Decedent's Trust B from further estate taxes. To best understand the restrictions on Trust B, you need to recognize the source of any challenge.

The children, if any, listed as beneficiaries in the Living Trust are only *contingent* beneficiaries; that is, the children are beneficiaries only if they are still living when the surviving spouse dies *and* if any assets are remaining in trust to pass on to the heirs. However, the contingent beneficiaries do have rights, and the surviving spouse, as trustee, has a fiduciary responsibility to protect those rights.

Abuse of the Rights to Trust B

An excellent example of a potential abuse of the fiduciary responsibility is illustrated in the following scenario involving the marriage of two people who have had previous marriages. Each spouse has children from his or her former marriage, and each brings substantial sums of separate property (that is, property attained before this marriage) into the new marriage.

It is the husband and wife's intent that their assets remain in place for the benefit of the surviving spouse. However, upon the death of the surviving spouse, each spouse's share of the estate shall pass to his or her own children, as shown in Figure 5-7.

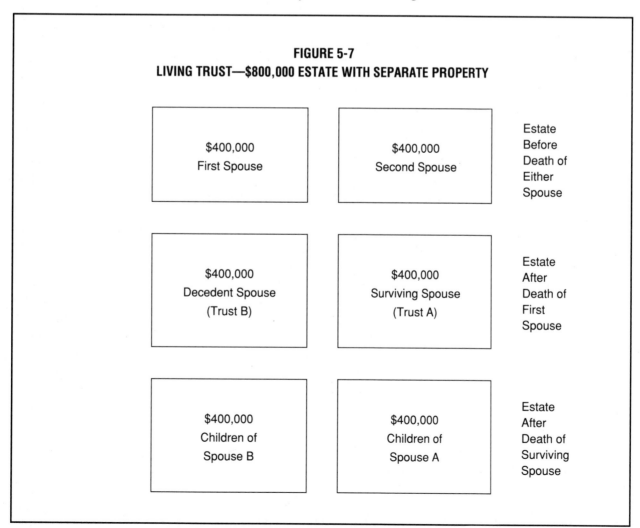

FIGURE 5-7
LIVING TRUST—$800,000 ESTATE WITH SEPARATE PROPERTY

$400,000 First Spouse	$400,000 Second Spouse	Estate Before Death of Either Spouse
$400,000 Decedent Spouse (Trust B)	$400,000 Surviving Spouse (Trust A)	Estate After Death of First Spouse
$400,000 Children of Spouse B	$400,000 Children of Spouse A	Estate After Death of Surviving Spouse

If one of the spouses were to die and the surviving spouse were to take $200,000 from the Decedent's Trust B and lose the funds gambling in Las Vegas, this action would clearly be an abuse of the fiduciary responsibility of the surviving trustee.

Another example of fiduciary abuse is shown in Figure 5-8. If the surviving spouse had removed $200,000 from Trust B and added it to the Survivor's Trust A, so that the additional assets would eventually pass to the children of the surviving spouse (instead of to the decedent's children), that act also would be considered to be an abuse of fiduciary responsibility.

FIGURE 5-8
EXAMPLE OF FIDUCIARY ABUSE TO DECEDENT'S TRUST B

Decedent's Trust B		Survivor's Trust A
$ 400,000		$ 400,000
(200,000)	Fiduciary	200,000
$ 200,000	Abuse	$ 600,000

Yet who would object? The Internal Revenue Service? No! As far as the Internal Revenue Service is concerned, if the surviving spouse removes the funds from Trust B and places them into Trust A, the IRS will jump with glee. The reason is simple: The funds in Trust B are insulated from further estate tax. However, when the funds are moved from Trust B into Trust A, they will once again be subject to federal estate tax upon the death of the surviving spouse! Therefore, any funds removed from Trust B should be used up by the surviving spouse.

However, if assets are removed from Trust B and placed in Trust A, the contingent beneficiaries of the Decedent's Trust B (the decedent's children) could object—for their rights to these assets are being abused. The children are contingent beneficiaries because their rights to the assets of Trust B (upon the death of the surviving spouse) are contingent upon assets still being in Trust B and the beneficiaries still being alive. The surviving spouse, as surviving trustee, has a fiduciary responsibility to preserve these funds within the rights specified in the Trust for the contingent beneficiaries.

Solution to Abuse of Trust B Rights

If the surviving trustee is not maintaining proper fiduciary responsibility, the simplest (and most common) recourse is for the contingent beneficiaries to hire an attorney to oversee the surviving trustee. A letter to this effect, from the attorney to the surviving trustee, usually rectifies any abuses rather quickly. Invariably, the surviving spouse overreacts to such a letter. Not only is the abuse readily corrected, but the surviving spouse then stands in fear of making even normal, acceptable Trust transactions. On the rare occasion where such a situation arises, I find it necessary to do everything possible to convince the surviving spouse to calm down and simply to continue to act as trustee without any further concern—as long as the fiduciary responsibility is not abused.

Historically, these fiduciary responsibilities are seldom abused. The very few instances of abuse of which I am aware have been resolved quickly and easily.

If Trust B assets are used properly, there is no practical restriction on use of the assets in the Decedent's Trust B by the surviving spouse. For example, the beneficial right of the surviving spouse to invade the principal (as necessary to maintain the same "standard of living") is not considered to be an abuse of fiduciary responsibility. Who determines what is the standard of living? The surviving trustee. Who is the surviving trustee? The surviving spouse. Thus, the surviving spouse has substantial latitude in using funds in the Decedent's Trust B, but again the latitude must not be abusive. In effect, the surviving spouse has the right to use the funds in Trust B almost *without* restriction.

Could the Trust B assets be entirely consumed for medical needs? Yes, most definitely. If, for example, the surviving spouse contracted cancer and incurred enormous medical bills, all of the assets in Trust B could be consumed to meet those medical expenses. That is as it should be and as the decedent spouse would have wanted.

Latitude in Setting Powers of Trust B

In effect, the creators of the Trust have the latitude to make the powers of the Decedent's B

Trust as broad or as narrow as desired for the surviving trustee. Although various restrictions may be imposed upon the surviving spouse as trustee, remember that the situation is a two-way street. Restrictions imposed by one spouse are usually imposed as well by the other spouse—and either spouse could end up as the restricted surviving spouse, depending on which spouse is the first to die. Such restrictions could limit the rights of the surviving spouse to income only, with no rights to the residual assets even for medical needs; could impose a co-trustee on the surviving spouse; or could distribute some or all of the assets upon the death of the first spouse.

The right to limit the powers of the Decedent's B Trust is pointed out in the example of a man with a $1 million estate. The man remarried late in life and wanted to provide for his wife if he were to predecease her. However, he was concerned that, if his wife were given the chance, she would "spend everything within 30 days." Unfortunately, as I became acquainted with his wife, I had to agree with his assessment!

The client named his eldest son from his former marriage as surviving trustee, instead of his wife, and limited his wife's rights to the income from Trust B. At the very least, 10 percent of $1 million would provide $100,000 income per year—a rather nice lifetime income for a spouse who had entered into the marriage with only $100,000 of her own assets.

Limits on Revocability

The A and B divisions of the A-B Trust are both revocable as long as both spouses are alive. However, upon the death of one spouse, the Decedent's B Trust becomes *irrevocable*. The difference between a revocable and an irrevocable Trust is changeability. A revocable Trust may be changed (amended) or terminated (revoked) as long as the settlor (the person who puts the assets into the Trust) lives. A Trust may be revoked or terminated simply by removing the assets from the name of the Trust. Upon the death of the first spouse, the B Trust becomes neither changeable nor terminable. On the other hand, the A Trust, the survivor's Trust, remains revocable during the life of the surviving spouse.

When the surviving spouse is also the surviving trustee and beneficiary of the B Trust, the only significant features that become unchangeable upon the death of the first spouse are the beneficiaries (who are named as future recipients of the assets in the B Trust) and the time, method, and percentage of distribution to the beneficiaries.

Absolute Right to Assets in Trust A

The surviving spouse's absolute right to the assets in Trust A includes being able to remove those assets from Trust A or to amend in any way the provisions in Trust A, including the naming of beneficiaries or changing the time, method, and percentage of distribution to the beneficiaries. Thus, the surviving spouse may change the heirs of Trust A (the survivor's Trust) but *not* of Trust B (the decedent's Trust) and usually not of Trust C.

Typically, the only things the surviving spouse cannot do are to change the beneficiaries of Trust B; change the time, method, and percentage of distribution from Trust B; or jeopardize the rights of the beneficiaries by an unauthorized removal of funds from Trust B.

OTHER COMMON CONCERNS ABOUT LIVING TRUSTS

Many people who are interested in the Living Trust have concerns about this little-known entity for holding their assets. The common concerns expressed by client after client include questions regarding the size of estate needed to have a Living Trust, whether a Living Trust is revocable or not, how a Living Trust can be changed or amended, what effect a Living Trust has on income tax, how a Living Trust can be terminated, what effect a divorce has on a Living Trust, and the cost of a Living Trust in relation to the cost of a Will.

Size of Estate Needed

It has been my experience that *everyone* should have a Living Trust—regardless of the size of the estate. The probate codes in most states encompass almost all estates; unless people take appropriate estate-planning measures (placing their assets in a Living Trust), they will end up giving away part of their hard-earned estates by paying unnecessary probate fees. If a person is young and his or her estate has not grown sufficiently, most likely the estate will increase in value if given enough time.

Even smaller estates should consider the numerous advantages of the Living Trust, as shown in the following example.

Luke's entire estate was worth only $20,000. Luke died; then only six months later his wife also died. Probate of this small estate was handled by a reputable legal firm. However, the probate cost was an amazing $9,000! This outrageous fee left only $11,000 of Luke's small estate for the heirs.

Everyone who reviewed this sad case concurred that, if Luke had only had a Living Trust, there would have been little or no administrative cost. Even though $9,000 may not be a lot of money to some people, in this case it represented almost half of the estate—money that was desperately needed by the heirs.

You may modify or revoke your Living Trust whenever you wish.

Revocability of Trust
The Living Trust is revocable, which means that the creators of the Trust may modify it or revoke it at any time they so choose. It is a plan—a plan to manage your estate—and any plan should be subject to change to meet the varying needs of you or your family. As has been mentioned earlier, upon the death of one or both creators of the Trust, part or all of the Trust becomes irrevocable—and that, too, is as it should be.

An irrevocable Trust is seldom recommended for the body of the estate. The exceptions to that statement are the use of the Insurance Trust and the Children's Trust. Each of these special types of Trusts will be explained in later chapters.

Amendments and Changes
Unlike a Will (which requires formal change because of the past history of abuse), the Living Trust is readily changeable, either formally or informally. Formal changes are called amendments and are accomplished by having legal counsel formalize the changes to the Trust. Informal changes to a Living Trust can be made by the creators themselves, simply by striking out or adding a section, in pen, and then initialing such changes. This informal type of change should stand up in any court. However, as soon after making the change as possible, you should seek formalization of the change through appropriate legal counsel to ensure that the change is consistent throughout the entire Trust document.

The ready changeability afforded to people having Living Trusts is often used to handle unexpected situations.

An excellent example is that of a couple who had a modest estate and three grown children. One of their sons was killed in an industrial accident, leaving behind a wife and a baby. The company responsible for the accident settled the case by awarding $1 million to the survivors (the wife and the baby). Since the wife and child were now provided for financially, the clients decided to change their Living Trust to leave their modest estate to their remaining two children.

In formulating the change, legal counsel pointed out that a similar change should be incorporated to pass the couple's personal effects to their surviving two children—a desired change that might otherwise have been overlooked without the benefit of legal counsel reviewing the changes.

Effect on Income Taxes
The Internal Revenue Service's interpretation of the Living Trust states that the Living Trust "has no effect upon income taxes." With a Living Trust, all income still flows to the individual, who will continue to report all income, as in the past, on the U.S. Individual Income Tax Return (Form 1040)—whether the individual is a single person, married and filing a joint return, or filing as head of household.

Even though an individual has a Living Trust,

he or she continues to use his or her social security number, as in the past, when filing the Form 1040 personal income tax return and reporting any income received from assets in the Trust. Later, on the death of the first spouse, the surviving spouse will use his or her social security number to identify any taxable income from assets in the Trust.

By far, the simplest way to avoid unnecessary correspondence with the IRS is to retain your assets under the social security number corresponding to your normal Form 1040 individual tax return. Thus, use your social security number as the Trust Identification Number if you are single; if you are married, use the husband's social security number. (In today's liberated society, however, the social security number used could just as well be the social security number of the wife.)

In 1981, Congress legislated that Form 1041 (the Trust tax return form) would no longer be required for a revocable Living Trust. If you are ever requested (because of a mistake on the part of the IRS) to file a Form 1041 for your

---

FIGURE 5-9
INSTRUCTIONS FOR HANDLING IRS REQUEST

What to Do if the IRS Asks for a Trust Tax Return

Less than 1 percent of our clients receive a request from the Internal Revenue Service for a tax return for their Living Trust. Another kind of trust might be required to file Form 1041, which is the proper tax return for a trust. However, the estate-planning trust that is revocable need not file such a return.

For federal income tax purposes, the Living Trust is called a "Grantor Trust," and this term should be used with the IRS if they raise any questions. For IRS purposes, this tells them that the trust is solely for estate-planning purposes and that the income tax due on income from assets or transactions on the trust assets will be reported on your Form 1040 just as if you owned those assets without the trust.

Letter to Be Sent to IRS if a Request for a Return Is Received

Internal Revenue Service   Date _____

Re: Tax Return for Living Trust
    IRS Employer Identification # _____

Gentlemen:

We have received a request for a tax return for the estate-planning revocable trust ("Grantor Trust") we have had prepared for us. This trust is revocable during our lifetimes, and we are the beneficiaries of the trust as well as the trustees. Our understanding is that all income and expenses relative to assets or transactions on the assets held by the trust must be reported on our individual Form 1040 just as if we owned those assets without the trust. This we have done.

It is further our understanding that we should not prepare a return for this kind of trust separate from our Form 1040 and ask you to correct your records accordingly. [Regs. Sec. 1.671-3 (a) (1)].

Very truly yours,

_____

_____

Social Security #

revocable Living Trust, simply advise the IRS that your Trust is a "Grantor" Trust and that you are not required to file a Form 1041 as called out in Section 1.671-3(a)(1) of the IRS regulations.

About 1 percent of our clients each year receive a letter demanding to know why they have not filed a 1041 Trust tax return for their revocable Trust. There seems to be no rhyme or reason for this random selection, nor is there any basis for such a request. The inquiry stems from our firm having originally ordered the IRS trust identification number as a service for our clients.

Some years ago, a former president of an insurance company received such an IRS demand. Being reasonably knowledgeable and astute, he answered the IRS inquiry in writing. His experience was similar to writing to a computer. After a whole series of letters and senseless responses, he sent the entire series of correspondence to our office in a plea for help.

In all of his well-written letters, the man had failed to use the magic words *Grantor Trust.* You see, the IRS recognizes the Living Trust as a Grantor Trust; until the right term is used, it is similar to talking to a brick wall. Recognizing that the IRS demand for 1041 Trust tax returns will continue in the future, our firm provides our clients with a letter of instructions for response, as shown in Figure 5-9.

Only the lower portion of the illustration needs to be duplicated, completed, and returned to the IRS. That action should be the end of the IRS inquiry—until possibly next year.

Termination of the Trust

The Living Trust will typically terminate when the assets are distributed from the Trust (because an unfunded Trust simply ceases to exist). No court action by a trustee is necessary.

Nevertheless, in order to satisfy the IRS Code, a revocable Living Trust must specify a termination at some point in time. This concept is referred to as the "law of perpetuity." Unless otherwise specifically stated in the Trust document, the IRS can create a scenario whereby the Trust theoretically could continue indefinitely—and the Decedent's Trust B would then lose its insulation from further taxation.

Specifically, the law of perpetuity says that, upon the death of both creators of the Trust, a snapshot in time is effectively taken that identifies every potential heir then living—such as the creators' children, grandchildren, great-grandchildren, and any fetuses, as well as aunts, uncles, nieces, and nephews. The Trust must cease twenty-one years after the death of *every one* of those heirs. Frankly, such a lengthy time period is beyond the scope of most people's imaginations, and I have yet to find a client who really cares about his or her Living Trust being terminated—possibly as far in the future as eighty to one hundred years or more.

Effect of Divorce on a Living Trust

Unfortunately, if a couple divorces, a Living Trust cannot in all practicality be cut in half. Therefore, one individual usually retains the Trust, and the other individual must revoke his or her interest in the Trust. The party who retains the Trust will retain his or her assets in the name of the Trust, and the other party will remove his or her assets from the Trust and will revoke his or her interest in the Trust. Such an action is accomplished by executing a "Disclaimer of Trust Interest" form as shown in Figure 5-10.

Cost of a Trust vs. a Will

Although a Will is initially less expensive to draw (create) than a Living Trust, the average individual will modify his or her Will four times during his or her lifetime, which ultimately becomes more costly than a Living Trust. In addition, by saving the cost of probate, a Living Trust ultimately saves an estate *many* times its original cost, by eliminating probate fees and eliminating or reducing estate taxes.

HISTORY OF THE LIVING TRUST

One of the most frequently asked questions is "When did we get this new concept, the Living Trust?" Surprise! The Living Trust is not really a new concept: it comes from English common law, which is the very basis for the legal system in the United States. The concept of a Trust existed long before this nation was conceived; the origins of a Trust go as far back as A.D. 800, to the days of the Roman Empire. In fact, a

---

FIGURE 5-10
DISCLAIMER OF TRUST INTEREST

Disclaimer of Trust Interest
(Probate Code Section 280 et seq.)

To Whom It May Concern:

Effective this date, I hereby disclaim my interest in the revocable Living Trust known as "_____ Family Trust, dated August 18, 1988, _____ and _____ Trustors, and _____ and _____ and/or Trustees."

The Trust was originally created by _____ and _____, and I disclaim each and every interest I may have therein.

I resign as Trustee of the Trust, and I disclaim and revoke my interest as Trustor, Settlor, and Beneficiary. I relinquish all my rights to the remaining Settlor, _____.

I have withdrawn all assets which I placed into the Trust as a Settlor, and I have legal title to them at this time as an individual free of trust. I have no claim on any further Trust assets.

This disclaimer is executed and delivered with the intent to comply with the provisions of the Probate Code Sections and to be bound thereby.

Date: _____

_____
Trustee

Trust became the preferred method of holding property in Europe during the Middle Ages.

Adopted from Roman Law

The English people adopted the Trust from Roman law as early as the twelfth century to preserve their property from the many abuses under the crown. For example, a landowner was obligated to provide relief, or money, to help supplement the lord of the land for numerous causes (such as the marriage of the lord's daughter or the knighting of the lord's son). In addition, the king imposed nearly 100 forms of tax. The landowner was prohibited from selling his land or dividing the land among his children or grandchildren. If the landowner were convicted of a crime, he forfeited all he owned to the lord or king, leaving his family destitute.

Accusing a peasant of a crime was a very common means of acquiring the peasant's land and, in the end, was quite profitable for the landlord. The peasants soon found that the Trust provided a means to protect their lands from this wrongful acquisition by the noble of the land.

The practice of holding title to land in a Trust eventually became commonplace. The Trust permitted one party (the trustee) to hold the property for the benefit of the owner and eventually to pass this property to the owner's children. With the passage of time (and continued abuse by the crown), passing title of land to a Trust became an ordinary practice.

Survived Challenge

By 1535, the king and his nobles challenged the legality of the Trust and attempted to prohibit its use with the "Statute of Uses." The king and his nobles considered the Trust to be evil, because it permitted privacy of transfer, legal avoidance of unreasonable taxes and regulations, preservation of the estate of convicted criminals and, most importantly, because it caused the loss of revenue to the king and his lords.

The challenge to the Trust fell upon the common law judges of England in the chancery court, the highest court in the land. The judges, who had absolute jurisdiction over legal estates, upheld the validity of the Trust concept. Within the next five years, the Statute of Uses was effectively abandoned—and the Trust was securely embedded as part of English common law, having survived the formidable challenge by the king and his nobles.

Brought to America with Colonists

The colonists brought the Trust to America, where Patrick Henry is given the first recorded credit for drafting a Trust on this continent. In 1765, he wrote a Trust for Robert Morris, governor of the colony of Virginia. Thus, the Trust was written more than two decades before the adoption of the U.S. Constitution.

Historically, the Living Trust has been used by people of great wealth, such as the late President John F. Kennedy, William Waldorf Astor, John D. Rockefeller, H. L. Hunt (the Texas oil billionaire), and J. Paul Getty. Until very recently, very few people in the United States had Living Trusts; however, as people are becoming more sophisticated, more and more of them are adopting the Living Trust as a way to preserve their estates and avoid the unnecessary agony of probate.

Will Congress Take It Away?

Most people are afraid that Congress will take away the Living Trust. However, if the English king and his nobles failed in their attack on the Trust in the sixteenth century, then you should have little fear that Congress will deprive Americans of such an established institution as the Living Trust. The Living Trust is not a tax shelter, but rather it is the only means by which married couples can fully utilize the federal estate tax equivalent exemptions given to them by Congress. Reportedly, fewer than 1 percent of the people in the United States have discovered the value of the Living Trust and have taken advantage of its many benefits.

On the other hand, great legal minds occasionally figure out a loophole and then, in a manner of speaking, take a horse (the Living Trust), add a hump, and call it a camel. The Clifford Trust, which will be discussed later in this chapter, is such a creature. The Clifford Trust was created to shelter income taxes and prevailed for some twelve to fourteen years until 1986, when Congress effectively lopped off the hump, returning the camel to the horse—

the Living Trust, the basic legal instrument.

Most senators and representatives in Congress have Living Trusts. When Congress enacts estate tax reform, it does so with the assumption that everyone should have a Living Trust. An example of such legislation is the Economic Recovery Tax Act of 1981, which provided today's $600,000 federal estate tax equivalent exemption. For both husband and wife to use and preserve their exemptions, they must have an A-B Trust.

Two hundred years ago, representatives from the thirteen founding states met to form one of the finest documents ever created—the U.S. Constitution. Specifically, the Constitution was created to form a central government to represent the people, and the Constitution granted certain rights to the federal government. The rights that were not specified in the Constitution (and, therefore, not relinquished by the states to the federal government) were retained by the states and are now often referred to as states' rights. Since such rights were fundamental to English law, they were therefore adopted as law when this nation was formed.

One of those states' rights is the right of a state to create a legal entity, such as a corporation or a Trust. Such a legal entity, once created, is equally recognized by all of the other forty-nine states. The right to create a legal entity is sacrosanct to the states, and it would be inconceivable to think that the federal government might trespass in this area. After 1,200 years of use and legal testing, the Living Trust is basically the same entity as its predecessor from English times. I can foresee little or no chance of Congress infringing upon this document.

THE LIVING TRUST AS A LEGAL ENTITY

The Living Trust is a legal entity created by the state to hold title to assets. It has been used to enable an individual or a family to hold title to assets so that the assets can eventually pass to the heirs without the intervention of any further legal process.

It may help you understand the concept of a Living Trust to compare a Trust to a corporation, as they both have the same basic characteristics. Both are legal entities created by the state. A Trust and a corporation are both entities that a person can neither touch, taste, nor smell. Regardless of which state creates the Trust or corporation, all other states recognize and accept the Trust or corporation that has been created.

A corporation has initial founders; a Trust has a creator (trustor). Stockholders place money in the corporation; settlors place their assets in the Trust. Corporate officers are authorized to buy, sell, and transfer the corporate assets; trustees (the administrators) are authorized to do likewise with the Trust assets.

If you were to form a corporation, you could take your assets and place them inside the corporation. As owner of a corporation, you do not own the assets; instead, the assets are owned by the corporation. However, if you were also the corporate officer or officers, you would have the power to buy, sell, transfer, and borrow against those assets without restriction. In a Living Trust, the income flows through to the creators and is reported, as before, on the regular Form 1040 tax return used by individuals. A corporation has an indefinite life; however, a Living Trust must eventually cease and the assets be distributed to the beneficiaries. However, the significant difference between a corporation and a Trust is that a corporation has red tape and taxes—whereas a Trust has neither.

As long as the creators (trustors) of the Trust are living and competent, the Living Trust is revocable. Assets may be placed in the Trust or removed from it as desired. In fact, whether the assets are in the Trust or outside it does not change control of the assets one iota.

The Living Trust is known by many names: Living Trust, Revocable Trust, Changeable Trust, Inter Vivos Trust (which means Living Trust in Latin), Family Trust, and Grantor Trust. This last name is the Internal Revenue Service designation for a Living Trust. All these names refer to the *same* Trust.

In fact, in my early days, I used to advise my clients that they should have an "Inter Vivos Trust." Those words were impressive to my clients. (They did not know what I was talking about, but it sounded good.) Today I go out of my way to try to make the Trust sound simple and therefore use the term *Living Trust*. I choose this term to be consistent and to emphasize that the Living Trust, properly funded, lives with you and is therefore basically unchallengeable.

Two Other Trust Forms

Two other forms of Trusts are sometimes confused with the Living Trust: the Constitutional Family Trust and the Clifford Trust. However, these Trusts are not Living Trusts, nor are they different names for the Living Trust.

Constitutional Family Trust

The Living Trust should not be confused with the Constitutional Family Trust, sometimes improperly referred to as the Family Trust. The Constitutional Family Trust is specifically forbidden by the Internal Revenue Code and was a very poor legal attempt to create an irrevocable Trust that would circumvent the payment of income taxes. Unfortunately, the people who fell prey to this unwise use of a Trust ultimately suffered dire consequences; the IRS eventually collected unpaid income taxes and levied stiff penalties.

Occasionally, I encounter someone who needs a Living Trust but shies away from it because of a previous disastrous experience with the Constitutional Family Trust. One client's uncle, a judge in a midwestern state, wrote, "Don't get involved with that notorious Living Trust, because it was disallowed by the IRS." It is tragic that an incompetent abuse of a Trust form can reflect unfavorably upon such an outstanding estate-planning tool as the Living Trust.

Clifford Trust

The Living Trust should also not be confused with the Clifford Trust, which is a special form of Trust that *temporarily* transfers only the beneficial interest (the right to receive the income). This type of Trust typically names the children of the person who created the Trust as the beneficial interest parties. They have the right to all of the income from the assets in the Trust during the lifetime of the Trust (formerly ten years and one day).

The Clifford Trust was designed for a Dr. Clifford in San Francisco, who had a high income through his medical practice and owned several apartments. Through good legal research, his counsel created the Clifford Trust, whereby, for at least ten years and one day, the apartments were placed in trust, with the income going to Dr. Clifford's children and being taxed at the children's tax rate. The Trust allowed Dr. Clifford to retain control over the apartments; after ten years and a day, the apartments (and all their income) returned to Dr. Clifford. The Trust also specified that, if Dr. Clifford died during the ten-year period of the Trust, the apartments would be included in his estate.

Since then, the Clifford Trust has been used quite successfully by many high-income people to shift income to their children without giving up either the asset or the control of it. Even though the Clifford Trust was effectively eliminated with the 1986 tax code, because of its temporary income transfer, this Trust can still be created if you are willing to have the Trust run for thirty-two years! This type of Trust, running for the longer period of time, is still legal under the 1986 tax code.

For special situations in which it may be advisable to transfer appreciating assets to your children, the Children's Trust is recommended. (The Children's Trust will be more fully explained in Chapter 10.)

Trust Applicability

Unlike a Will, the Living Trust is applicable from state to state. Since the basis of the Trust is English common law, a Trust is also recognized in Canada, England, and all commonwealth nations. Although most European and South American countries use civil law, the Trust is recognized in these countries as well. With clients all over the world today, our experience has been that, by and large, most nations recognize the Living Trust.

The 1961 Hague Convention (which went into effect for the United States in October 1981) abolished the procedures requiring foreign governments to legalize documents of other nations. In effect, the convention decreed that documents notarized as public documents in a particular country would be recognized as valid documents by the other countries (where both countries are signatories to the Hague Convention).

In contrast, since probate varies from state to state and since Wills have a history of abuse, the required legal content of Wills varies from state to state. Someone who has a Will and moves from one state to another should have his or her Will reviewed by legal counsel in the new state and probably redrawn to comply with local state law. A Will accompanying a Living Trust (known as a Pour-Over Will) is a supplementary document to be used only as a contingency if assets were inadvertently left outside the Trust. Therefore, it is not absolutely essential to conform this document to local state law.

PROPER FORMS OF THE LIVING TRUST

The Living Trust document can take one of three basic forms: an A Trust, an A-B Trust, and an A-B-C Trust. The form that best suits your particular situation depends on your marital status, the net worth of your estate, and the potential distribution you desire for your heirs.

A Trust

The A Trust can be used for single persons or married couples. As you learned earlier in the chapter, a husband and wife should always consider an A-B Trust, rather than only an A Trust, even if an A-B Trust is not financially needed for the size of their particular estate.

The A Trust must always be used when only one person is involved, such as an unmarried or a widowed person. For estates valued at less than $600,000, the entire estate will flow down to the heirs, since there will be no probate fees or estate taxes to pay. However, for estates valued at more than $600,000, estate taxes will be due.

The A Trust may also be used for a married or unmarried couple whose estate is valued at much less than $600,000, although this practice is not recommended. The entire estate will flow down to the surviving spouse, since there will be no probate fees and—because the estate is small—no estate taxes.

A-B Trust

The A-B Trust is used when two individuals are involved in the Trust, whether they are married or unmarried. The A-B Trust should be considered by any couple whose estate exceeds $600,000. Upon the death of one individual, half of the assets will flow down into the B (or decedent's) Trust, and the other half of the assets will flow down to the survivor in the A (or survivor's) Trust. Thus, the entire estate will remain available to be used by the surviving spouse.

A-B-C Trust

The A-B-C Trust is used for a married couple whose estate exceeds $1.2 million (two federal estate tax equivalent exemptions). This form of Trust is used to provide the right to forgo *any* estate taxes upon the first to die, regardless of the size of the estate. Of the decedent's portion of the estate, $600,000 will flow down into the Decedent's B Trust, and the excess will flow into the C Trust, in order to prevent estate taxation upon the death of the first spouse.

The C Trust is also known as a Q-Tip Trust. "Q-Tip" stands for *Qualified Terminal Interest Property*, which means that, to qualify for this right, the surviving spouse must have two rights:

1. *Right to Income*—The surviving spouse must have a right to all of the income, a right that must be granted for the life of the surviving spouse. The income right may not be terminated, for example, in only ten years or during the life of the surviving spouse. For the Trust to qualify, the surviving spouse need *not* be given the right to use the principal. In other words, the asset is preserved for the heirs, but the spouse may use any income derived from the asset (such as rental income from an apartment).

2. *Right to Change Beneficiaries*—In addition, the surviving spouse may be given a testamentary right to change the beneficiaries of Trust C, which means that, during the remaining life of the surviving spouse, he or she may change the beneficiaries of Trust C.

Occasionally, a situation arises where, for example, a couple have married, each spouse has children by a previous marriage, and both spouses have accumulated substantial estates prior to their new marriage. If one spouse (for example, the husband) desired that a large share of his estate pass directly to *his* children upon his death, his assets would not qualify for inclusion in the Q-Tip Trust, since the surviving spouse would not have the right to the income from these assets. Therefore, the husband's excess assets would be subject to federal estate taxes upon his death.

The husband may pass the assets directly from the B Trust to his heirs without those assets being subject to further federal estate taxation, leaving the excess assets in the C Trust for the use of his surviving spouse.

The C Trust is expandable. The surviving spouse may pass any amount in excess of $600,000 to the C Trust (whether the amount is $150,000, $1.5 million, or $15 million) and thereby defer any assessment of estate taxes until the death of the surviving spouse.

When to Use the C Trust

The surviving spouse can elect to defer paying any estate taxes upon the death of the first spouse as a means of preserving the estate.

An example of such a situation involves Richard and Joan Hogan, who had an estate of approximately $2 million. Upon Richard's death, his estate would come down to Joan without paying any estate taxes:

$400,000 Decedent (C Trust)	$600,000 Decedent (B Trust)	$1,000,000 Surviving Spouse (A Trust)

Upon the death of Joan (the surviving spouse), the portion of the estate in the B Trust would be insulated from federal estate taxes. Therefore, federal estate tax would be computed on the value of whatever amount is left in Trust C ($400,000) and in Trust A ($1 million), a total of $1.4 million. When the surviving spouse's equivalent exemption ($600,000) is deducted, the remaining $800,000 would be subject to federal estate tax at 40 percent. The federal estate tax due would therefore be $320,000:

Trust C	$ 400,000
Trust A	1,000,000
Subtotal	$ 1,400,000
Less: Surviving spouse's equivalent exemption	(600,000)
Taxable estate	$ 800,000
Federal estate tax (40%)	$ 320,000

When Not to Use the C Trust

Occasionally, however, a situation may arise where use of the C Trust may not be financially beneficial to the estate. If, in the previous example, Joan Hogan had cancer and knew that she had only a short time to live, paying the estate taxes on the excess amount in Trust B would preserve more of the estate.

Joan chose to forgo using the C Trust and instead elected to pay the federal estate taxes on her husband's taxable share of the estate ($400,000) upon his death. The estate would therefore be distributed only into the A and B portions of the Trust:

$0 Decedent (C Trust)	$845,000 Decedent (B Trust)	$1,000,000 Surviving Spouse (A Trust)

Computation of the federal estate tax would be as shown here:

Decedent's share of estate	$ 1,000,000
Less: Decedent's equivalent exemption	(600,000)
Taxable estate	$ 400,000
Federal estate tax (39%)	155,000
Decedent's original estate	$ 1,000,000
Less: Estate tax	(155,000)
Net estate	$ 845,000

After paying estate taxes of $155,000 (on the $400,000 taxable portion of Richard's estate), the $245,000 remaining after taxes may now be added to the $600,000 already placed in the Decedent's B Trust. The entire $845,000 would then be insulated from further estate taxes. Upon Joan's death, only the $1 million in the Survivor's A Trust would be subject to federal estate taxes. Joan's federal estate tax computations would appear as follows:

Survivor's share of estate	$ 1,000,000
Less: Survivor's equivalent exemption	(600,000)
Taxable estate	$ 400,000
Survivor's original estate	$ 1,000,000
Less: Estate tax (39%)	(155,000)
Net estate	$ 845,000
Plus: Decedent's estate from Trust B	845,000
Total estate for the heirs	$ 1,690,000

The following computations show how Joan benefited the heirs by paying taxes on the excess amount in Trust B rather than putting the excess in Trust C:

	Using C Trust	Not Using C Trust
Total estate	$ 2,000,000	$ 2,000,000
Tax on decedent's estate	-0-	(155,000)
Balance of estate for surviving spouse	$ 2,000,000	$ 1,845,000
Tax on survivor's estate	(320,000)	(155,000)
Residual estate to heirs	$ 1,680,000	$ 1,690,000
Additional gain for heirs		$ 10,000

In effect, by not using the C Trust and instead paying the federal government $155,000 in estate taxes upon the death of the first spouse, Joan saved the estate $10,000 in additional federal estate taxes. (On the other hand, if Joan had retained the $155,000 and invested it in a tax-free entity paying 6 percent or in a taxable entity paying 9 percent, she would have earned back the $10,000 by the end of the year—and *still* retained the funds for future income.)

The amount of tax saved will increase for larger estates, but the principle is the same. However, generally speaking, dollars in hand today are more valuable than money saved tomorrow.

Following a seminar some time ago, a young man came up to me and rather pompously announced that he knew about the Q-Tip Trust and knew that it was better to pay the decedent's estate tax up front. My response to the young man was that, if the surviving spouse knows he or she will die within only a few months of the decedent spouse, then paying tax on the decedent's share of the estate may have merit. However, as a practical matter, the intent of most people is to preserve as much of the estate as possible for the survivor. After settling hundreds of estates, I have found only this one estate where it was appropriate to recommend paying taxes on the decedent's estate following the death of the decedent, rather than waiting until the death of the surviving spouse. The Q-Tip Trust is an ideal estate-planning tool and a protection for the surviving spouse.

POUR-OVER WILL

The Living Trust becomes, in effect, your Will and specifically spells out to whom, when, and how your assets are to be distributed—and does so with far greater latitude than a standard Will. Nevertheless, another document, known as the "Pour-Over Will," is needed to accompany the Living Trust. The Pour-Over Will transfers into the Living Trust assets that have been inadvertently left outside. The Pour-Over Will simply says, in effect, that if you forgot to place an asset into your Living Trust, it is your intent (upon your death) that such assets "pour over" into your Trust. As a client said so well, "It's similar to a P.S. to a letter." The Pour-Over Will is therefore a useful catchall and should be included in every Living Trust.

Assets passing into the Living Trust through a Pour-Over Will must, however, first go through probate. Ideally, you have done your job—have placed all your assets in trust—and will never have to use this pour-over feature. After all, one of the prime purposes of the Living Trust is to avoid probate! Unfortunately, not all people take full advantage of this feature.

Several years ago, for example, clients who had established a Living Trust to avoid probate learned that they had been named executors of the estate of their brother-in-law, Bob Anderson. Wanting to avoid probate on his estate, the clients brought Bob in to establish his own Living Trust. Thereafter, they helped Bob transfer all of his assets into the Trust—that is, all but one asset. For some unknown reason, no matter how hard they tried, Bob resisted transferring one stock certificate into the Trust. At the most, it would have taken less than an hour to go to the bank, have his signature guaranteed, and forward the stock papers to the transfer agent.

Bob died six months later. His brother and sister-in-law, as trustees, sold his condominium within sixty days, liquidated his assets, and distributed them. The clients took care of all the assets—except the one stock certificate, which represented 5,000 shares of American Express stock, then worth $350,000. This single certificate had to go through twelve months of agonizing probate—and cost $8,500 in probate fees. As executors of Bob's estate, his brother and sister-in-law would be the first to say, "Don't leave *any* assets outside your Trust."

Provisions of the Pour-Over Will

A Pour-Over Will is a rather simple legal document that consists of five provisions:

- It identifies the individual by name.
- It revokes any prior Wills and related codicils.
- It pours into the Living Trust any personal or household effects left outside the Trust.
- It pours into the Trust any real assets left outside the Trust (but unfortunately, *after* probate).
- It names the executor and provides the necessary authority to take assets left outside the Trust through probate.

Identification of the Individual

The Pour-Over Will states your name. If you are married, the Pour-Over Will states that fact and names your spouse. All children (whether by this or any previous marriages) are each named. Often, a husband or wife who has married a spouse with children from a previous marriage feels close to these children and wishes to name them as his or her children and heirs, even though they are not formally adopted. This action is quite acceptable and common.

If a female child changes her name because of marriage or divorce, you do not need to change your Pour-Over Will or amend your Trust. Once identified as your child, that child remains identified as your child regardless of a name change.

If you wish to disinherit a child, this fact need *not* be stated in the Pour-Over Will. You need only *exclude* that child as a beneficiary of the Trust. Since the Living Trust is, in effect, a contract, you may include or exclude anyone as you so choose. To avoid a later challenge by an excluded child as having been forgotten, your Pour-Over Will includes that child's name as a simple acknowledgment and nothing more.

Revocation of Prior Wills and Codicils

The Pour-Over Will revokes any prior Wills or codicils (changes to a Will) you may have made. I am often asked whether a person who creates a Living Trust needs to notify the attorney who drew up his or her Will. My answer is no. Even though such a response does a minor disservice to the attorney, who will continue to retain that now-revoked document in his or her files, the attorney all too often takes such news ungraciously and tries to convince the client that he or she has done a stupid thing by creating a Living Trust and says, "Probate really isn't that much."

Pouring of Personal Effects into the Trust

Personal and household effects, including future acquisitions, should be transferred into the Trust by a document called Assignment of Furniture, Furnishings, and Personal Effects (explained in Chapter 11). The Pour-Over Will simply restates that, if some personal or household effects were somehow left outside the Trust, they are to pour over into the Living Trust.

Pouring of Real Assets into the Trust

The Pour-Over Will specifies that, upon your death, any real assets held outside the Trust are to pour over into the Trust. Real assets would include checking accounts, savings accounts, money market funds, certificates of deposit, Treasury bills, stocks, bonds, mutual funds, limited partnerships, notes due to you, real estate, trust deeds, and business interests (such as a sole proprietorship, a partnership, or a corporation). Unfortunately, if these real assets exceed the probate criteria, they must go

through probate first, and this task is the executor's job.

Naming of Executor and Granting of Authority

The Pour-Over Will names the executor and provides the executor with the authority to take any assets left outside the Trust through the probate process. If assets that have been left outside your Living Trust exceed the probate criteria, they must be taken through probate by the executor. Once the probate process is completed, the assets will pour over into the Living Trust to be utilized or distributed as you have specified in your Living Trust.

Typically, the surviving spouse should be named to serve as the executor; upon the death of the surviving spouse, the successor trustee should be named to serve as the executor. However, unlike the successor trustees (who may consist of several co-trustees), only one person should be appointed to serve as executor. That person should reside within the state where probate will occur because of the numerous court appearances and document signatures that are required.

Even though the Pour-Over Will often names the guardian for minor children, a far more appropriate way of naming a guardian is through an entirely separate document, titled Appointment of Guardian, which will be described in Chapter 9.

Potential Uses of the Pour-Over Will

Although one of the prime reasons for a Living Trust is to avoid probate, two potential uses of the Pour-Over Will still remain, even with all of the assets properly transferred to the Trust. If an individual were killed in an automobile accident, for example, there could potentially be proceeds from a wrongful death suit (which would become part of the decedent's estate).

Another situation would be individuals with great wealth and therefore potential exposure to liability suits, such as real estate developers, doctors, or contractors. In a situation of this nature, it may be advisable to probate a *specific sum* of money for the sole purpose of cutting off future claims at the conclusion of the probate process. For example, following the announcement that Bing Crosby had a Living

Trust, $1 million was probated in Mr. Crosby's estate, specifically to terminate any future suits. Mr. Crosby had not only accumulated a large estate, but his holdings were quite diverse—and he was a famous person.

In today's litigious society, such circumstances can give rise to any type of suit, regardless of its merits. Suits go through the civil courts, which are extremely crowded today, may take up to five years just to get to court, and may cost anywhere from $50,000 to $200,000 in legal fees. Therefore, whenever there is a potential for any type of suit, it is far more beneficial to have such claims heard in the probate court, whether or not the claim is groundless. Unlike the civil court, the probate court will typically hear the claim within four months of death, and it is far more inclined to discharge the claim or to carefully examine its merits and to settle it on the basis of the true merits of the claim, rather than on the emotional whims of a jury (as would be the case with a civil trial).

To settle potential suits via the probate process, an executor must be named and then authorized to act on behalf of the deceased person. Once the claims have been expeditiously settled in the probate court, the remaining assets would then pour over into the Trust and be used or distributed as specified in the Trust.

A MOST VERSATILE DOCUMENT

Even though the concept of the Living Trust is new to most people, it stands as a pillar of the democratic system.

It is important to recognize that it is not just the Living Trust that matters, but it is the *entire process* of establishing and funding a Living Trust that really counts. The process ensures that the assets are transferred into the Trust and that the estate is organized. A Living Trust becomes *your* plan, and, as any plan should be, it is readily changeable (and revocable). In addition, a properly drawn and funded Living Trust is unchallengeable.

After working with the Living Trust for almost twenty years, helping to create the documents and settle the estates, I firmly believe that the Living Trust is one of the most versatile and remarkable documents available.

6

Parties to the Trust

Individuals often serve many functions simultaneously. A man may be a husband, father, engineer, and church leader; a woman may be a wife, mother, teacher, and community leader. Each role is distinct and important. Similarly, when you have a Living Trust, you will generally serve as the trustor, the settlor, the trustee, and the beneficiary. Two other roles, distinct from the Trust but related to it, are the roles of the executor and the guardian. Since many of the legal terms associated with Living Trusts are not commonly understood, this chapter explains each of the terms identifying the parties to the Trust.

TRUSTOR

The *trustor* is the individual or individuals who create the Living Trust. These individuals will be asked to sign as trustors (that is, the *creators* of the Trust). Having created the Trust, the trustors have nothing further to do unless they wish to make a change to their Trust. The trustors will also be asked to sign any future amendments to the Trust.

SETTLOR

The *settlor* (who is almost always the same individual or individuals as the trustors) is the indi-

vidual or individuals who place the assets inside the Trust. As such, settlors have *absolute power* over those assets, with the freedom to do as they wish with the assets until their death. As you learned in Chapter 5, the settlors may buy, sell, borrow against, and transfer the assets. The settlors also have the power to amend or revoke the Trust and to name the heirs.

If the settlors are a couple, the surviving spouse inherits the power to buy, sell, transfer, borrow against, and distribute the assets. However, the right to amend the Decedent's Trust B or to name the heirs and method of distribution of the Decedent's Trust B dies with the decedent settlor. The surviving settlor retains *absolute power* over the assets in the Survivor's Trust A, since they are the survivor's assets. The right to make any changes to Trusts A, B, or C dies with the surviving settlor. The entire Trust then becomes irrevocable; the successor trustee may make no alterations whatsoever, and must thereafter abide by the specific directions of the Trust.

The settlor is sometimes referred to as the *grantor*, which is simply the Internal Revenue Service name for the settlor. Grantor Trust is the IRS name for a Living Trust.

TRUSTEE

The *trustee* is the individual or individuals who handle the administration of the Trust. When a Trust is first created, the trustees are usually the same individuals as the trustors and settlors of the Trust. For a married couple, usually husband and wife both act as trustees.

You have presumably managed your assets reasonably well, and this management should continue after you have created a Living Trust. Therefore, once your Trust is created, you will now step in as trustee of the Trust assets—with the same freedom and power to buy, sell, borrow against, or transfer the Trust assets as you had before creating a Living Trust.

Surviving Trustee

The *surviving trustee* is the individual who continues to manage the Trust after one of the original trustees has died. Upon the death of one spouse, the surviving spouse should become the surviving trustee, having the same freedom as before to manage the assets in the Trust. Typically, the surviving spouse also retains the right to change the successor trustee (the individual who will take over the administration of the Trust when the surviving spouse dies).

Historically, the wife was considered unsophisticated in financial matters, and a financial institution was usually named to serve as cotrustee with the wife. This attitude is a throwback to the promotion of the Living Trust by banking institutions during the 1920s. In today's society, it is recommended that the wife be named as surviving trustee as long as she is competent. If the wife feels the need, she may still hire (and fire at her discretion) good financial counsel. Of course, the same recommendations apply if the husband is the surviving spouse.

A good example of a financial institution being hired to manage Trust assets is that of Mrs. Adams, whose husband had been with a major bank for some thirty years. In drawing up their Trust, the pair's natural inclination was to name the bank as trustee or at least as a cotrustee with the wife. At my urging, they named the wife as sole surviving trustee. When Mr. Adams died some twelve months later, Mrs. Adams, as the surviving trustee, hired the bank to manage the Trust assets.

Within six months, however, Mrs. Adams was so frustrated with the bank's poor management that she moved her account to another financial institution. Nine years later, this financially unsophisticated widow has done very well—by demanding good service of the financial institution. Demanding good service was something she could do *only* as the sole surviving trustee.

Successor Trustee

A successor trustee also must be named to succeed you as the manager of the Trust assets upon your death or incompetence (if you are single) or upon the death or incompetence of both spouses (if you are married). This individual or individuals will step into your shoes upon your death or incompetence without requiring any court proceedings or legal action. The successor trustee will immediately have the same powers that you as trustee had to buy, sell, borrow against, and transfer the Trust assets. An even more important function for the successor trustee is to use or distribute the assets as you have instructed in your Living Trust. However, a successor trustee may not in any way change the Trust (since he or she was not the creator of the Trust).

A successor trustee, however, does have the freedom to manage the assets in the estate, but must do so in a prudent manner. For example, just as you might do, the successor trustee may take a first or second mortgage on real estate to improve the property or acquire other property in the name of the Trust. To borrow against an asset has to do with Trust *management*, not with asset distribution. The successor trustee may not borrow against assets in trust for the benefit of a beneficiary (rather than for the benefit of the Trust), unless you have so specified in your beneficial instructions, as described in the next chapter. For example, it could be appropriate for a successor trustee to borrow against Trust assets, rather than liquidate the assets, to pay for medical bills of minor children who are beneficiaries.

As you become aged and possibly infirm, though still competent, you may wish to relinquish the administration of your assets to the successor trustee or successor trustees. You may do so by a simple statement in writing to that effect. However, as long as you are competent, you retain the right to resume the role as trustee or to replace the successor trustee. This is your absolute right as the settlor. Since you created the Trust, you have full control over it.

The successor trustee's job of administering a Trust takes little effort. Location of residence therefore need not be a factor in naming successor trustees. From time to time, decisions must be made and papers signed in order to buy, sell, transfer, or distribute assets within the Trust. Such decisions usually can be made fairly easily from one or many locations.

For example, four children might be acting as successor trustees of a Trust. One of the children may live in San Francisco, another in Chicago, another in New York, and the other child in Miami. It is possible for the four trustees, by telephone, to agree to sell a particular piece of real estate and to authorize one of the trustees to take the appropriate action. Then, as would be the case in almost all real estate transactions, a real estate agent would be appointed, a buyer eventually found, and the real estate sold. However, before escrow could close, the deed must be signed by all four trustees. The signature process would be accomplished by having, for example, the trustee in San Francisco sign the deed; forward it to Chicago, on to New York, and then to Miami for signatures. The trustee in Miami would then return the deed to San Francisco. The entire process should take no more than one to two weeks, depending upon the vagaries of the postal system.

The predominant characteristic of the successor trustee is *trust*. Thus, you should consider selecting your adult child or children, close family members, or close friends to serve as the successor trustee or successor trustees.

Fiduciary Capacity

The successor trustee serves in a *fiduciary capacity*. This means that, in all financial matters relating to the Trust, the trustee must act with prudence and strictly in accordance with the Trust instructions. The successor trustees have *no* protection for acting irresponsibly or con-

trary to the instructions of the Trust. *Not even bankruptcy* is an excuse.

I often cite the situation of three children named as successor trustees and also as beneficiaries. Each child was to receive $50,000 outright upon the death of the surviving parent and another $50,000 five years later.

One child was involved in a business venture that needed $100,000, and he coerced his two siblings into giving him not only the $50,000 legally due him, but also the $50,000 that was not due for another five years. The business venture failed, and the son who received the extra share of money returned to his siblings and advised them that, since they were *all* at fault in violating their fiduciary responsibilities, he wanted his $50,000 in five years when due—from *their* share. The child was correct, and he would most likely get his money.

Recognizing these consequences, anyone serving as successor trustee should respond to such a request by saying, "Brother, I love you, but. . . ."

More than One Successor Trustee

If you are wondering who watches over the trustee, one way to alleviate your concerns is to appoint as trustee someone you trust. You can also obtain security in numbers by appointing two or more trustees. Multiple trustees tend to monitor each other, so it is less likely that one of the trustees will do something that is not in the best interest of the estate.

If more than one successor trustee is named, all successor trustees must act *in concert* as cotrustees. Any action on behalf of the Trust will require the agreement and signature of each successor co-trustee.

The concept of compromise and joint agreement can be illustrated by the example of three children who are serving as successor trustees and have different investment concepts. The first child wants to be safe and place the funds under the mattress. The second child wants to double the money overnight on a "high-flyer." The third child wants to place the assets in the bank in certificates of deposit. Since the children must all agree, the funds are obviously not going under the mattress or into a high-flyer.

The three must compromise and come up with a middle-of-the-road decision, which is in keeping with the fiduciary responsibilities of the trustees.

We usually require the successor trustees to act in concert, as this provides a greater degree of security, but you may elect to permit the successor trustees to act by majority rule.

A wealthy couple desired to have their seven sons serve together as successor trustees. The couple admitted that their sons did not get along well with each other, and the pair suggested that their Trust be drawn so as to permit a majority opinion of successor trustees to prevail. Unfortunately, such an arrangement cannot legally be permitted; co-trustees must *all* agree before there can be any decision. Even under these challenging circumstances, it is amazing to watch successor co-trustees compromise and ultimately reach the best decision for all concerned.

Clients frequently ask, "May we name all our children as successor trustees, so as not to hurt anyone?" The answer, of course, is yes. Unlike the committee that started out to design a horse and ended up with a camel, several trustees invariably make unified decisions that are in the best interest of the Trust.

Legal Age to Serve as Trustee
An individual must be of legal age (eighteen in most states) to serve as a trustee. One husband and wife felt that their only child, aged sixteen, was mature enough to be named successor trustee if something happened to them. In this situation, it was recommended that the father's sister be named as alternate successor trustee and that the sixteen-year-old son be named as the successor trustee. Then, if the parents died while the son were still a minor (less than eighteen years old), the father's sister, as alternate successor trustee, would serve as trustee until the son's eighteenth birthday. At that time, the son would step in as the successor trustee with all of the trustee powers his parents had possessed before him.

Recently, a husband and wife asked if they could name their children, ages five and seven, as successor trustees with an adult named as the alternate successor trustee. I suggested that the children were a little young for such responsibility and that the parents should wait until the children reached the age of fifteen or sixteen to see how well they were maturing.

Conflict Among Successor Trustees
Many people wonder what would happen in the event of unresolved conflict, such as sibling rivalry, where there are two or more successor trustees. In such rare situations, the Living Trusts written by our firm specify that a conflict shall be resolved by the American Arbitration Association via arbitration—a process that is swift, reasonable, and relatively inexpensive. As an added protection, a provision in the Living Trusts drawn up for our clients stipulates that there will be one arbitrator per individual, plus an independent arbitrator, if appropriate.

You may appoint multiple successor trustees— for example, all of your children.

If there is an unresolved conflict, the American Arbitration Association—headquartered in New York—will send, upon request, its rules of arbitration and identify its nearest local office. When the local office is contacted, it will supply a list of arbitrators (typically ten to fifteen people); each conflicting party then may choose his or her arbitrator. An arbitrator is simply a businessperson who serves as an impartial decision maker to resolve disputes. Conflict is typically emotional, and the arbitrator will take a businesslike approach. The arbitrator will simply look at the issues, eliminating the emotions, and will make a decision that is fair and in the best interests of all parties concerned.

In the five years since our firm has begun including this provision for resolving conflicts in the Living Trusts drawn up for our clients, I am not aware of any Trust that has gone to arbitration. People often operate on emotions; they will play the game as long as they can. However, when people recognize that they can no longer play their game, but must go to arbitration where their emotions will be set aside, they stop playing and proceed to work out a compromise.

BENEFICIARIES

The surviving spouse is typically the primary *beneficiary* as well as the surviving trustee. The children or other named heirs are the *contingent beneficiaries*, meaning that they are beneficiaries only if they are living when the surviving spouse dies and assets are left in the Trust to be distributed to them.

As you learned in Chapter 5, since the purpose of a Living Trust for a married couple is to *provide for the surviving spouse*, the entire Trust may be consumed to provide for the needs of the surviving spouse. The only exception is that the Decedent's B Trust (and/or C Trust) may be limited, such as by specifying "income only." Only after the surviving spouse's needs are fully satisfied do the children benefit from the Trust.

Upon the death of a parent (if single) or both parents (if married), the purpose of the Trust is to provide for the welfare of any minor children or handicapped children of any age or, where appropriate, any minor children of a deceased child.

The next chapter explains the allocation and distribution of the Trust assets to the beneficiaries upon the death of the settlor or settlors.

FINANCIAL INSTITUTION AS PARTY TO A TRUST

A financial institution may sometimes be named to serve in one of several capacities with a Living Trust, including as administrator, as co-trustee, as successor trustee, or as custodian of the Trust.

The primary objective of the Living Trust is to provide for the needs of the surviving spouse. Typically, the children benefit from a Trust only after the death of the surviving spouse.

Financial Institution as Administrator

In the early 1920s, the banking industry seized upon the Living Trust and the Testamentary Trust as the ideal vehicles by which to obtain control of money. The idea of the Trust was promoted extensively, particularly to people who had money but were not necessarily sophisticated in financial or legal matters. In almost any bank lobby today, you will find numerous brochures promoting the advantages of the Trust and emphasizing the opportunity to have the bank manage your funds "as trustees." Even though there are numerous advantages to the Living Trust, management by a financial institution is not necessarily one of them.

As trustee, you or your surviving spouse always has the option of hiring a financial institution for help in managing your estate.

Before the 1976 Tax Reform Act, many attorneys had a ready answer for clients who were venturesome enough to consider a Living Trust. The attorneys would simply ask their clients, "Do you know that a financial institution must be trustee and will charge you 1 percent of your assets *annually* as a management fee?" That statement is simply not true, but the question frightened many people away from creating Living Trusts—and eventually allowed the attorneys to extract fat probate fees from the estates of their clients.

Financial institutions are readily available to manage your estate—for a fee—if you so desire, but that fact has nothing to do with the need for a Living Trust. Most people want to manage their own assets. Therefore, when people create a Living Trust, they usually want to continue to manage their own assets as trustees. If you desire financial assistance, you always have the option to hire—and fire, as you see fit—any financial institution to act in your behalf.

The freedom to hire and fire a financial institution is also available to a surviving spouse. In the past, it was common practice to designate a financial institution as trustee or as co-trustee with a surviving spouse. In the last decade, however, as the Living Trust has been used more extensively, people have become more sophisticated. It is now recommended that the surviving spouse serve as sole surviving trustee—without being bound to a financial institution.

A sophisticated investor with a large portfolio of stocks and bonds did not want to saddle his wife with the responsibility of managing his extensive portfolio upon his death. The husband was very knowledgeable in buying and selling stocks and simply didn't want to burden his wife with an unfamiliar task. The husband was inclined to appoint a financial institution as surviving trustee upon his death instead of his wife.

It was suggested to the husband that he name his wife as surviving trustee and allow her to hire and fire, if necessary, a financial institution if she saw fit to do so. The husband concurred. This practice makes sound financial sense.

With the same reasoning, it is recommended that the adult children, close family members, or close friends, in lieu of a financial institution, be considered as successor trustees upon the death of both parents. The successor trustees can readily turn to a financial institution for financial assistance, if necessary.

Historically, banks have been far too conservative—and not necessarily astute—managers of Trusts. Typically, upon becoming a trustee, most banks liquidate all of the securities in an estate and then invest the assets in banking vehicles (such as certificates of deposit, Treasury bills, and bank stock). Appeals from the surviving beneficiaries for changes, regardless of how reasonable, usually fall upon deaf ears. Keep in mind that financial institutions tend to manage *your* assets to *their* best advantage—and not necessarily with your best interests in mind.

I remember a client's $1 million portfolio that was managed by a major bank. The husband, who had been a doctor, had died and left his share of the estate in trust for his surviving wife, with the bank as trustee. All of the wise investments in stocks and bonds had long been liquidated. The bank statement showed current earnings of only 3.1 percent—before the trustee fee was deducted. To add insult to injury, the surviving wife was receiving only $2,400 *annu-ally* from a $1 million Trust, because the bank had invested for growth rather than for the income so badly needed by this eighty-two-year-old widow!

In my earlier years, I was more vocal in our estate-planning seminars about the abuse of banks as trustees.

Following one such seminar, an attendee came in to create his Trust and complimented me for "telling it like it is." The man said that he now owned several banks but had started his career in the trust department of a bank. He related that in his earlier years he had watched many Trust beneficiaries come into the trust department and plead for more money (that is, request a better return of income) from the Trust investments. The man confided that the bank officials were overly solicitous and offered to do everything possible, and the beneficiary would depart feeling much better and satisfied. However, once the beneficiary was outside the bank, the bank officials would break into hysterics, as if to say, "There goes another sucker."

Admittedly, great change is now taking place in the banking industry, and many banks and financial institutions are installing good financial managers. However, a trusted family member or close friend acting as successor trustee always has the option to select one of these financial institutions to manage the assets, if needed.

In a situation in which a couple has no trusted family members or close friends, a financial institution is the logical successor trustee for any minor children. In addition, if adult children are considered irresponsible, a logical choice for a successor trustee may well be a financial institution.

For the extremely few people who feel the need for a financial institution as trustee, there are a number of companies that perform reputably. Unfortunately, locating these companies requires extensive research. As a suggestion for consideration, our firm has been very pleased with the performance of one of the oldest Trust services in the country—Trust Services of America, Inc. (700 Wilshire Boulevard, Los Angeles, California 90017). This company was originally the respected Title Insurance and Trust Company, which was acquired by California Federal Savings and Loan Association and is continuing the tradition of service established by the original company. Another Trust service to consider is Merchants Bank, North, an affiliate of Merchants Bancorp, Inc. (24 West Market Street, Wilkes-Barre, Pennsylvania 18711). Merchants Bank has become very aggressive and client-oriented; the firm has established an impressive track record as a financial administrator.

Financial Institution as Co-Trustee
A more stringent alternative for administering the Trust would be to appoint a financial institution as co-trustee. The other trustees could be authorized to replace the financial institution co-trustee when appropriate.

Financial Institution as Successor Trustee
A financial institution should be named as successor trustee *only* as a last resort. In only about one in five hundred Trusts has it been appropriate to recommend a financial institution.

There are two situations in which a financial institution should be named as successor trustee. The first situation is where husband and wife have immigrated to this country, have minor children, and have neither relatives nor friends in this country who could provide for their minor children. The second situation is one in which an only child is handicapped and there are no family members to be responsible for the child. In each of these situations, naming a financial institution as successor trustee is the obvious solution.

Financial Institution as Custodian
Naming a financial institution to serve as custodian is another alternative to the management of a Trust. The *custodian* maintains the necessary records and provides regular reports to the beneficiaries. Although the trustee maintains control, the custodian would quickly identify any fiduciary abuses and might suggest appropriate action. The previously mentioned Merchants Bank, North, provides an excellent custodial service at reasonable fees. The custodian need not be in your local area.

POSITIONS OUTSIDE THE TRUST
Although not an integral part of a Living Trust, two other key positions should be considered as part of *any* estate planning: executor and guardian. It is hoped that neither position ever has to be used. Nevertheless, it is *essential* that an executor be named and that a guardian be named for any minor children or handicapped individuals.

Executor
The *executor* should not be confused with the trustee. The successor trustee is responsible for all assets *within* the Trust; the executor (who is named in the Pour-Over Will) is the administrator for all assets that have been left *outside* the Trust. The executor is necessary in case any probate action is required to settle the estate. The executor would take through probate any assets that were inadvertently left outside the Trust. After the probate process has been completed, the executor would then pour the probated assets over into the Trust. Of course, if you have properly placed all your assets within the Living Trust, no probate action will be necessary.

Only one person should be named as your executor.

Since probate is a time-consuming and frustrating experience that requires numerous legal signatures and occasional court appearances, it is preferable to name an executor who resides in the state where the probate will be conducted. Unlike successor trustees, however, the executor should be only one person.

An executor should always be named, just to take care of any unforeseen contingency. If you are married, your spouse should be named as executor; after the death of the surviving spouse, one of the successor trustees should be named as executor. Although you may name several of your children as successor trustees of the Trust, only one of them should be designated to handle this chore, preferably the child living nearest to the probate court.

Guardian

A guardian or guardians should always be named for minor children in case the parents should die before their children reach the age of eighteen. It is also important to appoint a guardian if you have handicapped children, regardless of their ages. The guardian and the successor trustee may be, and often are, different people.

Probably one of the most difficult decisions with which you will ever be confronted is whom to name as the guardian of your children. Any judge in the land would say, "Please, don't put this burden upon me." A more detailed discussion of the guardian appears in Chapter 9.

AN ORGANIZED SOLUTION

As with your various roles in life, you will hold numerous roles with a Living Trust. The positions of trustor and settlor cease upon your death. The positions of trustee and beneficiary will eventually pass to others. As you age, management of the Trust may become too burdensome, and you may wish to pass that function over to those whom you trust. With the Living Trust, you may easily relinquish your role as trustee, thus allowing your children to take over the administration of the Trust. Upon incompetency or death, administration of the Trust passes to the successor trustee. Upon the death of the settlor (if single) or both settlors (if married), the beneficial interest in the Trust passes to the individuals (such as children) you have named as beneficiaries.

In addition, you should name an executor to handle any unexpected probate, and you must name a guardian for minor or handicapped children. Designating trusted individuals for the various positions in your Living Trust will protect you and give you peace of mind.

7

Allocation and Distribution of Assets

Upon your death (if you are single) or upon the death of both husband and wife (if you are married), the successor trustee needs to know how you wish your assets to be allocated and then distributed, or whether you wish the assets to be held in the Trust for future growth and/or income.

If you have a Living Trust, your assets need not all be distributed outright; your choices for allocation and distribution are unlimited.

All too often, clients have what I call the "Will syndrome"—the understanding that, upon death, all of the assets in an estate must be distributed outright at the conclusion of the probate process. This distribution of all assets is true for a Will, because there is no legal entity left in which to hold the assets. If you have a Living Trust, however, the assets need not be distributed. In fact, when you have a Living Trust, the methods of allocating and distributing the assets are unlimited! When you are creating a Trust, you are opening horizons you never before imagined.

Our computer system recently printed out every allocation and distribution section from all of the Living Trusts that were written in the past three months. In that brief time period, there were seventy different approaches to the allocation and distribution of assets.

The area of allocation and distribution of assets is probably the most difficult part of creating a Living Trust for the average individual. However, even though many clients have said they have for years been unable to determine what to do, by sharing my experience with these clients, I have in every case been able to show them how to solve their estate-planning problems and eventually come up with appropriate solutions for allocation and distribution of the assets in their estates.

ALLOCATION OF TRUST ASSETS
One of the first requirements is to determine how you wish your assets to be allocated among your heirs. Do you have specific be-

quests for specific individuals? How do you want your assets eventually shared with your children or other family members?

Specifically Named Beneficiaries for Special Bequests

Grandchildren, parents, aunts and uncles, and nieces and nephews are often named for specific amounts of distribution or income. To compensate for inflation, bequests should be specified as a percentage of your estate, rather than as fixed amounts. Determine the amount of the bequest, determine its current percentage of the estate, and then specify the bequest as that percentage. For example, a $10,000 bequest in a $200,000 estate would be stated as 5 percent.

In most cases, bequests should be specified as a percentage of your estate.

It is also quite acceptable, if desired, to specify a bequest as "5 percent or $10,000, whichever is greater." Then, for example, if ten years have elapsed and the estate has doubled in value, the 5 percent would be worth $20,000. On the other hand, a $10,000 bequest today could shrink in purchasing value to only $5,000 in ten years.

Small bequests of $500 to $1,000, however, should be listed as amounts only, ignoring the percentage approach. The reason is that these are minor gifts, where it is really the thought that counts. After all, a $500 gift from a $500,000 estate would only be 0.1 percent.

Equal vs. Unequal Allocation

Several times each week, couples come into our office and, with some embarrassment, tell us that they desire unequal allocation of their assets to their children. The couples are convinced that they are the only ones who have ever considered this type of allocation. However, unequal allocation is far more common than you might believe. Almost one-fourth of our clients choose unequal allocation—and for very good reasons, as you will see in the following representative examples.

Herb and Marge Allen have two children. The son is a very successful doctor and will probably earn far more than his parents. The daughter is married to a teacher and has seven children. The daughter and her husband will probably never have a farthing to their name. Therefore, the Allens' allocation heavily favored their daughter.

Jim and Louise Harmon have four grown children. Since one of the Harmons' children is mentally retarded, the parents chose to have their assets remain in trust to provide for the mentally retarded child as long as he lives. Only after the retarded child dies will the Harmons' remaining estate be equally divided and distributed to their three other children.

Kurt and Lisa Crowther have a son and daughter, but Kurt chose to disown their daughter. I advised Lisa that, with the A-B Trust, she could do anything she wanted with "her" half of the estate—even offset her husband's decision (by allocating her half of the estate to her daughter). In tears, she chose to allocate her half equally to the son and daughter.

Steve and Betty Hutton have three children. The Huttons chose equal allocation of their estate to their three children—until the youngest child was killed in a work-related accident. Although the deceased son left a wife and child, his company's $1 million settlement provided more than enough for their needs. Therefore, the Huttons amended their Trust to exclude their deceased son and their beloved grandson.

DISTRIBUTION OF TRUST ASSETS

Even though there are numerous approaches to distribution of Trust assets, the three most common methods of distribution are outright, at a specific age, and deferred distribution. If you have minor children, however, it is recommended that all assets remain in trust until the youngest child attains the age of twenty-one. There can be innumerable unexpected needs for minor children, particularly expensive medical needs. When all of the assets are in Trust, they are available for such use. This same restriction would apply to any share for minor children of a deceased child (your grandchildren).

Outright Distribution

Outright distribution is often used as the form of distribution for adults. This method does not imply, however, that the assets must be distributed *immediately* following the death of the settlor or settlors. The concept of an asset being held in trust rather than distributed is a frequent concern of clients when they have substantial real estate holdings. The assets are *available* for distribution, but the successor trustees (who are also often the beneficiaries) have the discretion to delay distribution, or sale of the assets, until they deem it appropriate—for years, if necessary. For example, high interest rates may offer a poor market for real estate sales. It may be more prudent to lease the property for the next few years and to then ultimately sell the property in a more favorable market—only then distributing the proceeds of the sale to the beneficiaries.

If you believe that your children are fully mature, you might decide to distribute your assets to them outright (all at one time). However, this practice is generally discouraged.

Whenever possible, the trustee should distribute in kind, rather than liquidate the assets and distribute cash. For example, real estate can be distributed by simply rewriting the deed in the name of the beneficiary or beneficiaries. Undivided interest, discussed in Chapter 2, can be written on the deed for distribution to more than one beneficiary. Securities, such as stocks, bonds, and mutual funds, can be rewritten in the name of the individual beneficiary.

Outright distribution means that the assets are available *for distribution; distribution may be delayed if, for example, market conditions are unfavorable.*

Distribution at a Specific Age

Distribution at a specific age is another form of distribution for minors (children below the age of eighteen). Distribution should not be made at an age less than twenty-three. Delaying any distribution until age twenty-three gets the child, or children, through college and then adds a year or two for good measure—for the sake of maturity. However, many parents are so satisfied with their children's maturity and good judgment that they have named them to receive a distribution at the age of eighteen.

If the settlors died when their children were older than the ages specified for distribution, the children would receive their distributions outright (that is, they would receive the entire amount all at one time).

Deferred Distribution

The most common type of distribution specified by clients is deferred distribution. With deferred distribution, the assets are not distributed to the heirs at the time of death; instead, distribution is delayed for a specific number of years or until the heir reaches a specified age. A deferred distribution may be made outright at a specified age or portioned to the heir as he or she attains different ages.

The most frequently specified form of deferred distribution is a partial distribution when the heir attains a specified age.

Examples

Heir receives $\frac{1}{3}$ of his or her share at age 25.	Heir receives $\frac{1}{2}$ of his or her share at age 25.
Heir receives $\frac{1}{3}$ of his or her share at age 30.	Heir receives $\frac{1}{2}$ of his or her share at age 30.
Heir receives $\frac{1}{3}$ of his or her share at age 35.	

Another form of deferred distribution is where the distribution is made in increments, following the death of the settlor or settlors.

Examples

Heir receives $\frac{1}{3}$ of his or her share outright.	Heir receives $\frac{1}{2}$ of his or her share outright.
Heir receives $\frac{1}{3}$ of his or her share in 5 years.	Heir receives $\frac{1}{2}$ of his or her share in 5 years.
Heir receives $\frac{1}{3}$ of his or her share in 10 years.	

If the surviving settlor dies after the children have already reached any of the ages specified for partial distributions, the children would receive outright those portions to which they were then entitled. Any remaining distributions would be made when the children reach the ages specified for those distributions.

> For example, assume that a child is to receive a deferred distribution as one-third at age twenty-five, one-third at age thirty, and one-third at age thirty-five. If the surviving settlor dies when the child is thirty-two years old, the child will receive two-thirds of the distribution outright (the distributions specified for ages twenty-five and thirty); the remaining one-third would be distributed when the child attains the age of thirty-five.

Children of any age mature with time. Consequently, with a partial distribution at specified ages or time periods, if an heir receives a distribution and spends the entire amount (often frivolously), the heir later gets a second chance and is much less inclined to unwisely waste the inheritance. The deferred distribution method of one-half at age twenty-five and one-half at age thirty is used frequently with estates valued at less than $300,000.

A most tragic incident illustrates how important the concept of deferred distribution can be.

> A nineteen-year-old woman was attending UCLA; she was in the middle of her junior year and was getting straight *A*'s. Her parents were killed in an automobile accident, and she received $400,000 in one lump sum. She thereupon left school, took friends with her, and went on a European spree. She bought automobiles for her friends, and they all had a magnificent time—for two years. At the end of those two years, the money was gone.

How different the young woman's situation could have been if, instead, she had received one-third of her inheritance outright, another one-third in five years, and the final one-third in ten years. She could have squandered the first third, but she would have learned a valuable lesson and presumably would have handled the other two distributions quite differently.

As a registered investment adviser, all too often I see people of every age who receive money and, on the advice and good intentions of others, invest unwisely and lose it all. Through experience, I have become a very strong advocate of the deferred distribution method. For our own children, my wife and I have selected the distribution to be one-third at age twenty-five, another one-third at age thirty, and the final one-third at age thirty-five. If our children attain the age of thirty-five before we pass away, our family Trust further states that the children will receive *no more* than one-third outright, one-third in five years, and one-third in ten years.

Far too often, I have had clients say, "Our son (or daughter) at age forty-five is still immature; we wish to choose one-third at age fifty, one-third at age fifty-five, and one-third at age sixty." Why not? It is *your* plan, and *you* specify the desired type of distribution. Nothing in the plan is set in concrete. As long as the settlors live, they can change that plan—even daily, if they wish.

Income vs. Distribution

In many instances, it is deemed more advisable to bequeath to heirs the *income* derived from assets in the estate, rather than directly giving the heirs the asset as a distribution. It is quite proper to bequeath only the income.

You might decide that one (or more) of your children is very immature and possibly also a spendthrift. In such a situation, it may be far more appropriate to retain the assets in the Trust and to provide "income only" to one or more of your children. If you choose to provide income only, you should authorize the trustee to meet a variety of emergency needs—whether for general care, medical care, educational assistance, or necessary professional services.

Income, or a combination of income and distribution, may be more preferable in large estates—particularly estates with substantial real estate holdings. Often, families that have accumulated substantial real estate desire to retain these holdings to provide future income for their children. The Living Trust provides this option; the successor trustees (often the same individuals as the beneficiaries) have the right to buy, sell, borrow against, and transfer these assets, as conditions dictate for investment purposes.

Under circumstances where most of the estate is held in trust and provides only income to the beneficiaries, it is often recommended that you specify at least *some* asset distribution. Alternatively, the successor trustees could be authorized to make a reasonable loan to each child—for example, to help each child purchase his or her home or begin a business.

Varying Distribution Methods for Each Child

You may select a different method of distribution for each child. If you believe one child is extremely mature, you may feel that it is appropriate to distribute the assets to that child outright. Another child may seem totally immature (or may be involved with drugs or alcohol), so that it seems far more appropriate to retain your assets in trust and to distribute only the income from the assets (but also authorizing the trustee to provide for unexpected and extraordinary circumstances). A third child, although still immature, may be progressing nicely, so it may be appropriate to distribute assets to that child as a deferred distribution of one-third outright, one-third in five years, and one-third in ten years.

Not only may the distribution vary per individual, it may also vary for each asset where appropriate. For example, if one child has dependents and another has administrative skills, the parents might distribute their home to the first child and their business to the second child. However, this form of distribution is the exception.

PROVISIONS FOR SPECIAL SITUATIONS

Certain provisions in the area of allocation and distribution of assets take care of special situations, such as handling a deceased child's share of the estate and excluding the surviving spouse of a deceased child, deducting gifts and loans to children, providing for children with special needs, and disinheriting children.

Deceased Child's Share

If one (or more) of your children fails to survive you, that child's share of your estate will typi-

cally pass to the children of your deceased child (that is, your grandchildren). For the sake of illustration, let's look at some different situations relating to the inheritance of assets.

Tom and Martha Hurst have two children, Susan and Jeff. Each child is to share equally in the assets of the estate. Both children are married and have two children each.

Upon the death of Tom and Martha Hurst, their assets are to pass one-half to Susan and one-half to Jeff, as shown in Figure 7-1.

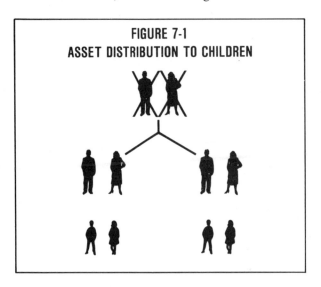

FIGURE 7-1
ASSET DISTRIBUTION TO CHILDREN

If Susan were not living upon the death of her mother and father, her share would pass equally to her two children, bypassing her husband, as depicted in Figure 7-2. If Jeff also were not living upon the death of his mother and father, his share would pass to his two children, bypassing his wife, in the same manner.

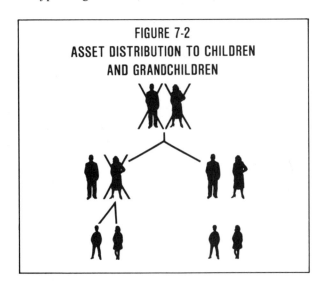

FIGURE 7-2
ASSET DISTRIBUTION TO CHILDREN AND GRANDCHILDREN

If Susan and her two children were not living when Tom and Martha Hurst died, Susan's share would pass to her brother Jeff, bypassing Susan's husband, as indicated in Figure 7-3.

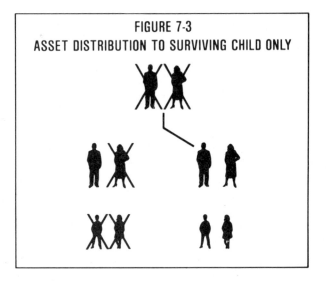

FIGURE 7-3
ASSET DISTRIBUTION TO SURVIVING CHILD ONLY

Note that, in these examples, the spouse is out. Neither Susan's husband nor Jeff's wife received *anything*! Excluding the spouse is, as strange as it may seem, the standard method of distribution—that is, distribution is typically along blood lines or adoption. Historically, human nature has adopted the approach of excluding the surviving spouse of a deceased child.

The surviving spouse of a deceased child does not *need* to be excluded from distribution; your Living Trust may include the spouse. However, in all my experience with the Living Trust, I am aware of only two such alterations to the usual pattern: one family left $10,000 to a daughter-in-law; another family left only $1,000—and in both instances, their estates exceeded $1 million! This method of distribution is done by choice only.

A related concern is what will happen to the parents' assets if their children were to someday get divorced. There are several solutions to this dilemma.

One solution is for the parents to leave their assets in trust, with their children receiving income only. The assets held in the parents' Trust would not be considered the children's property and thus would not be subject to being divided between the divorcing parties.

A second solution is for the parents to leave their assets in trust and have them distributed in five-year increments. The assumption is that the longer the children are married, the more apt they are to remain so.

A third solution is for the married children to have their own Living Trusts with Separate Property Agreements (described in Chapter 9). More and more frequently, parents are coming to our office to create Living Trusts for their children. One reason is that these parents want to ensure that any "parental assets" passed on to their children will be designated as separate property—and thereby be preserved if something were to happen to a child's marriage.

For example, a father created a Living Trust for each of his four children, who were in their early to middle twenties. One child was married, and two more got married before the end of the year. In each case, the father had already distributed between $200,000 and $300,000 to his children; the father wanted to make sure that these funds *remained* as his children's separate property.

If there is a divorce, the community property is typically divided in half, whereas the separate property remains with the individual to whom the separate property belongs. Where there are children from the marriage and the children remain with the mother, the mother's separate property will almost always remain as hers. However, the court has the right to reach over into the father's separate property to make it available to provide for the children—since the children are the first concern of the court.

Gifts and Loans

Frequently, our clients make gifts or loans to one or more children. An example could be to help a child make a down payment on a home. The parents may desire that, upon their death, these gifts or loans be considered part of the overall estate and be deducted from that child's share of his or her eventual distribution of the estate. To make this process simple, each of our Living Trusts includes a special form, shown in Figure 7-4. This form, which we call Schedule A, provides a convenient place where the parents may itemize any gifts or loans to their children (if they are to be considered part of the child's distribution). Use of this form is optional.

Children with Special Needs
Supporting a child who is mentally or physically handicapped can be a very costly experience. In many situations, the individuals may qualify for government benefits or assistance, such as Supplemental Security Income (SSI) or Medicare, which is often crucial to the survival of the individual.

If a handicapped individual is named as a beneficiary of a Living Trust and has been receiving government assistance, dire consequences can occur when the handicapped individual finally receives his or her inheritance. Upon the death of both settlors (if married) or upon the death of the settlor (if single), one of two things will happen: Either the benefits will immediately cease (and this situation could be incredibly costly to the survivors), or the government agency can (and usually does) step in and grab the entire inheritance!

I remember the case of a young woman who was physically paralyzed from the waist down and confined to a wheelchair. She was originally given a life expectancy of fourteen years by her doctors. However, she was a determined youngster and eventually put herself through college and was able to obtain employment as a counselor at a school for handicapped children.

She didn't earn much money, but with her SSI assistance, government medical benefits, and an opportunity to live with her grandmother, she lived quite nicely. Most important, however, was that her mental outlook was outstanding. The young woman's father died when she was ten years old and left funds in trust to be distributed to her at age twenty-one. Both

---

FIGURE 7-4
SCHEDULE A—GIFTS AND LOANS

Gift or Loan?	Recipient	Amount	Date	Trustor's Initials
G	Mary	$ 10,000	1/10/87	
L	Robert	15,000	2/15/88	

G — Gift
L — Loan

the young lady and her grandmother looked forward to the day when those funds would become available.

However, once the daughter reached the age of twenty-one, the government agency stepped in and took possession of her *entire inheritance of $100,000!*

As incredible as this callous act may seem, government agencies have the right to seize the inheritance because government funds have previously been expended on behalf of the handicapped child. Therefore, mentally or physically handicapped children should be excluded from directly receiving either assets (as a distribution) or income.

Instead, the successor trustee should be authorized and directed to provide for such a child's welfare. Thus, the trustee can directly pay rent, board, education, medical and psychiatric care, transportation, and entertainment—without making any *direct payment* to the child. In this way, the SSI payments are not jeopardized.

Disinheriting a Child

Occasionally, parents wish to disinherit a child; they can do so very simply with a Living Trust. Any child who is to be disinherited is simply excluded as a beneficiary of the Trust. The Trust is a contract, and, as such, if it does not name a child as a beneficiary, that child is not a part of that Trust. No statement needs to be made to the effect that the child is to be excluded.

It is very important, however, to avoid any implication that a child was forgotten. The way to avoid this problem is to name each of the children—regardless of whether he or she is to be included as a beneficiary of the Trust—in the Pour-Over Will. Naming the children in the Pour-Over Will clearly indicates that the children were not forgotten, since the Pour-Over Will and the Living Trust are put into effect on the same date.

A father came to me with an interesting dilemma. Following World War II, he had fathered one child in Germany and possibly a second child, both out of wedlock. He did not want either of these children coming forth at some later date to claim an inheritance.

This dilemma was resolved simply by naming his three children born of wedlock as his children in his Living Trust and in his Pour-Over Will. The children born out of wedlock were excluded, simply by not naming them as beneficiaries in the Trust, though they were identified in his Pour-Over Will.

If a son, for example, marries a woman who has two children from a former marriage, those children are not heirs by either blood or adoption. The son may, if he so desires, eventually adopt those children, whereby they would be included under the adoption provision. However, if the son does not adopt the children, they are *not* included as heirs under the Living Trust document—unless the Trust specifically states that the children are to be included as heirs.

Occasionally, a client has a child or children with one spouse, then remarries and has children in the second marriage. For some reason, the client may hold great anger toward one or more of the children of the first marriage, or the individual may not have seen or heard from them in decades. It is painful for the individual to confront the topic of the children by the first marriage, but the subject must be addressed. However, all children of this and any previous marriages *must* be named in the Pour-Over Will. Children of any prior marriages who are not to be included as heirs to the estate would simply not be named in the Trust as beneficiaries.

Naming *all* of the children in the Pour-Over Will takes away their ability to contest the Trust on the basis that they had been "forgotten."

IMPORTANT DEFINITIONS

The trust, being a legal document, is fraught with legal terminology. Unfortunately, the use of legal language is necessary in order to make the document one that legally establishes the Living Trust and then makes it unchallengeable by dissident heirs. Therefore, it is helpful if you understand some key definitions that will directly apply to the way your assets may someday be distributed.

Blood or Adopted

The Trust usually defines your children as blood or adopted and specifically includes, by definition, legally adopted children. Although people usually recognize children adopted by themselves, or by their children, as comparable to their blood issue, occasionally a client asks that the words pertaining to adoption be deleted.

One example is a mother who was most disconcerted that her daughter-in-law refused to bear children but was willing to adopt them. The mother directed us to strike out the words pertaining to adopted children. She wanted to make it very clear that, if her daughter-in-law

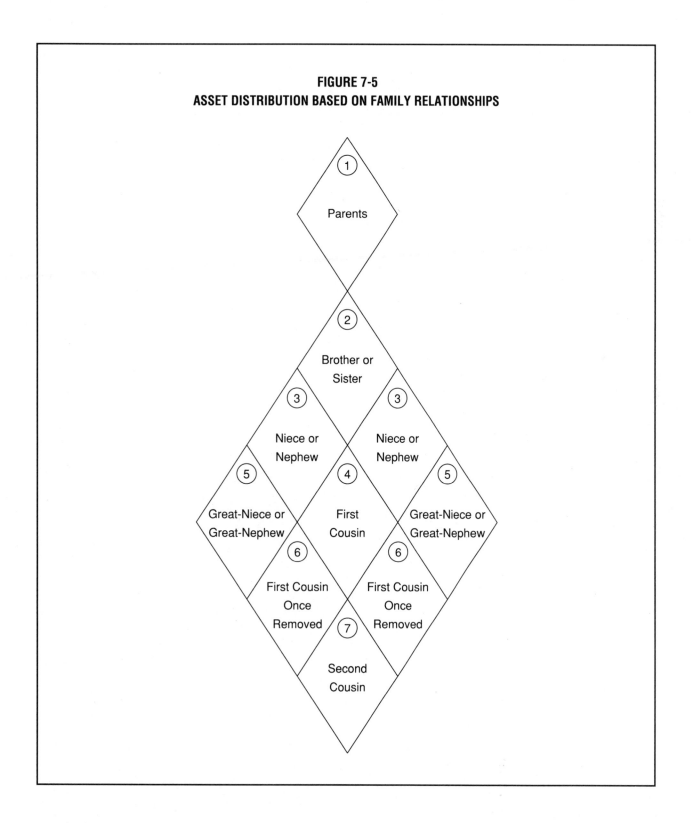

FIGURE 7-5
ASSET DISTRIBUTION BASED ON FAMILY RELATIONSHIPS

were willing to bear children, they would be included as heirs, but any adopted children would be excluded from the estate.

Issue

The term *issue* refers to your children, your children's children, your children's children's children, and so on, by blood—in other words, your biological children and their offspring. The term *issue* can also refer to your children and/or their offspring by adoption, if so defined in the Trust.

Per Stirpes

Per stirpes is a Latin term. By legal definition, the term refers to your children downward (your children, grandchildren, great-grandchildren, and so on).

Intestate Succession

If there are no surviving heirs downward (per stirpes), then distribution will be by *intestate succession*. Your assets will be distributed to relatives "upward and outward." Specifically, any distribution would first be to father and mother (if living); otherwise, distribution would be to brothers and sisters. If neither mother, father, brothers, nor sisters were living, then distribution would be to aunts and uncles, and then to nieces and nephews. If none of those relatives were living, then distribution would be made to any cousins.

The specific pattern of succession for distribution of an estate and the related percentages are spelled out in the probate code of each state. Figure 7-5 illustrates the general succession of heirs when an intestate distribution is to be made.

> One of the most prominent examples of probate distribution by intestate succession is the case of Howard Hughes, where one or more cousins may eventually become the recipients of his vast estate.

With a Living Trust, of course, you can establish the pattern of distribution that *you* want.

CHARITABLE DISTRIBUTIONS

Charitable distributions should always be stated as a percentage of the estate—never as a dollar amount. All too often, settlors of a large estate have designated a specific sum to charity, only to find that, for some unexpected reason, the value of the estate has shrunk by the time of the first spouse's death. The surviving spouse is then forced to ask the court to intervene in order to preserve enough of the estate for his or her survival.

State any large charitable distributions (over $5,000) as a percentage of the estate.

Figure 7-6 shows an example of a Charitable Distribution Form; we call it Schedule B and include it with all our Living Trusts. Experience has shown that the most effective method of specifying charitable contributions is to designate the percentage of the estate that is to be bequeathed to charity. The clients then designate their choices of charitable institutions and the percentage of the total amount bequeathed to charity that is to be given to each organization. A typical example would be "10 percent of the estate to charity as per Schedule B." Schedule B might then read:

Name of Charity	Percent of Distribution
American Heart Association	50%
American Lung Association	10%
Girl Scouts of America	10%
United Way	30%

Note that, in Schedule B, 100 percent equals the total *charitable* contributions. Thus, if you wanted to contribute to only one charity (for example, the American Heart Association), you would show the distribution as "American Heart Association, 100%." If you wanted the charitable contribution to be divided equally between the American Heart Association and the American Cancer Society, you would show the distribution as "American Heart Association, 50%" and "American Cancer Society, 50%."

FIGURE 7-6
SCHEDULE B—CHARITABLE DISTRIBUTION FORM

Name of Charity	Percent of Distribution	Date	Trustor's Initials

The charities and percentages bequeathed to each organization may be changed with the simple stroke of a pen. Interestingly, although clients usually know how much they wish to leave to charity (the percentage of their estate), the hardest decision seems to be which charities to give donations to and how much to bequeath. The simplest way to solve the problem is for the Trust to state the percentage of the estate that is to benefit charity, and for Schedule B to be used to permit the client to make and change the specific details later—as often as is desired.

If no living heirs survive you, distribution of your estate will be made to qualified charitable institutions, as indicated in Schedule B. If you have not named any charitable organizations, the court will act for you. However, Schedule B allows you the opportunity to easily specify a favorite charity or charities ahead of time.

THE BEST SOLUTION

The most versatile part of the Living Trust is the section titled "Allocation and Distribution of Trust Assets." Once you understand that there are no limitations to how you may allocate and distribute your assets in a Living Trust, you realize that there are endless potential options for how you may pass your assets to your heirs. Every family, as well as each family member, is different. The Living Trust allows you to design the best solution for everyone.

8

Separating the Good from the Bad

In recent years, the general population has become increasingly aware that there is an alternative to the evils of probate—the Living Trust. Unfortunately, this popularity has given rise to a proliferation of Trusts, many of which are of substantially reduced quality. In effect, more and more attorneys are exploiting the general public with the Living Trust. People are being constantly bombarded with newspaper, radio, and television ads from various attorneys and firms inviting the public to seminars on the Living Trust as a means of generating revenue. Regrettably, few attorneys today have the experience needed to write an adequate Living Trust.

Far too many attorneys, inexperienced in the details of writing Trusts, fail to refer clients to more knowledgeable counsel. Unlike the medical profession, which recognizes today's need to specialize, the legal profession has not yet been able to accept this concept of specialization. No one can be an expert in every area of the complex field of law, but most attorneys are unwilling to acknowledge the absolute need for specialization or to admit their own inexperience in a particular area.

More than fifteen years ago, I was appalled to recognize how many attorneys were presenting "factual conclusions" to prospective clients in areas in which the attorneys had little knowledge. I finally took my concern to a very respected attorney, who gave me a very simple reason, which still rings in my ears: "The attorney is afraid to refer a client to another attorney more knowledgeable in a particular area for fear he will lose that client." In comparison, how would you like to have your family physician perform open-heart surgery on members of your family? Yet a similar situation is just what is happening all too frequently with your attorney with respect to Living Trusts. With the legal fraternity suddenly waking up to the need for Living Trusts, every attorney seems to be an expert—but most of them lack even the most rudimentary knowledge or experience needed to prepare an adequate Trust.

This lack of knowledge by attorneys is tragic, because these individuals do a great disservice to their profession. There are many very qualified, knowledgeable, and experienced estate-planning attorneys who will do an outstanding job in their specialty and will provide you with an outstanding Living Trust. This chapter is intended to provide you with the knowledge that you need in order to screen the "pretenders" from the true experts.

The legal profession seems to be at an interesting crossroads. Experienced, knowledgeable estate-planning attorneys are accustomed to writing Trusts only for wealthy clients. How, then, do these experienced attorneys use their talents and expertise to create a Trust that is economically feasible for the average individual? On the other hand, inexperienced attorneys naively write Trusts that, when subjected to various tests and legal challenges, fall *far short* of expected results.

WHAT TO AVOID

In 1985, I was asked to speak on the use of the Living Trust at the national FBI convention. Afterward, I was deluged by the members attending the seminar, asking for the Living Trust. Unfortunately, I had opened Pandora's box. These people lived all over the nation, were about to return to their homes, and desired Living Trusts! How could they obtain *good* Living Trusts—without being exploited? I tried to give the members some guidelines on selecting competent legal counsel and obtaining a comprehensive Living Trust. However, I have anguished over that situation in the intervening years since the convention; the more I see of today's Trusts (many written by attorneys who are unfamiliar with the Living Trust), the more concerned I become.

Trusts written by most attorneys suffer from a variety of shortcomings. Some of the Trusts are lengthy documents but still do not encompass all possible contingencies, and most of them are very disorganized; most Trusts are poorly understood by the clients on whose behalf they were written; more often than not, there is a lack of communication between the client and the attorney; and most Trusts are thin and therefore incomplete (that is, they do not cover many very important contingencies). Unfortunately, the price of a Trust is also not indicative of the quality of the Trust. Be very aware that the quality of a Trust is of *utmost importance*, since a poorly written Trust can be a nightmare!

Lengthy and Disorganized Trusts

All too frequently, an attorney turns to his or her legal Trust reference manual and identifies those paragraphs that he or she feels should be included in the Trust. As a result, the Trust has neither organization nor pattern. To review the document adequately, the client or any financial institution must read it from cover to cover.

This lack of organization has become very evident during the last several years, as clients have tried to refinance their homes to take advantage of lower interest rates. If your home were recorded in a Living Trust and you wanted to refinance it, the financial institution would have to reissue a mortgage in the title of your Living Trust (instead of in your own name). Therefore, the financial institution must hire an attorney to read your Trust document. The attorney must then determine whether your Trust has little substance or validity or is a legally recognized entity that can, in fact, hold title to your home in trust. The lender must be further assured that there is nothing written in the Trust that will stand between the lender and your home if foreclosure may someday become necessary.

Unfortunately, the only means of ascertaining either of these necessary facts was to have an attorney read every paragraph of the Trust from beginning to end, which was a costly process. In an effort to reduce its costs, the banking institution usually asked the applicant to remove his or her home from the Trust by having the deed rerecorded in the individual's name, so that the financial institution could issue the mortgage without having to read the Trust. Once the home was refinanced, the individual was then permitted to put it back in the Trust!

This legal maneuvering by the financial institutions had nothing to do with the validity of the Trust document. The banking institutions simply recognized that, since the Trust document was so poorly organized and lacked any conformity, it would require great expenditure to adequately scrutinize the Trust to ensure that it would satisfy a particular institution's legal requirements before the institution could issue a mortgage. I have looked at too many such Trusts and have had to agree with the approach taken by the financial institutions.

Trust in "Legalese"

Besides usually being disorganized, all Trusts must be written in "legalese" (language that is peculiar to the legal profession). Trusts are usually written with little thought for the client's understanding. The result is that few, if any, individuals understand their Trusts; therefore, the Trusts do not work for the individuals. In effect, the Trusts are not being properly utilized.

A husband and wife came to me with a draft of their Living Trust, drawn for them by an attorney who had been referred to them by a friend. The pair were badly frustrated; they had paid $1,500 for the draft of their Trust, but no matter how they tried, they could not understand it—and the two were highly educated. The husband had received his master's degree from Stanford University, and the wife had obtained her master's degree from Bryn Mawr College.

Legally, the couple's Trust was quite adequate. However, for the clients, the Trust was most *inadequate*. The document contained no organization, no subtitles, and no summary of the contents of the Trust. The couple had heard about our program and asked us to prepare a Living Trust for them. The frustrated pair were willing to scrap their existing Living Trust draft and forgo the $1,500 they had already spent—in order to have a Living Trust that they could understand.

I appeal to every attorney who is fortunate enough to be knowledgeable of the Living Trust: write the document in such a manner that the client will understand it—or provide a supplemental means of communication, such as a summary written in simple language!

**Lack of Communication Between
Client and Attorney**

Even when the Trust document is well drawn, communication between the client and attorney often leaves much to be desired. The attorney may understand the Trust, but he or she is seldom able to simplify the concept or explain it so that the client understands it.

Many years ago, I would often describe and illustrate the Living Trust—ultimately convincing a client that he or she should have one—only to take him or her to an attorney and then watch the client walk away from the office shaking his or her head, as if to say, "I am now more confused than ever." I also remember going into the home of two clients—several months after the husband and wife agreed to have the attorney draw their Trust—only to see the unexecuted draft of their Trust still sitting in the living room. The pair explained that they did not understand the Trust; not only were they unable to get a satisfactory (or understandable) answer from the attorney, but they were billed as much as $200 per telephone call! Such an unpleasant experience can turn *anyone* off.

Even an individual of average intelligence who is not necessarily schooled in legal matters can understand the Trust and how it works—and with minimal effort on the part of the attorney drawing up the Trust—*if* the Trust is organized and the client is provided with a brief summary written in simple language.

Thin Trusts

A quick rule of thumb to use in determining if a Trust is comprehensive or not is to see whether the document is a "thin Trust" or a "thick Trust." A good Living Trust must necessarily be a rather thick document if it is going to adequately handle the many contingencies that may occur during the lifetimes of the creators. Two of the primary purposes of a Living Trust are to give the trustee or trustees the greatest latitude in which to operate (that is, to provide for every possible contingency) and to satisfy the specific requirements of the Internal Revenue Service.

Provision for All Contingencies

Our experience in doing thousands of Trusts has been that "Murphy's law" ("If anything can go wrong, it will") continues to prevail. Therefore, it is important to incorporate into every Living Trust all the provisions that are needed to encompass every imaginable contingency. Most of the contingencies will never happen to the majority of our clients, but sooner or later a client will be well served by a particular provision. Only a very few of these contingencies are predictable, but it is always better to be prepared. Since our Living Trust is based on drawing thousands of Trusts, as each new situation arises for a particular client, the "new" provision is added to all of our Trusts, if that provision has wide applicability.

An example of the unexpected happening is the situation of Dr. and Mrs. Campbell. Dr. Campbell was a renowned oral surgeon, who lectured worldwide and was deeply in love with his bride of fifty years. Since the couple had no children, they named Dr. Campbell's secretary of some twenty-five years' association to become the successor trustee.

I had numerous occasions to come in contact with this couple in the ensuing years, and it was always a delight to be in their presence, because the love between the two of them simply radiated. Unfortunately, Mrs. Campbell contracted Alzheimer's disease, and Dr. Campbell was genuinely concerned that his wife would outlive him, even though her mental abilities would be severely impaired. The doctor was satisfied that his trusted secretary would see that his wife was adequately cared for at all times. However, Mrs. Campbell ended up dying before her husband.

Six months later, after his wife's death, Dr. Campbell was waltzed off to the altar by another woman. I'm certain that he approached this marriage with rose-colored glasses, assuming that all women were similar to his beloved first wife. Tragically, this idealism was not to be upheld. In the ensuing months, I watched him turn into a very unhappy person.

Seven months later, Dr. Campbell came into our office to make some adjustments to the distributions within his Trust. After we reviewed his Trust, a few modifications were made, and Dr. Campbell was then satisfied that his Trust accomplished everything he wanted it to do. Only then did Dr. Campbell express his concern that his prostate cancer had not been controlled as the doctors had originally believed. Only a month later, Dr. Campbell was in the hospital, and he passed away shortly thereafter.

Upon his death, the new Mrs. Campbell made it known to everyone in the hospital, and to everyone in general, that "no little secretary was going to be the successor trustee of his Trust" and furthermore that she was going to break it. Mrs. Campbell had two brothers who were attorneys, and she simply considered that she was above the law.

Realizing that trouble lay ahead, I asked to see Mrs. Campbell a week after the funeral; I expressed my sympathy for her loss and then tactfully reviewed her deceased husband's desires for the distribution of his assets—which he had *reconfirmed* just a month earlier. I hoped that this meeting would clarify any misunderstanding on Mrs. Campbell's part and therefore stop any problems before they began.

However, Mrs. Campbell was not to be deterred. With the assistance of her attorney brothers, she proceeded to attack the Trust. The only time that our firm has ever had to go into court was when our legal counsel asked that the secretary be confirmed as the successor trustee. Six weeks later, the secretary was confirmed by the court as the successor trustee. Our legal counsel then advised the widow's brothers of the court action. Since the attorneys were still determined to attack the Trust, our firm once again found it necessary to go to court to request a formal court order—which was granted.

After the second court order was granted, the widow and her brothers realized that the integrity of the Trust document could not be assailed, and they finally backed away.

The power of the Living Trust had again been witnessed, but unfortunately under circumstances I never would have anticipated. I cite this case as an ideal example of "Murphy's law."

Another example of the perils of a "thin" Trust is the recent experience of a couple who came to our office after attending one of our seminars. The couple asked me to review and comment on a Living Trust they had acquired in 1983. The entire Trust document was five pages long, double-spaced. I pointed out to the couple that the outline alone of our Living Trust was thicker than their entire Trust. After reading the couple's Trust, I was appalled! Our legal counsel confirmed that the Trust was the worst Trust document that had ever come to our attention.

These innocent people understood the need

to avoid probate, had gone to an attorney for a Living Trust, and had paid good money for their Trust documents, but they were now worse off than if they had done nothing. Their totally inadequate Trust was quickly replaced with our Living Trust. Seeing the couple's needless expense and frustration only reconfirmed my dedication to completing this book—so that everyone can differentiate between a good Trust and a poor Trust.

This example shows why a good Living Trust should be drawn to cover the lifetimes of the creators and possibly the lifetimes of the heirs. Frequently, people look at a Living Trust document only in light of how the document might apply to them at that particular moment in time; when they do so, they readily recognize many features that do not apply to their present situation. However, a *good* Living Trust should anticipate every contingent event that may conceivably be possible for the next ten, twenty, thirty, or forty years—in this generation as well as the next generation. Such a comprehensive Trust document comes only from an experienced attorney who has had many years of practice in drawing up Living Trusts. Unfortunately, these experienced individuals are as hard to find as a needle in a haystack!

Provision of Broad Powers to the Creators

When you create a Living Trust, whether as husband and wife or as a single individual, you want the broadest powers possible. The Living Trust permits this great breadth of power under the legal authorization that two parties are entering into a contract with each other. These two parties would be husband and wife, if you are married, or implied between you and your beneficiaries, if you are single. The scope of this extensive latitude is best illustrated later in this chapter in the outline of Trust provisions that should be included in all Living Trust documents.

Provision of Broad Powers to Successor Trustees

Although the powers of a trustee appointed by a probate court are defined under the state's probate code, such powers are necessarily far too restrictive. In contrast, however, a Living Trust provides the opportunity to specify the powers of the trustee. Those powers may be made as broad as each client wants them—thus creating a manageable document that allows the successor trustees to provide for the heirs in the manner deemed most appropriate by the creators of the Trust.

If, for example, minor children were orphaned and no Living Trust were in effect to provide for their well-being, the court would be required to appoint a guardian and to set up a Trust to hold the assets of the estate. Under these circumstances, the powers of the guardian and the trustee will be very restrictive, and the court should supervise their actions.

However, if an appropriate Living Trust has been drawn up, a trustee (or trustees) and a guardian (or guardians) who are *trusted* by the creators will have been named. In this situation, since the named persons are trusted individuals, it is reasonable to give them far broader powers. In the long run, this action will be far more beneficial to the heirs.

Price Is No Indicator

During a six-month period in 1977, three clients came to me and acknowledged that they needed Living Trusts. Each client was the president of a small corporation and desired to ask his or her own corporate legal counsel, whom each had known for years, to draw up the Trust. In each case, I was asked to review the Trusts drawn up by their personal corporate legal counsels, and I naively agreed.

Although the situation for each individual was different and each attorney was different, the Trust documents were astonishingly identical. All these documents were given to me for review within a period of weeks—and I was shocked! *Not one* of the Trusts was worth the paper on which it was written. To cross-check my conclusion, I took the three Trust documents to legal counsel I knew was expert in Trusts; this experienced counsel quickly came to the same opinion—that the Trusts were not properly written—and put this fact in writing to each of the clients. I had learned a sad lesson, which also became the impetus for the writing of this book.

Unfortunately, price is no measurement of a

well-written Trust. In the preceding example, the clients were charged three to five times more than the price of a perfect (properly written) Trust that could be obtained from *experienced* and *knowledgeable* counsel. The clients had apparently been charged for all of the attorney's time—including the attorney's learning process (all of the time spent researching the provisions that should be included) for the attorney's first attempt at a Living Trust.

SELECTING A COMPETENT LEGAL FIRM

Everyone needs a Living Trust—and each person is faced with the same dilemma of finding the right attorney. Even with my experience as an estate planner and licensed/registered investment adviser, I would be afraid to draw up my own Trust. I know the advantages of a good Trust—*and* the dire consequences of a poor one! Your Trust, to be effective, *must* be drawn by a knowledgeable, experienced estate-planning attorney.

To obtain an effective Living Trust, you must have it drawn by a knowledgeable, experienced estate-planning attorney.

In dealing with our clients many years ago, we discovered a disturbing dilemma: In recommending the Living Trust to everyone, we were inadvertently throwing people to the wolves—to be exploited by those members of the legal fraternity who were only too willing to take advantage of the unknowledgeable.

Books are now available which provide forms for do-it-yourself Trusts. Write-your-own Trust forms are even available from mail order sources. Even with such forms, however, be aware that there is just too much chance for error—and consequently for the ensuing nightmare that can result from a poorly drawn Trust.

Thus, in your quest for a Living Trust, the most important thing to look for is an attorney who has the right experience and will provide some important services. Some words about our own company should give you a flavor of what you need.

The Estate Plan

In recognizing many years ago the problems of finding a well-written Living Trust, my associate and I formed a corporation called The Estate Plan to provide Living Trusts for our clients. Because of our continuing dissatisfaction with the caliber of Trusts being written, we learned that, too often, if you are going to do it right, you must do it yourself. I have worked diligently to incorporate into the Living Trust every experience we or our clients have ever encountered, so that our future clients will never be subjected to the same problems.

Even though our Living Trust document is all-encompassing, it is also logically organized. You can readily find the section needed for a particular occasion. My associate, who has a brilliant legal mind, develops the necessary legal solutions and generates appropriately written legal provisions. Together, we have created a synergism—with my contribution being to summarize the Living Trust in simple English, so that our clients understand this important estate-planning tool. Our clients really *do* understand their Living Trusts, as well as how to make their Trusts work for them as living and readily changeable instruments for passing their assets on to their heirs.

The Estate Plan also has a staff of knowledgeable individuals who are readily available to answer our clients' questions and to notify us of any special problems that might arise. Our staff allows us to continually be aware of the needs of our client base and to make whatever adjustments are appropriate in our Living Trust to eliminate any recurrence of the same problems.

An additional service we have provided to our clients is to offer to "settle" their estates—at no cost. With the Living Trust and our Estate Plan Book (a special loose-leaf binder that organizes the estate), it is possible to settle an estate in less than an hour. Time and again, by enabling the easy settlement of an estate in such a short time, our Living Trust assures us that our Living Trust works in every imaginable situation. An additional benefit to the client and to ourselves is that, if there is any problem, we will be the first to learn of it—and thus be able to create a solution for all subsequent Trusts that are written.

A good Living Trust is truly the result of

years of experience and dealing with every problem imaginable. Only through years of *actual* experience (and not just contemplative thought) can someone write a Living Trust that contains provisions to handle every possible contingency.

In an effort to protect our Living Trust documents against future alteration or substitution, our Trust and all accompanying documents are printed on special paper imprinted with the logo of The Estate Plan. Thus, although the document is signed only on the last or signature page, if anyone were to attempt to alter a line or lines or to substitute a page, the alteration or substitution would be obvious.

The specially marked paper is used as a matter of pride. Our Living Trust document is the result of almost twenty years of working together with legal counsel to cover every imaginable contingency. I have yet to find an instance in which our Living Trust has not worked perfectly. I am often asked about the downside of having a Living Trust, but I have yet to find a disadvantage in having a *properly written* Living Trust.

Experienced Legal Counsel

A well-written and comprehensive Trust document comes about only through extensive experience. Therefore, one of the first questions I would ask any attorney being considered for drawing up a Living Trust is: "How many Living Trusts do you draw in a year?" (The Estate Plan draws between 500 and 1,000 Living Trusts each year.) The number of Trusts drawn by an attorney at least gives you a measure of the attorney's experience. The legal counsel you select should have drawn up many hundreds of Living Trusts.

The legal counsel you select should have drawn up and settled hundreds of Living Trusts.

The next question I would ask is: "How many Trusts do you settle in a year?" (The Estate Plan settles almost one estate per week.) I would follow that question by asking, "What do you charge to settle the estate?" What you really want to know is whether the attorney has had much experience in settling the estates, whether his or her Trusts settle without problems, and, in effect, whether the attorney stands behind the Trust. It is our experience that, if your Trust is properly drawn and your estate is well organized, the process of settling your estate should take less than an hour! The subject of settling an estate in a Living Trust will be discussed in greater detail in Chapter 13.

A client and her husband had executed a Trust with a well-known Beverly Hills firm in 1978. The husband died in 1982, and the widow went back to the firm to settle the estate. After attending meetings and spending many dollars, the woman still did not have her assets identified as being distributed in either the Survivor's A Trust or the Decedent's B Trust. No matter how hard she tried, the widow could not get the legal firm to respond to her requests. Eventually she was told, in so many words, to "go away."

In 1986, the woman went to another legal firm to get her assets properly distributed into the A and B Trusts. She was again told that she needed certain *unnecessary* papers drawn up and was given substantial bills for professional services rendered. However, even then, no assets were identified as being distributed to either the A Trust or the B Trust. She was finally referred to our office, and her assets were easily apportioned between the Survivor's A Trust and the Decedent's B Trust—in less than one hour!

Although both of the firms in the previous example were willing to draw Living Trusts and to charge substantial fees for their Trusts, I believe that neither of the firms understood how to settle the Trust. I do not wish to disparage the many fine, outstanding, legitimate, and experienced estate-planning attorneys who are doing excellent jobs. Unfortunately, the American Bar Association says that fewer than 1 percent of the legal fraternity understands the Living Trust—and my experience forces me to agree.

In addition to drawing up an extensive and all-encompassing Living Trust and the several related legal documents, any attorney or firm offering to draw up your Living Trust should also provide you with at least the following basic services:

- A simple, clear, English summary of the Trust
- Copies of transfer letters to assure that every asset gets properly placed into your Trust
- An agreement to advise you of future tax changes
- An agreement to periodically update your Trust at a reasonable cost
- A simple but methodical means to organize your estate for rapid settlement

Clear Summary of Trust

A Living Trust, by its very nature as a legal document, is written in legalese. No matter how hard I have tried, as long as I have worked with legal counsel, I have never been able to get a Trust written in a way that is totally understandable by a client. However, it is essential that the client be able to understand his or her own Trust. Therefore, legal counsel should provide the client with a summary in clear, concise, and simple English, which will allow the client to understand the Trust and how it works.

Because the Living Trust document must be written in legalese, it should come with a summary in plain English.

Every client is different. Some clients are only interested in a vague understanding of the concept, and other clients want to know the smallest details of every provision. Many people simply accept the Trust at face value but want to know that the necessary information is correct. The detail-oriented person may want to cross the *t* and dot the *i* and, therefore, may want to know how the Trust works in detail. A general understanding of the documents and the key provisions enables every client to establish a "comfort level." Without this comfort level, the Trust documents effectively cease to function for the client.

Our clients are provided with an additional five-page, simple summary of their Trusts. After the computer creates all of the legal documents,

the computer searches through the document and generates a summary of the pertinent Trust information:

- Page 1 identifies the personal data. This information would include such items as your name and social security number, your spouse's name, children's names, parents' names and dates of birth, and so on.
- Pages 2 and 3 identify whom you have named where. This information includes such key individuals as trustee, surviving trustee, successor trustee(s), executor, durable power of attorney, alternates, the doctors for your Competency Clause, and so on. (Provisions of the Trust will be explained in the next chapter.)
- Pages 4 and 5 identify the particular paragraphs that have been personalized to make the Trust documents meet *your* particular needs.

Thus, in five to ten minutes, you can be assured that all of the information in your legal documents is correct.

Transfer Letters

For your Living Trust to be effective, all of your assets must be transferred into the Living Trust. Without this transfer of assets, you effectively have only a Testamentary Trust—which means that your assets must go through probate upon your death, and only *after* the probate process will the remainder of your assets then pass into your Trust. Appropriate transfer letters should be provided to each client who creates a Living Trust, so that he or she may readily transfer his or her assets into the Trust. In Chapter 12, you will learn more about how to accomplish this very important action.

Notification of Future Tax Changes

You should have an agreement with the firm that draws your Trust that the firm will advise you of any future tax changes. Any related changes to your Trust should be made at a reasonable cost. Unfortunately, Congress gets around to changing the estate tax laws about every five years. Most people readily become aware of the income tax changes (for example, the 1986 tax code), but too few people are aware of the *estate* tax changes, usually made in different years. Unless clients have some means of notification, their Trusts may eventually become noncompliant with the IRS Code because of a new tax change of which they are unaware. I believe that it is the responsibility of every legal counsel who draws up Living Trusts to notify his or her clients of any estate tax change and to offer to make related changes to the Trust for a reasonable fee.

All of our Trusts have been cataloged inside our computer system. Whenever there is a major estate tax change (and if it is of *benefit* to our clients), the computer searches all of our Trusts and provisions and then identifies which Trusts would be subject to that particular tax change. The computer prints out the names and addresses of the affected clients, and each client is advised in writing that his or her Trust should be updated because of the tax change.

Because the computer processing is done en masse for all of our clients, the Trusts of all clients will remain current. A reasonable fee for typical tax-related changes to the Trust would be $50 to $100, depending upon the extent of the tax change. This service is almost as important as the Living Trust itself.

Periodic Trust Updates

You should also review your Trust periodically for any personal changes that have occurred in your life and to see that your Trust still meets your objectives. A personal review of your Trust is suggested at least every five years—or sooner, if there is a significant change in your family status. Changes you may wish to make might include a change of a successor trustee, a change of a beneficiary, or a change in the method of distribution. These personal changes to your Trust, too, should be provided at a reasonable cost.

In contrast, all too often legal counsel charges $500 or more to upgrade a Trust! As ironic as this situation may seem, such an apparently exorbitant charge is frequently justified—because, when the Trust was drawn, it lacked organization, and therefore it is necessary for legal counsel to go through the entire Trust in order to identify which areas need to be updated! As you can see, it does not have to be that way.

If changes to your Trust are too expensive, your Trust eventually becomes outdated and ineffective, because you are unlikely to change it. Assume, for example, that an individual has had a Trust for five or six years and visits the attorney's office to ask him or her to review and update it—and following such updates, the client receives a bill for $500. The average person would probably be far less inclined to ever go back again. If this situation happens to you, your Trust has just stopped working for you!

Organization of Your Estate

As important as the Living Trust is, organization of your estate is equally important. Without an organized estate, the surviving spouse and/or children crawl around on hands and knees and turn drawers upside down, looking for missing documents. After the loss of a loved one, clients frequently search for documents that they "know exactly where they are," only to be unable to find them. After repeatedly seeing client after client spend hour after hour searching for documents that "have to be here someplace," I knew that there just had to be a better way. Thus, the Estate Plan Book was created for our clients—to provide them with a simple and orderly way to organize their estates (and to keep them organized), as well as to put everything needed to settle an estate in one place. The Estate Plan Book will be described and illustrated in Chapter 11.

With a Living Trust and an organized estate, the estate can be settled in less than an hour. However, it takes both: the Living Trust *and* organization.

STRUCTURE OF A GOOD LIVING TRUST

Even though the organization and structure of a good Living Trust will vary from attorney to attorney, a well-written Living Trust requires a multitude of carefully worded provisions, so that the Trust can accommodate your changing circumstances without needing to be legally modified. One of our A-B-C Living Trusts covers approximately sixty pages of legal language! The rest of this chapter will identify and explain the particular provisions that should be included in *every* Living Trust. This information should help you distinguish the good Trusts (and attorneys) from the bad ones.

Even though some of these Trust provisions may not apply at this particular moment in your life, any of the provisions could apply *someday*—and that is why they are included.

An extreme example, but a true situation, was Harry Strom, who had no children and objected to the provisions for minor children. I convinced him, however, to leave the provision in his Trust—just in case. Years later, when Harry died, his assets were divided between his brother and his sister. Since his brother had predeceased him and left minor nephews, the provision for minors in Harry's Living Trust was then essential.

However your Trust is organized, it should contain all of the provisions listed in Table 8-1.

Remember: Look not to today, but to what might happen tomorrow. Your Trust is designed for the future, and at some time any one of these provisions may be a necessity. Having a well-written Living Trust prepares you for the unknown or unexpected contingencies that may arise in the future.

The necessary provisions are listed in Table 8-1 by type of Trust: single person's A Trust, married couple's A Trust, married couple's A-B Trust, married couple's A-B-C Trust, and unmarried persons' A-B Trust. (This last Trust is used by two single individuals living together, retaining their assets for joint use, but keeping their assets legally separate.) The asterisks within each column indicate *necessary* provisions for the particular type of Trust.

If you use the table as an outline of your criteria for a Living Trust, a knowledgeable, experienced estate-planning attorney will acknowledge that these provisions are a part of his or her Trust, whereas an inexperienced attorney will decline to draw the Trust. The time an inexperienced attorney would have to spend researching all the provisions would make the cost of the Trust prohibitive. It would take the average attorney 1,500 to 1,600 hours to create such a document from scratch! If he or she has not already created such a vehicle through

years of experience, the attorney certainly cannot afford to begin now—and still provide you with a Living Trust at reasonable cost.

Therefore, you should use the outline in this chapter to demand that your Trust include these necessary provisions. Beware of the attorney who tries to pooh-pooh some or all of the provisions as unnecessary. After settling hundreds of estates, I can testify to the necessity of every provision.

Although other Trusts may be organized in different ways, any well-drawn Trust should include every one of the provisions described in the outline. If a Trust does *not* include all of these provisions, then I believe that you are being shortchanged. Each of these provisions is explained in greater detail and illustrated with real-life situations in Appendix G.

The list of provisions in Table 8-1 is probably one of the most important sections of this book. It is not placed here to read, but rather to glance through and recognize the number and types of provisions you should have in your Living Trust. More importantly, this outline is placed here to be used as a tool to enable you to differentiate a good Living Trust from a poor one—and thus be able to screen out the inexperienced attorneys.

CAVEAT EMPTOR ("LET THE BUYER BEWARE")

It is my intent to convince all people that they ought to have Living Trusts. The advantages of a well-written Trust are innumerable, and there are no disadvantages. On the other hand, I fully recognize the danger of sending you out into the cold at the mercy of those members of the legal fraternity who, when you say, "I want a Living Trust," will respond by saying, "OK, I'll draw it for you"—without having years of experience in this delicate area of legal technicalities. More than ever, the caution *caveat emptor* ("Let the buyer beware") applies in this situation. If you are offered a Trust that is not all-inclusive or that is not well organized, then quickly look elsewhere.

Almost daily I see advertisements of free seminars on the Living Trust. The information offered at these seminars may be worthwhile, but the abuses unfortunately are many:

TABLE 8-1
NECESSARY PROVISIONS FOR A GOOD LIVING TRUST

	Single	Married A Trust	Married A-B Trust	Married A-B-C Trust	Unmarried A-B Trust
Creation of the Trust					
Name of Trust	●	●	●	●	●
Parties to the Trust	●	●	●	●	●
Trustee authority to act independently		●	●	●	●
Tax treatment of revocable "Grantor" Trusts	●	●	●	●	●
Use of trust identification number	●	●	●	●	●
Settlor(s) still living	●[1]	●	●	●	●[2]
Upon death of first spouse	●[1]	●	●	●	●[2]
Upon death of both settlors		●	●	●	●[2]
Trust Property					
Property transferred to the Trust	●	●	●	●	●
Community property and quasi-community property		●	●	●	●[2]
Separate property	●	●	●	●	●
Successor Trustee					
Surviving trustee		●	●	●	●
Successor trustee	●	●	●	●	●
Successor trustees must act together	●	●	●	●	●
No bond requirement	●	●	●	●	●
Resolution of conflict	●	●	●	●	●
Litigation	●	●	●	●	●
Discharge or resignation of trustee	●	●	●	●	●[3]
Trustee compensation	●	●	●	●	●
Competency Clause	●	●	●	●	●
Settlor Powers					
Settlor retains absolute right as trustee	●	●	●	●	●
Description of powers	●	●	●	●	●
Catastrophic illness			●	●	
Trustee Powers					
Discretionary powers of trustee	●	●	●	●	●
Community property		●	●	●	●[2]
Separate property	●	●	●	●	●
Incompetency	●	●	●	●	●
Specific trustee powers	●	●	●	●	●
Securities authorization	●	●	●	●	●

	Single	A Trust	A-B Trust	A-B-C Trust	Unmarried A-B Trust
			Married		
S Chapter authorization	•	•	•	•	•
Precious metals and limited partnerships	•	•	•	•	•
Trust investments	•	•	•	•	•
Marital deduction		•	•	•	
Payment to minor/handicapped individuals	•	•	•	•	•
Reimbursement of guardian's expenses	•	•	•	•	•
Occupancy of residence	•	•	•	•	•
Discretional dissolution of Trust	•	•	•	•	•
Valuation of assets	•	•	•	•	•
Application to court	•	•	•	•	•
Insurance	•	•	•	•	•
Policy owner's rights	•	•	•	•	•
Trustee held harmless	•	•	•	•	•
Canceling a policy	•	•	•	•	•
Policy options	•	•	•	•	•
Insurance payment discharge	•	•	•	•	•
Suing an insurance company	•	•	•	•	•
Payment of Death Costs					
Discretionary powers of trustee	•	•	•	•	•
Specific provisions for settling the estate			•[4]	•[4]	•[4]
Written statement as evidence	•	•	•	•	•
Flower bonds	•	•	•	•	•
Death of Settlor					
Survivor's Trust A			•	•	•
Decedent's marital share			•	•	•[1]
Maximum marital deduction			•	•	
Division of "marital share"			•	•	
Decedent's Trust B			•	•	
Decedent's Trust C				•	
Election of fiscal year			•	•	•
Use of Trust B—simultaneous death			•	•	•
Survivor's Trust A					
Right to income		•	•	•	•
Right to principal		•	•	•	•
Right to withdraw principal		•	•	•	•
Control of assets		•	•	•	•
Right to change beneficiary		•	•	•	•
Distribution of residual of Trust A		•	•	•	•

		Married			
	Single	A Trust	A-B Trust	A-B-C Trust	Unmarried A-B Trust
Decedent's Trust B					
Payment of income			•	•	•
Payment of principal			•	•	•
Discretionary payments			•	•	•
Control of assets			•	•	•
Distribution of residual of Trust B			•	•	•
Decedent's Trust C					
Payment of income				•	
Payment of principal				•	
Discretionary payments				•	
Control of assets				•	
Testamentary power of appointment				•	
Distribution of residual of Trust C				•	
Allocation and Distribution of Trust Assets					
Upon the death of the first settlor		•	•	•	•
Upon the death of both settlors		•	•	•	•
Personal property distribution	•	•	•	•	•
Retention of Trust assets	•	•	•	•	•
Support and education	•	•	•	•	•
Extraordinary distribution	•	•	•	•	•
Gifts or loans	•	•	•	•	•
Handicapped beneficiaries	•	•	•	•	•
Primary beneficiaries	•	•	•	•	•
Special bequests	•	•	•	•	•
Allocation of Trust assets	•	•	•	•	•
Distribution of Trust assets	•	•	•	•	•
Per stirpes	•	•	•	•	•
Intestate succession	•	•	•	•	•
Charity	•	•	•	•	•
General Provisions					
Annual accounting	•	•	•	•	•
Partial invalidity	•	•	•	•	•
Headings	•	•	•	•	•
Counterparts	•	•	•	•	•
Spendthrift provision	•	•	•	•	•
Simultaneous death	•	•	•	•	•[2]
Last illness and funeral expense	•	•	•	•	•

		Married			
	Single	A Trust	A-B Trust	A-B-C Trust	Unmarried A-B Trust
Glossary of Terms					
Trustee	•	•	•	•	•
Child or children	•	•	•	•	•
Internal Revenue Code terminology	•	•	•	•	•[2]
Creation and Dissolution of Trust					
Situs of Trust	•	•	•	•	•
Reproduction of Trust provisions	•	•	•	•	•
Termination of Trust	•	•	•	•	•
Agreement between parties	•	•	•	•	•[2]
Enactment of Trust	•	•	•	•	•
Schedule A					
Gifts or Loans	•	•	•	•	•
Schedule B					
Charitable distributions	•	•	•	•	•
Separate Property Addendum		•	•	•	•[2]
Competency Clause Addendum	•	•	•	•	•

[1] The wording is specifically altered to reflect a single person as the settlor.

[2] The wording is specifically altered to reflect two unmarried single persons as the settlors.

[3] Under the unmarried A-B Trust, the right of the surviving settlor to replace the named successor trustee of the Decedent's B Trust has been specifically deleted.

[4] The wording is specifically altered to apply to the appropriate Trust: married A-B, married A-B-C, or unmarried A-B.

- The Living Trust fee quoted to you may ultimately be far greater when the cost of additional documents is added.
- One firm tells you that an appraisal of real estate is necessary to transfer your property into the Trust. The firm just happens to be affiliated with a company that will do the appraisal for $250 per property! (No appraisal is *ever* necessary to transfer property into your Living Trust.)
- One young attorney who graduated from a small law school advertised that he was "most experienced," having drawn up Living Trusts since 1983. (How much experience does one truly have just a few years after graduating from law school?)
- Another law firm offers *free* client follow-up interviews after its seminar. However, if you do not sign up for the firm's Living Trust, you are billed for "professional services rendered"!
- Some firms charge a fee of 0.5 percent to 1 percent of your *total* estate to settle your estate. Other firms charge you as much as one-third of what it would have cost if you had gone through probate! (If the Living Trust process is done correctly from the very beginning, very little should be involved in settling the estate, and—in the typical estate—you certainly don't need the assistance of legal counsel.)

A poorly written Trust can be worse than no Trust at all. Upon the death of a spouse (if a married couple have an A-B Trust), the decedent's half of the Trust becomes irrevocable; if a single person (with an A Trust) dies, the entire Trust becomes irrevocable. In these cases, a poorly drawn Trust can become a restrictive nightmare for the surviving spouse or successor trustee and beneficiaries.

As long as the clients are living, it does not matter what a Living Trust says, because it can always be changed or revoked. However, upon the death of the client, these poorly written Trusts are going to end up in probate court, with petitions being presented to revise or clarify the Trust wording. (Even though the main advantage of a Living Trust is to *avoid* probate, a Trust falls under the legal jurisdiction of the probate code; any need for clarification of a Trust therefore must be handled in the probate courts.)

A poorly drawn Trust can even become a nightmare while the creator is living. Fortunately, the Trust is still revocable at that time.

In spite of the abuses and the perils of a poorly written Trust, everyone *needs* a Living Trust. There are many reputable, knowledgeable, and experienced estate-planning attorneys throughout the United States. Unfortunately, there are far too many attorneys who purport to be experts but are exploiting the public. Remember the warning: "Let the buyer beware."

It is my hope that, by presenting the many details in this chapter, I have given you the necessary tools to make the appropriate decisions. If an attorney agrees to incorporate the provisions in this chapter into a Living Trust, then you have reason to believe that he or she is reasonably knowledgeable.

I hope that this chapter has given you the proper groundwork and equipped you with the basic knowledge to seek out and select a competent attorney to draw up your next step in sound financial planning—*your* Living Trust document.

9

Desirable Provisions

There are a number of desirable provisions (each considered to be a separate legal entity) which are not legally required parts of the Living Trust but which should be included in or with the Trust to provide for future contingencies. These provisions are so important that, with two minor exceptions, our clients are not charged for them. The desirable provisions to include with every Living Trust are:

- Living Will
- Durable Power of Attorney
- Competency Clause
- Catastrophic Illness Provision
- Assignment of Furniture, Furnishings, and Personal Effects
- Appointment of Guardian
- Appointment of Conservator
- Anatomical Gift
- Separate Property Agreements

LIVING WILL

With modern technology, the Living Will is becoming more and more important as a protection for you and your loved ones. The term *Living Will* refers to what many people know as the "Right-to-Die Clause." This document says in effect that, if your life is being sustained *solely* by artificial means, it is your desire—a decision made when you were competent—that the plug be pulled. By making this election before the onset of major medical problems, you may thereafter tell the doctors and hospitals that you want to die with dignity—and not be subjected to being kept alive by a machine.

People often say, "Well, that's all well and good, but I know that the doctors and/or hospitals will not abide by such a document." In the past several years, the courts and the medical professions have *slowly* come to the realization that each person *does* have a right to decide about his or her "quality of life." Only recently have several court decisions finally begun to uphold an individual's right to die. The following examples (which include factual names and cases that have been widely published in the media) will provide you with some interesting insight.

The case of William F. Bartling is a good example involving an individual's right to die and points out the typical position of many hospitals.

117

In 1984, William F. Bartling, age seventy, entered the Glendale Adventist Medical Center, suffering from five potentially fatal diseases, and he was placed on an artificial life-support system. Subsequently, Mr. Bartling asked that the artificial life-support system be disconnected. The doctors and the hospital refused—saying that they felt that "in their 'Christian, pro-life-oriented hospital' [the] doctors see 'disconnecting a life-support system in a case such as this inconsistent with the healing orientation of physicians.' "

William Bartling and his wife then sued the medical center and five doctors. The court found in favor of the doctors and the hospital. Mr. Bartling consequently remained connected to the artificial life-support equipment until he eventually died—five months later.

The day before Mr. Bartling died, his case was appealed. The appeals court found in his favor, but this decision was rendered two months after he died. Part of the judge's decision is significant enough to quote here: "The right of a competent adult patient to refuse medical treatment is a constitutionally guaranteed right which must not be abridged. Bartling's right to refuse unwanted medical treatment outweighed the hospital's and his doctors' concerns about the preservation of life and the maintenance of the medical profession's ethics. Adults have the right to control their own medical care, 'including the decision to have life-sustaining procedures withheld or withdrawn in instances of terminal condition.' "

In effect, the court ruled that a terminally ill patient has the right to determine the *quality* of his or her own life. (On the following day, every doctor and medical institution in the state of California was aware of the *Bartling* decision.)

Another notable case involving an individual's right to die is that of Paul Brophy. His case was aired on the television program "20/20" in 1985.

Paul Brophy was forty-five years old when an artery in his brain burst. Mr. Brophy underwent twelve hours of surgery, and sixteen hours later had a massive stroke. He never again regained consciousness. As months passed, Mr. Brophy's condition did not change. No ma-chines were keeping him alive; he breathed on his own. However, a feeding tube had been surgically implanted in his stomach to keep him alive.

After two years, his wife met with her family; the family decided that there was no chance of recovery and that Mr. Brophy should be taken off the feeding-support system. Being Irish Catholic, the family consulted its church leaders and was eventually directed to the Reverend John Paris, the church's ethicist located in Washington, D.C. Father Paris stated, "We have a medical intervention, and it is not really working, and so we are going to stop it. Removing the feeding tubes from patients is done regularly. I consult in medical ethics in several hospitals, and I myself have signed consult sheets stating that I believe that it was appropriate to have feeding tubes removed, and they were removed and those patients died."

Mrs. Brophy asked that the feeding tube be removed, but the hospital refused. With the approval of her family and of the church, Mrs. Brophy filed suit, but the judge ruled against withdrawing life support. His reason: Paul Brophy, in the judge's opinion, was not *terminally* ill; he was not a person about to die almost at any moment.

The decision was appealed, and in September 1986, the Massachusetts appeals court finally ordered that the feeding tube be removed. Eight days later, after removal of the feeding tube, Paul Brophy died.

Another famous "quality of life" case is that of Elizabeth Bouvia, a twenty-eight-year-old quadriplegic, whose tragic case received wide media attention several years ago.

Miss Bouvia had been stricken with cerebral palsy since birth and also suffered from progressive arthritis. She asked the court to order the hospital to stop force-feeding her by inserting a permanent tube through her nose into her stomach. The court upheld the involuntary use of the feeding tube; yet in 1986, in a unanimous opinion, the California appeals court stated that Miss Bouvia had the right to refuse medical treatment—even if the treatment were life-sustaining.

Most people will remember the landmark case of Karen Ann Quinlan, which was also widely reported by the media.

Miss Quinlan lapsed into a coma, apparently after ingesting a mixture of alcohol and barbiturates at a party. Her mother and father fought a year-long court battle to have their comatose daughter removed from a respirator. In 1975, the New Jersey Supreme Court ruled unanimously in favor of her parents. After being removed from the respirator, Karen Ann Quinlan astounded the medical profession by continuing to live another nine years, until she died at the age of thirty-one.

The day that the Quinlan's daughter died was a sad day for the mother and father. However, all people have reason to thank this mother and father for their courage—because they began the legal process that has eventually made the medical and legal professions aware that each individual should have the right to determine his or her own quality of life.

Legality of the Living Will

In every instance where the Living Will has been challenged in the courts, eventually the state court (usually the state supreme court) has unanimously supported the legality of the Living Will. There is no question today that the Living Will is a legally accepted document. Therefore, each person has the right to determine his or her own quality of life—but the decision *must* be made before the onset of a terminal condition and while the individual is fully competent and not under mental duress.

There is no question today that the Living Will is a legally accepted document.

On the other hand, the medical profession (including doctors and medical facilities) still sees its role as one of maintaining life at all costs—which is, in effect, the physician's code. Society is undergoing a major revolution in determining how to deal with the terminally ill patient. At the moment, the patient and his or her family are still being intimidated by the medical profession—that is, they are being told that the medical profession must still do everything necessary to maintain life (regardless of the cost involved or the continued suffering of the patient and family). Remember, though, that, if you have a Living Will (the Right-to-Die Clause), you have an absolute right—supported by the highest state courts—to determine *your own* quality of life.

The conflict over the legality of the Living Will arises from two opposing forces: the right-to-death force and the right-to-life force. The right-to-death force has successfully created the Living Will (the Right-to-Die Clause), which allows a terminally ill individual to determine his or her own destiny. In contrast, the right-to-life force does recognize an individual's right to determine his or her quality of life but takes the position that, if an individual has not exercised the right to put into effect the Living Will *while competent*, then the individual does not have the right to determine his or her own destiny once he or she becomes terminally ill. The right-to-life group further takes the position that, if an individual is in the hospital and under intense medication, he or she is no longer competent to exercise that right (if not previously done while competent). In addition, the group believes that *no one else* has the right to act on behalf of the terminally ill person.

Some states have enacted laws stating that an individual may not execute a Living Will within five days of being notified that he or she is terminally ill. The states are saying, in effect, that such notification causes undue stress and influence; therefore, the individual is not truly competent to execute the Living Will.

The right-to-die group and right-to-life group are both extremely strong and active forces in America today. I do not take issue with either group, but I *do* strongly believe that everyone ought to have the Living Will (the Right-to-Die Clause) signed and available. In the past few years, many clients have used their Living Wills when they have been diagnosed as terminally ill with cancer.

Importance of the Living Will

A poignant story will emphasize the importance of having a Living Will.

One of my clients wrote to me to say that her aunt, who had terminal cancer, had entered Cedars-Sinai Medical Center, a prominent hospital in southern California. The aunt went in for surgery and then wished to return home to die in familiar surroundings.

Following surgery, the hospital directed that the aunt be placed on life-support equipment. The aunt's niece advised the hospital of her aunt's wishes, but was somewhat brusquely shunted aside—the hospital was determined to put the aunt on life-support equipment. However, the niece stood her ground, held up her aunt's Living Will, and said, "You will not place my aunt on life-support equipment." Seeing the executed copy of the aunt's Living Will, the hospital yielded to the niece's demand.

The key point of this example is that the medical profession is still re-evaluating and re-educating itself about how to cope with terminally ill patients. With the Living Will, *you* have the right to make your own decision. There may be times when you or your family may be intimidated by doctors or hospitals, but hold your ground and recognize that the medical profession knows, as you now know, that the Living Will has been upheld by the highest courts.

Your Right to Act

The Living Will is not an *order* to act, it is simply your *right* to act. Clients sometimes worry that, if one of them has the Living Will and something happens (and he or she gets close to the edge of dying), the doctor is immediately going to pull the plug, even though there still might be a slight chance for the individual to recover. This worry is unfounded. The Living Will is available to be used—but *only you* or your family decides *when* it should be used.

Only you or your family decides when your Living Will is to be used.

The Living Will is a legal document that is kept at home with your Living Trust and its related documents and is available only to your family. When you have decided to have a Living Will, you have removed the burden of a "let live" or "let die" decision from your family. When the time comes to use your Living Will, the members of your family will be the only ones who will have access to your Living Will—and they will know when to use it.

The Doctor-Patient Relationship

Occasionally, a client will comment, "When mother was in that condition, her doctor let her go without putting her on an artificial life-support system; therefore, I don't see any need for the Living Will." When my own grandmother died at ninety-seven years of age, her doctor suggested that we keep her as comfortable as possible but quietly let her go. However, this doctor had been her doctor and mine for over twenty years, and we knew each other extremely well. Unfortunately, because people in the United States today have become a transient society, people change doctors regularly. The formerly close relationship between a person's family and the family doctor has nearly become history. The result is a strained doctor-patient relationship.

Some years ago, two doctors were subjected to the rigors of a murder trial because of actions they took on behalf of their patient (and with the agreement of the patient's spouse). Even though the doctors were eventually found innocent, the agony of having to go through a murder trial was more than anyone would want to face.

As I recall the circumstances, the husband had gone in for elective surgery. Something had gone wrong with the anesthesia, and, after the surgery, the husband was effectively brain-dead. The doctors so advised the wife and suggested that her husband be taken off the life-support system—and the wife concurred.

However, when the husband was taken off the life-support system, his life continued. The doctors then directed the nurse to remove the intravenous feeding tube, which was providing nourishment to the husband's body, but the nurse refused the doctor's request. Eventually, the intravenous feeding tube was removed, and the man died. At that point, the nurse told the wife that her husband would still be living if the doctors had not removed the feeding tube.

Upon hearing this news, the wife filed a criminal complaint.

Under these circumstances, if I were a doctor, I, too, would require the Living Will before taking such life-or-death action on behalf of a patient.

As of this writing, thirty-seven states have adopted the Living Will, and it appears to be just a matter of time before all states will universally adopt the Living Will with basically the same language. However, every state, except the state of Washington, requires that the Living Will must be re-signed and redated (and preferably rewitnessed) every five years. This five-year re-signing of the Living Will has been required simply because the concept is new. It is likely that this requirement eventually will be withdrawn. In the meantime, as a service to our clients, our computer prints out the names of our clients who have a Living Will (the Right-to-Die Clause) that is about to expire. These clients are then advised that they should have their Living Wills re-signed, redated, and rewitnessed.

Eloquent Words
This discussion of the Right-to-Die Clause—one of the more important (but optional) provisions included with the Living Trust—is best concluded by sharing with you a significant letter, written by Sidney Hook, emeritus professor of philosophy at New York University, published in the *New York Times* in March 1987, and reprinted here with his permission:

A few short years ago, I lay at the point of death. A congestive heart failure was treated for diagnostic purposes by an angiogram that triggered a stroke. Violent and painful hiccups, uninterrupted for several days and nights, prevented the ingestion of food. My left side and one of my vocal cords became paralyzed. Some form of pleurisy set in, and I felt I was drowning in a sea of slime. At one point, my heart stopped beating; just as I lost consciousness, it was thumped back into action again. In one of my lucid intervals during those days of agony, I asked my physician to discontinue all life-supporting services or show me how to do it. He refused and predicted that someday I would appreciate the unwisdom of my request.

A month later, I was discharged from the hospital. In six months, I regained the use of my limbs, and although my voice still lacks its old resonance and carrying power, I no longer croak like a frog. There remain some minor disabilities, and I am restricted to a rigorous, low-sodium diet. I have resumed my writing and research.

My experience can be, and has been, cited as an argument against honoring requests of stricken patients to be gently eased out of their pain and life. I cannot agree. There are two main reasons. As an octogenarian, there is a reasonable likelihood that I may suffer another "cardiovascular accident" or worse. I may not even be in a position to ask for the surcease of pain. It seems to me that I have already paid my dues to death—indeed, although time has softened my memories, they are vivid enough to justify my saying that I suffered enough to warrant dying several times over. Why run the risk of more?

Secondly, I dread imposing on my family and friends another grim round of misery similar to the one my first attack occasioned.

My wife and children endured enough for one lifetime. I know that, for them, the long days and nights of waiting, the disruption of their professional duties and their own familial responsibilities counted for nothing in their anxiety for me. In their joy at my recovery, they have been forgotten. Nonetheless, to visit another prolonged spell of helpless suffering on them as my life ebbs away, or even worse, if I linger on into a comatose senility, seems altogether gratuitous.

But what, it may be asked, of the joy and satisfaction of living, of basking in the sunshine, listening to music, watching one's grandchildren grow into adolescence, following the news about the fate of freedom in a troubled world, playing with ideas, writing one's testament of wisdom and folly for posterity? Is not all that one endured, together with the risk of its recurrence, an acceptable price for the multiple satisfactions that are still open even to a person of advanced years?

Apparently those who cling to life no matter what think so. I do not.

The zest and intensity of these experiences are no longer what they used to be. I am not vain enough to delude myself that I can, in the few remaining years, make an important discovery useful for mankind or can lead a social movement or do anything that will be historically eventful, no less event-making. My autobiography, which describes a record of intellectual and political experiences of some historical value, already much too long, could be posthumously published. I have had my fill of joys and sorrows and am not greedy for more life. I have always thought that a test of whether one had found happiness in one's life is whether one would be willing to relive it—whether, if it were possible, one would accept the opportunity to be born again.

Having lived a full and relatively happy life, I would cheerfully accept the chance to be reborn, but certainly not to be reborn again as an infirm octogenarian. To some extent, my views reflect what I have seen happen to the aged and stricken who have been so unfortunate as to survive crippling paralysis. They suffer, and impose suffering on others, unable even to make a request that their torment be ended.

I am mindful, too, of the burdens placed upon the community, with its rapidly diminishing resources, to provide the adequate and costly services necessary to sustain the lives of those whose days and nights are spent on mattress graves of pain. A better use could be made of these resources to increase the opportunities and qualities of life for the young. I am not denying the moral obligation the community has to look after its disabled and aged. There are times, however, when an individual may find it pointless to insist on the fulfillment of a legal and moral right.

What is required is no great revolution in morals but an enlargement of imagination and an intelligent evaluation of alternative uses of community resources.

Long ago, Seneca observed that "the wise man will live as long as he ought, not as long as he can." One can envisage hypothetical circumstances in which one has a duty to prolong one's life despite its costs for the sake of others, but such circumstances are far removed from the ordinary prospects we are considering. If wisdom is rooted in knowledge of the alternatives of choice, it must be reliably informed of the state one is in and its likely outcome. Scientific

medicine is not infallible, but it is the best we have. No rational person would forgo relief from prolonged agony merely on the chance that a miraculous cure might presently be at hand. Each one should be permitted to make his own choice—especially when no one else is harmed by it.

The responsibility for the decision, whether deemed wise or foolish, must be with the chooser.

With such eloquent words about the Living Will from the first-hand perspective of one who has been to the edge of life, need I say more?

DURABLE POWER OF ATTORNEY

The Durable Power of Attorney was established by the states in recent years for the specific purpose of allowing you to name an individual to act for you when you become incapacitated. The Durable Power of Attorney gives the power to the individual whom you have specified to act for you *only* when you become incompetent. The document has no application whatsoever while you are competent. Remember, however, that you must create the Durable Power of Attorney while you are competent.

The person you name in your Durable Power of Attorney while you are competent can act for you only when you are incompetent.

In contrast, the more commonly known and used "power of attorney" gives the named individual the right to act on another's behalf only while the individual is competent. Many people think that if they extend their power of attorney to someone they trust, the assignment will apply when they become incompetent. This assumption is not so. When a person becomes incompetent or dies, the power of attorney given by that individual ceases. Remember, however, that you must create the Durable Power of Attorney while you are competent.

Most legal documents are uniform throughout the fifty states—but not the Durable Power of Attorney. Each state legislature seems to have adopted its own approach. As you move from state to state, your Durable Power of Attorney is one of those documents that should be reviewed to make sure that it complies with that particular state's legal requirements.

The Durable Power of Attorney document provided to our clients also contains the Right-to-Die Clause. However, since the Right-to-Die Clause in the Durable Power of Attorney has never been tested in the courts, each client also receives the same provision in the form of a separate document, the "Living Will"—which has been successfully upheld in every state court where there has been a challenge. This duplication is part of our effort to design a Living Trust and accompanying documents that cover all eventualities.

The Durable Power of Attorney is really one legal document, but it consists of two parts: the Durable Power of Attorney for Health Care Decisions and the Durable General Power of Attorney.

Durable Power of Attorney for Health Care Decisions

The primary purpose of the Durable Power of Attorney is to appoint someone to make health care decisions. The Durable Power of Attorney specifically identifies whom you would want to make medical decisions for you if you were unable to do so yourself (for example, if you were in a coma). This person is legally known as the "attorney-in-fact." The document authorizes that person to make such health care decisions for you.

For example, if you were involved in an automobile accident, were rushed to the hospital, were unconscious, and surgery were required, the hospital and the doctors would need an authorization to perform such surgery. Such authorization can only be provided by a person who *legally* holds the Durable Power of Attorney on your behalf.

The Durable Power of Attorney for Health Care Decisions is probably one of the most important documents an unmarried person could possibly have! Most people assume that their children have the right to sign an authorization for them in an emergency, but this assumption is simply not true. Your children do *not* have the authority to authorize the doctor or hospital to perform surgery or important life-saving acts on your behalf!

Some years ago, I did a Trust for an emergency room physician who made it very clear that everyone ought to have the Durable Power of Attorney. The doctor lamented that, when people come into the emergency room with one of their family members, they do not realize that they do *not* have the authority to act for that family member if that individual is unconscious or incompetent. Of even greater surprise to most people is that parents *cannot* authorize emergency treatment for their legally adult children!

For a married person in most emergency situations, the spouse would be recognized as having the right to sign any medical release if the other spouse is unconscious or unable to sign those papers. The spouse would not normally be required to provide a Durable Power of Attorney. On the other hand, it is also entirely possible that something could happen to the spouse.

Even though some people might consider the Durable Power of Attorney to be less important for a married couple, this document is provided for all of our married clients for two specific reasons. First, realize that the husband and wife could both be involved in an automobile accident. If, for example, one of the couple were killed and the other were rushed to the hospital unconscious, who could make the appropriate medical decisions? Second, and far more important, is the case where something could happen to one spouse, leaving the surviving spouse a widow or widower. It is highly unlikely in such a stressful time that the surviving spouse will suddenly remember that he or she needs the Durable Power of Attorney. Therefore, wise planning dictates that everyone should have the Durable Power of Attorney—at all times and regardless of his or her medical circumstances.

For a married couple, the spouse is typically named as the attorney-in-fact. Since something could happen to the spouse, it is suggested that you also name alternate individuals ("successor attorneys") whether you are married or single. The next in line can step in on your behalf if the primary attorney-in-fact should be unable to perform the function. The successor attorney would presumably be one of your adult children, close family members, or close friends.

Occasionally, clients ask whether they can name two or three of their children to act together. Unfortunately, the states say that only *one* individual may act as the attorney-in-fact at any given time. It is possible to name more than one individual, but they would be named as first successor, second successor, third successor, and so on.

In case something should happen to the attorney-in-fact, you should name a successor attorney-in-fact.

Durable General Power of Attorney

The Durable *General* Power of Attorney is the second part of the Durable Power of Attorney document and identifies whom you would want to assume your Durable Power of Attorney for matters other than health care decisions if you should become incompetent. This document allows a spouse (or other such designated person) to act on behalf of an individual who becomes incapacitated. The individual appointed to act for the incapacitated person is called the "principal" or "attorney-in-fact."

The Durable General Power of Attorney is of secondary use only. The person named in your Durable General Power of Attorney has absolutely no access to your assets already in your Living Trust. Our sole purpose for the Durable General Power of Attorney is to permit the designated person to transfer any assets inadvertently left outside your Trust into your Trust if you become incompetent. If you have done your job and have all of your assets in your Trust, then this part of the Durable Power of Attorney is meaningless.

The following example (returning once again to using fictitious names, but real-life experiences, of my clients) points out the usefulness of the Durable Power of Attorney.

Some years ago, Shirley Drake called me to say that her husband had just had a stroke and was in the hospital in a coma. I said, "Shirley, did you get everything into the Trust?" She responded, "Bob got everything into the Trust except the Treasury bills; he just never got around to getting those transferred."

Since I knew that the Drakes had the Durable Power of Attorney in their Trust, I then told her that I would bring the appropriate transfer papers and immediately meet her at the hospital, outside the intensive care unit. Then I took Shirley and the transfer papers directly to the bank. With the Durable Power of Attorney and the transfer papers, Shirley had the Treasury notes transferred into the name of the Trust.

By putting all of the Treasury bills into their Living Trust, the Drakes avoided my greatest nightmare—a client going through probate. Bob died only five days later.

If the Durable Power of Attorney document had not been available for Bob Drake, then the Treasury bills could *not* have been transferred into the Drakes' Living Trust—and nothing could have been legally done. This situation does not occur often. When it does, however, the Durable Power of Attorney document can be *extremely* important.

Only one person at a time can be named as having your Durable Power of Attorney.

The person to whom you assign your Durable Power of Attorney should be the person you want to make medical decisions for you, since only one person can be named as having your Durable Power of Attorney for *both* functions described here. Remember that the Durable Power of Attorney for Health Care Decisions is *by far* the more important function—and is the primary purpose of this document.

COMPETENCY CLAUSE

If an individual were to become incompetent, for example, as the result of an accident, a stroke, or senility, management of the individual's assets must continue. Someone would still need to be able to buy, sell, or transfer the assets and to write the monthly checks. Without the Competency Clause, a member of the family would eventually be forced to go into the courts and suffer through the rather degrading process of establishing incompetency. However, with the Competency Clause, the legal process is very much simplified. You simply identify two doctors of *your* choice now (while you are competent); if you should someday become incompetent, the doctors you named would simply write a letter to that effect. Then whomever you have designated to act on your behalf would have the power to carry on for you.

The Competency Clause applies only to indisputable situations.

The Competency Clause is an extremely important document. All too often, however, clients hesitate to incorporate this provision into their Trusts because they are concerned that someone might "take advantage" of it. However, rest assured that this provision is for a black-or-white (yes-or-no) area, not a gray (maybe) area. The only time the doctors are going to be involved is when the case is very clear (usually if you are in a coma or are clearly senile).

I consider an ideal combination of physicians to act in this capacity to be a dermatologist and a dentist. Note that a dentist is considered a physician for this purpose. However, the state legislatures still do not recognize a chiropractor or Christian Science practitioner to act in this capacity. The doctors are not going to be involved in a borderline medical decision or a family dispute over a questionable condition. Thus, the Competency Clause works *for* your protection.

Robert Sinclair's mother-in-law called him one day and asked him to rush up to meet her in a small town some forty miles away. Upon his arrival, Mr. Sinclair was informed that his mother-in-law had lost control of all her funds, and he was handed a two-page legal form. The last paragraph of the form stated, "This woman has been making poor investments, has been losing money, and in order to preserve her assets, I ask that I be appointed her conservator." The legal document was signed by an attorney who had befriended the woman. The

court had approved the request, and the attorney had taken control of her assets. In actuality, the woman had not made *any* poor investments; she had, as a matter of fact, more than doubled her estate since her husband had passed away some ten years before. Regardless, the court granted the attorney's request, and the attorney had control of the woman's assets.

Steps were taken in the courts to have control returned to the woman, but the process took over six months and incurred substantial legal costs—as well as the fees extracted by the attorney who had made himself conservator of her estate.

If, in contrast, the woman had done as her daughter had been urging for the past two years—and had created a Living Trust—she would have named her daughter as the logical successor trustee. If, under these circumstances, an attorney were foolish enough to ask a court to determine that the woman was incompetent, then the daughter would take over as successor trustee—not some little-known attorney. Obviously, no attorney is going to waste time under such circumstances. Had the woman followed her daughter's advice, she would have saved herself substantial grief and expense.

The Competency Clause can be a protection against unscrupulous people attempting to exploit elderly and often infirm individuals. With the Competency Clause, *you* control who is to look after your estate if you become incompetent.

What Can Happen Without It

An excellent example of the need for the Competency Clause happened some years ago when a client who had initially elected to exclude the provision called to tell me of the following dilemma.

The client and his wife had sold their home, escrow had closed, and they had received a check for $125,000. The time was a Friday afternoon, and the client wanted to put the money to work. The client took the check to the bank, endorsed it, and handed it to the teller. The teller explained that the check also needed the signature of the client's wife. The client explained that his wife had suffered a stroke a week earlier and could not sign the check—and, in fact, was dying. The bank teller sympathized with my client, but she explained that the bank could not accept the check without the signature of both parties.

At this point, the client called me in sheer frustration. I explained to the client that, if he had the Competency Clause, it would be a very simple matter to get a letter (from the two doctors chosen by his wife) stating that his wife had suffered a stroke and was no longer competent. With the signed letter and the Trust document, the client could resubmit the check to the bank, and it would be accepted under the Competency Clause.

However, since the client lacked the Competency Clause, he had only two other options available to him. The client could go into the courts and be subjected to the process of establishing incompetency (which would take six to eight weeks); alternately, he could wait until his wife died (which the doctors said would probably take six to eight weeks). The client elected to wait until his wife died; however, he called me every other week complaining that he was losing $300 a day in interest. I could only commiserate with him.

Seven weeks later, the client's wife finally died. The following day, with the death certificate in hand, the client finally deposited the check in the bank.

If the client had included the Competency Clause in his Living Trust, none of the delay would have been necessary.

If You Regain Competency

All of the necessary protections are built into the Competency Clause. If you regain your competency, the doctors can certify your competency and reinstate you as before, simply by writing a letter. On the other hand, if you disagree with the decision of the doctors, you have the right to solicit legal recourse in the courts— that is, the right to have the *court* determine your competency.

CATASTROPHIC ILLNESS PROVISION

The Catastrophic Illness Provision described in Chapter 5 applies specifically to a married couple with an A-B Living Trust. This provision is now provided as an integral part of all of our A-B Living Trusts. Unfortunately, this important provision cannot be included in an A Trust, simply because the A Trust cannot be divided.

Because of the advancements of medical science, people are living longer; therefore, it is becoming more and more frequent that one spouse may suffer a catastrophic illness—one that involves such horrendous medical costs that the couple may have to seek state or federal assistance. Because most states require that the net worth of a couple be less than $2,500 before assistance will be granted, such a situation leaves the other spouse a pauper.

Furthermore, many elderly people are faced with the prospect of long-term nursing care. In most states today, before a nursing home will accept an individual for care, that individual must sign over *all* of his or her assets to the nursing home! This assignment of assets can be absolutely devastating to the surviving spouse.

The special Catastrophic Illness Provision of the Living Trust can be used to preserve the other spouse's half of the estate. At the onset of a catastrophic illness, the couple's assets are, in effect, divided in half—and only the afflicted spouse's half of the assets must be depleted in order to qualify for federal or state assistance. For example, if a couple had an A-B Living Trust with the Catastrophic Illness Provision and a $400,000 estate (assuming the assets were owned equally by both spouses)—and if one of the spouses were to suffer a catastrophic illness, $200,000 of the $400,000 estate would be preserved for the other spouse.

I can think of no better protective provision for the surviving spouse than the Catastrophic Illness Provision.

ASSIGNMENT OF FURNITURE, FURNISHINGS, AND PERSONAL EFFECTS

Many people overlook the transfer of personal property into a Living Trust. However, because it is quite easy nowadays for the average couple to accumulate personal property whose value exceeds the probate limits, all of the Living Trusts drawn for our clients include a separate document titled "Assignment of Furniture, Furnishings, and Personal Effects." This document is used for items that typically do not have written title—such as personal and household effects (furniture, appliances, furnishings, pictures, china, silverware, glass, books, jewelry, clothing, and so on). Historically, personal effects and household items have simply been left outside the Trust and passed to the surviving spouse; if there is no surviving spouse, the assets are passed to the children through the Pour-Over Will.

Depending upon the state, the value of an estate that requires probate ranges from $30,000 to $60,000. Visualize, if you will, the following scenario.

For simplicity, assume that a deceased individual's personal effects are worth $80,000. In most cases, this situation is not a real problem, because the assets are simply distributed "under the table" to the heirs (without reporting the assets to the probate attorney). However, assume that one child says, "I want all the books." The child is told, "No, you cannot have all the books; they will be divided equally." Unfortunately, this child knows a friend who knows an attorney. The child announces that he or she understands that, since the personal effects exceed the dollar amount subject to probate (and if the child is not given all the books), the child will blow the whistle and thereby cause *all* the personal effects to go through probate!

Given the choice of taking all of the personal effects through the onerous process of probate or giving the child the books, guess what alternative the heirs will choose. Obviously, the child gets all the books.

The language of our Living Trust is structured to avoid just such a situation. With the Transfer of Personal Property document, our clients transfer all of their personal effects into the Living Trust—that is, all of today's personal assets and all personal assets they may acquire in the future. The personal effects are transferred without a detailed inventory. Chapter 11 describes how you can use a Memorandum to identify any personal effects that you wish to pass to someone special.

APPOINTMENT OF GUARDIAN

In the past, the Appointment of Guardian provision was usually included as a part of the Pour-Over Will. However, our experience has taught us that it is far more effective to use a single-page document to identify the guardian. The Appointment of Guardian provision is used for minor children and also applies to handicapped individuals regardless of age.

It is customary to name a guardian until children reach the age of twenty-one. Most states have established that a child legally becomes an adult at age eighteen and is, thereafter, no longer subject to the guardian. Even though a child who is eighteen years of age may walk away on his or her own, by naming a guardian you have identified to whom you would want the child to return for advice and counsel if both parents were no longer living.

A guardian should also be appointed for adult children who are mentally or physically handicapped. Designation of a guardian also allows the parents to identify whom they would want to care for their adult handicapped child if something happened to both parents.

If both parents die without having legally appointed a guardian for their surviving children, the courts must appoint a guardian without knowing the parents' desires.

The appointment of a guardian is a very important decision for any parent to make. As you go through life, you establish certain goals and objectives, and you find others with similar goals and objectives. These people may be close family members, or they may be close friends. As many of our clients have discovered, if you go to the person whom you would appoint as a guardian and tell him or her that you have a Living Trust that will provide for your children financially and that you hope that he or she would provide for your children morally, spiritually, and educationally if both parents die, such an approach has almost always been received favorably.

Many times, people name a brother and his wife, or a sister and her husband, as co-guardians. Stop for a moment and think what would happen if your brother or sister died or got divorced. Would you want the spouse to be a guardian? Be aware that such awkward situations are always possible. Before you make a decision, carefully think about the alternatives available to you. You may simply decide to name your brother or sister as guardian, for example.

If both parents die without having legally appointed a guardian for their surviving minor children, the courts *must* appoint a guardian—without the benefit of knowing the parents' desires and preferences. There is not a court in the land that would not say, "Please don't place this burden upon me." People think that such a situation will never happen to them. Most people tend to feel immortal. Unfortunately, in the past ten years, I have had two sets of very close friends killed in automobile accidents; in both instances, they left orphaned children. In each case, the guardian appointed by the court was unfortunately not the one the deceased parents would have selected—and the results have been tragic!

If you have grown children, *please* convey the following message to them: Every parent should name an appropriate guardian (or guardians) for their minor children. To do otherwise ultimately may seriously jeopardize their children's future, if something were to happen to the parents.

Alternate Guardian

If your children are eleven years of age or younger, you should always name an alternate guardian. With a guardian being responsible for your children until they reach the age of twenty-one, there are often just too many years to elapse until the child reaches twenty-one, or at least eighteen. During those intervening years, the guardian specified in your Appointment of Guardian document could die. When that situation happens, if you are still living, you usually do not suddenly remember that you must change your guardian provision. If you are not living, who would select another guardian for your children? Thus, it is wise at any time to name an alternate guardian—and it is *essential* to do so when your children are eleven years old or younger.

Single-Page Document

The Appointment of Guardian provision included with our Living Trusts has evolved into a single-page document, which allows the named guardian to be easily changed from time to time as your particular situation may dictate. The Appointment of Guardian form works extremely well when parents have divorced and remarried.

A common situation involves a mother with very young children who becomes divorced and then remarries. Many years may have passed, and her present husband (although not having adopted the children) has effectively become their father. The mother elects to name her present husband as the guardian of her children upon her death. Of course, the children's biological father has certain legal rights to these children if the mother dies. On the other hand, the court is always concerned with the best interests of the children, and guardian papers naming the mother's current husband (the acting father) as the guardian can carry much weight.

The guardian of your children and the trustee of your Trust need not be the same person; one is responsible for your children, and the other is responsible for your assets.

APPOINTMENT OF CONSERVATOR

The Appointment of Conservator document identifies the individual who is to be responsible for your *person* if you become incompetent. This document should not be confused with the Competency Clause, which authorizes the successor trustee to administer the *assets* of your estate if you become incompetent.

The conservator becomes responsible for ensuring your safety and well-being. For example, if you were to become afflicted with Alzheimer's disease, eventually the Competency Clause would be used to authorize your successor trustee to step in and manage your assets and finances. The conservator you name should be the person you would trust to place you in a nursing home if necessary—to provide you with the kindest and the finest care possible.

Historically, Living Trusts have been concerned with managing and distributing the assets of an estate. Sadly, however, more and more people are becoming incompetent because of Alzheimer's disease and other maladies of age. Under these circumstances (and without the appropriate provisions in a Living Trust), the family finds it necessary to go into court to be appointed conservator of the afflicted individual.

It is the aim of our Living Trusts and accompanying documents to make it as simple as possible for our clients to manage their estates (and, where possible, to avoid the court process). Of even greater importance to our clients, however, is their desire to be the ones to identify (while they are competent) whom they want to be responsible for their person if they should later become incompetent. Therefore, the Appointment of Conservator provision is included with all of our Living Trusts.

No one likes to think of the possibility of going to a nursing home. In fact, almost everyone abhors the aging process. Unfortunately, all too often I have witnessed the agony of the transition process from home to a nursing home—not only with my clients, but also with my own family. At least with the Appointment of Conservator provision, along with a Living Trust, an individual is able to name that person in whom he or she has the greatest trust.

ANATOMICAL GIFT

With the Anatomical Gift document, you gift your vital organs upon your death, allowing them to be used to save other people's lives or to provide sight to elderly people with glaucoma. In many states, you may accomplish the same thing by simply filling out a small form and attaching it to the back of your driver's license. However, because so many of our clients asked for the Anatomical Gift as a separate legal document, the Anatomical Gift document was included with our Living Trusts as a separate (but optional) legal document some six years ago.

Shortly after we had drafted the Anatomical Gift document, a doctor came in with his wife to create a Living Trust. When the doctor saw the Anatomical Gift provision, he immediately complimented us for providing the document, and he then related the following personal incident.

When the doctor first met his wife, she had the anatomical gift card on the back of her driver's license, and he immediately made her remove it. As a doctor, he recognized the enormous need for vital organs. However, he stated that, when an individual is in that gray area between life and death, there is often a tendency on the part of the medical profession to want to take those vital organs prematurely. The doctor said, "I don't want anyone making that decision except myself."

The man made that statement as a husband, not as a doctor. I have since had three other medical personnel express the same view.

As a result of such experiences, the Anatomical Gift provision is recommended for those people who are kind and generous enough to want to give their vital organs to others upon their death. However, it is further recommended to our clients that they keep this legal document at home in the possession of their families—not on the back of their driver's licenses, where the decision to remove vital organs may be made by someone who has never seen the clients before. Our clients are advised that the ideal place to keep the Anatomical Gift document is inside the Estate Plan Book (which will be described in Chapter 11).

Not for Everyone

The Anatomical Gift provision does not appeal to everyone. Therefore, as a matter of course, we ask our clients whether they are interested in it. About 20 percent of our clients respond very positively, about 20 percent respond negatively, and the rest of our clients simply have no opinion on the subject.

I am often asked at what age one is too old to donate organs. A recent news article reporting the accidental death of a sixty-five-year-old woman stated that, since her death, she was responsible for saving two lives and giving two other people the gift of sight. How nice it would be if more people would consider being so generous.

Cost of Removing and Transporting Vital Organs

Occasionally a client asks, "If I donate my vital organs, will my family be burdened with the cost of removing and transporting those organs?" The answer is no. If the family gives permission, the organs are harvested, and the bill goes to the hospital. The hospital has an arrangement with the federal government, which reimburses the hospital through Medicare.

SEPARATE PROPERTY AGREEMENTS

Separate Property Agreements are documents that list those assets which, by definition, are the separate property of each spouse (that is, property received by one spouse as a gift or inheritance or property obtained before marriage). The list of separate property is attached to, and becomes an integral part of, the Living Trust. Since a Trust is simply a contract between two parties, if the parties agree to identify certain assets as separate property, the assets are so identified.

The effect of a Separate Property Agreement is that separate property assets placed in the Trust will retain their characteristic as separate property, even though they will take on the name of the Trust. In simple terms, this situation means that the assets separately belonging to each spouse may be brought together for the enjoyment of both spouses. Upon the death of one spouse, the assets *remain* in the Trust to provide for the surviving spouse. However, on the death of the surviving spouse, the separate property will go to the heirs specified by the spouse who owned the property.

Assets held as separate property are often commingled as the marriage progresses. For instance, you may enter into marriage and then receive an inheritance of stock, which you later decide to invest in your home for expansion or upgrading. Before you know it, this asset has become a part of the marriage property as a whole; the money received from the stock has lost its identity as separate property. However, with Separate Property Agreements included as part of your Living Trust, that property may easily be identified as separate property and be treated as such.

Use of Separate Property Agreements

The use of Separate Property Agreements can best be explained with an example.

Assume that a married couple have an estate valued at $400,000. Of this estate, the husband has separate property with a value of $200,000, the wife has separate property worth $100,000, and together the husband and wife have accumulated common property with a value of $100,000.

If the husband is the first to die, the common property would be divided in half, as shown in Figure 9-1. One-half of the property would come down to the Decedent's Trust B as the husband's share, and the other half would come down to the Survivor's Trust A as the wife's share. The husband's separate property would come down to his side of the Trust (the B Trust), and the wife's separate property would come down to her side of the Trust (the A Trust). Thus, the Decedent's Trust B would contain the husband's $200,000 of separate property, plus $50,000 of common property, for a total of $250,000. The Survivor's Trust A would contain the wife's $100,000 of separate property, plus her $50,000 share of common property, for a total of $150,000.

The husband, if he had so desired, could have distributed all or part of his share upon his death and left nothing in Trust B. However, in this example, the entire $250,000 may be used by the surviving spouse for as long as she lives. Upon her death, the assets in Trust B would be distributed to the heirs specified by the husband, and the assets in Trust A would be distributed to the heirs specified by the wife.

Separate Property Agreements are commonly used when a husband and wife have each been married before, and both have children by their former marriages. When the two people married, they brought their previously acquired assets together so that together they might enjoy a higher standard of living. The couple desire that, upon the death of one of them, the surviving spouse should continue to enjoy that same standard of living. However, upon the death of the surviving spouse, each partner in the marriage desires that his or her share of the estate will pass on to the children of his or her former marriage.

As mentioned in Chapter 7, the finest way I know to ensure that distributions made to your married children will remain their separate property is to have each of your children create a Living Trust with his or her spouse. In these situations, I normally recommend an A-B Trust, which clearly establishes that the beneficiary of each part (the Decedent's B Trust and the Survivor's A Trust) will be so recognized. Each spouse will then specify his or her separate property in Separate Property Agreements, which accompany their Living Trust. When these assets are then placed into the Trust, they will retain their characteristic as separate property.

The separate property may eventually be commingled with the other assets of the couple. However, as long as the trail is reasonably maintained (preferably with notes written directly on the Separate Property Agreement within the Trust), that property will remain separate property. If that child were to die, his or her assets would typically pass to the Decedent's Trust B to be used by the surviving spouse as long as the surviving spouse lives. However, upon the

---

FIGURE 9-1
DISTRIBUTION OF SEPARATE PROPERTY

$400,000 Estate
(Assumes Husband Is First to Die)

A-B Living Trust

Separate Property:	Husband	$200,000
	Wife	$100,000
Common Property		$100,000

Husband

Wife

Separate Property	$200,000
Common Property	50,000
Total	$250,000

Separate Property	$100,000
Common Property	50,000
Total	$150,000

$250,000
Decedent Spouse
Trust B

$150,000
Surviving Spouse
Trust A

$250,000
Heirs of Husband

$150,000
Heirs of Wife

death of the surviving spouse, those assets would go to the heirs of the first to die. In the early part of the marriage, before the children arrive, the designated heirs may be a brother or sister; as children are born, they usually become the heirs.

In case of a divorce, the divorce court usually recognizes a separate property agreement, although the agreement may be reallocated to provide for the children, particularly if the father is moving from the home and leaving the mother with one or more minor children. If the husband's income is adequate to provide for his ex-wife and children, the court will usually divide common property in half, and separate property will return to its owner.

Separate Property Agreements vs. Prenuptial Agreements

Separate Property Agreements have resolved many marriage conflicts. In contrast, the well-known divorce attorney Marvin Mitchelson states that 90 percent of his clients who have prenuptial agreements end up in divorce. A prenuptial agreement says in effect, "What is mine before marriage is not yours." My experience with thousands of clients supports the observation of Marvin Mitchelson. Prenuptial agreements are nothing more than a burr under the

saddle; however, I fervently recommend Separate Property Agreements where they are appropriate.

SATISFYING EVERY CONTINGENCY

Although not legally necessary, it is greatly to your benefit for your Living Trust to include a Living Will (the Right-to-Die Clause); a Durable Power of Attorney; the Competency Clause; the Catastrophic Illness Provision (if you are married and have an A-B Trust); the Assignment of Furniture, Furnishings, and Personal Effects (into your Living Trust); the Appointment of Guardian (for your minor and/or handicapped children, where appropriate); and the Appointment of Conservator. All of these provisions are essential in a well-written Trust. In fact, I feel so strongly about these provisions that they are provided (at no additional cost) to all of our clients as part of their Living Trust program.

In addition to these essential provisions, you may wish to add an Anatomical Gift provision, which should be available at nominal cost. If appropriate, Separate Property Agreements should also be included as an integral part of your Living Trust.

These provisions, when included with your Living Trust, should satisfy every potential contingency—now and in the years to come.

10

Estate Tax-Saving Documents

To shelter your hard-earned estate from unnecessary estate taxes, you should consider several other documents to supplement your Living Trust:

- Insurance Trust
- Spousal Gift
- Children's Trust

The Insurance Trust is significant and common, and therefore the majority of this chapter will be devoted to it. The Spousal Gift and the Children's Trust have limited use; however, they can be very important in specific situations.

Each of these documents has its own place in estate planning. Therefore, each should be considered in conjunction with creating a Living Trust.

LIFE INSURANCE

Before you can appreciate the Insurance Trust, you need a basic understanding of the concept of life insurance. Why should you have life insurance? How much life insurance should you have? How much should you pay for it?

Purposes of Insurance

There are basically two prime purposes for insurance: to supplement your estate (and provide for your family in the event of your premature death) and to pay estate taxes if your estate exceeds the federal estate tax equivalent exemption.

Providing for Family

A person's primary estate-planning objective should be to build an estate that is sufficient to eventually provide for his or her needs. In the interim, if the assets are insufficient to meet the needs of the family, then the individual has a responsibility to insure against the loss of income by premature death.

When your family is young, particularly when you have children, the loss of the family provider can be disastrous.

Years ago, I walked into the hospital room of a dear friend who was dying of bone cancer. When I opened the door, his wife was with him and he was in tears, so I quickly withdrew. Some moments later, I was invited back into the room, and my friend told me that he was in tears because he knew that his cancer was terminal and that he had not provided adequate insurance for his wife and seven young children.

My friend died several months later. However, I watched in admiration as that mother of seven went back to school to get her master's degree—all the while struggling to raise her children on what little money was available.

The woman has done a magnificent job, but how different it could have been if her husband had left enough insurance to adequately provide for the family's well-being. This husband and father loved his family dearly and had provided for his family in all but one area.

Because life insurance is designed to protect against such a loss of income, insurance on children and unmarried individuals is a waste of money. When a couple get married, the two people should consider life insurance on either or both of their lives, *especially* when they decide to have children.

Paying Estate Taxes
Ideally, as you build the value of your estate, you will have less need for insurance as a means of providing for the family welfare, and you can eventually replace it with the assets of your estate. Many individuals will eventually get to a crucial crossing point—that is, when their assets exceed the federal estate tax equivalent exemption described in Chapter 3 ($600,000 for a single person and $1.2 million for a married couple). At this point, the need for life insurance again arises, because the cheapest way to pay estate taxes on the assets that exceed the exemption is with insurance. Although this use of insurance may seem strange to you, the reasoning will be explained in more detail later in this chapter.

The cheapest way to pay estate taxes is with insurance.

In deciding whether your estate is large enough to need this benefit of insurance, remember that upon the death of an individual, life insurance becomes an *asset* of the estate.

Thus, its value will be included as part of the estate for the purpose of determining estate taxes. Over 50 percent of the clients who come into my office are shocked to learn that life insurance is subject to federal estate taxes.

If, for example, you are single, with assets of $400,000 and insurance of $300,000, your total estate on your death would be $700,000. Using the single person's federal estate tax equivalent exemption of $600,000 would leave a taxable estate of $100,000. The federal estate tax on the additional $100,000 would be approximately $37,000.

Estate Tax—Single Person	
Total estate (other assets plus insurance)	$ 700,000
Less: Federal estate tax equivalent exemption	(600,000)
Taxable estate	$ 100,000
Federal estate tax (@ 37%)	$ 37,000

If you are married and have an estate of $800,000 plus life insurance with a value of $600,000, upon your death, your total estate would be $1.4 million. If you and your spouse have an A-B Trust, $1.2 million of the estate could be sheltered from federal estate taxes. However, $200,000 of your estate would still be subject to federal estate tax. The federal estate tax on the additional $200,000 would be approximately $80,000!

Estate Tax—Married Couple	
Total estate (other assets plus insurance)	$ 1,400,000
Less: federal estate tax equivalent exemption	(1,200,000)
Taxable estate	$ 200,000
Federal estate tax (@ 40%)	$ 80,000

The Right Amount of Insurance
One problem that confronts every family is how to determine the right amount of insurance. I suggest to my clients a very simple but effective way: determine what your gross income is; from that, deduct what you are saving. Gross income

minus amount saved is presumably the amount of money needed for the family to maintain its normal standard of living—and this amount of money should be provided by insurance for the family. If both spouses are working, then both spouses should be insured for the loss of their incomes.

Two examples may help you see how to select the right amount of insurance.

Husband as Sole Provider
Assume that a husband is the sole provider for himself, a wife, and children. The husband's gross income is $60,000 per year, and the family saves $10,000 a year—leaving $50,000 a year, which is necessary to maintain the same standard of living if the husband were to die.

Note that I use the term *gross income* (income before deducting income taxes). When the proceeds of life insurance are invested, the income earned on those investments will, as salary income is, be subject to income taxes. Therefore, by using gross income, the example is comparing apples to apples.

Gross Income Needed as Replacement	
Gross income	$ 60,000
Less: Savings	(10,000)
Amount of gross income to replace	$ 50,000

Individuals should be able to earn at least a 10 percent return on their investments. Therefore, the amount of life insurance needed to maintain the same standard of living upon the death of the provider would be the amount which, earning 10 percent annually, would provide $50,000 per year.

Insurance Needed	
Amount of income needed	$ 50,000
Annual return	÷ 10%
Insurance (investment)	$ 500,000

Thus, the husband should have a $500,000 life insurance policy.

A mother raising her children full-time has a very definite economic value. If the mother dies, the father is left with the responsibility of being both mother and father, as well as housekeeper. The usual result is that the father's work suffers. Therefore, whenever possible, I recommend that the mother be insured for at least $50,000—to provide for housekeeping and child care in the event of her premature demise.

Husband and Wife as Joint Providers
Assume that a husband and wife both contribute to the family income. Together they have a gross income of $60,000, with the husband providing $40,000 and the wife providing $20,000. The pair manage to save $10,000 of their earnings each year. Therefore, the family would require $50,000 per year to maintain the same standard of living.

Gross Living Expense	
Husband's gross income	$ 40,000
Wife's gross income	20,000
Combined gross income	$ 60,000
Less: Savings	(10,000)
Living expense	$ 50,000

If the family needs $50,000 and the wife provides $20,000, the difference is $30,000. A total of $300,000 invested at 10 percent would provide $30,000 per year. Therefore, the husband should have $300,000 of insurance on his life.

IF HUSBAND WERE TO DIE	
Gross Income Needed as Replacement	
Living expense	$ 50,000
Less: Wife's gross income	(20,000)
Amount of gross income to replace	$ 30,000
Insurance Needed	
Amount of income needed	$ 30,000
Annual return	÷ 10%
Insurance (investment)	$ 300,000

Since the wife provides $20,000 of income (and the couple were saving $10,000), the death of the wife would result in a net loss of earnings of $10,000. An income of 10 percent on $100,000 would provide the necessary $10,000 per year. Thus, the wife should have at least $100,000 of insurance on her life.

IF WIFE WERE TO DIE	
Gross Income Needed as Replacement	
Living expense	$ 50,000
Less: Husband's gross income	(40,000)
Amount of gross income to replace	$ 10,000
Insurance Needed	
Amount of income needed	$ 10,000
Annual return	÷ 10%
Insurance (investment)	$ 100,000

Who Should Own the Insurance

Today, the person who is being insured should be the owner of the life insurance policies. The reason is that most life insurance policies have little value until the individual dies, and then the value is considered a death benefit, which is specifically exempted from probate. Therefore, it is not necessary for the Living Trust to be the owner of the policy.

Instead, your Living Trust should *always* be named as the "beneficiary" (to receive the funds paid out by the insurance company) unless you have an Insurance Trust. The Living Trust could be the owner, but taking such an action requires additional paperwork, which would be meaningless, because the insurance policy does not attain its full value until the death of an individual. At that time, if the Living Trust is the named beneficiary, the payout funds will flow into the Trust.

Upon the death of an insured spouse, the insurance is considered to be owned by both husband and wife, because the premium is assumed to have been paid from joint funds. The payout will, therefore, flow half into the husband's estate and half into the wife's estate—which is preferable in order to gain the maximum tax benefits of an A-B Trust.

The Best Beneficiary: The Living Trust

All of our clients are advised that their Living Trusts should be the beneficiaries of their insurance policies unless they have an Insurance Trust. There are two reasons for this advice. First, of course, is to eliminate the possibility of any probate. The insurance payout will pass to the *named beneficiary* without having to go through probate—one of the benefits of a life insurance policy.

However, consider the following scenario.

Assume a husband and wife are driving down the highway and are involved in an automobile collision, and both the husband and wife are killed. The insurance money from the husband's policy would pass to the named beneficiary (presumably the wife's estate) probate-free, but the wife's estate must now go through probate before the insurance money can be passed to their children. Admittedly, some people could be sophisticated enough to have named *contingent* beneficiaries, but years of experience have shown that these people are definitely in the minority.

The second, and even greater, reason for making your Living Trust the beneficiary of your life insurance is that your insurance policy (as so many other documents) takes *precedence* over your Will—which, of course, should be your Living Trust.

If you don't have an Insurance Trust, the best beneficiary of your life insurance is your Living Trust.

As people go through life, they often (and many times without much thought) name beneficiaries of their assets in all forms, which take precedence over their Trusts or Wills. Examples of such assets are life insurance, Keogh plans, IRAs, pension plans, profit-sharing plans, 401(k) plans, property held in joint tenancy, and others—the list goes on and on. As the following example points out, the insurance money may not always be paid to the desired individuals.

Four years ago, some clients who already had a Trust of their own brought in their brother-in-law to create a Living Trust. After the Trust was drawn, the brother-in-law's condominium was transferred into the Trust. Within the next few days, the clients worked with the brother-in-law to get his other assets transferred into the Trust. However, they somehow overlooked his National Service Life Insurance policy (taken out during the waning days of World War II).

Having just drawn the brother-in-law's Living Trust, I knew exactly to whom he wanted to leave his assets. Since the man's wife had died and he didn't have children, he named specific family members to receive the assets of his estate. When he took out his National Service Life Insurance policy in 1945, he designated his wife as primary beneficiary and his two nephews as secondary, or contingent, beneficiaries.

Since the brother-in-law's wife had predeceased him by some five years, when he died, his $10,000 National Service Life Insurance policy was paid to his two nephews. The nephews had not been named in the brother-in-law's Trust, and they were not part of his currently desired heirs. In fact, there was reason to believe that the brother-in-law had not communicated with his nephews in over twenty-five years!

If the brother-in-law had named his Living Trust as the beneficiary, the proceeds from that $10,000 life insurance policy would have flowed into his Living Trust, and the insurance money would have then been distributed to the desired heirs as specified in the Trust.

Estate Taxation of Insurance

More than half of our clients are convinced, or have been told by someone else, that their life insurance is "tax-free." Unfortunately, although the income on life insurance has been exempt from income taxes, life insurance is—similar to any other asset of an estate—subject to federal estate taxes. Upon the death of an individual, an insurance company converts the deceased person's insurance policy into a check for a specific amount of money. That money is added to the individual's estate and becomes subject to estate taxes.

Therefore, in analyzing your estate, you should compute your net worth and then add the value of any insurance carried on the husband and the wife. The reason for including the value of insurance of both husband and wife is that, if your estate planning is done properly, no estate taxes will be computed until the death of the second spouse; therefore, insurance on both spouses will ultimately be included in the estate computations.

Life insurance benefits are not exempt from estate taxation.

An A-B Trust can be used to avoid unnecessary estate taxation on insurance. To see how, let's examine the difference between an A Trust and an A-B Trust on a $700,000 estate.

Without an A-B Trust
If a husband and wife have $300,000 of insurance and $400,000 of other assets, they have a total estate of $700,000. With only an A Trust, the entire estate of $700,000 would come down to the surviving spouse, as shown in Figure 10-1. Upon the death of the surviving spouse, since the surviving spouse has only one federal estate tax equivalent exemption of $600,000, the excess estate of $100,000, would be subject to federal estate tax. A federal estate tax of 37 percent (or $37,000) would leave only $663,000 for the heirs.

FIGURE 10-1
ESTATE TAXATION OF $700,000 ESTATE WITH A TRUST

Other assets		$ 400,000
Insurance		300,000
Total estate		$ 700,000

Surviving Spouse A Trust

Total estate	$ 700,000	$ 700,000
Less: Federal estate tax equivalent exemption	(600,000)	
Taxable estate	$ 100,000	
Federal estate tax (@ 37%)	$ 37,000	(37,000)
Estate passing to heirs		$ 663,000

With an A-B Trust

If the husband and wife have an A-B Trust, the estate tax picture would look much brighter, as shown in Figure 10-2. Upon the death of the first spouse, half of the estate ($350,000) would come down to the surviving spouse in the Survivor's A Trust, and the other half of the estate would come down to the Decedent's Trust B. Since the Decedent's Trust B is valued at less than $600,000, no federal estate tax would be due, and Trust B would then be insulated from further estate taxes. Upon the death of the surviving spouse, only the assets in the surviving spouse's Trust A could be considered for estate tax purposes. Since the surviving spouse also has an equivalent exemption of $600,000, no federal estate tax would be due. The net result is that the *entire* $700,000 in the original estate would pass down to the heirs.

FIGURE 10-2
ESTATE TAXATION OF $700,000 ESTATE WITH AN A-B TRUST

Other assets	$ 400,000
Insurance	300,000
Total estate	$ 700,000

Surviving Spouse A-B Trust

	Decedent's Trust B	Surviving Spouse's Trust A
Total estate	$ 350,000	$ 350,000
Less: Federal estate tax equivalent exemption	(600,000)	(600,000)
Taxable estate	-0-	-0-
Federal estate tax	-0-	-0-
Estate passing to heirs		$ 700,000

How Much to Pay for Insurance

In most cases, if you have done proper estate planning and have a Living Trust, the estate taxes for a married couple need to be paid only when the second spouse dies. When life insurance is being used for the purpose of ultimately paying federal estate taxes, the insurance should be carried on the spouse for which the premium will be cheaper, typically the wife.

One reason that life insurance is usually cheaper for the wife is that most wives are younger than their husbands. In addition, the rates for women are typically lower than for men of the same age. For example, a woman who is thirty-eight years old would be charged the same premium as a man only thirty-four or thirty-five years old.

As with homeowner's or automobile insurance, shop around for the least expensive life insurance.

INSURANCE TRUST

The primary benefit of an Insurance Trust is that it enables you to place a life insurance policy (which is effectively valueless while you are living) inside the Insurance Trust, without any gift tax consequences. (Only the premium is considered to be a gift and usually can be excluded under the annual $10,000 gift exclusion rule.) The insurance takes on value only upon the death of the insured, at which time the insurance company will pay the face value of the insurance policy to the trustee of the Insurance Trust.

Unlike the Living Trust, an Insurance Trust is an irrevocable Trust, which means that it is unchangeable. Nevertheless, you effectively still maintain control over the Trust. Even though the trustee cannot cancel an insurance policy, you already know that, the moment you cease paying the policy premiums, the insurance company will cancel that policy. Thus, you can change insurance policies, if necessary. In addition, even though you cannot change the beneficiaries of the Insurance Trust once it is put into effect, you can name the Living Trust as the beneficiary of the Insurance Trust. You can always change the beneficiaries of your own Living Trust. Because of a recent court decision, individuals with large estates (those exceeding $2 million) should name their heirs rather than their Living Trust as the beneficiaries of their Insurance Trust to avoid an IRS challenge.

Estate Tax Savings

The Insurance Trust should be the owner/beneficiary of your insurance policies. Since the Insurance Trust is irrevocable and is the owner/beneficiary of the insurance, funds paid by the insurance company upon the death of the insured are effectively removed from your estate for estate tax purposes. Yet you may still use these funds to provide for your surviving spouse, to pass on to your children, and to pay estate taxes. Thus, the Insurance Trust gives you the best of both worlds.

Some examples will show how the Insurance Trust can save you unnecessary estate taxes.

Single Person

As you will recall from earlier in this chapter, the federal estate tax on a combined estate of $400,000 in assets and $300,000 of insurance is $37,000. Assume you have an Insurance Trust and place the $300,000 insurance policy in the Insurance Trust. Upon your death, the $300,000 life insurance will be excluded from your estate, as shown in Figure 10-3.

FIGURE 10-3
TAXATION OF SINGLE PERSON'S $700,000 ESTATE

	Without Insurance Trust	With Insurance Trust
Other assets	$ 400,000	$ 400,000
Insurance	300,000	300,000
Total estate	$ 700,000	$ 700,000
Insurance trust	-0-	(300,000)
Taxable estate	$ 700,000	$ 400,000
Less: Federal estate tax equivalent exemption	(600,000)	(600,000)
Taxable excess	$ 100,000	-0-
Estate tax (@ 37%)	$ 37,000	-0-

FIGURE 10-4
TAXATION OF COUPLE'S $1.5 MILLION ESTATE WITH A-B-C TRUST

Other assets	$1,000,000
Insurance	500,000
Total estate	$1,500,000

$150,000
Decedent's
C Trust

$600,000
Decedent's
B Trust

$750,000
Surviving Spouse's
A Trust

Federal Estate Tax on $900,000 Estate $115,000

$1,385,000 for Heirs

Married Couple

Although an A-B Living Trust can shelter an estate of a married couple where the net worth and insurance are valued at less than $1.2 million, when the total of all assets including insurance exceeds $1.2 million, an Insurance Trust is strongly recommended. Let's look at the different tax consequences of an estate of a married couple worth $1.5 million, first using an example of an A-B-C Trust without an Insurance Trust, and then using an example of an A-B Trust coupled with an Insurance Trust. In both examples, assume an estate of $1 million plus $500,000 of life insurance.

As you learned in earlier chapters, with a total estate valued at $1.5 million, the couple can benefit from using an A-B-C Trust. As shown in Figure 10-4 and previously explained in Chapter 4, upon the death of one spouse, the surviving spouse can elect to defer paying any taxes. However, on the death of the second spouse, there will be $115,000 of unnecessary estate tax.

In contrast, let's see what happens to the same estate using an A-B Trust along with an Insurance Trust. Figure 10-5 shows that the combination of the two types of Trusts avoids any federal estate taxes.

The Insurance Trust is a separate Trust, so the insurance of $500,000 in the Insurance Trust is no longer considered to be an asset of the estate, but of the Insurance Trust. With no insurance in the estate per se, the entire value of the estate is therefore $1 million.

Upon the death of the surviving spouse, no estate taxes would be due. Trust B would then be insulated from further estate taxes. The proceeds from the insurance in the Insurance Trust would also eventually flow down to the heirs (sixty days after the second spouse dies), without any estate tax being due. By creating an Insurance Trust, the couple in this example would have ultimately saved $115,000 of taxes—and therefore, the heirs would receive an "extra" $115,000.

As the example suggests, the significance of the Insurance Trust becomes more important as the amount of insurance becomes larger.

In most instances where people have estates valued in excess of $1.2 million, an A-B-C Trust should be recommended. However, if there is any insurance in the estate, the Insurance Trust

FIGURE 10-5

TAXATION OF COUPLE'S $1.5 MILLION ESTATE WITH A-B TRUST AND INSURANCE TRUST

Other assets	$1,000,000
Insurance	500,000
Total estate	$1,500,000

$500,000 Insurance Trust	$500,000 Decedent's B Trust	$500,000 Surviving Spouse's A Trust

$1,500,000 for Heirs

is typically recommended. This recommendation holds true even when the amount of insurance is relatively small but the value of the estate is over $1.2 million.

For example, upon the death of both spouses, with only a $10,000 life insurance policy but an estate of $1.2 million in other assets, the federal estate tax would be $4,000 (a 40 percent tax rate). Wouldn't you rather spend only one-tenth of that amount today for an Insurance Trust—to save $4,000 in federal estate taxes upon the death of both spouses? Sound estate planning dictates that you should indeed do so.

The Cheapest Way to Pay Taxes

As mentioned earlier in the chapter, for people with large estates, the cheapest way to pay estate taxes is with insurance. There are three reasons for this fact. First, insurance provides liquidity. Second, insurance prevents liquidation. Third, if you use an Insurance Trust, the insurance is excluded from your estate—and, therefore, from estate taxes.

Provides Liquidity

Most people tend to think of their estates as being akin to an orange; when they have to pay estate taxes, they neatly cut a proportionate slice from the orange, leaving the balance of the orange for the estate. Unfortunately, this simple analogy does not approximate what ac-

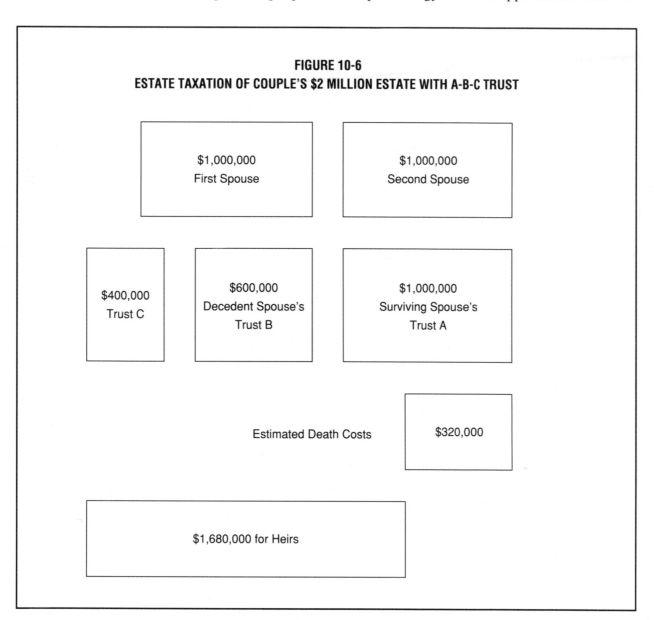

FIGURE 10-6
ESTATE TAXATION OF COUPLE'S $2 MILLION ESTATE WITH A-B-C TRUST

$1,000,000
First Spouse

$1,000,000
Second Spouse

$400,000
Trust C

$600,000
Decedent Spouse's
Trust B

$1,000,000
Surviving Spouse's
Trust A

Estimated Death Costs

$320,000

$1,680,000 for Heirs

tually happens in the real world. People's estates are seldom very liquid, meaning that the assets of their estates cannot immediately be converted into ready cash. Therefore, the orange gets squeezed, and the juice comes out the bottom into a glass. The juice goes to pay taxes—leaving the beneficiaries with the pulp. In literal terms, the assets of the estate are sold for less than their actual worth in order to effect a quick sale and obtain the needed cash to pay the estate taxes.

On a $2 million estate, for example, the federal estate taxes would be $320,000. Figure 10-6 shows how an estate of this size with an A-B-C Trust would be treated for tax purposes. When the surviving spouse dies, $320,000 of liquid assets would be needed to pay off the tax liability.

Most people who build their estates have their assets working for them, rather than earning simple interest in a savings account, so they typically do not have that large a sum of money in a liquid form. Insurance, in contrast, could provide the cash when it is most needed.

Prevents Liquidation

A related reason, and probably one of the most important, for using insurance to pay estate taxes is that failure to have adequate liquidity means that one or more of your assets must be liquidated (sold) in order to pay the estate taxes. An estate planner who knows the size of your estate can quickly estimate your estate taxes. (You can do so yourself by simply looking in Appendix A, B, C, or D for your particular estate and noting the estimated amount of estate taxes.)

Selling an asset to pay the estate taxes, however, is a much too simplistic description of the process. Sadly, the real world does not work that way. A more realistic scenario is that the survivor goes to an attorney, and, *eight months later*, the attorney notifies the survivor that he or she must come up with $320,000 in the next thirty days, because the taxes must be paid within nine months from the date of death. If he or she had known eight months earlier that it would be necessary to come up with $320,000, the survivor would have had a more realistic opportunity of raising those funds.

When you have only thirty days to liquidate assets, you are seldom able to sell the assets at full value. Such forced sales usually generate a return of only about ten cents on the dollar! I used to know businessmen who made their living buying businesses from estates for ten cents on the dollar. The businessmen admitted that their objectives were to buy assets as cheaply as they could from estates that were forced to liquidate in order to pay estate taxes. I call these people vultures, but that is also the real world.

Excludes Insurance from Estate Taxes

The third reason to pay estate taxes with insurance money is that the Insurance Trust excludes the insurance from estate taxes, as described earlier in the chapter. Therefore, the entire amount of the insurance proceeds may be used to pay the taxes. Figure 10-7 shows how using an Insurance Trust to pay federal estate taxes passes the full value of the estate to the heirs. In this example, the couple have purchased insurance with a death benefit of $320,000, which flows into the Insurance Trust, where it avoids estate taxes.

In contrast, if you use taxable assets to pay the estate taxes, you would have to generate an additional estate of $533,000 just to have $320,000 left to pay the estate tax! From the original $533,000, 40 percent, or $213,000, would be paid in taxes, leaving $320,000 to pay the estate taxes.

Additional estate to pay taxes	$ 533,000
Federal estate tax (@ 40%)	(213,000)
Available funds to pay estate taxes	$ 320,000

The arithmetic indicates that it is much cheaper to pay estate taxes with insurance. However, to avoid the extra taxation, the insurance must be in an Insurance Trust.

Even though the Insurance Trust was designed originally to hold insurance solely to pay estate taxes, all too often people take out large sums of insurance specifically to provide for the wife and children upon the early demise of the husband. The following example shows how good planning and an Insurance Trust can avoid the adverse tax consequences of such "generosity."

An insurance executive who had built an estate with a net worth of $500,000 had taken out life insurance in the amount of $1 million—so that, if he were to die prematurely, there would be sufficient funds to provide for his wife and four children. This amount of insurance was an unusually large insurance policy in relation to the size of the estate, but the executive felt that the amount was appropriate to provide the standard of living he desired for his family.

The family's net worth plus the large amount of insurance—an estate with a value of $1.5 million—exceeded the $1.2 million that could be sheltered from federal estate taxes with an A-B Trust. Therefore, it was recommended to the executive that he should have an Insurance

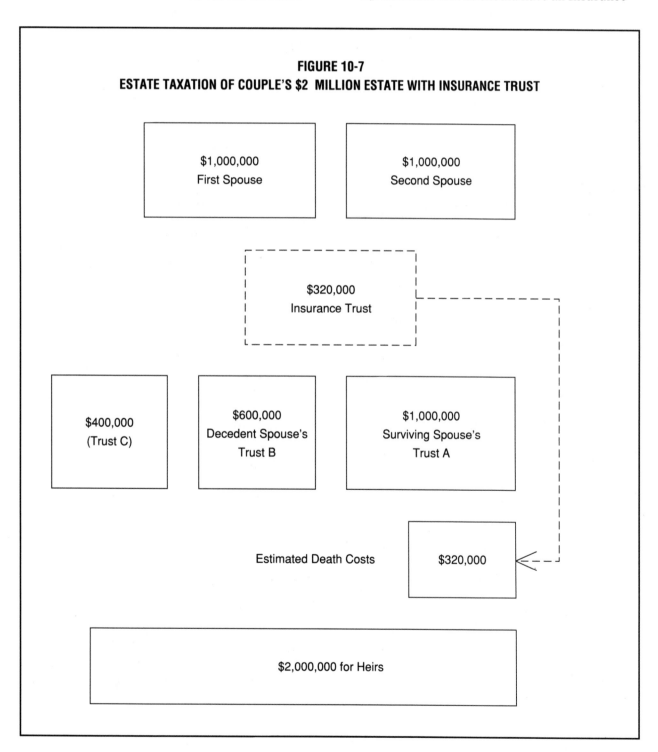

FIGURE 10-7
ESTATE TAXATION OF COUPLE'S $2 MILLION ESTATE WITH INSURANCE TRUST

Trust (along with his Living Trust), in order to avoid having to pay unnecessary federal estate taxes.

Features of the Insurance Trust

As the previous pages have shown, there are economic advantages to having an Insurance Trust for estates with significant amounts of insurance. The Insurance Trust should be the owner/beneficiary of your life insurance policies.

Note that the trustors (the creators) of the Insurance Trust *cannot* also be trustees of the Insurance Trust. Therefore, another member of the family, one or more of the adult children, close family members, or close friends should be named as the trustee or trustees.

Although not essential, a separate bank account should be set up to pay the premiums for the insurance in the Insurance Trust. You should make contributions to this checking account in different amounts and at different frequencies than are required to make the premium payments—in order to protect the Insurance Trust from challenge by the Internal Revenue Service.

In the past few years, *single-premium* whole life insurance and *single-premium* universal life insurance have become investment vehicles used to take advantage of the tax benefit of deferred income. Because these two vehicles are investments per se, they would not normally be placed inside the Insurance Trust. You do not want to create a gift or lose the right to your funds. Instead, you would designate your Living Trust as the beneficiary of these types of insurance policies.

Company group insurance policies are considered to be "owned" by the insured. The only right the insured has over his or her insurance policy is the right to change the beneficiary. The IRS says that, as long as the insured has that right, the person has what is called the "incidence of ownership"; upon the death of the insured person, that insurance policy will be included in the deceased person's estate for estate tax purposes. Therefore, on company group insurance, be certain that you specifically transfer the "right to change the beneficiary" as well as transfer the beneficiary to the Insurance Trust.

The main provisions of The Estate Plan's Insurance Trust are:

- To provide the surviving spouse with income for life
- To supplement the surviving spouse's estate, if necessary
- To pass to the heirs the Trust funds that are exempt from estate taxation

Since life insurance is so often taken out to provide for the surviving spouse and children, our Insurance Trust is designed to provide the income to the spouse for life. Upon the death of a spouse, the insurance company pays the face value of the insurance policy to the trustee of the Insurance Trust. The trustee then invests those funds and pays the income from the investments to the surviving spouse as long as the surviving spouse lives.

Our Insurance Trust is further designed to provide the surviving spouse with the right to borrow against the insurance, if his or her own estate were to substantially diminish. Why, you may ask, should someone borrow against his or her life insurance? The answer is: "for sound estate planning." If, for instance, the surviving spouse needed to withdraw $100,000 from the Insurance Trust, the spouse would be increasing his or her estate by $100,000—but, by signing a note back to the Insurance Trust indicating that $100,000 was borrowed from the Trust, the surviving spouse creates a comparable liability. Therefore, the transaction has not increased the survivor's estate for estate tax purposes.

Sixty days after the death of the second spouse, the monies from the insurance in the Insurance Trust pour over to the heirs without being subject to federal estate taxation. Since the insurance was never owned by the trustors (creators of the Trust), the insurance will not be considered to be an asset of the trustor's estate (for purposes of estate and inheritance taxes). The funds will therefore pass to the heirs without being subject to federal estate taxes.

Applicability of Insurance Trust

As a general rule, in considering whether an Insurance Trust applies to your particular estate, keep in mind the following guidelines:

- If the assets of your estate, including the value of insurance, will not be subject to federal estate tax—for example, if the total value of your estate is less than $600,000 (if single) or is less than $1.2 million (if married)—your Living Trust should be named the beneficiary of your insurance policies.
- If the assets of your estate plus the value of any insurance exceed the federal estate tax equivalent exemption, then the Insurance Trust should be used as part of your estate planning—to avoid estate taxes on the insurance proceeds.

SPOUSAL GIFT

The Spousal Gift is a separate document that allows a spouse with a large estate to gift a portion of that estate to the other spouse, who has a very small estate, in order to use both federal estate tax exemptions. This document is infrequently used. However, the Spousal Gift can have great significance in certain estates.

For example, an heiress to a large fortune held substantial stock in a publicly traded corporation. She had been married for many years to a police officer who was retired on disability. The couple were obviously quite happily married and had been so for many years.

The wife's assets were in the millions, whereas the husband's assets were in the thousands. If the husband were the first to die, although he would have a $600,000 federal estate tax equivalent exemption, he would have very little estate to exempt it against. The wife would not be able to use the benefit of any of her husband's federal estate tax equivalent exemption to ultimately reduce the estate taxes that would be assessed on her large estate. The solution was for the wife to make a spousal gift to her husband of $600,000, thereby reducing her estate by that amount but also enabling full use of her husband's federal estate tax equivalent exemption.

To allow you to better understand the tax-saving advantages of a Spousal Gift (in situations that warrant it), Figure 10-8 illustrates this example with numbers and shows the effect before gifting and the effect after gifting.

Assume an estate with a value of $2 million. Notice that, by prudent use of the Spousal Gift, the wife was able to effect a tax savings on her estate of $270,000!

FIGURE 10-8
TAX ADVANTAGES OF SPOUSAL GIFT

Before Gifting

	Husband's Estate	Wife's Estate
Net worth	-0-	$ 2,000,000
Less: Federal estate tax equivalent exemption	($ 600,000)	(600,000)
Taxable estate	-0-	$ 1,400,000
Federal estate tax (@ 42%)	-0-	$ 590,000

After Gifting

	Husband's Estate	Wife's Estate
Net worth	$ 600,000	$ 1,400,000
Less: Federal estate tax equivalent exemption	(600,000)	(600,000)
Taxable estate	-0-	$ 800,000
Federal estate tax (@ 40%)	-0-	$ 320,000
Tax savings ($590,000–$320,000)		$ 270,000

CHILDREN'S TRUST

The Children's Trust is an irrevocable Trust used to gift assets to one's children or grandchildren for their future education and general benefit. The 1986 tax code had a major impact on the Children's Trust. The tax code now attributes the income of a Children's Trust to the parents while the children are under the age of fourteen. Initially, many financial advisers saw this tax interpretation as the demise of the Children's Trust. However, more and more people are now discovering that an excellent use of the Children's Trust is to take appreciating assets (such as real estate) and to transfer them into a Children's Trust for the future benefit of the children. Effectively, you remove an appreciating asset from your own personal estate, and all future growth of the asset will be in the estate of your children.

The following example illustrates how a Children's Trust is used in some special financial situations.

Assume that a dynamic investor, a young man about forty-three years old with four children, has a net worth of about $1 million—all of which is invested in real estate. This individual expects to double his net worth in the next year and to continue growing his estate in that fashion.

The investor decides that it would be most appropriate to gift the $1 million of real estate holdings to his four children in a Children's Trust. Based on the investor's expectations, the $1 million of real estate will grow by appreciation to many millions of dollars in the coming years. Even though there may be some income to be realized, the major gain will be in unrealized appreciation that will be attributable to the Children's Trust. All of the real estate holdings (the growth assets) will be in the Children's Trust and will eventually pass on to the children without being subject to federal estate taxes on the investor's estate.

Many years from now, when the investor and his wife pass on, that real estate will not be in their estate; it will instead be in the children's estate and will be there without having been subject to federal estate taxes. Admittedly, the investor and his wife will have given up $1 million of their $1.2 million federal estate tax equivalent exemption in that gift. However, that $1 million of real estate could now be worth four or five times the value of the initial gift. In this situation, using a Children's Trust would be very good estate planning.

You may name yourself as the trustee of the Children's Trust and still continue to manage, invest, buy, and sell that real estate. You may specify in the Children's Trust when you want those assets to eventually pass on to your children or grandchildren.

Types of Gifting
To better understand the potential of the Children's Trust, you need to recognize that there are two types of gifts available for your estate-planning use:

- $10,000 gift per person per year
- $600,000 gift in a lifetime

$10,000 Gift Exclusion
Under a tax provision known as the $10,000 gift exclusion, you may gift $10,000 per person to as many individuals as you choose each year without the gifts being subject to estate taxes. Most people limit this gifting to their children or grandchildren.

For example, you may have four children. The father could gift $10,000 to each of the children (for a total of $40,000), and the mother could also gift $10,000 to each child (for an additional total of $40,000). This gift exclusion allows the parents to give their children a grand total gift of $80,000 per year. Be aware, however, that on April 15 of the following year, the parents must file a Gift Exempt Form 709 and declare the gifts to each of their children.

Figure 10-9 shows a sample of the Gift Exempt Form 709A, a simpler version of Form 709, which we suggest you use.

$600,000 Lifetime Gift
An alternative method of gifting part of your estate is the one-time lifetime gift of $600,000. If you are single, you can gift up to $600,000; if you are married (with an A-B Trust), you and your spouse can gift up to a total of $1.2 million. However, be aware that, once you exceed this amount, you must then pay gift tax, and the gift tax is the same as the estate tax! In fact, the estate tax code is known as the Gift and Estate Tax Code.

Do not be under the misapprehension that, if you make such a one-time gift from your estate, you have reduced the value of your estate for estate tax purposes. The IRS Form 706, Federal Estate Tax form, requires the trustee of your estate to identify your estate and also to identify *all gifts* (other than the $10,000 exempt gifts) that have been made from your estate since December 31, 1976. The IRS adds these gifts from your estate back into your estate for the purpose of determining the value of your estate.

For example, if you have an estate of $800,000 and have made gifts of $1.2 million, upon the

FIGURE 10-9
GIFT EXEMPT FORM 709

Form **709-A** (Rev. April 1988) Department of the Treasury Internal Revenue Service	**United States Short Form Gift Tax Return** (For "Privacy Act" notice, see the Form 1040 instructions) Calendar year 19 _____	OMB No. 1545-0021 Expires 02-29-91

1 Donor's first name and middle initial John J.	2 Donor's last name Smith	3 Donor's social security number 123 : 45 : 6789
4 Address (number and street) 5751 Oak Street		5 Legal residence (domicile) same
6 City, state, and ZIP code Santa Barbara, California 91382		7 Citizenship USA

8 Did you file any gift tax returns for prior periods? . . . . □ Yes ☒ No
If "Yes," state when and where earlier returns were filed ▶ _____

9 Name of consenting spouse Mary Ann Smith	10 Consenting spouse's social security number 123 : 45 : 8769

Note: Do not use this form to report gifts of closely held stock. Instead, use Form 709.

List of Gifts

Donee's name and address and description of gift (a)	Donor's adjusted basis of gift (b)	Date of gift (c)	Value at date of gift (d)
Cash	$ 20,000	Jan. 10, 88	$ 20,000

Consent

I consent to have the gifts made by my spouse to third parties during the calendar year considered as made one-half by each of us.

Consenting spouse's signature ▶ *Mary Ann Smith*   Date ▶ January 10, 1988

Under penalties of perjury, I declare that I have examined this return, and to the best of my knowledge and belief it is true, correct, and complete. Declaration of preparer (other than donor) is based on all information of which preparer has any knowledge.

Donor's signature ▶ *John J. Smith*   Date ▶ January 10, 1988

Preparer's signature (other than donor's) ▶ _____   Date ▶ _____

Preparer's address (other than donor's) ▶ _____

Form **709-A** (Rev. 4-88)

death of both spouses, your taxable estate will be $2 million. With an A-B Trust, you and your spouse have a federal estate tax equivalent exemption of $1.2 million, which is applied against the value of your estate. Therefore, your net taxable estate is back to its original net worth of $800,000.

Estate	$ 800,000
Gifts since December 31, 1976	$ 1,200,000
Taxable estate	$ 2,000,000
Less: Federal estate tax equivalent exemption	(1,200,000)
Estate subject to federal estate tax	$ 800,000

As you can see, gifting in this form does not reduce your estate for estate tax purposes. However, gifting $1.2 million and placing it in a Children's Trust shifts the *growth* of the assets to the children. Ten years later, that $1.2 million could be worth $4 million. The growth would be in the children's estate and not in yours. Thus, today, more and more people with large estates are finding that the Children's Trust has considerable application in estate planning.

Gifting Forfeits Stepped-Up Valuation
When you make a gift, you pass on to your children your cost basis for that gift. Therefore, the children do *not* get stepped-up valuation on the gifted assets upon your death.

For example, assume that today you gift $200,000 worth of real estate to your children, and twenty years later that real estate is worth $1 million. When you die, the children own the real estate (it is not in your estate); if they decide to sell it, they have a taxable gain of $800,000.

If, however, the children had received the real estate as part of their inheritance upon your death, the cost basis to the children would be market value at the date of death ($1 million, not the original cost of $200,000). Thus, if the children decide to sell the real estate, their taxable gain would be zero.

The concept of stepped-up valuation was explained in detail in Chapter 2.

ESTATE TAX–SAVING POTENTIAL
As significant as the Living Trust is in avoiding unnecessary estate taxes, several other estate-planning tools will also help. These tools are the Insurance Trust, the Spousal Gift, and the Children's Trust. Of these estate-planning tools, the most widely used by far is the Insurance Trust. Everyone should be aware that any insurance is included in the value of your estate. Everyone should also understand how to avoid being taxed on insurance. The Spousal Gift has a very limited use. The Children's Trust seems to be coming into increasing use for insulating an estate against taxation on appreciating assets.

11

Organizing Your Estate

There are two crucial, and equally important, elements in settling an estate: having a Living Trust *and* having an organized estate. The Living Trust avoids the agonizing probate process and unnecessary estate taxes; an organized estate facilitates a quick settlement and identifies what assets exist and where they are located.

THE PUZZLE OF SETTLING AN ESTATE

For most people, the biggest problem involved in settling an estate of a loved one is just being able to find all of the pieces. Even spouses do not always keep track of what the other spouse is accumulating. For example, many widows do not really know all of the stocks and bonds their husbands have purchased or all the pension benefits their husbands have earned over many years. Further, many people find it difficult to talk about such things, because they relate to the eventual death of a loved one—a very unpleasant thought for most people.

Losing a loved one—especially a spouse—is a traumatic experience. People in mourning can think only of the loss and not of the many details that *must* be resolved to settle the estate.

Unfortunately, at such a time, very few people can confidently go to one source and *know* that they will find *all* the puzzle pieces required to settle an estate.

The Estate—What and Where

What do you do when someone you love is dying—and then dies? Most people's natural reaction is to become mentally paralyzed. After almost twenty years of experience with clients and beginning with my own personal experience of my father's death twenty-three years ago, I realized the need for a "what-to-do" sequence.

How large is the estate, and where are the assets? Where is the deed to the house? Where are the checking and savings accounts and certificates of deposit? (The banks love to retain unclaimed accounts.) Who was your last stockbroker, and where are all those U.S. Government savings bonds?

People know where their important papers are—until they go to retrieve them. I have watched both spouses, even in the most organized families, search high and low for missing documents. Imagine the dilemma if one spouse were removed. Similarly, trying to step in and assemble the estate of a single person is a nightmare.

Even if you cannot locate a missing document, it is easy enough to order a replacement. One of the most common missing documents is the grant deed (ownership papers) to your home. Everyone who has purchased a home received a grant deed and meant to put it in the safe-deposit box. However, when someone ultimately looks in the safe-deposit box, the grant deed is not there. Instead, the person finds only the title insurance policy or a reconveyance (release of lien when the mortgage has been paid in full). How easy it is *now* to write to the county recorder's office for a copy of your grant deed; do not wait until you are under the stress of the loss of a loved one.

Years ago, a client was trying to go through the probate process for his father. The mother and father had lived in New York and worked as domestic help. When the parents reached retirement age, being of the old school, they informed their only son that they were moving west to live with him. The son knew that his parents had no money, so he purchased a small home for them nearby. The father soon died, and the mother was rapidly deteriorating with cancer, so the son moved his mother into his own home.

Months later, as the son was going through the probate process for his father, he literally stumbled onto a stack of stock certificates. The son learned that, as his parents worked, they would take their meager savings and buy one or two shares of blue-chip stocks and hide them away. The buying of stock had begun in the early 1930s, and now the stock certificates totaled $300,000. What a shock for a son who thought his parents were penniless!

Then the mother died. When the son was finally about to close probate on his father's estate, he cleaned out his parents' home prior to selling it. As the son removed the paper that lined the bottom of a drawer, he came upon yet another stock certificate. Neither the son nor the local stockbrokers had ever heard of the company; however, detailed research revealed that the company held oil rights in West Germany, and the stock certificate was then worth

$400,000. What a pleasant discovery. Unfortunately, probate on the father's estate, which was about to close, now had to be reopened. By the end of the probate process, this new-found fortune had all but vanished as the price of oil spiraled downward.

One client died of a stroke while driving home, and his wallet was stolen. (I think he owned every credit card produced.) You can imagine the urgency of trying to reconstruct, and cancel, those cards before massive charges were illegally made—and at a time of great stress.

How about those insurance policies? Many people have small insurance policies that their parents took out for them years ago or that they purchased themselves when they were first married. The policies are paid up but have been shoved away in a drawer someplace. Did you know that you do not need the actual insurance policy to collect the insurance money? However, you *do* need to know to what insurance company the claim should be submitted. In addition, do not forget "accident policies," which are often purchased through credit card companies or ordered through the local newspaper.

Have you identified all of your retirement plans? Retirement plans would include your many IRAs, Keogh plans, annuities, pension plans, and profit-sharing plans, as well as many other programs such as stock or savings plans in which you may be involved. Adding them all together could make the difference between decent survival or severe hardship.

Do you have any business agreements such as a buy-sell agreement (an agreement to buy back your company interest at a predetermined price) or deferred compensation (income earned but not yet paid)? These agreements, too, are assets of the estate.

How about all those legal documents you worked so hard to put together: Living Trust, Amendments, Pour-Over Will, Durable Power of Attorney, Appointment of Conservator, Living Will (Right-to-Die Clause), Gift of Vital Organs, Abstract, Insurance Trust, and Appointment of Guardian? These important documents are *essential*; they will be needed at the greatest moments of stress. Are they readily at your fingertips? Do you really *know* where they are?

Who are your advisers? These people are the individuals your spouse or children can turn to for assistance and would include such key people as successor trustee(s), special friends or relatives, guardian, financial adviser, and CPA. How can you reach them? Do you have readily at hand the current addresses and telephone numbers of these key people?

Do you have personal property you would like to leave to a son or daughter or to a special friend? How do you simply and easily identify the item and who is to receive it? Would you like to be able to add to this list periodically? One of my greatest regrets was that my father did not identify something personal—and meaningful between the two of us—to be left to me. Do not make the same mistake.

There Must Be an Easier Way

My first experience in settling the estate of a loved one came when my own father died in 1966. He was a very private person, and he was the only one who knew anything about his estate. (Does this scenario sound familiar?) When my father passed away, I was confronted with an impossible task. Figuratively speaking, I had to piece together a jigsaw puzzle.

I started with a three-ring binder with dividers. As I discovered an asset, I categorized it. Slowly, agonizingly, and tediously, I assembled the pieces of my father's estate. The search was similar to looking for needles in a haystack. Did my father have other accounts in banks unknown to me? I will never know.

It took me three months to assemble my father's estate. I believe that I eventually found most of the estate, but I will never really be certain. This trying experience was the birth of what is now referred to as the "Estate Plan Book"—a simple means to *organize* your estate.

Without organization, you have a nightmare; however, with organization, you create an orderly process for your surviving spouse, children, or other heirs. The orderly process allows the survivors to quickly identify your assets, legal documents, and distribution desires and then to settle your affairs—and then get back to living their own lives.

I have a magnificent wife and four lovely children; they are my life. When my time comes, I want it to be as easy as possible on my family.

Most people feel the same way about their own families. So that you, too, will not have to leave a jumble of jigsaw pieces as your legacy to your family, I offer you the fruits of my experience and the means by which you can organize your estate—the Estate Plan Book.

By organizing your estate now, you can save your heirs the arduous task of assembling your estate after your death.

After my clients complete their estate-planning process, I watch them walk away from the office holding the Estate Plan Book, with their Living Trust inside it, as if it were a precious possession. The clients act as if a great weight has just been lifted from their shoulders. Many clients express their appreciation for giving them peace of mind. The Estate Plan Book offers you that same peace of mind.

Time and again, I have seen the Estate Plan Book in action and know how vitally important it was to the survivor. I settle approximately one estate a week, and I could recite innumerable stories of how the book saved a survivor. The following true story illustrates the book's importance.

About three years ago, a couple came in to our office to draw up a Living Trust. The husband was a CPA. As a result, the necessary documents were quickly put together, and the couple's assets were transferred into the Trust.

The husband died last year. Five days later, his wife, Nancy, came into our office with the Estate Plan Book under her left arm and a stack of checkbooks, passbooks, and trust deeds in her right hand. Nancy laid the documents on the table, and said, "Henry, I am embarrassed to tell you that I don't understand numbers; I never have. My husband always took care of that. I have no idea of what I have." I simply added together the balances shown in the passbooks, checkbooks, and trust deeds. The total came to $350,000. I said, "Nancy, you have an estate of $350,000."

I then proceeded to go through the Estate Plan Book, and, when I came to the section entitled "Financial Statement," I found that, as a CPA, Nancy's husband had computed their net worth as of December 31; the financial statement showed a net worth of $550,000. I said, "Nancy, you are missing $200,000. Where would it be?" She said, "Henry, I wouldn't have the slightest idea where to begin!"

I again went to the Estate Plan Book and turned to the two sections titled "Savings and Investment Documents" and "Real Estate Documents." Nancy and her husband had done as I had instructed them when their Living Trust was first created, and they had placed copies of all their assets in these sections of the book. I checked off the various documents Nancy had placed on the table against the copies filed in the book. When that comparison was completed, I took little yellow tabs and marked each page that had not been checked off. The page identified the name of the financial institution, its address, the account name, and the account number. I said, "Nancy, I want you to take this book and, during the next week, go to each of these financial institutions and get a current financial statement of the assets in that institution."

Nancy returned a week later with the current financial statements from each institution. I added them all up—and they totaled $200,000. The missing $200,000 had been found! Right there, the Estate Plan Book had more than done its job. Similar situations have repeated time and again.

THE ESTATE PLAN BOOK

The remainder of this chapter is devoted to a description of the Estate Plan Book. Use this information as a basis for organizing your estate as you work with your own estate-planning professional.

The Estate Plan Book organizes your estate and takes the survivor step by step through the settlement process. The book itself is an $8\frac{1}{2}$-by-11-inch three-ring binder with large rings and twenty-one tabbed dividers. The dividers label the following sections:

- Letter with Special Administrative Instructions
- Durable Power of Attorney
- Conservator
- Living Will and Gift of Vital Organs
- Final Instructions
- Personal Data
- Advisers
- Trust
- Amendment
- Abstract
- Memorandum/Personal Property Disposition
- Insurance Trust
- Guardian
- Pour-Over Will and Codicils
- Financial Statement
- Asset Distribution by Trust
- Savings and Investment Documents
- Retirement Programs
- Real Estate Documents
- Insurance Policies
- Business Agreements and Documents

Letter with Special Administrative Instructions

When a Living Trust is executed, our clients are provided with an extensive letter of instructions, which specifically covers what they are to do to transfer all their assets into the Trust and thereafter to implement the Trust while they are living. All clients are also provided with special administrative instructions advising them what to do if the IRS asks for a Trust tax return and also telling them what to do when they are sent a form to reinstate their homeowner's property exemption.

Durable Power of Attorney

The Durable Power of Attorney document goes in this section. This document acts as the Competency Clause for any assets that have been inadvertently left outside the Trust. More importantly, however, the document identifies whom you would want to make medical decisions for you if you were unable to do so yourself.

Conservator

This section contains the Appointment of Conservator document, in which you identify whom you would want to be responsible for your *person* if you were to become incompetent.

Living Will and Gift of Vital Organs

If you have elected the Anatomical Gift document (Gift of Vital Organs), this document is placed on top. Following the Anatomical Gift document, if any, this section also contains the Living Will (the Right-to-Die Clause).

Final Instructions

In this section are three pages of instructions identifying the steps that need to be followed upon the death of a spouse or a parent. This information is included because experience has shown that, upon the death of a spouse or parent, the surviving spouse and/or children are often mentally paralyzed.

When our clients first receive their Estate Plan Book, we recommend that they go through this section and complete the right-hand side of those final instructions, as shown in Figure 11-1.

Beginning with the middle of the second page, the final instructions identify the steps that will need to be accomplished to settle the estate. Since, to a great extent, everything needed has already been done by putting the assets in the Living Trust, there is little to do following the death of a spouse, both spouses, or a parent. My experience has been that I can usually go through this section of the Estate Plan Book with a client (or a surviving family member) in less than an hour, as detailed in Chapter 13.

Not long ago, one of my clients asked me if I knew how to identify where a safe-deposit box might be if I were given a key. I must admit that I did not have a ready answer. The client went on to tell me that, when her husband died, he left behind over a dozen keys to safe-deposit boxes—and three years later, the widow still did not have the slightest idea where to look!

In the final instructions section, identify the number of safe-deposit boxes you have and where they are located, and also mention where the keys are located.

At the bottom of the third page of final instructions is a special area where clients may designate any special instructions they desire to be carried out upon their death.

The final instructions provide a page on which you should list all of your credit cards. The simplest way to make this list is to lay down eight cards at a time on a copy machine and photocopy them. The page is then simply inserted into the Estate Plan Book. You may also want to write on the page the telephone number to call if the card is ever lost or stolen. This page (or pages) now becomes an excellent record of all of your credit cards in case your wallet is stolen or somehow lost.

Personal Data

The section of the Estate Plan Book titled "Personal Data" should include copies (not the originals) of family birth certificates, baptismal records, marriage license, divorce papers from any previous marriages, military papers (particularly discharge papers), vital papers of personal interest, and vehicle registration certificates.

Divorce papers can be particularly sensitive, but it is very important that they be included. On numerous occasions, a previous spouse has submitted a claim to the estate—claiming that there had never been any divorce. The divorce papers filed in the Estate Plan Book can be your protection against such false claims.

For a simple and complete record of your credit cards, make photocopies of the cards, and next to each card write the number to call if the card is lost or stolen.

Military papers are the honorable discharge papers you may have received years ago and then filed away and forgotten. If the husband is the first to die, which is so often the case, the funeral home will ask the wife whether her husband served in the military. If the answer is yes, the Veterans Administration will apply $150 toward the cost of the funeral expenses as well as provide an American flag. At such a traumatic moment as this one, how does the grieving widow know where to look for those important military papers? The Estate Plan book is the logical choice for keeping copies of *all* of your important documents.

Thanks to the computer, our clients are now provided with a personal data sheet in this sec-

FIGURE 11-1
FINAL INSTRUCTIONS

Carl Sandburg said, *"There is no agony in the world greater than decision."* Now is the time to resolve **together** some of these essential decisions.

(✓) Telephone Check as Accomplished	Name	Phone
_____Doctor	_____	_____
_____Religious Representative	_____	_____
	_____	_____
_____Hospital for Anatomical Gifts	_____	_____
_____Funeral Home	_____	_____
Place & Manner of Internment	_____	_____
_____Immediate Family	_____	_____
	_____	_____
	_____	_____
	_____	_____
_____Close Friends	_____	_____
	_____	_____
	_____	_____
	_____	_____
_____Business Associates	_____	_____
	_____	_____
	_____	_____
	_____	_____
_____Review "Personal Data" in Estate Plan Book for Death Certificate accuracy		
_____Make Funeral Arrangements	_____	
_____If a veteran, take Military Papers to funeral home*	_____	
_____Order 12 Death Certifi- cates through funeral home	_____	
_____Determine if a memorial is to be suggested in lieu of flowers	_____	
_____Prepare and deliver notice to newspaper (include date, time and place of funeral)	_____	

Veterans Administration will provide $150 towards funeral expense, headstone marker and an American Flag, if desired.

(Attach list of names and addresses)

Name		Phone

_____Notify out of town friends
and relatives

_____ _____

_____Notify Successor Trustee

_____Notify Insurance Trustee
(if you have Insurance Trust)

_____Notify Company Personnel
Department

_____Advise Social Security (if receiving
or eligible for benefits)

_____Check safe deposit box for
special instructions or messages.   Box #_____ Location _____

Key Location   _____

Individual(s) authorized to
open box.   _____

_____Notify Advisors (see Advisors)

_____ **Meet with your Advisor on**   _____ to:
                                          (Month)   (Year)   (Time)

_____Review Trust Instructions

Note: Another executed copy of your Trust and Wills is located at:

_____Review Estate Plan Book

_____Notify Life Insurance Companies — include copy of Death Certificate.

_____Insure that all assets are within the Trust ("Savings and Investments," "Real Estate Documents," "Insurance Policies," and "Business Agreements" and, if not, which assets must be probated).

_____Review size of Estate (see "Financial Statement").

_____Determine if the Estate is subject to Federal of Inheritance Taxes. Do forms need to be filed and taxes paid?

Keep an accurate record of last illness and funeral costs.

_____Review business agreements for action, disposition and benefits. (See "Business Agreements").

_____Obtain written valuation of real assets (includes stock market quotation — at date of death, and six (6) months later to determine best valuation).

_____Review credit cards — determine if they should be changed or cancelled. (See Credit Card List)

_____Distribute personal effects, as per will, and special Memorandum (see "Memorandum"). Make special estate distributions if called for.

_____If assets are to be distributed or retained in Trust for heirs: Determine which assets, and real estate, should be distributed, sold, or converted to income.
(Determine debts outstanding to be paid prior to distribution of estate.)

_____Identify which assets are to be placed in the A Trust and the B Trust and/or the C Trust.

_____Review investments to see if they meet objectives of income, growth and security. Determine if some assets should be reinvested to provide adequate income as well as appropriate growth for hedge against inflation. Review assets at least annually to determine if assets should be reinvested for best growth/income and if assets should be shifted between A, B and/or C Trusts to preserve anticipated appreciation.

_____It may be appropriate to change the indentification number on your Trust assets: Substitute surviving spouse's social security number or IRS Employee Identification Number. See Trust section "Trust Identification Number". Use form W-9 or its appropriate alternate form as specified by IRS Regulations.

_____If any part, or all, of the Trust becomes irrevocable, and assets are retained therein, file form 1041 Trust tax return annually for the irrevocable part of the Trust.

If a spouse survives:

_____Continue to maintain income tax records — you will usually file a joint return in the year of the loss of spouse.

SPECIAL INSTRUCTIONS

If the decedent was living alone:

_____Remove important documents and valuables to a safe location.

_____Notify utility companies and landlord.

_____Advise post office where to send mail.

Other _____

_____

_____

_____

_____

_____

_____

We strongly urge you to take this opportunity to leave a tape recorded message to loved ones to be sealed until your death.

tion of the Estate Plan Book. This one-page data sheet lists all of the pertinent personal information of the clients, including the names of the husband's and wife's parents (and maiden names of the mothers) and the cities and states (or countries) of their birth.

When my mother-in-law passed away, I did not want to burden my wife, so I went down to the funeral home to answer the necessary questions. I was embarrassed when the funeral director asked me the questions, because of all the people who should have been prepared I should have been, but I was not. I had not brought the necessary information with me. When I was asked for the name of my mother-in-law's father (and where he was born) and her mother's name (and where she was born), I just did not know. I had to tell them I would return later with that information. How silly I felt!

The personal data sheet provides all such information—needed at the time when you are least mentally able to supply it. You might ask why the state wants to know where the mother and father were born. The answer is that someone, somewhere, does a census of migration—tracking how people move from country to country and from state to state.

My real excitement comes from being able to provide the heirs with information that allows them to begin tracing their roots. Most of our children are Americanized and give little thought today to their origin. As this personal data information is included with our Trusts, I am delightfully surprised to see how many of our clients (or their parents) came from countries far and wide to eventually become a part of this great nation. One day your children are going to seek their roots, and the personal data page may be their beginning.

Advisers

In the next section of the book, you list your special friends and relatives, successor trustees, guardians, financial planners or advisers, attorneys, and CPA, along with their names, addresses, and telephone numbers. Since these individuals change from time to time, it is suggested that you enter the information on this page with a pencil, so that you can easily and clearly keep your Estate Plan Book up to date. Figure 11-2 shows a sample of the Advisers page included in the book.

Trust

This section of the Estate Plan Book is where the original copy of your Living Trust document should reside. It may be an A Trust, an A-B Trust, or an A-B-C Trust.

Amendment

From time to time, there may be changes to your Living Trust; these changes are called amendments. The amendments may be personal changes (such as a change of beneficiary, a change of method of distribution, or a change of successor trustee), or they may be tax changes as a result of tax laws passed by Congress that could be of benefit to your estate planning.

As mentioned earlier, all of our Trusts have been codified (arranged systematically) in the computer. Whenever there is a major tax change, the computer prints out the name and address of each client who would be affected. The service of reviewing *all* of our Trusts for applicable tax law changes is as important to our clients as are the Living Trust and the Estate Plan Book themselves.

Abstract

The abstract is a three-page legal summary of your Living Trust. However, the abstract does *not* identify the allocation or distribution of assets upon your death. The abstract is simply a legal summary of the Trust, which identifies the key issues.

From time to time, a financial institution may ask to see a copy of your Trust. You need only loan the institution a copy of this abstract; in most cases, the abstract will be sufficient. Occasionally, however, a financial institution may ask to see a complete copy of your Living Trust, rather than just the abstract. Do not be concerned if an institution insists on seeing your entire Trust—simply loan it a copy of your Living Trust. By and large, an institution only wants to see the first page, the signature page, and the trustee powers. The institution wants to make sure that your Trust is a valid document and that you have the necessary authority to perform certain actions. In the case of a mortgage, the mortgage company wants to make sure that there is no provision in the Trust that would stand between the institution and the right to foreclose on your home if you were unable to make the required mortgage payments.

Memorandum/Personal Property Disposition
In the Trust document, under the section "Allocation and Distribution of Trust Assets," the Trust specifically requests the trustee to abide by any "Memorandum." Almost everyone has certain personal effects that he or she wants to leave to a son, daughter, or close personal friend. The Memorandum included as part of the Estate Plan Book provides a form, as shown in Figure 11-3, that can be used to describe the personal property and to identify to whom you want to leave it.

If you really stop and observe your children or, better yet, simply ask them, you will no doubt find that each child has at least one or two items that he or she would want because of

---

FIGURE 11-2
ADVISERS PAGE

We suggest that you complete this section in pencil so that changes can be made as necessary.

	Name	Address	Telephone No.
Successor Trustee*	_____	_____	(___) _____
Special Relatives or Friends	_____	_____	(___) _____
	_____	_____	(___) _____
	_____	_____	(___) _____
	_____	_____	(___) _____
	_____	_____	(___) _____
	_____	_____	(___) _____
Guardian	_____	_____	(___) _____
Financial	_____	_____	(___) _____
Attorney	_____	_____	(___) _____
CPA	_____	_____	(___) _____

*Other than Husband, Wife, or Client.

FIGURE 11-3
MEMORANDUM

DESIRED DISTRIBUTION OF PERSONAL PROPERTY

Certain of my personal effects have special meaning. I desire that upon my death these items be given to those herein indicated.

Description of Personal Property   **Desired Recipient and Relationship**

_____   _____

_____   _____

_____   _____

_____   _____

_____   _____

_____   _____

_____   _____

_____   _____

_____
Signed

_____   _____

_____   _____

_____   _____

_____   _____

_____   _____

_____   _____

_____   _____

_____   _____

_____
Signed

a personal attachment. How nice it is to be able to write, in the "Memorandum" section of the Estate Plan Book, a simple description of that property and to whom you would like it to be given.

I remember, as a child, spending rare moments with my father each September when we went dove hunting. He loaned me his double-barreled twenty-gauge shotgun. It wasn't a fancy shotgun by my father's standards. In fact, when my father died many years later, he had many very expensive shotguns, and some even had gold triggers.

However, that double-barreled shotgun in some way was a bond between my father and me. Today, the thought of shooting a bird or animal is repugnant to me, so that shotgun would be worthless to me. Still, because of the link it represented between my father and me, I would give my eyeteeth to have it.

Sadly, my favorite shotgun was sold along with the rest of my father's expensive gun collection. I don't think that is what my father would have wanted; however, he wasn't around anymore, and he hadn't put anything in writing.

Keep the Estate Plan Book in a place where it is readily available to you to review or amend.

The Estate Plan Book is a workbook. The book does not belong in a safe-deposit box; it belongs at home, on a shelf, or in a drawer, where it is readily available. When you wake up in the middle of the night and suddenly remember that your oldest son indicated that he would someday like to have a particular painting, make a note of it. When you get up in the morning, take out the Estate Plan Book, open it to the Memorandum section, write down a simple description of the picture, and enter the son's name.

Behind the Memorandum page, this section also includes the document entitled "Assignment of Furniture, Furnishings, and Personal Effects," which assigns these untitled assets

into your Living Trust without your having to inventory all of the personal effects. This document includes today's personal effects as well as future acquisitions.

Insurance Trust

If you have an Insurance Trust, it will be placed in the Estate Plan Book behind a divider labeled "Insurance Trust."

Guardian

If you have named a guardian for your minor children (or a handicapped child), the Appointment of Guardian document would be placed in the Estate Plan Book behind a divider labeled "Guardian."

Pour-Over Will and Codicils

The Pour-Over Will simply says that, if you forgot to put an asset into your Trust, it is your intention upon your death that the forgotten asset should "pour over" into your Living Trust. Unfortunately, if the asset is not in your Trust at the time of your death, the asset must first go through probate if its value exceeds the probate limits.

The executor is the person responsible for shepherding any of your forgotten assets through the probate process. The Pour-Over Will identifies the executor and gives the executor the power to take those assets through probate. Once the probate process is complete, the executor is then empowered to pour over what is left of those assets into the Trust.

If you have done your job, no assets are left outside your Trust; therefore, the Pour-Over Will should never have to be used.

A codicil is simply a change to your Pour-Over Will.

Financial Statement

Included in the Financial Statement section of the Estate Plan Book is a very simple form for our clients to complete, which provides them with a summary of their financial net worth. Net worth is discussed in greater detail in Chapter 14. Our clients are instructed, when filling out this form, to round the figures to the nearest thousand dollars and to fill out the form in pencil. It is further suggested that the clients review and update this form yearly. The form in the Estate Plan Book is simple and, if kept up to date, simplifies determining whether a Federal Estate Tax Return (Form 706) needs to be filed and, thus, whether any federal estate taxes need to be paid. (The federal estate tax return will be discussed more fully in Chapter 13.)

Asset Distribution by Trust

The "Asset Distribution by Trust" section identifies, upon the death of a spouse, which assets go into the Survivor's A Trust, which assets go into the Decedent's B Trust, and, where appropriate, which assets go into the C (or Q-Tip) Trust. This section of the Estate Plan Book also includes simple forms that are used as aids to settling the estate of a client with a Living Trust. Figure 11-4 is an example of the form used for distribution into the A Trust. Similar forms with different titles are used for the B and C Trusts. Once the assets are divided and identified on these forms, nothing else needs to be done.

Generally, the appreciating assets should be placed in the B Trust, because this Trust will be insulated from any further estate taxes. On the other hand, when the desired objectives of the estate are discussed with a surviving spouse, the placement of assets in the A, B, or C portion of the Trust may be quite different for each situation.

Of almost equal importance is the inclusion in this section of the Estate Plan Book of forms that provide the trustee with a simple means of transferring assets back and forth, as necessary, among the A, B, and C Trusts. Figure 11-5 shows an example of the transfer form included in the Estate Plan Book for the use of our clients. These forms will be explained in greater detail in Chapter 13.

When a client first receives a copy of the Estate Plan Book, we usually postpone discussing the area of asset distribution. There are so many advantages to the Living Trust for people while they are living, and there is so much information to learn and retain, that a detailed discussion of this particular area is deferred until the death of a spouse or parent—at which time all of the advantages of estate planning with a Living Trust are individually discussed with each client.

Savings and Investment Documents

This section of the Estate Plan Book should include *copies* of any forms that provide the pertinent information (such as name and address of an institution, your account number, and so on) for all of your checking accounts, savings accounts, company and credit union savings accounts, money market funds, certificates of deposit, Treasury bills, stocks, bonds, mutual funds, and notes due.

To provide an accurate picture of your estate, however, you should also include copies of documents that identify your liabilities—such as home mortgage, bank loans, credit union loans, and personal loans.

To make a record of your checking account, simply photocopy a check; for your savings accounts, copy the inside cover of each passbook.

Since this section of the Estate Plan Book should contain only *copies* of the original documents, it is also important to note where all of the originals may be found (such as in a bank safe-deposit box, a filing cabinet in your den, or wherever the documents are kept).

I am often asked, "How do I make a copy of my checking account?" The answer is simple: Just lay one of your checks down on the surface of a copy machine and make a copy of the check—which immediately makes a record of the name of the bank, the bank's address, the name under which the account is listed, and the account number. It is a simple trail to follow when the need eventually arises. The amount of money in the account is immaterial at this time.

The pertinent information for your savings accounts is recorded in the same manner. Simply make a copy of the inside cover of each passbook. For stocks and bonds held in a "street account" by your broker, the quarterly statement of your brokerage account is sufficient. Similarly, the value of each of these accounts is immaterial at this time.

The term *street account* is used by stockbrokers to indicate an account where you allow the stockbroker to hold your stocks at the brokerage firm. The broker/dealer holds your stocks and bonds in the firm's name (otherwise re-

FIGURE 11-4
TRUST FORM FOR SETTLING AN ESTATE

Asset Description	Valuation		
	Amount	Date	Source*
_____	_____	_____	_____
_____	_____	_____	_____
_____	_____	_____	_____
_____	_____	_____	_____
_____	_____	_____	_____
_____	_____	_____	_____
_____	_____	_____	_____
_____	_____	_____	_____
_____	_____	_____	_____
_____	_____	_____	_____
_____	_____	_____	_____
_____	_____	_____	_____
_____	_____	_____	_____

Date:_____ Signature of Trustee:_____

*Source of Valuation

FIGURE 11-5
ASSET TRANSFER FORM

| Asset Description | Valuation | | | Transfer | | Trustee Signature | Date |
	Amount	Date	Source*	From Trust	To Trust		

*Source of Valuation

ferred to as the "street name"), and the dealer can easily and quickly buy, sell, and transfer those assets—either upon your authority or at the discretion of the broker/dealer if you have given the firm power of attorney. A copy of a quarterly statement is sufficient.

For stocks and bonds held in your name, if you have possession of the certificates, you should also make a copy of every stock and every bond. If these documents should ever happen to be lost, the copy could be used to re-establish your rightful ownership.

> Years ago, a newly widowed woman called me with a problem. The widow said that her husband was so well organized that she always knew where everything was—but, for some unknown reason, she could not find the Treasury notes. I simply said to the widow, "Bring in your Estate Plan Book." I knew that there was a copy of each Treasury note in the book; with copies of the original Treasury notes, the widow could then have new Treasury notes issued.

Retirement Programs

The "Retirement Programs" section of the Estate Plan Book should include *copies* of your retirement programs with "beneficial interests"—such as your IRAs, Keogh plans, SEPs, pension plans, profit-sharing plans, annuities, tax-sheltered annuities, 401k plans, ESOPs, and any deferred-compensation plans. "Beneficial interest" means investments that (upon the death of the primary individual) will continue to provide a benefit to the surviving spouse or children or heirs. For example, a husband may have a retirement plan option to receive a lower pension while he is living in order that the widow may continue to receive the same payment until her death.

Real Estate Documents

The section of the book labeled "Real Estate Documents" should contain copies (definitely *not* the original documents) of grant deeds and any first and second trust deeds due you; time-share documents should also be included here. You may also wish to include copies of any mortgages you owe, but doing so is optional. Remember, the asset is the important item to record in the book; the liability will always fol-

low the asset. If you have homesteaded your home, include a copy of the homestead papers.

Insurance Policies

The Insurance Policies section of the Estate Plan Book should include copies of the *face page* of your insurance policies for any life insurance, accident insurance, disability insurance, and medical insurance policies in force. All too often, people think of an insurance policy for some reason as being sacred. All you really need in the book is a copy of the face page of the insurance policy, which identifies the name of the insurance company, the name of the insured, the policy number, and the face value of the policy.

If the insurance policy is lost, you can always contact the insurance company, and the policy can be replaced. Unfortunately, there are hundreds of insurance companies, and therefore you *must* know the name of the insurance company that issued the policy. It is surprising how many people have small insurance policies given to them by their parents or acquired early in a marriage. These policies, although not worth much today, are still valuable and usually have been stuck away in a corner and forgotten. How much more effective to have copies of *all* of your insurance policies in this section of the book.

Business Agreements and Documents

The last section of the Estate Plan Book should contain copies of any corporate stock certificates (of privately held corporations), partnership agreements, buy-sell agreements, and any stock-redemption agreements.

SETTLING AN ESTATE IN LESS THAN AN HOUR

When the Living Trust has been executed by and explained to clients, and copies of all the client's documents have been placed in the Estate Plan Book, I close the book and hand it to the wife or the single client with these words: "It is our experience with this book—with the Living Trust—that we can settle your estate in less than one hour—and that certainly beats two years of probate." In every instance, the clients react as though the world has just been lifted off their shoulders; they leave our offices smiling and with peace of mind.

In working with thousands of clients, it has been my experience that when a husband and wife (or a surviving parent and child) get together, they can ultimately find all of their assets. Everyone "knows" where his or her assets are located—until he or she goes to look for them! However, with each other's assistance, members of a family are ultimately able to put together a complete record of their assets.

One couple were incredibly organized. The couple came into our office to execute a Living Trust, bringing a metal box that contained every legal document or asset title in envelopes (filed alphabetically). As the couple took each title or deed from its envelope, the document was photocopied. However, when the husband and wife were supposedly finishing copying all of the documents, I watched them in amazement as they went back and searched through everything—looking for the "pink slip" (the title of legal ownership) for one of their automobiles.

Finally, after they had undergone an exhaustive ten-minute search, a light dawned with the husband. Sheepishly, he reached into his pocket and took out his wallet. From one of the wallet's recesses, the husband pulled out a small piece of paper that had been folded into a half-inch square. The husband laid down the folded piece of paper on the table, unfolded it, pressed out the wrinkles, and said with a sheepish grin, "Here it is!"

If the husband had died, how would anyone have ever found that document? This scene is another of the many examples of how two people—when given the chance to work together—can reconstruct their assets.

A natural question is what will happen if the Estate Plan Book and Living Trust are somehow destroyed. At The Estate Plan, we execute two complete sets of the Living Trust and all ancillary legal documents for each client. One complete set goes into the Estate Plan Book, which is given to the client, and the other complete set goes into our legal files. Then, if anything were to happen to the client's book, between the legal documents in our offices and the legal titles of assets that are presumably held in the client's safe-deposit box, it should be possible to reconstitute the Estate Plan Book with all legal and supporting documents within about two days. You can benefit by setting up this kind of arrangement with your own adviser.

Even though your successor trustee does not need to *see* your Trust, know the *size* of your estate, or *see* the Estate Plan Book while you are living, you should tell your successor trustee where to find your Estate Plan Book upon your death!

One day when I was in my mother's apartment, she asked me to go into the den and get her Estate Plan Book, so that we could make a change to it. Fifteen minutes later, I came from the den and asked her where she had hidden it. "Oh, I forgot to tell you—it's in the bottom drawer of the dresser, at the very bottom of the drawer." I wondered how I would have ever found that book if something had happened to her.

The Estate Plan Book is a workbook—*it belongs at home.* However, please let your successor trustee know where to find it!

12

Transferring Your Assets into Your Living Trust

All too often, attorneys create Trusts but then do not have the clients' assets transferred into the Trusts. Instead, the attorneys simply list the assets in "schedules" attached to the Living Trust—Schedule A (assets) and Schedule B (life insurance). Typically, attorneys also write the clients a letter advising them to open a bank account for $50 in the name of the Trust in order to "fund the Trust." Theoretically, these actions release the attorneys from any further liability, because an unfunded Trust is no Trust at all.

However, the client's assets are not actually recorded in the name of the Trust, and—as you learned in Chapter 5—this situation means that the Trust is legally nothing more than a Testamentary Trust. On the death of a spouse, the assets must still go through probate before they will pass into the Trust! Such situations happen all too frequently, because of a lack of proper communication between the client and the attorney.

In many cases, the lawyer has even told the client that listing the assets in Schedules A and B transfers them into the Trust. However, this information is absolutely false! The primary purpose of Schedules A and B in many Trusts drawn up by inexperienced attorneys is to identify the client's assets in Schedule A and the client's insurance policies in Schedule B—but the schedules serve no legal purpose.

Listing your assets in a Schedule A or B merely identifies them; it does not transfer them into your Trust.

Many attorneys get their clients from insurance agents and financial planners. "Professional courtesy" often means scratching each other's back. Thus, the attorney, having received a referral from an insurance agent, can look at the amount of insurance carried by the client and suggest to the client that he or she should have more insurance—and who better to provide that insurance than the insurance agent who brought the client to the attorney? Such back scratching is called third-party influence. The same situation would be true for assets (instead of insurance) when a financial planner provides the referral.

In 1979, I took a client to an attorney to draw up a Trust for his mother, who was dying of cancer. The attorney elected "not to bother" the mother with signatures needed to transfer each asset into the Trust and instead chose only to list the assets in a Schedule A. I reminded the attorney that only listing the assets in Schedule A would *not*, in fact, transfer them into the Trust; however, the attorney was not about to listen to me and told me in no uncertain terms that *he* was the attorney and that he knew the law.

Six months later, the mother died. Then the troubles began, as the client discovered that, indeed, the assets were *not* legally in the Trust.

To assist the client, I went to the secretary of state, who advised me that the assets listed on Schedule A were *not* inside the Trust. I pleaded that it was very definitely the woman's intent to have the assets placed inside the Trust. However, my pleading was fruitless; I was told that the assets definitely must go through probate. To my understanding, the assets are *still* going through probate today!

Listing assets and insurance in Schedules A and B for a Trust is absolutely meaningless. (In fact, such schedules are not included in our Living Trust, expressly to avoid such situations.) Instead, you need to transfer the title of all your assets into your Trust. This chapter explains how to do so.

WHAT TO LEAVE OUTSIDE YOUR TRUST

As a general rule, you should leave *nothing* outside your Trust. However, only your assets (such as a house, stocks, bonds, savings accounts, and so on) need to be transferred into the name of your Living Trust. Liabilities (such as any debts you owe) and general insurance policies (such as house and automobile insurance) are not transferred into the name of the Trust. In addition, for convenience, there are two exceptions to the general rule for assets. These exceptions are your checking accounts (as long as they collectively remain under $30,000, or $60,000, as applicable) and your automobiles.

Checking Accounts

The probate code in most states specifies that, for the estate to avoid probate, assets (including personal effects) must be valued at less than $30,000. (In some states, the maximum is $60,000, so check with your estate planner or attorney.) Therefore, you should feel reasonably comfortable excluding checking accounts from your Trust if you make sure that the total of all your checking accounts never exceeds $30,000 (or $60,000, as applicable).

If, for some reason, the total of all your checking accounts does get over this amount, either transfer one of the checking accounts into the name of your Trust, or simply put some of the money into one of your savings accounts (which should already be in the name of your Trust). It is very easy to say, "That won't happen to me; I would know how much money is in my bank accounts." Even so, exceptions occur. For example, assume that you sell your home and receive a check from the escrow company for $200,000. It's late on a Friday afternoon, and you want to put the money to work for you, so you endorse the check on the back and deposit it into your checking account. In so doing, you have just transferred that asset from inside your Trust to outside your Trust. If you were to die before you could move that asset from your bank account into your Trust, the entire $200,000 would have to go through probate! Such a situation actually happened, some years ago, to one of my clients.

Consequently, you might wonder why your checking account should not also be inside your Trust. The answer is based on Murphy's law ("If anything can go wrong, it will"). Consider an example:

You go to the bank and ask the teller to transfer your checking account into the name of the Trust. The teller informs you that you must now get new checks showing the Trust name. Is the teller right? Absolutely not. However, since you don't know any better, you order the new checks.

Several weeks later, you pick up your checks, and you stop on your way home at your favorite department store to pick up some shoes, which you had ordered. You give one of your new checks to the sales clerk, who looks at the check and says, "Oh, I'm sorry, I can't cash this check, because it's in the name of a Trust." You are then sent upstairs to the credit manager, where, after a half-hour of frustration and no further satisfaction, you take out your credit card and charge the shoes.

Continuing on your way home, you stop by your favorite grocery store; it's seven o'clock at night, and the lines are long. You finally get up to the front of the line and hand another clerk your new check. The clerk responds, "I cannot accept this check, because it is in the name of a Trust." In frustration, you finally reach into your wallet and dig through your pockets to come up with enough money to pay for the groceries.

After you have experienced this frustration, you can't wait to get home to call me—to find out just what kind of a mess I created for you. Were any of the clerks right? Absolutely not! Yet is such a situation actually going to happen? Yes, over and over again.

As this example shows, putting your checking account into the name of your Trust just is not worth the possible trouble. I know of only one incident where a client had a problem as a result of keeping a checking account outside the Trust.

The client walked into his bank with a dividend check made out to him and his wife in the name of the Trust, and the teller told him he could not deposit the check in his regular checking account. The client politely suggested that the teller call the bank's trust department. A knowledgeable employee quickly set the teller straight.

Our aim is to make things easy for our clients, so they are advised to take the simple route.

Motor Vehicles

The reason for leaving your automobiles outside the Trust is that the motor vehicle code in most states is exempt from the probate code. If you look at the horrendous size of the motor vehicle code of your state and then at the voluminous size of your state's probate code, you can begin to see why. Correlating these two codes would be almost impossible. The legislatures of the various states took the simple way out and decreed that the motor vehicle code was exempt from the probate code.

However, if you own an expensive automobile, more than one moderately priced vehicle, or a motor home, it is in your best interest to record those vehicles in the name of the Trust. The transfer process is very simple. More importantly, you will avoid any future question of whether the value of your estate exceeds the limit that would require probate.

In some states, mobile homes were once registered as motor vehicles but are now registered in a different department. For example, all new mobile homes purchased in California must register with the Department of Housing and Community Development. Under these circumstances, a mobile home should definitely be in the name of the Living Trust.

WHAT TO TRANSFER INTO YOUR TRUST

Aside from the limited exceptions, *all* of your assets should go into your Trust. Assets outside the Trust are subject to the agonizing probate process. Fortunately, as you will see, transferring your assets into your Living Trust is really quite simple.

All of your assets should be transferred into your Living Trust.

TRANSFERRING SAFE-DEPOSIT BOXES

Although it is not necessary to put your safe-deposit boxes in the name of the Living Trust, such action is good preventive medicine. Therefore, to be on the safe side, you may wish to put your safe-deposit boxes in the name of the Trust.

To transfer your safe-deposit boxes into your Trust, you simply go to the bank and have the bank representative rewrite your file card for the safe-deposit boxes in the name of your Trust.

TRANSFERRING DEEDS

Transferring real estate deeds into your Living Trust is the one area of funding your Trust that should *not* be a do-it-yourself project! Only attorneys should transfer deeds, unless you specialize in this particular area (that is, you are a real estate agent or escrow agent). The cost of

FIGURE 12-1
TYPICAL DEED FOR PROPERTY HELD IN JOINT TENANCY

AND WHEN RECORDED MAIL TO

Name

Street
Address

City &
State

MAIL TAX STATEMENTS TO

Name   William W. Wimmons
Street   200 Talvert Street
Address Wood Mills, CA 99111
City &
State

_____SPACE ABOVE THIS LINE FOR RECORDER'S USE_____

Individual Quitclaim Deed

FOR A VALUABLE CONSIDERATION, receipt of which is hereby acknowledged,

WALTER D. FELLER

hereby REMISES, RELEASES AND QUITCLAIMS to

WILLIAM W. WIMMONS and FRAN WIMMONS, husband and wife as joint tenants

the following described real property in the
County of   Riverside   , State of California:

The Northwest 100 feet of the Southwesterly 18.18 acres on Lot 3
in Block 8 of Rancho Amiga, as shown by map on file in Book 10,
Page 1000, of Maps, records of Riverside County, California.

Subject to conditions, covenants, and all other items of record.

Dated: _____June 31, 1974_____   Walter D. Feller

STATE OF CALIFORNIA
COUNTY OF ___Los Angeles___ } SS.

On _____June 1, 1974_____ before
me, the undersigned, a Notary Public in and for said State,
personally appeared _____
   Walter D. Feller
personally known to me or proved to me on the basis of satisfactory evidence to be the person __ whose name__ is
subscribed to the within instrument and acknowledged
that __he__ executed the same.
WITNESS my hand and official seal.

Signature _____

OFFICIAL SEAL

(This area for official notarial seal)

FIGURE 12-2
TYPICAL DEED FOR PROPERTY HELD IN NAME OF A TRUST

RECORDING REQUESTED BY

AND WHEN RECORDED MAIL TO

Name

Street
Address

City &
State

MAIL TAX STATEMENTS TO

Name   Mr. & Mrs. William W. Wimmons
Street   200 Talvert Street
Address Wood Mills, CA 99111
City &
State

————— SPACE ABOVE THIS LINE FOR RECORDER'S USE —————

Trust Transfer Deed

Grant Deed

GRANTOR(S): WILLIAM W. WIMMONS and FRAN WIMMONS, husband and wife
hereby GRANT(S) to THE WIMMONS FAMILY TRUST, dated January 1, 1989,
WILLIAM W. WIMMONS and FRAN WIMMONS, Trustors and Trustees.

the following described real property in the
County of   Riverside   **, State of California:**

The Northwest 100 feet of the Southwesterly 18.18 acres on Lot 3 in
Block 8 of Rancho Amiga, as shown by map on file in Book 10, Page
1000, of Maps, records of Riverside County, California.

Subject to conditions, covenants, and all other items of record.

Dated _January 1, 1989_

William W. Wimmons

Fran Wimmons

State of California
County of _____ Los Angeles _____
On this the _1st_ day of _____ January _____ 19_89_,
before me, _____
the undersigned Notary Public, personally appeared
   William W. and Fran Wimmons

Grantor - Transferor (s)

XX personally known to me
☐ proved to me on the basis of satisfactory evidence
to be the person(s) whose name(s) _are_____ subscribed to the
within instrument, and acknowledged that _they_ executed it.
WITNESS my hand and official seal.

OFFICIAL SEAL

_____
Notary's Signature

(This area for official notarial seal)

transferring deeds should be nominal (less than $100), but the importance of making the transfer legally proper cannot be overemphasized. An improper and possibly ineffective transfer of real estate deeds can be disastrous!

As you learned in Chapter 5, transferring the deed to your house, for example, into your Living Trust will not affect your right to borrow against your house or to refinance it. If the deed is properly transferred, the transfer will not accelerate your mortgage (cause it to become due, as if you had sold your home).

Figure 12-1 shows a typical deed for property held in joint tenancy by a husband and wife. Figure 12-2 shows how the same deed would look when ownership of the property has been transferred into the name of the Living Trust.

Effect on Tax Base of Property

Some years ago, California voters approved Proposition 13, which rolled back the property tax base and permitted it to be increased at a maximum rate of only 2 percent per year. Many states have followed California's lead in rolling back property taxes and limiting future increases. If you live in such a state, placing your assets in a Living Trust will have no effect whatsoever on your favorable property tax base.

Putting your home in your Living Trust will not cause your property taxes to increase.

In California, four months after Proposition 13 was passed, the state legislature quickly addressed the problem of transferring real estate into a Living Trust and, by legislation, made it very clear that transferring property into such a Trust would have no effect on the tax base of real estate (that is, the assessed valuation used to assess property tax). In simple terms, your property taxes will *not* increase when you place your home in a Living Trust. Recently, California voters also passed Proposition 58, which allows assets to pass from parents to children or from children to parents with no effect upon the tax base of the asset.

Clients also wonder what happens when a widow remarries and wishes to put her home in a Trust created with her new husband, which effectively transfers ownership of the home. Proposition 13 and its counterparts in other states typically provide that, when a surviving or divorced spouse remarries, his or her part of the interest in the property may pass to the new spouse without being subject to reappraisal and potentially higher property taxes.

A similar concern arises when parents and children share ownership of real estate. In today's extremely high-cost housing market, it is becoming more and more common for grown children to need their parents to join them as co-owners when they purchase property, because the children's income is insufficient to satisfy the mortgage requirements. In such cases, the parents may remove their names from the title to the home and allow the children to put the home in a Living Trust without any impact upon the tax base. However, under such circumstances, it *is* necessary to specify (on an accompanying form, which is attached to the real estate deed) the reason that the parents' names were on the title—specifically, to allow the children to be able to qualify for the mortgage.

Effect on Property Tax Exemptions and Homesteading

The homeowner's property tax exemption is a state exemption, which in some states is limited to veterans only and in other states is made available to all homeowners. Placing the deed to your home in a Living Trust has absolutely no effect upon the state tax exemption.

The Homestead Act is a federal law that protects your home from creditors if the equity in your home is less than $45,000 and you file bankruptcy. As part of good financial planning, everyone should consider recording his or her home under the federal Homestead Act with the county recorder's office. Placing your home in a Living Trust has no effect upon the protections offered by the federal Homestead Act.

If, when you first transfer your home into your Living Trust, the county assessor sends you a letter indicating that your homeowner's property tax exemption has been terminated, you can re-establish your exemption. The attorney who prepared your Living Trust should be able to advise you on this matter.

The Grant Deed

When you transfer your home into the Trust, give your lawyer a copy of your grant deed for the property. If the grant deed says "See Exhibit A Attached," then you must also provide the attached exhibit, since it is considered to be part of the deed.

Some clients mistakenly believe that they do not have a grant deed, because they have not yet paid off the mortgage. However, in most states, when you buy real estate, you are given a grant deed, which gives you ownership to the property. In some states, title to the property may be known as a land grant or land lease, but, under any name, this document gives title to the property.

If you are unable to locate the grant deed—as often happens with our clients—you may easily acquire a copy by calling the county recorder's office. Someone there will tell you how to request a copy of the grant deed. You will have to request it in writing and pay a nominal fee.

Transferring When an Owner Is Not a Family Member

If you have property in a state with legislation similar to California's Proposition 13, be very careful about recording real estate in the name of your Trust when you are transferring all of the property into the Trust and one of the owners is *not* a family member. Under Proposition 13, if property ownership is passed to a nonrelated party, this transfer of ownership is not an exempt transaction (family transfer) and would therefore trigger reappraisal of the property to the current market value.

An unmarried couple owned a home in joint tenancy. When the woman decided to create a Living Trust, the man volunteered to transfer his entire interest in the property to her. Therefore, the deed to the property was written in the name of her Trust. However, the deed was *not* recorded, because doing so would cause the interest in the property given to the woman to be reappraised.

TRANSFERRING TRUST DEEDS

If you have lent money to people, using their home as collateral, and have taken back a first or second trust deed, the trust deed is an asset to you. It is another individual's obligation to pay you money. Usually the value of trust deeds is high enough that this asset would cause your estate to go through the probate process; therefore, trust deeds should *always* be in the name of your Trust.

To transfer a trust deed (a legal document), you must have the trust deed redrawn by an attorney or real estate specialist and recorded with the county recorder's office in the name of your Trust. A trust deed should always be recorded, because it is your protection to ensure that the property against which you hold a lien may not be sold until the debtor has repaid the money owed to you.

TRANSFERRING TIME-SHARES

Today, more and more people have invested in time-share property, in which they typically own a piece of property for one week of the year. Time-share ownership is, in fact, ownership in real estate; therefore, title to the property should be transferred into the name of your Trust. Again, the title should be redrawn in the name of your Trust and then recorded with the county recorder's office.

TRANSFERRING A BUSINESS INTEREST

If you own part or all of a business in the form of stock that is publicly traded over the counter or on one of the stock exchanges, the company's transfer agent should change the ownership of your stock to the name of the Trust. This action can usually be done through your company's personnel office or treasurer.

If your business interest is in a privately owned corporation, it may be easily transferred by voiding your existing stock certificates and reissuing new stock certificates in the name of the Trust. Blank stock certificates are typically found in your corporate minutes book.

To transfer a partnership interest or sole proprietorship, an attorney should draw a legal Bill of Sale/Letter of Assignment, which describes the business and transfers it into your Trust.

UNUSUAL TRANSFERS

If you own shares in a limited partnership, ask the general partners to transfer your interest into your Trust. On rare occasions, a general partner responds that it cannot transfer your limited partnership into the Trust. What the general partner is really saying is that it doesn't know how to do the transfer. Legal counsel can resolve this dilemma by creating a Bill of Sale/Letter of Transfer for your limited partnership interest.

The same approach would apply to any other assets that the agents will not readily transfer, as well as to expensive artworks or an extensive collection of antiques. This approach would also apply to patents and copyrights.

TRANSFERRING GENERAL ASSETS

General assets include savings accounts, money market accounts, certificates of deposit, Treasury bills, Ginnie Maes, credit union accounts, stocks, bonds, mutual funds, limited partnerships, and notes due. All these general assets can be transferred into your Trust with simple letters of transfer.

Real Assets Other than
Real Estate and Securities

To transfer each general asset into your Living Trust, you need only write the name and address of the financial institution as well as the particular asset and account number on the letter of transfer. We advise our clients to use one letter per financial institution. If you have more than one account at a particular financial institution, you would simply list each of the accounts on the same letter. The letter states that the specified assets are to be transferred into the name of the Living Trust (the full name of which is included as part of the letter).

The letter of transfer also specifies that the identification number of the Trust will be the social security number of the trustee. For reasons pointed out in earlier chapters, if an individual is single, his or her social security number should be used as the Trust Identification Number. If individuals are married, the husband's social security number should be typically used, but it is appropriate to use either the husband's or the wife's number. The individuals then sign the transfer letter in two places—as the transferors (they are the ones who are transferring the assets) and as the transferees (they are the ones who are receiving the assets on behalf of the Trust). As a service to our clients, we then notarize the signatures on the transfer letters.

We provide each of our clients with six letters of transfer. If clients need additional copies, they can simply photocopy one of the original letters; the photocopies usually are just as acceptable as the originals.

You should mail or hand-deliver these letters of transfer to the various institutions that have your accounts. In many cases, a financial institution has its own form, which it requires you to sign. If so, your letter of transfer simply causes the institution to send you its form (which it typically fills out for you); you then need only sign the institution's special form, have your signature witnessed or notarized, and then return the form to the institution holding your account. When you send a letter of transfer to a financial institution and the necessary paperwork has been completed (either your transfer letter or the signing of the institution's own transfer form), the institution should acknowledge that it has made the requested transfer.

Stocks and Bonds

The easiest way to transfer stocks and bonds into your Trust is to take them to your stockbroker and ask the brokerage firm to transfer them for you. The firm may want to charge you for such a transfer; however, since you most likely have bought your stocks and bonds in the past from this particular brokerage house, the firm should be more than happy to make your stock transfers free of charge (if it would like your continued business).

If you do not have a stockbroker, you will need to send your stocks or bonds to a transfer agent, whose name is typically listed on the stocks and bonds. When you send stock certificates to a transfer agent, you should do so by using an Irrevocable Stock or Bond Power, such as the one shown in Figure 12-3. You must sign this Irrevocable Stock or Bond Power in *exactly* the same manner as the stock or bond has been registered. You must have your signature guaranteed—which may be done only by a stock brokerage firm with a seat on any stock exchange or by any bank. Unfortunately, a savings and loan institution may not guarantee your signature on such a form.

Your stocks or bonds are nonnegotiable as long as they are unsigned. Once signed, your stock or bond certificates are now negotiable by anyone! For your protection, send the *unsigned* stocks or bonds in one letter and the Irrevocable Stock or Bond Power in a separate letter. Thus, only when both envelopes arrive at the destination can the two be put together, at which time the stock and bond certificates will be negotiable. An alternative solution is to name the transferring brokerage firm as the designated power of attorney.

Your letter of transfer for the stocks or bonds should be sent to the transfer agent along with the other paperwork.

Many people have accumulated stocks and bonds over a long period. Even though the people bought only small quantities at any one time, they fail to realize how the value of their stock and bond portfolio may have increased to a sizable amount.

About four years ago, a widower came to our office to do a Living Trust. The widower transferred all of his assets into the Trust, with one exception—a single stock certificate for 5,000 shares of IBM stock. It would have taken the man less than an hour to drive down to the bank, have his signature guaranteed, and then send that stock certificate forward to be transferred into the name of his Trust, but he never got around to it. The man died six months later.

Since the rest of the man's estate was in his

FIGURE 12-3
TYPICAL IRREVOCABLE STOCK OR BOND POWER FORM

FOR VALUE RECEIVED, the undersigned does (do) hereby sell, assign and transfer to

_____

_____ | _____

(Social Security or Taxpayer Identifying No.)

IF STOCK, COMPLETE THIS PORTION
{ _____ shares of the _____ stock of _____
represented by Certificate (s) No (s)_____ inclusive,
standing in the name of the undersigned on the books of said Company.

IF BONDS, COMPLETE THIS PORTION
{ _____ bonds of _____
in the principal amount of $_____ , No (s)_____ inclusive,
standing in the name of the undersigned on the books of said Company.

The undersigned does (do) hereby irrevocably constitute and appoint _____

_____ attorney to transfer the said stock or bond (s), as the case may

be, on the books of said Company, with full power of substitution in the premises.

Dated_____

X _____

X _____

(Person(s) Executing This Power Sign(s) Here)

OFF	Account No.	T

92-0162

Living Trust, most of his estate was settled immediately. Within two months thereafter, all of the assets, including his house, had been sold, and the assets were distributed to his heirs. In contrast, that single piece of paper not in the Trust was then worth $500,000 and had to go through probate. The process took one full year and cost more than $10,000! The man's family learned—the hard way—about the agony of probate. How much simpler it would have been had the man transferred that stock certificate into the name of his Living Trust.

TRANSFERRING ASSETS WITH A BENEFICIARY

Your Trust should be the beneficiary of all life insurance policies and the *contingent* beneficiary of all other assets that specify a beneficiary. In every instance, the named beneficiary of these legal instruments (such as an insurance policy or IRA) will take precedence over any Will or Trust. For example, if you have named your spouse as the beneficiary of your life insurance policy, and you and your spouse happen to be killed simultaneously, the insurance policy will pass (in the legal sense) without probate to your spouse, but then must go though probate to pass on to your children. Although some people are smart enough to name contingent beneficiaries (such as their children), most people have not bothered to do so. Contingent beneficiaries would be the recipients of the insurance (without probate) upon the simultaneous death of both husband and wife.

To transfer assets with a beneficiary—such as life insurance, annuities, IRAs, Keogh plans, 401k plans, ESOPs, and profit-sharing plans— our clients use a beneficiary letter of transfer. The beneficiary letter of transfer is similar to the general asset letter of transfer.

For transferring life insurance policies into the Trust, for either single or married persons, the letter states, "The beneficiary should now read," followed by the name of the Trust and the creator's social security number.

For transferring all other beneficial interests (IRAs and so on), the letter differs depending on whether the Trust is for a single person or a

married couple. For a single person, the letter states, "The beneficiary should now read," followed by the name of the Trust and the creator's social security number. For a married couple, the letter states, "The contingent beneficiary should now read," followed by the name of the Trust and the creator's social security number.

For each asset with a named beneficiary, you simply write in the name and address of the institution, such as an insurance company, as well as the policy or account number. If you have more than one policy or account with that company, you would list the numbers for all policies or accounts with that particular company. We suggest to our clients that they send only one letter of transfer to each company.

You must sign the letters twice—once as the transferors (the individuals who are transferring the assets) and again as the transferees (the individuals who are receiving the assets on behalf of the Trust). As a service to our clients, we notarize the transfer letters. We provide our clients six copies of the transfer letter for their use in transferring their beneficial interests into their Living Trust.

Upon receipt of your letter of transfer, an insurance company almost always will send back to you its own form (which it has usually filled out) to be signed by you and then witnessed. Each insurance company does a beneficiary change in its own way.

Single-Premium Life Insurance

Unlike ordinary life insurance policies, single-premium life insurance is an investment vehicle under the insurance company umbrella. Single-premium insurance policies can be either single-premium whole life insurance or single-premium universal life insurance. With this investment vehicle, you make a single investment (such as $100,000), and, because of the income tax–favored basis of insurance, the growth—as well as the income from the investment—can be tax-deferred.

The single-premium life insurance policy also is life insurance; it pays a death benefit. Depending upon the age of the insured individual when the single premium is paid, the death benefit will vary from six times the amount of the investment (for someone around the age of forty) to twice the amount of the investment (for someone around the age of sixty). Since these insurance policies have a death benefit, your Living Trust should be named as beneficiary, using the beneficiary letter of transfer.

Annuities

As another type of insurance company investment, annuities have designated beneficiaries. You should use the beneficiary letter of transfer to name your Living Trust as the contingent beneficiary of all annuities.

IRAs

Besides insurance policies, Individual Retirement Accounts are probably the next most common asset in a person's estate to have designated beneficiaries. Therefore, IRAs need to have the beneficial interest, or contingent beneficial interest, changed to the name of the Trust. People often get confused between ownership of an IRA (the person in whose name the IRA was established) and the beneficiary of the IRA (the person who will receive the IRA distributions in future years). Ownership of the IRA remains vested in the individual, whereas the Trust only becomes the contingent beneficiary for a married couple and the beneficiary for a single person.

If you were to transfer "ownership" of an IRA from an individual to a Trust, the transfer is comparable to an outright distribution, which would immediately be taxable in that year as income. With the Trust as the beneficiary (or contingent beneficiary) only, and the individual retaining ownership, the contingent beneficiary transfer has simply changed the beneficial interest; therefore, there is no adverse tax impact upon the IRA. Upon the death of the individual who owns the IRA, the IRA will pass on to the named beneficiary and, if that individual is not living, then to the Trust, which is typically the children. Under these circumstances, there is no tax impact from changing the contingent beneficiary of the IRA to the Trust.

With IRAs, unlike life insurance, the Trust is named as contingent beneficiary in order to comply with a recent letter ruling of the Internal Revenue Service.

Pension Plans

Although your pension plan should name your Trust as a contingent beneficiary, the personnel department of a corporation may be reluctant to transfer the contingent beneficiary to your Living Trust. Do not be concerned *if* payments from your pension plan cease upon your death. However, if your pension plan has a death benefit or if payments from the plan will continue to other than your surviving spouse after his or her death, then the named contingent beneficiary of your pension plan should definitely be your Living Trust. In that case, you should insist that the personnel department make the transfer.

A Word of Caution

Remember to make sure that you are transferring only the beneficial interest in these assets, not ownership. Most financial institutions understand that a transfer of beneficial interest is *not* a change in ownership and will help you to avoid mistakes in this area. However, sometimes even financial institutions are not as knowledgeable as you would expect.

About a year ago, a client called me and said she had a $45,000 Keogh in a no-load mutual fund. The woman had called the sales office in Boston and asked the firm to change her beneficiary designation into the name of her Trust. The woman then sent a copy of her beneficial letter of transfer to the mutual fund company. Three months later, the woman received IRS Form 1099 (used to indicate the receipt of income), showing that she had received $45,000 of taxable income!

The woman called the sales department; after numerous fruitless attempts to get the erroneous "distribution of income" rectified, she eventually called me for assistance. I thereupon called the salesman, who rather abruptly made it very clear that he had followed the woman's instructions and had transferred her "ownership" into her Living Trust. From the IRS viewpoint, this action had distributed the Keogh outright to the woman—and that is *not* what she wanted!

I didn't make any headway with the salesman either, so I asked to speak to his manager. It took me three minutes of discussion with the manager to clarify the situation. The manager said he would rectify the problem immediately but asked that I please verify our conversation in writing. I did so, and the woman's problem was quickly resolved.

Recently, the Internal Revenue Service ruled that if the primary beneficiary of your retirement plan is a nonperson, such as a Living Trust, you may lose your right to utilize "joint life payout." Thus, it is appropriate and safe to name your spouse as primary beneficiary and your Living Trust as contingent beneficiary. Single persons should name their Living Trust as primary beneficiary.

TRANSFER ALL YOUR ASSETS

I cannot emphasize strongly enough the importance of transferring all of your assets into your Trust—with the exception of your checking accounts (as long as they collectively *never* exceed $30,000, or $60,000, as applicable) and your motor vehicles of moderate value. *All* of your other assets (particularly your house) should be transferred into your Trust. If you create a Living Trust but fail to fund it with your assets, you will not have a working Living Trust (with all of its intended benefits), but only a Testamentary Trust, which is a very costly mistake indeed.

Remember, the greatest benefit of the Living Trust is to avoid probate. As a general rule, if you follow the recommendations made in this book, your estate will avoid probate, regardless of the probate laws of the state where you are living. However, the probate laws vary from state to state, so it is worthwhile to check with an attorney who is knowledgeable about the laws of your state. It is true nationwide that you avoid probate only by getting *all* of your assets properly transferred into your Living Trust.

13

Settling the Estate

Settling an estate is an area of concern for every client. Since certain actions are legally required with probate, clients assume that certain things must legally be done with a Living Trust. However, as you will see in this chapter, aside from the usual steps that need to be taken upon the death of any individual, settling an estate in a Living Trust is really quite easy.

If all of your assets are in a good Living Trust and if the estate is organized with the Estate Plan Book, settling the estate typically takes less than an hour. I use the term *to settle* rather loosely, because there is not really anything to settle, per se. However, a number of things must be done.

CHECK "FINAL INSTRUCTIONS"
SECTION OF THE ESTATE PLAN BOOK
Immediately upon the death of a loved one, the survivor should notify certain people, in order to set in motion the many steps that must be taken. The basic steps that should be followed upon the death of an individual are delineated in the "Final Instructions" section of the Estate Plan Book:

- Make important telephone calls.
- Review personal data summary (in Estate Plan Book).
- Make funeral arrangements, including memorial or flowers and funeral notice.
- Notify other people.
- Check the safe-deposit box and checking accounts.
- Make an appointment to meet with your primary adviser.

If all your assets are in a good Living Trust and your estate is well organized, settling your estate should take less than an hour.

The death of a loved one is always a traumatic time for the survivors, and the death of a spouse is almost always mentally paralyzing to the surviving spouse. Many people get totally confused and literally do not know what to do first. Fortunately, the "Final Instructions" pages of the Estate Plan Book help to guide the survivors in the steps that are necessary to begin the process of settling the estate of the deceased.

Review Personal Data

Review the "Personal Data" section in the Estate Plan Book to ascertain the accuracy of information that will be needed for completing the death certificate. This section was described in Chapter 11.

Information for Death Certificate

Have you ever looked at a death certificate? You will find that it is probably one of the best sources of misinformation available, because the surviving family members often have no idea of the correct information.

The information required on a death certificate is so much easier to gather and record when you and your spouse are both still living.

The information contained in the "Personal Data" section of the Estate Plan Book is required on most death certificates. That information is so much easier to gather and record in the book while you and your spouse are both still living. When our clients first begin to fill out the "Personal Data" section, they often guess at where their mothers or fathers were born and then call back days later when they have had a chance to find the correct information. How nice it is to be able to correct the data now, instead of guessing later—at a time of emotional upset and bereavement.

Military Papers

Copies of military discharge papers are filed in the "Personal Data" section of the Estate Plan Book. If an individual who served in the armed forces dies, the Veterans Administration will provide $150 toward funeral expenses, a headstone marker, and an American flag, if desired. How nice it is to easily be able to put your fingers on copies of the required military separation papers.

In the process of making funeral arrangements, you will need to take the military separation papers to the funeral home. These papers are needed to show proof that the deceased person was a veteran of military service.

Order Death Certificates

Order at least twelve death certificates. A separate death certificate will be needed for each insurance policy and each real asset (real estate, stocks, bonds, and so on) that you desire to ultimately sell or transfer. A simple copy of the death certificate is *not* sufficient; it must be a certified copy, obtained from the county recorder's office. Unfortunately, certified copies of the death certificate are seldom available until about ten days after the death of an individual. However, you can usually obtain one or two copies of the death certificate for immediate use directly from the funeral home. With a copy of the Living Trust and a certified copy of the death certificate, the surviving trustee or successor trustee then has exactly the same power to manage the estate as the deceased individual had while living.

Check Safe-Deposit Box and Checking Accounts

In the early 1970s, the death of a spouse could have drastically limited the surviving spouse's ability to gain access to funds needed for daily subsistence.

In 1971, on a Friday afternoon, I was called to a local hospital and advised that one of my dearest friends had just passed away as the result of bone cancer. Upon arriving at the hospital, I told my friend's grieving widow to immediately go to the bank and clear out their checking account and safe-deposit box. What a horrible thing to have to say to a grieving widow! However, in those days, the banks read the obituary columns in the newspapers and immediately locked up the safe-deposit boxes and the checking accounts of deceased individuals.

I am happy to report that this primitive practice no longer exists. Now, upon the death of a spouse or parent, neither the checking account nor the safe-deposit box is inaccessible.

You should look in the safe-deposit box for two reasons. First, the deceased may have left a message or a statement of posthumous desires that should be carried out by the survivors. The second, and more important, reason to look in the safe-deposit box is to inventory the contents to be sure that all of the valuable assets (such as real estate deeds and stocks and bonds) are in the name of the Trust.

Because only *cash* is acceptable for settling the funeral expenses, you should confirm the amount of readily available funds in the checking account of the deceased person and make arrangements to have access to the checking account funds.

As good business practice, it is worthwhile to put your safe-deposit box in the name of your Living Trust. With the Trust document and a death certificate in hand, the bank should readily give the successor trustee access to the safe-deposit box. In your estate-planning process, do not forget to let your successor trustee know where your safe-deposit box is located, as well as the location of the key to the safe-deposit box.

Although for simplicity you should keep your checking account outside the Living Trust, the account of a married person should be in joint tenancy with the spouse. If you are single, your checking account should be in joint tenancy with at least one of your named successor trustees. Joint tenancy gives the successor trustees simple, rapid access to funds that may be needed upon your demise (in case the financial institution should try to delay access to the funds of the deceased individual—as often happens in estates going through the probate process).

Make Appointment with Your Primary Adviser

The next step is to make an appointment to meet with your primary adviser. The actual settlement process—involving the estate and financial affairs—will begin at the meeting with this person.

We use the term *your primary adviser* in a broad sense, because he or she is the person with whom *you* may choose to counsel. He or she may be from any of several different backgrounds, be it legal, financial, or accounting, or simply a family member or a close friend. No particular discipline is required—the primary adviser is *your* choice.

THE SETTLEMENT PROCESS

If you have done your estate planning properly—if you have all of your assets in a good Living Trust—your survivors have nothing to do from a legal standpoint. They do *not* have to change your Trust or change title to any of your assets. The one exception would be, upon the death of a single individual or the *second* spouse (if married), when the estate is large enough to be subject to federal or state taxation.

Although I make it a point to be readily available to help our clients settle an estate, some clients worry about what will happen if The Estate Plan might not be available. Even without our services, the surviving spouse or adult children should be able to settle the estate without difficulty—*if* it has been organized. The surviving trustee or successor trustee needs only a copy of the death certificate and a copy of the Living Trust to allow him or her to take whatever action is necessary on behalf of the Trust.

In contrast, consider the following scenario: The survivor goes to an attorney and is told that a special document needs to be drawn. The "special document" drawn up by the attorney may be a simple statement to the effect that the surviving spouse is the surviving trustee, or it may be an abstract (which is simply a legal summary of the Trust) or some other innocuous document that has little or no legal meaning but establishes the basis for the attorney to charge a legal fee. The document is unnecessary, and the legal fee usually ranges from $250 to $500. Even though the document is legally unnecessary, the minor expense certainly beats two years of probate and a cost of 8 percent to 10 percent of the gross estate!

For example, about a year ago, a widow made an appointment to discuss her estate shortly after the death of her husband. Two days later, the widow called and said that it wouldn't be necessary for her to come, because she had found a local attorney who would draw up a legal document stating that she was now the surviving trustee. The widow probably paid the attorney $250 to $500 for this unnecessary document. (However, she did save herself a forty-mile trip to our office.)

Unfortunately, similar stories are repeated much too frequently. However, today I have a far greater concern: Most clients, and most attorneys, do not know how to properly settle an estate that is in a Living Trust. This unfortunate situation is best illustrated by the following story.

In 1978, a couple went to a rather large legal firm in Beverly Hills to draw up a Living Trust. The husband died four years later. The widow immediately returned to the same legal firm to have her Living Trust settled.

The widow was astute enough to realize that she had an A-B Trust and that the assets somehow needed to be divided between these two parts of the Trust. At that time, inheritance taxes were due upon the husband's death. The legal firm computed the value of the estate, estimated the taxes, and then filed the appropriate papers; however, the firm then stopped.

Although the widow had been billed extensively for the firm's legal services, she recognized that she still didn't have the required division of her assets into the Decedent's B Trust and the Survivor's A Trust. She continued to call the firm until it finally told her to go away.

Still concerned about the lack of distribution of assets, the widow contacted a different legal firm in 1986. The firm produced a rather immature legal summary of the Trust and charged the widow a hefty fee for its services, but still did not distribute her assets! The widow persisted, calling the firm for clarification and action; the firm responded by billing her $200 for each telephone call!

In utter frustration, the widow gave up. Later she was referred to our office. Based upon the 1982 state inheritance tax return filed on behalf of her husband, we reconstructed the estate and made a reasonable distribution of the assets into the A and B Trusts. Even though distributing the assets was not difficult, I believe that neither legal firm knew how to do it!

Unfortunately, situations such as this one seem to be surfacing more and more frequently.

Because only a few people—even among the professionals—really know how to settle an estate in a Living Trust, the major thrust of this part of the chapter will be to take you, step by step, through the Living Trust "settlement process." Even though nothing needs to be done legally to your Trust or in changing title to the assets in your estate, your survivor needs to take a number of steps in order to put your accounts in order and to ensure that he or she will enjoy the appropriate tax benefits your Living Trust provides.

The following steps should be followed by your primary adviser to settle an estate in a Living Trust:

- Review the Trust instructions in the Estate Plan Book and in the Living Trust document.
- Notify life insurance companies.
- Ensure that all assets are inside the Trust.
- Review the size of the estate.
- File an income tax return.
- Obtain a written valuation of assets.
- Review business agreements.
- Review credit cards.
- Distribute personal effects.
- Review allocation and distribution of assets.

Review the Estate Plan Book and Trust Document

The importance of the Estate Plan Book, which was discussed in detail in Chapter 11, is especially apparent during the process of estate settlement. By organizing the estate, the book prevents a guessing game upon the death of a settlor. The Estate Plan Book allows the survivor the privilege of settling the estate in minutes (or possibly an hour), rather than trying to piece together the assets in the estate over several months.

After you have done the preliminary review of the Estate Plan Book, as described previously in this chapter, you and your primary adviser should then specifically look at the following sections:

- The actual Trust (specifically, the section titled "Successor Trustee" and the section titled "Allocation and Distribution")
- The "Amendment" section for any changes to the Trust
- The Memorandum for any specific desired distribution of personal property
- The Financial Statement to determine whether the net worth is reasonably current

and whether the estate may be subject to federal estate taxes or state inheritance taxes

- The "Business Agreements and Documents" section to determine whether there are any partnerships, buy-sell agreements, or stock-redemption agreements

Review the Living Trust document, which is found in the "Trust" section of the Estate Plan Book. Specifically check the section in the Trust on Successor Trustee for authority in administering the Trust, as well as the "Allocation and Distribution" section to find out the desires of the deceased person.

If the successor trustee is the surviving spouse, I make a special point of showing him or her the Trust language that states that he or she has exactly the same power to administer the Trust as before the death of the spouse. Now that only one of the original trustees is still living, it is *most important* to be sure that the Trust names competent successor trustees to assume responsibility for the Trust upon the eventual death of the second spouse.

The "Allocation and Distribution" section should be reviewed to determine whether any of the decedent's assets are to be immediately distributed, rather than remaining in trust for the benefit of the surviving spouse.

Remember, if you cannot find the original Living Trust and Will(s), a duplicate executed copy should be obtainable from the firm that created your Living Trust. The Estate Plan provides this service to all its clients; whoever draws your Trust should provide you with comparable protection.

Notify Life Insurance Companies

Your adviser should check to be sure that each of the life insurance companies has been notified of the death of the insured. Each insurance company will require a certified copy of the death certificate. In the Estate Plan Book, copies of the face pages of any insurance policies would be listed behind the divider tab entitled "Insurance Policies."

Ensure Assets Are Within the Trust

Your adviser should help you ensure that all of the assets are within the Trust. In the Estate Plan Book, evidence of ownership of these assets will be found in the sections entitled "Savings and Investments," "Real Estate Documents," and "Business Agreements." Remember to check the safe-deposit box, just in case an expensive asset is not recorded in the name of the Trust.

If any asset is not in the Trust and the value of all assets outside the Trust exceeds the value established by the particular state for probate, then the assets outside the Trust must go through probate. If everything is in the Trust, the surviving trustee or successor trustee steps in immediately and—with the Trust and a death certificate—has identically the same power to buy, sell, or transfer any of the assets as did the individual who placed those assets into the Trust.

Review Size of Estate

The adviser should check the information in the "Financial Statement" section of the Estate Plan Book; ideally, the financial statement has been updated within the last twelve months. The adviser should also review the last year's federal and state income tax returns, and determine whether any gifts were reported on IRS Form 709 or 709A. All this information determines whether the estate is subject to federal estate taxes and state inheritance taxes. If so, the adviser should ascertain which forms need to be filed and how much tax needs to be paid.

As you learned in Chapter 4, with proper estate planning, there need not be *any* estate taxes to pay upon the death of the first spouse, regardless of the size of the estate. However, if estate taxes are due, a Form 706 (Federal Estate Tax form) must be filed, and any taxes due must be paid within nine months of death. There are options available under the tax code for extending estate tax payments over a period of ten years, but for most estates, the taxes do not qualify for the extension.

Many states are now conforming to the federal estate tax code to the extent that, if no federal estate tax is due on an estate, then no state inheritance tax is due. Since each state is different, the particular state laws for inheritance taxes need to be checked at the time of death.

File Income Tax Return

Upon the death of a spouse, the adviser should explain that the surviving spouse has a right to file a joint income tax return (Form 1040, as had been done while the spouse was alive) for the year in which his or her spouse died. The surviving spouse should keep an accurate record of the decedent's last medical and funeral expenses, because the medical expenses can be deducted from the survivor's taxable income, and the funeral expenses can be deducted for estate tax purposes.

The surviving spouse should use his or her social security number to identify all of the assets in the Trust, including the assets in the Survivor's A Trust as well as the assets in the Decedent's B Trust. The reason for reporting the assets in this manner is that it enables the trustee to transfer assets back and forth between the A Trust and the B Trust (and the C Trust, where applicable) as easily as possible, as you will see later in this chapter. The IRS Trust Identification Number is used to identify the assets upon the death of a single settlor or upon the death of the second spouse.

A surviving spouse acting as the surviving trustee will typically pay out all the income from the Trust to himself or herself and continue to report the Trust income on his or her personal Form 1040 income tax return.

Upon Death of First Spouse

If a couple have an A-B Trust, upon the death of a spouse, one-half of the Trust (the Decedent's B Trust) becomes irrevocable. A Form 1041S (*S* for simple) tax return should then be filed, but only for the decedent's irrevocable B Trust. This form must be filed each year until no assets remain in the B Trust.

The Form 1041S, formally known as the "U.S. Fiduciary Income Tax Return for Nontaxable Simple Trusts," is a simplified short form of the regular Form 1041. The Form 1041S is not well known; many CPAs do not even know that it exists.

The IRS Trust Identification Number will be used on the Form 1041S tax return. The Form 1041S and the accompanying Schedule K-1 are the only places where the special Trust ID number will be used during the life of the surviving spouse.

All of the income in Trust B is usually paid to the surviving spouse. However, since the surviving spouse is still a settlor of the Trust, the net effect is paying all of the income to oneself. Therefore, on Form 1041S, the surviving spouse would subtract from the income of Trust B an income distribution deduction in the same amount.

Computation of Trust Income

Income: Interest and dividends	$ 50,000	Decedent's half of the income of the Trust
Deductions: Distribution	(50,000)	Amount paid to survivor and reported on survivor's Form 1040 tax return
Balance: Taxable income	-0-	

Since the amount paid out from the Trust (the decedent's share) is the same as the amount received (income), the taxable income is zero! Thus, it is easy to see that the Form 1041S tax return on the decedent's half of an A-B Trust is simply an information return. The surviving trustee would continue to report any income received from the Trust on his or her regular Form 1040 tax return, as was done before the spouse's death.

To show you how simple the Form 1041S Trust Tax Return really can be, Figure 13-1 depicts a sample Form 1041S that has been completed. All of the income received by the Trust was paid out to the surviving trustee, and therefore the taxable balance is zero. Note that line 16 of the Form 1041S indicates that a Schedule K-1 must be attached to the return, to show who received the distribution from the Trust. A sample of Schedule K-1, "Beneficiary's Share of Income, Deductions, Credits, etc.," is shown in Figure 13-2. Note that the Form 1041S and Schedule K-1 forms both require the taxpayer to include the Trust Identification Number (shown on the form as the Employer Identification Number).

To prevent confusion at the IRS office that receives Form 1041S, we recommend to our clients that they include a short letter that reminds the IRS that all of the distributions from

**FIGURE 13-1
FORM 1041S TAX RETURN**

Form **1041S** Department of the Treasury Internal Revenue Service	**U.S. Fiduciary Income Tax Return for Nontaxable Simple Trusts** For the calendar year 1987, or short year beginning ...., 1987, and ending December 31, 1987. Check here if this return is for a short taxable year under section 645 ▶ ☐

OMB No. 1545-0960

1987

Name of simple trust

The Smith Family Trust

Name and title of fiduciary

Mary Ann Smith, Trustee

Address of fiduciary (number and street)

5751 Oak Street

City, state, and ZIP code

Santa Barbara, California 91382

Employer identification number

95-4632475

Date trust created

August 18, 1988

Check applicable box(es):

XX Initial return
☐ Amended return
☐ Final return

Caution: *Complex trusts, grantor trusts, and estates must use Form 1041.*

Income	1 Dividends	1	10,000 —
	2 Interest income	2	40,000 —
	3 Income (or losses) from partnerships, estates, or other trusts	3	
	4 Net royalty income (or loss) (attach Schedule E (Form 1040))	4	
	5 Net business and farm income (or loss) (attach Schedules C and F (Form 1040))	5	
	6 Ordinary gain (or loss) (attach Form 4797)	6	
	7 Other income (state nature of income) _____	7	
	8 **Total** income (add lines 1 through 7) ▶	8	50,000 —

Deductions	9 Interest	9		
	10 Taxes	10		
	11 Fiduciary fees	11		
	12 Accountant, attorney, and return preparer fees	12		
	13 Other deductions (itemize on a separate sheet)	13		
	14 **Total** (add lines 9 through 13) ▶		14	
	15 Adjusted total income (or loss) (subtract line 14 from line 8)		15	
	16 Income distribution deduction (attach Schedule K-1 (Form 1041))		16	50,000 —
	17 Balance (subtract line 16 from line 15) (see instructions) ▶		17	-0-

Other Information

		Yes	No
1	If the fiduciary's name or address has changed enter the old information ▶		
2	Did the trust receive tax-exempt income? (If "Yes," attach a computation of the allocation of expenses.) Enter the amount of tax-exempt interest income ▶ $		X
3	Did the trust receive all or any part of the earnings (salary, wages, and other compensation) of any individual by reason of a contract assignment or similar arrangement?		X
4	Was the trust the grantor of, or transferor to, a foreign trust which existed during the current tax year, whether or not the trust has any beneficial interest in it? (If "Yes," you may have to file Form 3520, 3520-A, or 926)		X
5	At any time during the tax year, did the trust have an interest in or a signature or other authority over a financial account in a foreign country (such as a bank account, securities account, or other financial account)? (See the Instructions for exceptions and filing requirements for Form TD F 90-22.1.) If "Yes," write the name of the foreign country ▶		X
6	Check this box if this trust has filed or is required to file **Form 8264,** Application for Registration of a Tax Shelter ▶ ☐		

Please Sign Here

Under penalties of perjury, I declare that I have examined this return, including accompanying schedules and statements, and to the best of my knowledge and belief, it is true, correct, and complete. Declaration of preparer (other than fiduciary) is based on all information of which preparer has any knowledge.

▶ *Mary Ann Smith*
Signature of fiduciary or officer representing fiduciary

▶ **February 16, 1989**
Date

Paid Preparer's Use Only

Preparer's signature ▶		Date	Check if self-employed ▶ ☐	Preparer's social security no.
Firm's name (or yours, if self-employed) and address ▶			E.I. No. ▶	
			ZIP code ▶	

Form **1041S** (1987)

FIGURE 13-2
SCHEDULE K-1 (ATTACHMENT TO FORM 1041S)

SCHEDULE K-1 (Form 1041)	**Beneficiary's Share of Income, Deductions, Credits, etc.—1987**	OMB No. 1545-0092
Department of the Treasury Internal Revenue Service	for the calendar year 1987, or fiscal year beginning ...., 1987, ending ...., 19 ..... **Complete a separate Schedule K-1 for each beneficiary.**	**1987**

Name of estate or trust ▶

The Smith Family Trust, dated August 18, 1988

Beneficiary's identifying number ▶ 123-45-8374	Estate's or trust's employer identification number ▶ 95-4632475
Beneficiary's name, address, and ZIP code Mary Ann Smith 5751 Oak Street Santa Barbara, California 91382	Fiduciary's name, address, and ZIP code SAME

A. 4-Year Proration.—Fiduciary: Check here ▶ ☐ if this Schedule K-1 is for a short taxable year required by section 1403 of the Tax Reform Act of 1986. **Beneficiary:** If this box is checked, you must prorate all column (b) amounts shown below (except for line 9a) over a four-year period beginning with this tax year. (See the instructions on the other side of this schedule.)

	(a) Allocable share item	(b) Amount	(c) Calendar year 1987 Form 1040 filers enter the amounts in column (b) on:
1	Dividends	10,000	Schedule B, Part II, line 4
2a	Net short-term capital gain (or loss)		Schedule D, line 5, column (f) or (g)
b	Net long-term capital gain (or loss)		Schedule D, line 12, column (f) or (g)
3	Interest	40,000	Schedule B, Part I, line 2
4a	Other taxable income:		
	(1) Rental, rental real estate, and business income from activities acquired before 10/23/86		(see instructions)
	(2) Rental, rental real estate, and business income from activities acquired after 10/22/86		(see instructions)
	(3) Other income		Schedule E, Part III, column (e) or (f)
b	Depreciation (including cost recovery) and depletion:		
	(1) Attributable to line 4a(1)		(see instructions)
	(2) Attributable to line 4a(2)		(see instructions)
	(3) Attributable to line 4a(3)		Schedule E, Part III, column (e)
c	Amortization deductions:		
	(1) Attributable to line 4a(1)		(see instructions)
	(2) Attributable to line 4a(2)		(see instructions)
	(3) Attributable to line 4a(3)		Schedule E, Part III, column (e)
5	Estate tax deduction (including generation-skipping transfer taxes) (attach computation)		Schedule A, line 25
6	Excess deductions on termination (attach computation)		Schedule A, line 21
7	Distributable Net Alternative Minimum Taxable Income		See Form 6251, line 4q instructions
8	Foreign taxes (list on a separate sheet)		Form 1116 or Schedule A (Form 1040), line 7
9	Other (itemize):		
a	Trust payments of estimated taxes credited to you		Include on page 2, line 55, Form 1040
b	Tax-exempt interest		Enter on page 1, line 9, Form 1040
c	....		
d	....		(Enter on applicable line
e	....		of appropriate tax form)
f	....		
g	....		
h			

Schedule K-1 (Form 1041) 1987

FIGURE 13-3
LETTER TO ACCOMPANY FORM 1041S

Internal Revenue Service   Re: 1041 Tax Return
                                                Accompanying K-1

Dear IRS Agent:

      The attached 1041S Trust Tax Return and accompanying K-1 are submitted for information only. This tax information was submitted on various 1099s and is reported under my social security number _____ on my 1040 Tax Return.

      Sincerely,

_____

the Trust are being reported on individual Form 1040 returns. Figure 13-3 shows a sample of the letter that should accompany the Form 1041S and Schedule K-1.

Upon Death of Both Spouses or a Single Person

Upon the death of both spouses or a single person, the entire Living Trust becomes irrevocable. Depending upon the distribution instructions, income may or may not be retained in the Trust. In either case, however, the successor trustees of the Trust must then file a Form 1041S income tax return. For example, if the Trust were providing for minor children, possibly only a portion of the Trust income would be distributed to the children. The children would be responsible for reporting the income they received from the Trust on their own individual income tax returns, and the Trust would be responsible for paying taxes on any income that was retained in the Trust.

Any assets retained in trust must use the special IRS Trust ID number. The practice of using the Trust ID number after the death of the settlors is logical, because the social security num-

bers belonging to the settlors cease upon their deaths.

Payment of Taxes

Needless to say, if the Trust has retained income and is required to pay federal income taxes, then presumably a state income tax return must also be filed, and any taxes due must be paid.

On the other hand, if all of the income is paid out from the Trust, then the recipients of the income will report such income on their own Form 1040 tax returns and pay any taxes due. The Trust must still file a Form 1041S Trust tax return. However, as previously mentioned, if all of the income of the Trust is paid out, then the Trust has no taxable income to report on Form 1041S.

Income Retained in the Trust

It may be to your tax advantage to retain some income in the Trust. Even though the 1986 tax code eliminated the income tax advantages of retaining income in the decedent's irrevocable half of the Trust and having it act as a separate tax entity, Congress continues to change the tax laws. Therefore, your CPA should review the pros and cons of whether to use the irrevocable Trust as a separate tax entity.

Obtain Written Valuation of Assets

The adviser should explain that one of the most important functions that must be completed upon the death of an individual who has a Living Trust is to establish written valuation of all of the assets in the Trust. It is absolutely necessary to obtain written valuation of all real estate and securities in order to determine a new cost basis for these assets and to take advantage of stepped-up valuation, thus minimizing the taxable gain when the assets are eventually sold.

The adviser should describe why and how to get stepped-up valuation. It is essential to establish a written valuation of each asset upon the death of a settlor. The written valuation provides a valid and documented justification of the asset's current market value for determining stepped-up valuation. Chapter 3 explains the importance of stepped-up valuation.

Real Estate

The simplest method of establishing current market value for real estate is to telephone two real estate agents from separate firms. Tell the agents that you are always interested in the possibility of selling your real estate and that you would appreciate it if they would estimate the value for which you should be able to sell your property (preferably on the high side when no estate taxes are due). Ask the agents to give these figures to you in writing, as well as to back up their valuations with "comparables" (recent sales of comparable real estate within the neighborhood). On the death of the last settlor, if the estate is going to be subject to estate taxes, you may desire to seek an evaluation on the low side. In general, however, you should never ask for either overvaluation or undervaluation of the real estate.

If the valuations from the two real estate agents are fairly close together, take the average of the two estimates for the value of your real estate. If the two estimates are far apart, ask a third real estate agent for another valuation of your real estate.

It is most important to place these written valuations in your Estate Plan Book (or somewhere else safe and accessible), so that you may use the valuations to substantiate your new stepped-up cost basis to the Internal Revenue Service, possibly years later when you decide to sell your real estate. You must be able to *prove* your cost basis in writing.

For example, assume that a husband and wife buy a home for $50,000. The couple have their home in a Living Trust in a community property state. Years later, when the market value of the home is $200,000, the husband dies. Because the surviving spouse inherits the house at current market value at the time of death, the *new* cost basis is $200,000.

Five years later, the surviving spouse sells the home for $350,000—a gain of only $150,000. However, the surviving spouse must have established the new cost basis in writing at the time the first spouse died. Failure to establish the cost basis at the time of the first spouse's death might make it difficult or impossible to justify the new cost basis to the IRS, which would dearly love to restore the valuation to the *original* cost basis.

The same principle of establishing written proof of current market valuation at date of death applies to any real estate and to any survivor, whether a surviving spouse or children. Note that your children also get stepped-up valuation as their cost basis upon the death of the surviving spouse.

Securities

Establishing the current market value of stocks and bonds is very simple—just look in the newspaper. The stock and bond quotations in the newspaper on or near the date of death are sufficient. Simply put the stock quotation page from the newspaper in the Estate Plan Book, but be sure that the entire page with the newspaper's dateline is included, so that the date of the quotation is recorded for future use.

Alternatively, your stockbroker can give you the actual stock and bond prices on the date of death. Most brokers will provide these figures to you in writing if you ask them to do so. In many cases, a monthly statement of account from a brokerage firm will include the value as of the date of the statement. Remember, the market value of the stocks and bonds at date of death becomes the new cost basis, which will be used to compute any taxable gain when the assets are eventually sold.

Review Business Agreements

Your adviser should review business agreements for action, dispositions, and benefits. Copies of any corporate stock certificates, partnership agreements, buy-sell agreements, and stock-redemption agreements are found in the "Business Agreements and Documents" section of the Estate Plan Book.

Any businesses must be valued *very* carefully and wisely. You should hire at least two, and possibly three, certified public accounting firms to value your business. Since most privately held businesses have a minimal cost basis, stepped-up valuation can become extremely important. However, you must establish a sound and justifiable basis to satisfy the Internal Revenue Service!

Assume that a husband and wife have built a corporation that is worth $1 million and that they developed the business from almost nothing, so their cost basis was minimal. When the couple finally die, their children inherit the business. The children wisely hire appraisers to value the business, whose value is established at $1 million. Two years later, the children have the opportunity to sell the business for $1.5 million, and they do so.

If the children have established a sound valuation upon the death of their parents and upon the sale of the business, the children will have a capital gain of only $500,000. Failure to establish a sound valuation at the time of the parents' death, however, would cause the children to have a gain of $1.5 million—quite a difference in taxes!

When you have an interest in a business of substantial value, you should be aware that a number of estate-planning tools can be used to freeze or establish the value of the business and, if desirable, to shift the gain to your chil-

dren. The various alternatives should be pursued with a knowledgeable estate-planning attorney.

The IRS has some fourteen different methods by which to compute corporate valuation, and, upon your death, the IRS will always strive to come up with the highest valuation for your business. For valuation purposes, the IRS looks at a business the day *before* an individual dies, not the day after. For example:

A surgeon has no clients except patients referred to him by other doctors, and he earns $300,000 a year. The surgeon's assets are his hands. The IRS will typically value his business at two years of earnings, or $600,000—the day before the surgeon dies. In reality, the day after the surgeon dies, his business is worth nothing

Assume that the doctor died leaving a spouse and an appropriate estate plan. Since, under these circumstances, there will be no estate taxes upon the death of the first spouse, the value of the business at date of death is not really of concern. Assume that the surviving spouse is able to collect her husband's business receivables of $50,000, which she places in a certificate of deposit. Upon the death of the surviving spouse, the only remaining business item of value is the CD ($50,000 plus interest).

Thus, where there is an interest in a privately held business, a proper estate plan is essential. While you are living, you can usually do something about determining a proper valuation for your business. Failure to do so, however, may have a tragic result.

Review Credit Cards

The next step to take in settling an estate is to review the credit cards that were issued to the deceased individual and to determine whether they should be destroyed. Cards that should definitely be destroyed are those issued only in the name of the deceased or for business use only.

As a matter of practice, you should always have a list of your credit cards readily available for the surviving trustee or successor trustee. Chapter 11 describes the easiest way to keep and maintain such records.

Distribute Personal Effects

At this time, it is appropriate to distribute personal effects as specified in any special Memorandum. Any special estate distributions should also be made, if specified. Your adviser should help you begin this step by checking the section titled "Memorandum" in the Estate Plan Book. Our Living Trusts, in the section on personal effects, specifically refer to the Memorandum and request the surviving trustee or successor trustee to abide by any Memorandum that may have been specified by the decedent.

The "Memorandum" section in the Estate Plan Book provides a place where clients can specify the desired distribution of their personal property. Occasionally, a client meticulously identifies almost every item to go to a particular child or to a brother, sister, mother, or father. However, most people are not quite this efficient.

Review Allocation and Distribution

If assets are to be distributed or retained in trust for the heirs, your adviser should help you determine which assets and real estate should be distributed, sold, or converted to income. Remember, though, to first determine any outstanding debts or taxes that must be paid before the estate is distributed.

The "Allocation and Distribution" section of the Trust should be carefully reviewed even if only one spouse has died.

The importance of the allocation and distribution aspects of settling an estate cannot be overemphasized. The "Allocation and Distribution" section of the Trust should be reviewed carefully. Even if only one spouse has died, the decedent may have left specific instructions as to certain assets that are to be distributed outright upon his or her death. Since the trustee should be given the choice of distributing in cash or in kind (by the language in the Trust), the trustee preferably should distribute the assets outright, rather than selling them and then distributing cash.

If the decedent is single or the surviving spouse, then the allocation and distribution of the assets in the estate must conform to the "Allocation and Distribution" section of the Trust. Again, it is always preferable to distribute the assets, where appropriate, rather than simply selling the assets and then distributing cash. On the other hand, to be perfectly fair to all heirs, it is often difficult to divide assets equally, so it may be necessary to sell some assets and then distribute equal dollar amounts in cash to each heir.

FINAL ISSUES

After the survivor has met with the primary adviser, he or she still has several months within which to take care of some important issues: making sure assets are most advantageously placed into the various Trusts, reviewing the way these assets are invested, and filing Form 706 for estate taxes, if required.

Asset Placement into A Trust, B Trust, and C Trust

People who have only an A Trust do not need to worry about allocating their assets, because the assets will continue to remain in the A Trust. However, people who have an A-B Trust or an A-B-C Trust need to be concerned about allocating assets among the A Trust, the B Trust, and, where applicable, the C Trust.

The decedent's share of community and separate property should be identified and placed in the Decedent's B Trust, with any excess over $600,000 placed in the C Trust, if available. (As described in Chapter 4, there is occasionally an exception to this rule.) The surviving spouse's share of community property and separate property should then be identified and placed in the Survivor's A Trust.

The decedent's assets consist of the decedent's separate property and the *value* of the decedent's share of the community or common property. One-half of the asset value of the community or common property must flow into Trust B (and Trust C, if applicable). Most people think that, if they own a home, the decedent owns half of the house and the surviving spouse owns the other half of the house—and, therefore, they need to put one-half of the house into Trust A and the other half into Trust B. However, this belief is not true. You may put the entire house into either Trust A or Trust B, as long as you put an equal value of assets into the other Trust. If you think of the dollar value of the house, instead of the house itself, as what is being placed in the Decedent's Trust B, then apportionment of assets into the A and B Trusts is much easier to understand.

With an A-B Trust, the value of the assets must be apportioned equally between the A and B Trusts, not the assets themselves.

The procedure for placing assets in the A, B, and C Trusts is really very simple. To place an asset in an A, B, or C Trust, the trustee merely needs to describe the asset, the valuation amount, the date on which the valuation was made, and the source of valuation. This description can be made on a form such as the one shown in Figure 13-4, which lists the assets placed in the A Trust. The forms for Trusts B and C are the same except for their titles. The trustee should date and sign these forms.

Thereafter, the trustee may totally ignore this distribution of assets among the A, B, and C Trusts, other than to annually report the income on the Form 1041S Trust tax return, as mentioned before. The trustee must also abide by the rules for the use of those assets, as described in the Trust under the provisions of the B and C Trusts.

FIGURE 13-4
FORM FOR ASSET DISTRIBUTION BY TRUST

TRUST A

Asset Description	Valuation		
	Amount	Date	Source
Real estate at 1571 Oak St., Santa Barbara, California	$400,000	8-1-86	Real estate valuation
Bank of America Certificate of Deposit #364382	$200,000	8-6-86	Statement

Date: 8-6-88   Signature of Trustee: *Mary Ann Smith*

As you learned in Chapter 5, growth assets should be placed in the Decedent's B Trust, since these assets will henceforth be insulated from further estate taxes. Nevertheless, each surviving spouse has his or her own set of objectives.

An example of somewhat unusual placement of assets in the B Trust involved a widow who was quite angry at the daughter of her deceased husband.

The daughter, who was from a former marriage of her father, had apparently been extremely unkind to her father, right up to and including the last days of his life. The father had left 20 percent of his share of the assets in his Decedent's Trust B to his daughter, upon the eventual death of his spouse.

The widow felt that even 20 percent was too much of an inheritance for the daughter. The widow made it very clear that the assets placed in Trust B were to have *no* growth. Further, the widow would annually take *all* the income from the B Trust and would also exercise her frivolous right to $5,000 or 5 percent (whichever was greater) once a year. The widow intended to see that the daughter got no more than was absolutely essential under the terms of the Trust.

One of the most important features of the Living Trust is the right of the trustee to transfer assets between the survivor's portion of the Trust and the decedent's part of the Trust (that is, from the A Trust to the B Trust or from the B Trust to the A Trust—and to the C Trust, if included). Figure 13-5, which illustrates typical asset transfers among parts of a Living Trust, shows that the process is quite easy. You need only describe the asset, the amount of valuation, the date of valuation, and the source of valuation. Then you show from which Trust the asset is being taken and to which Trust the asset is being transferred. The transfers would then be signed and dated by the trustee.

Assume an estate of $800,000, an A-B Trust, and the death of a husband. Assume also that the estate consists of $400,000 in real estate and $400,000 in stock. If the stock market is expected to rise substantially in the next year, and

real estate is expected to remain relatively static, the stock should be placed in the Decedent's B Trust, and the real estate should be placed in the Survivor's A Trust.

VALUE AT DATE OF DEATH		
Assets	Decedent's Trust B	Survivor's Trust A
Stock	$400,000	
Real estate		$400,000

Assume that after a year has passed, the stock is worth $600,000, and the real estate is still worth $400,000. Now you believe that the stock market has reached its high and that the real estate will begin to grow. Since it is quite permissible to transfer *dollar for dollar* between the decedent's and survivor's Trusts, $400,000 of the stock would be transferred into the A Trust. In exchange, the $400,000 of real estate would be transferred into the B Trust. The B Trust would then have $400,000 of real estate plus $200,000 of stock; the A Trust would have $400,000 of stock.

ONE YEAR LATER		
Assets	Decedent's Trust B	Survivor's Trust A
Stock	$600,000	
Real estate		$400,000

AFTER TRANSFER		
Assets	Decedent's Trust B	Survivor's Trust A
Stock	$200,000	$400,000
Real estate	$400,000	

After another year has passed, the real estate has grown from $400,000 to $600,000. As a result, there is now $800,000 in the B Trust ($600,000 of real estate and $200,000 of stock), and there is still $400,000 in the Survivor's A

FIGURE 13-5
ASSET TRANSFER—TRUST TO TRUST

| Asset Description | Valuation | | | Transfer | | Trustee Signature | Date |
	Amount	Date	Source	From Trust	To Trust		
Stock Brokerage Account #1764397 Merrill Lynch	$400,000	8-1-87	Statement from Broker	B	A	*Mary Ann Smith*	8-6-87
Real estate at 1571 Oak St. Santa Barbara California	$400,000	8-6-88	Real estate valuation	A	B	*Mary Ann Smith*	8-6-87

Trust. Remember, whatever is in the B Trust is insulated from further estate taxes. If the surviving spouse were now to die, the estate tax would be zero.

TWO YEARS LATER		
Assets	Decedent's Trust B	Survivor's Trust A
Stock	$ 200,000	$ 400,000
Real estate	600,000	
Total	$ 800,000	$ 400,000

All of the transfers in the above example could be made with the Asset Transfer form shown in Figure 13-5.

Since there are many different approaches to placing assets in the various Trusts, you have a most versatile vehicle in the Living Trust. More importantly, however, the Living Trust is an outstanding estate-planning tool upon the death of a spouse.

Review Investments and Investment Objectives

Review the investments in the Trust to see whether they meet the objectives of income, growth, and security. Determine whether some assets should be reinvested to provide adequate income as well as appropriate growth for a hedge against inflation. The assets should be reviewed at least annually to determine whether they should be reinvested for the best balance between growth and income and whether assets should be shifted among the A, B, and C Trusts to preserve anticipated appreciation.

Upon the death of an individual, it makes sense to review the types of investments in the estate to see whether they still correspond with the objectives of the survivors. This review is particularly necessary when the survivor is a spouse, a minor child, or a handicapped individual of any age. Typically, upon the death of a spouse or parent, the family income is reduced substantially. It may be far more appropriate to sell assets that were invested for growth and to replace them with income-producing assets.

On the other hand, if both parents are deceased, the beneficiaries of the Trust are the children, and the children are to receive the assets with an outright distribution, then the simplest way to distribute the assets is just to change title to the assets. However, if the assets are to be retained in trust for a period of time, it may be more appropriate to leave the assets invested for growth.

It also may be appropriate to change the identification number on your Trust assets. The surviving spouse's social security number should be used. If there is no surviving spouse, then the IRS Trust ID Number (Employee Identification Number) should be used. This number should have been recorded in the Estate Plan Book. IRS Form W-9, or its appropriate alternate form as specified by IRS regulations, should be used to change the tax number for each asset. This form may be obtained from any financial institution.

As mentioned earlier, if part or all of the Living Trust becomes irrevocable and assets are retained in the Trust, it will be necessary to annually file a Form 1041S Trust tax return for the irrevocable part of the Trust.

File Federal Estate Tax Form 706

The Federal Estate Tax Form 706 is one of the more complicated tax forms and should be avoided if at all possible. This form consists of eighteen pages of various forms, schedules, and instructions! The basic Form 706 consists of three very complex pages of information needed by the IRS; it is followed by Schedules A through P. Figure 13-6 shows the front page of this form. Remember, the Form 706, "United States Estate Tax Return," is one IRS form with which you *do not* want to get involved!

The only redeeming feature of Form 706 is that it need only be submitted if there are federal estate taxes to pay. If no taxes are owed, no Form 706 is necessary. If any federal estate taxes are due, the Form 706 must be filed within six months, and any taxes due must be paid within nine months. With proper estate planning, Form 706 need not be filed for a single person's estate of less than $600,000 or for a married couple's estate of less than $1.2 million. As you have seen, good estate planning can raise these limits substantially.

NOTHING ELSE TO DO

If you have done your homework—you have a Living Trust and an organized estate—settling the estate should take only a matter of minutes and not drag on for years. If any cost is involved, it should be minimal—and not consume 6 percent to 10 percent of the gross estate. Much of the hour we spend settling an estate is devoted to convincing the survivor that there really is nothing else to do.

About six years ago, a husband and wife attended one of our seminars and then came in to our office to draw up a Trust. As they completed the Trust, the husband told me that, as a retired FBI agent, he received a monthly newsletter from an individual in Washington who, in effect, continued to tell them to "get their houses in order." The former FBI agent said to me, "You've done it. You've created that process. Would you be willing to come down to Los Angeles and attend our monthly luncheon and present your seminar?" I told him that I would be delighted. Within the month, I had received an invitation and accepted.

Seventy-seven FBI agents, active and retired, attended my presentation. Recognizing that

FIGURE 13-6
FORM 706 ESTATE TAX RETURN

Form **706** (Rev. October 1988) Department of the Treasury Internal Revenue Service	**United States Estate (and Generation-Skipping Transfer)** **Tax Return** Estate of a citizen or resident of the United States (see separate instructions). To be filed for decedents dying after October 22, 1986, and before January 1, 1990. For Paperwork Reduction Act Notice, see page 1 of the instructions.	OMB No. 1545-0015 Expires 8-30-91

Part 1.—Decedent and Executor

1a Decedent's first name and middle initial (and maiden name, if any)	1b Decedent's last name	2 Decedent's social security no.
3a Domicile at time of death	3b Year domicile established	4 Date of birth 5 Date of death
6a Name of executor (see instructions)	6b Executor's address (number and street including apartment number or rural route; city, town, or post office; state; and ZIP code)	
6c Executor's social security number (see instructions)		
7a Name and location of court where will was probated or estate administered		7b Case number

8 If decedent died testate, check here ▶ ☐ and attach a certified copy of the will.   9 If Form 4768 is attached, check here ▶ ☐

10 If Schedule R-1 is attached, check here ▶ ☐   *See page 2 for representative's authorization.*

Part 2.—Tax Computation

1	Total gross estate (from Part 5, Recapitulation, page 3, item 10).	1	
2	Total allowable deductions (from Part 5, Recapitulation, page 3, item 25)	2	
3	Taxable estate (subtract line 2 from line 1)	3	
4	Adjusted taxable gifts (total taxable gifts (within the meaning of section 2503) made by the decedent after December 31, 1976, other than gifts that are includible in decedent's gross estate (section 2001(b))). . .	4	
5	Add lines 3 and 4	5	
6	Tentative tax on the amount on line 5 from Table A in the instructions	6	
	Note: *If decedent died before January 1, 1988, skip lines 7a-c and enter the amount from line 6 on line 8.*		
7a	If line 5 exceeds $10,000,000, enter the lesser of line 5 or $21,040,000. If line 5 is $10,000,000 or less, skip lines 7a and 7b and enter zero on line 7c **7a**		
b	Subtract $10,000,000 from line 7a **7b**		
c	Enter 5% (.05) of line 7b	7c	
8	Total tentative tax (add lines 6 and 7c)	8	
9	Total gift tax payable with respect to gifts made by the decedent after December 31, 1976. Include gift taxes paid by the decedent's spouse for split gifts (section 2513) only if the decedent was the donor of these gifts and they are includible in the decedent's gross estate (see instructions)	9	
10	Gross estate tax (subtract line 9 from line 8)	10	
11	Unified credit against estate tax from Table B in the instructions **11**		
12	Adjustment to unified credit. (This adjustment may not exceed $6,000. See instructions.) **12**		
13	Allowable unified credit (subtract line 12 from line 11)	13	
14	Subtract line 13 from line 10 (but do not enter less than zero)	14	
15	Credit for state death taxes. Do not enter more than line 14. Compute credit by using amount on line 3 less $60,000. See Table C in the instructions and **attach credit evidence** (see instructions)	15	
16	Subtract line 15 from line 14	16	
17	Credit for Federal gift taxes on pre-1977 gifts (section 2012)(attach computation) **17**		
18	Credit for foreign death taxes (from Schedule(s) P). (Attach Form(s) 706CE) **18**		
19	Credit for tax on prior transfers (from Schedule Q) **19**		
20	Total (add lines 17, 18, and 19)	20	
21	Net estate tax (subtract line 20 from line 16)	21	
22	Generation-skipping transfer taxes (from Schedule R, Part 2, line 12)	22	
23	Section 4980A increased estate tax (attach Schedule S (Form 706)) (see instructions) . . .	23	
24	Total transfer taxes (add lines 21, 22, and 23)	24	
25	Prior payments. Explain in an attached statement **25**		
26	United States Treasury bonds redeemed in payment of estate tax . . . **26**		
27	Total (add lines 25 and 26)	27	
28	Balance due (subtract line 27 from line 24)	28	

Under penalties of perjury, I declare that I have examined this return, including accompanying schedules and statements, and to the best of my knowledge and belief, it is true, correct, and complete. Declaration of preparer other than the executor is based on all information of which preparer has any knowledge.

Signature(s) of executor(s) _____   Date _____

_____

Signature of preparer other than executor _____   Address (and ZIP code) _____   Date _____ most FBI agents are either attorneys or CPAs, I did not quite know what reaction to my seminar on the Living Trust to expect. In retrospect, however, I regret not having a tape recorder to capture the comments at the conclusion of the seminar.

In particular, I remember one man who stood up and said, "I have been a federal referee for the past two years. My responsibility has been to investigate estates being stripped by attorneys. By the time we complete our investigations, the estates are typically stripped bone dry. The Living Trust and the program presented here today are the one means of preventing that from happening."

So often, I have received a call from a client telling me that her husband is dying in the hospital. There is little that I can do except to extend my sympathy. However, the individual is really calling from fear—fear of the unknown. The woman is calling to find out if settling an estate is really as easy as we told her when we created the Trust. The answer is that settling an estate in a Living Trust really *is* that easy.

14

Determining Your Net Worth

All too often, I see a very good Trust that is, unfortunately, inappropriate for the client. The attorney who wrote the Trust failed to ask the proper questions to establish the necessary client picture before writing the Trust. To properly identify the type of Living Trust and the provisions that are best suited to clients and their individual circumstances, it is essential to establish not only the size of the estate (the net worth), but also the different types and sizes of assets that make up the estate.

FACT GATHERING

Fact gathering is essential to creating the right type of Living Trust and its accompanying provisions. When clients come to our office with their minds already made up that they want a Living Trust, it is sometimes tempting to skip the important process of establishing a client profile. For example, a couple will say, "We're convinced; we know we want the Living Trust. We've got our papers, and we are ready to write the check." Under these circumstances, it is difficult to back off and to start from the very beginning—the fact-gathering process—but it is a most necessary step.

I typically begin a session with a new client by saying something similar to the following: "Like a doctor, before I can diagnose your financial health, I need to know the symptoms. Therefore, I need to ask you some personal questions and then some financial questions." On a rare occasion—possibly one in a thousand—I encounter a client who does not want to reveal his or her financial information. When that situation arises, I simply stop the fact-gathering process and explain to the clients (most often a husband and wife) that, unless I can gather the appropriate information, I cannot do an adequate job in helping them design their Trust. If the clients are unwilling to cooperate at that point, I nicely terminate our meeting, because I cannot in good conscience do anything more for them. I can only hope that someday the clients will find someone in whom they can confide—before it is too late.

Clients wonder what information they need to bring to our office when they are ready to create their Living Trust. My standard answer is, "Simply yourselves." To do a proper financial analysis, you need no preparation—only to respond to a series of simple financial questions.

When working with new clients, I am most concerned with putting them at ease while also getting the job done. It is more important to ask them simple questions and to get the clients responding. Then the financial answers can be gathered rather easily.

Most people are not financially detail-oriented and are unprepared to answer detailed financial questions. If the clients were asked to bring in a financial statement, most would end up putting off their appointment—either because they still have not gathered their financial data together or because they do not know enough about what a financial statement should contain. Most people dread dealing with finances, since it is too much like working with a budget or doing their taxes.

At the other extreme are clients who are extremely detailed, will bring in reams of paper, and are prepared to discuss each and every asset—down to the last penny. This detailed analysis can take an hour and a half or more and really is unnecessary. An adequate financial picture of a client's estate can be gathered within twenty minutes and will be accurate within 10 percent (more than adequate for what is required to establish the type of Trust and appropriate provisions).

An adequate picture of a client's estate can be gathered within twenty minutes.

It has been my experience that everyone knows the value of his or her estate or business at any time, if he or she is just asked the proper questions. Occasionally, a client goes home and meticulously rechecks the figures developed during our financial fact-finding interview. After thousands of similar interviews, I have yet to have a client come back and tell me that the paper-and-pencil valuation of his or her estate was off by more than 10 percent.

Even though our office has an expensive computer program that will allow our staff to do almost any type of sophisticated financial analysis, I still find that I can do the basic financial fact gathering for a new client more simply with just paper and pencil. I have been doing this fact gathering with thousands of clients over many, many years—and it works like a charm.

Every once in a while, a client will come into our office with his or her own computer printout or financial statement done on a home computer. I occasionally feel rather silly using my simple pencil-and-paper method, but I find that it always works. The questions in this chapter follow the same steps I take with my clients.

To develop an accurate financial picture of a client's estate, it is desirable to separate ordinary investments from retirement funds. To ensure that the various categories are kept separate, retirement investments are itemized first. Later questions address ordinary investments. The sequence of questions about cash accounts begins with the credit union and then continues with CDs, money market accounts, savings accounts, and finally checking accounts.

Most insurance has very little, if any, cash value and therefore is valueless when computing the net worth of your estate while you are alive. As described in Chapter 10, many clients benefit from placing their life insurance in an irrevocable Insurance Trust, which allows them to avoid paying estate taxes on their life insurance. In most cases, however, it is not advisable to take an investment vehicle (such as a single-premium whole life policy) and place it in an Insurance Trust. If you were to do so, you would have made a gift of this policy, which might eventually have undesirable tax consequences. Even more important, however, the tax-deferred income and the cash investment are no longer available to you. To prevent this situation from happening, you should identify these investments in an insurance vehicle for what they are—investments—and distinguish them from insurance per se.

DETERMINING YOUR NET WORTH

To determine your own net worth, use the questions on the following pages as a guide to "interview" yourself. To help you sort out your assets without duplication, the questions are in inverse order, beginning with your insurance and concluding with your savings.

If you are married and you wisely elect an A-B Trust, and if you have separate property and choose to have separate distributions or want to ensure that at least your share of common assets plus your separate property gets to your heirs as you have specified, then you should identify these assets as separate property. Once the financial analysis of your estate is completed, it is a simple matter to go back and add up the separate property of the husband and of the wife and the common property of both.

For this fact-gathering process, simply estimate to the nearest thousand dollars; you need only be accurate within 10 percent.

Since the same financial questions apply whether the client is single or married, the questions in this chapter are posed as if a husband and wife are being interviewed. If you are single, you can simply ignore the occasional question regarding the spouse.

For purposes of this financial fact-gathering process, you only need to provide estimates to the nearest thousand dollars, and you only need to be accurate within 10 percent.

Use the following format only as a guide, entering the necessary figures on your own separate notepad. The financial questions asked in this chapter serve simply as a format to help you go about identifying your net worth.

Insurance

The questions in this section about insurance are asked separately of the husband and wife. If you are single, you need only answer one set of questions.

Note that the cash value in an insurance policy is the amount of money you may borrow (take out) at any given point in time. The cash value is usually very low in comparison to the face value of the policy.

To the husband: How much life insurance do you have?

	Face Value	Cash Value
How much company group life insurance do you have?	$ _____	$ ___-0-___
Do you have NSLI (National Service Life Insurance, also known as GI Insurance)? If so, how much?	$ _____	$ _____
What individual life insurance policies do you have? How much cash value do you have in these policies?	$ _____	$ _____
	$ _____	$ _____
Total Husband's Insurance	$ _____ (1)	$ _____ (2)

To the wife: How much life insurance do you have?

	Face Value	Cash Value
How much company group life insurance do you have?	$ _____	$ ___-0-___
Do you have NSLI (National Service Life Insurance, also known as GI Insurance)? If so, how much?	$ _____	$ _____
What individual life insurance policies do you have? How much cash value do you have in these policies?	$ _____	$ _____
	$ _____	$ _____
Total Wife's Insurance	$ _____ (3)	$ _____ (4)

	Face Value	Cash Value

Total Insurance
Bring down totals (1), (2), (3), and (4)

Husband $ _____ (1) $ _____ (2)

Wife $ _____ (3) $ _____ (4)

Total Insurance of Both Spouses
Add together the amounts for husband and wife:
(1) + (3) = (G); (2) + (4) = (F) $ _____ (G) $ _____ (F)

Do not include the value of any accidental death benefits. Your chance of dying by accident is about one in forty. In addition, do not include the accidental life insurance that you have taken out with your credit card or local newspaper, since these policies are also accident policies.

Tax-Sheltered Investments
The following questions about various types of tax-deferred investments apply to husband and wife together. If you do not know what these plans are, you most likely do not have them, so do not worry about them.

IRAs
How much money do you have in IRAs? $ _____

Do you have an IRA rollover account? If so, how much is in it? $ _____

Keogh Plans
Do you have a Keogh plan? If so, how much is in it? $ _____

SEP Programs
Do you have an SEP (Simplified Employee Pension)? If so, how much is in it? $ _____

Pension Plans
Do you have a pension plan? If so, what is your vested interest (that is, money you may take out in the form of a lump sum)? How much could you take out if you left the company today? $ _____

Profit-Sharing Plans
Do you have a profit-sharing plan? If so, how much is in the plan? $ _____

Tax-Sheltered Annuities
Do you have a TSA (tax-sheltered annuity)? If so, how much is in the annuity? $ _____

401(k) Plans
Do you have a 401(k) (company savings) plan? If so, how much is in the plan? $ _____

Deferred Compensation Plans

Do you have a deferred compensation plan? If so, how much is in the plan? $ _____

Employee Stock Option Plans

Do you have an ESOP (employee stock option plan)? If so, how much is in the plan? $ _____

Total Tax-Sheltered Investments
Add together all of these tax-sheltered investments $ _____ (E)

Fixed and Other Investments

Your fixed and other investments include your home, personal property, first and second trust deeds that you hold, limited partnerships, and business interests.

Home

What is the sales value of your home? That is, what could you sell your home for today? $ _____

Do you have a mortgage? If so, what is the unpaid balance? $ _____

Net Value of the Home
Subtract the unpaid balance from the sales value $ _____

Personal Property

What is the value of your personal property—including furniture, furnishings, antiques, artworks, clothing, furs, jewelry, automobiles, recreational vehicles, hobbies, tools, and so on? (Estimate to the nearest $10,000.) $ _____

The primary concern with this part of the fact-gathering process is to identify any expensive possessions you may own. When I ask the question about personal property, I am really listening for one spouse to turn to the other and say, "What is that Picasso worth?" Specifically, you want to identify any valuable art objects or antiques you may have. Such valuable possessions should be separately inventoried and *separately transferred* into your Trust by Bill of Sale/Letter of Transfer.

You should figure the value of your personal property as somewhere between the price at which you could buy it and the price at which you could sell it. If you have no objects of special value, it is common practice to value personal property (upon the death of both spouses) at $10,000. In almost all cases, this personal property is going to "disappear" into the homes of your children.

First and Second Trust Deeds

List all first and second trust deeds you hold on someone else's property. $ _____

$ _____

$ _____

Total First and Second Trust Deeds $ _____

Limited Partnerships

Do you have any limited partnerships? If so, what is the value? If you do not know today's value, enter what you paid for each partnership, in anticipation that you will at least get back your money. $ _____

$ _____

$ _____

Total Value of Partnerships $ _____

Business Interests

Do you have an interest in a sole proprietorship, partnership, or corporation? What is the value of the business? Or, in other words, if someone were to place cash on the table, for what amount of money would you sell it? If you own only a partial interest in a business, then, after having valued the business, record only your share.

Total Value of Business Interests $ _____

In the early 1960s, I was a consultant with Cresap, McCormick, and Paget—one of the leading consulting firms in the nation. The company did a number of corporate valuations for merger acquisitions. As financial analysts, we went through a long, arduous (typically three-month) process to determine the corporate valuation.

Then one day I made an interesting discovery. I asked the owner, "If I placed cash on the table today, for what amount would you sell the company to me?" The owner's answer came within 10 percent of our company's three-month-long valuation.

I continued this practice for years, doing similar valuations (but for days, not for months) and then posed the same question to the owner. I consistently found that the owner would value the business within 10 percent of my detailed valuation. I learned by experience that everyone knows the value of his or her business at any given time, if asked the right question.

All too often, I get a response such as, "I really don't know what my business is worth." To me,

that response is just a form of modesty. I respond to such an answer by saying, "If I laid $5 million in cash on the table, would you sell the business to me?" If the answer is no, I offer a higher amount. However, if the answer is a quick yes, I quickly make a lower offer (for example, $3 million). If the owner's response is again a quick yes, I offer $1 million. If the response is then a thoughtful no, I try an offer in the area of $1.5 million. If the response is slow in coming forth (allowing time for thought) and then a yes, I have finally arrived at the proper value. This approach works every time. Whether I ask the questions or you ask them of yourself, the result should be the same.

However, heed a word of warning: Do not get caught in the trap of valuing your business for the IRS. Every business owner always has two valuations readily at hand: an amount for which he or she would sell the business and an amount at which he or she would value the business for IRS tax purposes. Do not play games, and do not fool yourself. The IRS will value your business typically for a much larger amount than the amount for which you think you could sell it. Therefore, value your business realistically—for the price at which you think you could sell it. By doing so, you can identify the magnitude of your estate-planning needs, and then the appropriate type of Trust can be determined.

Total Investments—Fixed and Other

Add the totals for your home, personal property, first and second trust deeds, limited partnerships, and business interests.

$ _____ (D)

_____

Real Estate Equity (Other than Home)

Now consider any real estate that you own other than your home. Each property should be listed separately, since the list identifies the number of deeds that must be specifically transferred into the name of your Living Trust.

What real estate do you own other than your home? How would you describe it, and where is it located (for example, commercial building, home, or land in Las Vegas, Nevada)? For what amount could you sell it? Do you have a mortgage? If so, how much do you still owe? You can easily compute the net value (your equity) by deducting your mortgage from the sales value.

Description of Property	Sales Value	Mortgage	Equity (Sales Value Less Mortgage)
_____	$ _____	$ _____	$ _____
_____	$ _____	$ _____	$ _____
_____	$ _____	$ _____	$ _____
_____	$ _____	$ _____	$ _____
Total Equity in Real Estate Other than Home		$ _____ (C)	

It is important to know in what state each of your properties is located. This information should remind you that, if you hold property in different states—and do not have ownership in the name of your Living Trust—probate will be required in *each* of those states! For example, if you own a residence in California and a condominium in Utah, your residence would be probated in California, and your condominium would go through the probate process in Utah. As mentioned earlier in the book, absentee probate is an absolute nightmare! Furthermore, although you are considering only your equity in your real estate to determine your net worth, any probate fees would be based on the gross value (sales value) of your real estate.

Investments—Market Securities
Securities listed in this section should specifically exclude any assets already identified under the tax-sheltered category. Stock brokerage houses commonly shift your investments back and forth among stocks and bonds and their money market funds, and the ratio of investments varies from time to time. If your securities are handled in this manner, include the money market fund as part of your stocks and/or bonds.

Stocks

How much money do you have invested in stocks (the purchase price)? $ _____

Do you have any stock on margin? If so, how much is on margin? (For example, if you bought $1,000 worth of stock and paid only $500, you owe the remaining $500—you would thus have 50 percent of the stock on margin.) $ _____

Net value of stocks
Subtract margin figure from amount of stocks $ _____

Bonds

How much money do you have in bonds (municipal bonds, corporate bonds, government bonds, and Ginnie Maes)? $ _____

Mutual Funds

How much money do you have invested in mutual funds? $ _____

Annuities

How much money do you have invested in annuities? $ _____

Single-Premium Life Insurance

How much *investment* money do you have in single-premium whole life insurance or single-premium universal life? $ _____

Gold

What amount do you have invested in gold? $ _____

Silver

What amount do you have invested in silver? $ _____

Diamonds

What amount do you have invested in diamonds (investment-grade stones, not personal jewelry)? $ _____

Other Investments

What amounts do you have in other investments not previously mentioned?

Type of investment: _____ $ _____

Total Investments—Market Securities
Add together all of the investments in this section $ _____ (B)

Savings
The savings category includes any remaining assets. If these figures have already been included in any other area, they should not be included here.

Credit Union

How much money do you have in credit union accounts? $ _____

Government Securities

How much money do you have in Treasury bills or notes? $ _____

Savings Bonds

What is the face value of your savings bonds? $ _____

Certificates of Deposit

How much money do you have in certificates of deposits (CDs)? CDs are now referred to
by many names, but typically they are investments tied up for periods of three months
to several years that command a specific interest rate dependent on the investment time
period. $ _____

Money Market Accounts

What funds do you have in money market accounts? $ _____

Savings Accounts

What funds do you have in regular (passbook) savings accounts? $ _____

Checking Accounts

What is the average amount of money in your checking accounts? $ _____

The balance in most people's checking accounts varies from a large amount at the beginning of the month to a small amount at the end. Simply guess at an average of your ending balance. (At this stage of the financial fact-gathering process, the amount of money in your checking accounts is usually inconsequential in relation to the rest of your estate.) Remember that the combined value of your checking accounts should never exceed $30,000. If such a situation should arise, simply make sure that one or more of your checking accounts is placed in the name of your Trust.

Total Savings
Add together all of the savings amounts $ _____ (A)

Summation of Your Net Worth
Now that you have answered the questions and have determined totals for your insurance, tax-sheltered investments, fixed and other investments, real estate equity (other than home), market securities investments, and savings, you are ready to find out your net worth. Your net worth is the sum of the amounts for the six previously discussed categories. Each of these category totals has been identified by a letter, from (A) to (F), in the right-hand margin. Bring each of these category totals down to the following blanks to find your net worth.

Total Savings	$ _____	(A)
Total Investments—Market Securities	$ _____	(B)
Total Equity in Real Estate Other than Home	$ _____	(C)
Total Investments—Fixed and Other	$ _____	(D)
Total Tax-Sheltered Investments	$ _____	(E)
Total *Cash Value* of Insurance	$ _____	(F)
Total Net Worth	$ _____	
Total Face Value of Life Insurance	$ _____	(G)
Total Net Worth and Life Insurance Add together the preceding two figures	$ _____	

IDENTIFYING THE PROPER TYPE OF TRUST

The total net worth and life insurance amount is the primary figure you will use to determine whether you need an A Trust, an A-B Trust, an A-B-C Trust, and/or an Insurance Trust. Even though your financial analysis may indicate that you only need an A Trust, several other reasons why you may well want to select an A-B Trust are identified in Chapter 5.

As a general reminder from previous chapters, your choices (assuming moderate-sized estates) are as follows:

- Single person
  A Trust—Your only choice.

- Married (or unmarried) couple
  A Trust—Suitable only if your estate is less than $600,000. Catastrophic Illness Provision cannot be included.
  A-B Trust—Suitable for estates of less than $1.2 million. Catastrophic Illness Provision is included. Taxes must be paid on first to die if estate exceeds $1.2 million.
  A-B-C Trust—Suitable for estates that exceed a value of $1.2 million. Catastrophic Illness Provision is included. Taxes may be deferred until death of second spouse (regardless of value of estate).

For a refresher on why the different types of Trusts are suitable for different-sized estates, you may want to review the examples in Chapter 5. For estates valued at more than $1.2 million, an Insurance Trust—illustrated in Chapter 10—may also be advisable.

A SIMPLE PROCESS

Valuing your estate can be simple and swift. Take my word for it—you do not need any papers in front of you. Simply go through the questionnaire presented in this chapter and answer the questions. It should take you no more than twenty minutes, and your valuation will be within 10 percent of the actual value; you do not need to be any closer. Recognize that the value of your estate will fluctuate during the year for any number of reasons, but you need not worry about such changes.

If you follow the simple process presented in this chapter, you can identify the type of Trust you need. In addition, if you decide now that you need only an A Trust or an A-B Trust, recognize that, at any future date, you can always update your Trust by amendment.

As an old adage says, "People don't eat a whole cow in one sitting; they just take one bite at a time." Similarly, as you build your estate, you should review and build your Living Trust a piece at a time.

15

Creating Your Estate Plan

Once you have decided to create your own Living Trust and have selected the type of Trust that is most appropriate for your estate, you have arrived at the stage where you are finally ready to create your estate plan. People seldom create the perfect plan on the first attempt. Yet, remember, your Living Trust is changeable—monthly, weekly, or even daily. Often, the most difficult part of developing a plan is to get started. The decisions you make now are not etched in stone. Therefore, begin your plan now, put it into effect, and then, as time goes on, modify it as necessary to meet your current goals. In the end, you will come up with the perfect solution—but you need to start now.

MAJOR DECISIONS

For many people, deciding to create a Living Trust is the easy part. To create a Trust that is tailored to the individual circumstances and needs of each client requires the client to make several important decisions:

- Whom to name as the trustees for your Trust
- Whom to name as the executor of your estate

- Whom to name as guardian or guardians, if you have minor or handicapped children
- To whom you want to leave your assets, in what proportion, and when you want your assets to be distributed
- Which desirable provisions are to be included with your Living Trust

---

These decisions are difficult, but once you make them, you will enjoy peace of mind.

These decisions are difficult, so do not make them in a hurried manner. Instead, give the various alternatives some thought and discussion, make some tentative decisions, and then sleep on them. It is particularly important for a married couple to discuss each potential decision jointly—so that their Living Trust will reflect their mutual desires, and not just the desires of either the husband or the wife.

Unfortunately, at about this time in the process of creating your estate plan, the dreaded disease called apathy sets in, and all of your

207

best efforts cease. This situation often happens because many of the necessary decisions are difficult to make and many people find the subject to be somewhat unpleasant. However, you must make these decisions, or eventually the court will make them for you. Once you make the decisions, however, you will enjoy peace of mind.

Selection of Trustees

The trustee(s), co-trustees, and successor trustee(s) are responsible for administering the Living Trust. Whether you are married or single, the decisions you need to make are almost identical, although your selections will be based on different criteria. For guidance in making your decisions, refer to the information about trustees in Chapter 6.

Decisions for a Married Couple

If you are married, you and your spouse need to identify the individuals who will administer your Trust while you are both living, after one of you passes away, and after both of you are gone. These people are the initial trustee or co-trustees, the surviving trustee, and the successor trustee.

Since you have most likely done a reasonably good job of managing your assets to this point in your life, you would presumably want to continue to do so; therefore, it is typical to name both husband and wife as trustees of their Living Trust. On rare occasions, where one spouse is not well and everything is being handled entirely by the other spouse, it would be appropriate to name only the active spouse as the trustee.

If one spouse dies, the surviving spouse is typically named as the surviving trustee. Occasionally, a client considers naming a child (or children) as co-trustee with the surviving spouse. However, only in rare situations would doing so be recommended.

For example, a man who was dying of cancer named his daughter to serve as co-trustee with his wife upon his death. He was concerned about his wife's ability to manage the estate after his demise, because his wife's mental faculties were rapidly deteriorating.

In another situation, a husband had built a very large estate in real estate. His daughter was very active in the management of the real estate, while his wife had little or no involvement. The husband therefore felt that it was appropriate to name his daughter as co-trustee with his wife upon his death.

As a last resort, you may wish to name a financial institution as surviving trustee, either in lieu of the spouse or as a co-trustee with the spouse. Before you do so, however, review the discussion of this alternative in Chapter 6.

One or more of your adult children, close family members, or close friends should be named as successor trustees to serve upon the death, incompetence, or resignation of the surviving spouse. Administration of your Living Trust is quite easy, and whether you name one child or four children as successor trustees is entirely academic. Clients most often name the child they consider most mature or name all of their children. Either approach works well. However, you must be aware that the minimum age to be a trustee is eighteen years old.

If you have named one successor trustee, you should consider naming one or more alternate successor trustees in case the named successor trustee is unable or unwilling to serve when the need finally arises. If you do not name an alternate successor trustee, your Trust should have within it a provision in which the primary beneficiaries would have the right to elect a successor trustee. Such a provision is included in all Living Trusts drawn up for our clients.

You may sometimes find it appropriate to name a financial institution as successor trustee; however, such action is recommended only as a last resort. Situations in which such an arrangement may be appropriate are described in Chapter 6.

Decisions for a Single Person

If you are a single person, you must make almost the same decisions regarding the administration of your Trust as are required of a married couple. You need to identify the initial trustee or co-trustee and the successor trustee. However, you cannot name a surviving trustee, because your Trust becomes irrevocable upon your death.

Assuming that you have managed your assets reasonably well until now, you would presumably want to be the trustee of your own Trust.

One or more of your adult children, close family members, or close friends should be considered as successor trustees upon your death, incompetence, or resignation. The previous information about selecting a successor trustee for a married couple would also apply to a single individual.

Assuming you have managed your assets reasonably well, you would presumably want to be the trustee of your own Trust.

Selection of Executor

After selecting your various trustees, you must select an executor to handle any of your assets that have been inadvertently left outside your Living Trust. The responsibilities and selection of an executor are described in Chapter 6. If you have all of your assets inside your Living Trust, there will be absolutely nothing for the executor to do.

For a Married Couple

Upon the death of a spouse, the surviving spouse is typically named as the executor. If the surviving spouse is not physically or mentally able to withstand the eventual appearances in court, it may be more appropriate to name one of the adult children, a close family member, or a close friend as executor.

Upon the death of both husband and wife, the successor trustee is normally the person who is named to be the executor. For guidelines in selecting this person, see Chapter 6.

For a Single Person

If you are a single person, you need to be concerned only about whom to name as the executor to handle your estate upon your demise. Upon the death of the settlor, the successor trustee is typically named as the executor.

Appointment of Guardian

If you have minor children or mentally or physically handicapped children, it is essential that you name a guardian (or guardians) for the children. Selection of a guardian is probably one of the most important—and one of the most difficult—decisions you can ever make. For some guidance, you may wish to review the information about appointment of a guardian in Chapter 9.

Naming an Alternate Guardian

If your children are eleven years of age or younger, it is strongly suggested that you name an alternate guardian. As mentioned earlier in the book, many years must pass before your children attain adulthood, and in the meantime your named guardian could die. When such an event occurs, you are not likely even to remember that your Appointment of Guardian document now needs to be changed. It is much better—for the ultimate protection of your children—to take a little more time now and thoughtfully select an alternate guardian.

Naming a Guardian for a Handicapped Child

If you have a handicapped child, you should review the discussion of this subject in Chapter 9. This critical decision of naming a guardian for a handicapped child should be made *only* after careful thought.

In recent years, many of our clients have drawn up guardianship papers for their adult handicapped children, who were once very bright contributors to society but who experimented with drugs and are now mentally incapacitated. This sad situation is one of the most frightening and insidious occurrences that has happened to our society, but the true-to-life consequences are little known to the general public. When my clients are drawing up Living Trusts, the subject of guardianship for an adult child who has been incapacitated because of drugs is one of the last issues to surface—and then it is almost as if the subject were an embarrassment to the sad parents. Appallingly, the number of such cases is large and seems to be growing without end.

Allocation and Distribution of Assets

Unlike a Will, the Living Trust gives each spouse an *independent* right to determine to whom he or she wants his or her assets distributed, in what proportion, and when. For a couple with an A-B Trust, upon the death of the first spouse, the Decedent's Trust B becomes irrevocable—and the named beneficiaries, the percentage of allocation, and the time of distribution for the decedent's share of the assets become cast in concrete. However, the surviving spouse may continue to change the allocation and distribution for his or her own share of the assets in an A Trust.

A mother and father were estranged from their only child. The couple left only 10 percent of their assets to the child, and the mother died shortly thereafter. During the ensuing years, the child re-established a close relationship with the father. When the father eventually came into our office to increase the portion of the estate going to the child, I simply asked him to tell me what percentage of the total estate he wanted to go to the child. We thereupon drew an amendment adjusting the Survivor's A Trust to meet the client's desire.

Allocation of Assets

If you have children, presumably you will want your assets to go to them upon the death of both you and your spouse (if you are married) or upon your death (if you are single). Obviously, you may make any number of special bequests to whomever you desire (such as to your grandchildren, brothers and sisters, relatives, friends, favorite charities, or church). Chapter 7 provides guidance in making these decisions.

Probably the most important decision that needs to be made at this juncture is whether you want to allocate your assets equally to your children or to allocate each child's share unequally. About one-fourth of our clients have very good reasons for allocating the assets to their children in other than equal proportions. Chapter 7 provides some examples to help you decide what is right for you.

When a husband and wife have been married before, have children from their former marriages, and have remarried, an A-B Trust is the logical choice for allocating assets fairly. The A-B Trust allows the spouses to combine their assets so that they may upgrade their standard of living. The A-B Trust also retains the combined assets so that the surviving spouse may

maintain the same standard of living as when both spouses were alive. Upon the death of the surviving spouse, the A-B Trust can ensure that the assets in the Survivor's A Trust go to the children of the surviving spouse, and the assets in the Decedent's B Trust go to the children of the first spouse to die. Thus, the A-B Trust provides a simple, ideal way to solve what could be a complex situation. In fact, I have seen this particular solution restore harmony to many marriages that were under stress because of the issue of allocation and distribution.

Distribution of Assets

Once you have decided who is to get what portion of your estate, you need to decide *when* the specified distribution is to be made. Most people desire to distribute their estates to their children. As you may recall from Chapter 7, the most commonly used types of asset distribution are outright, at a specific age, income only, and deferred distribution. If you are unsure which arrangement would be best for your situation, you should review the material in Chapter 7.

Deferred distribution is the most common method of distribution selected by our clients, and I lean very heavily toward this type of distribution for two important reasons. First, all people mature with age. Second, if an individual gets a sum of money and wastes it, the individual gets a second chance. Some individuals need to learn by experience. Being a registered investment adviser, I have learned from observing many "mature" people that age is no guarantee of wisdom. All too often, people between fifty-five and sixty years old take their retirement money and invest it on well-intentioned advice, which has often been disastrous.

I feel so strongly about deferred distribution—and providing a second chance—that I have used deferred distribution in my own family's Living Trust for my children, specifying that distribution for each child will be one-third at age twenty-five, one-third at age thirty, and one-third at age thirty-five. However, at no time (regardless of the children's ages) will distribution be greater than one-third outright, one-third in five years, and one-third in ten years. Thus, if my wife and I were to die after our children had all attained the age of thirty-five, they would still receive their inheritances as deferred distributions.

Occasionally, however, a spouse desires to make an outright distribution of a particular asset or of a particular dollar amount to his or her children upon his or her death. Such a situation often occurs when the parents have been married before and have children from their former marriages. The situation is even more prevalent when there is a disparity of age between the parents.

Deferred distribution gives your heirs a chance to learn from experience.

For example, a husband had married a woman much younger than himself, and they had a young child. The husband was concerned that, because his wife was near in age to the children of his former marriage, if he were to leave all of the assets in trust for his surviving spouse, his own children from his first marriage would probably never benefit from his estate. The husband therefore decided to distribute his $50,000 retirement program to the children from his first marriage at the time of his death. Although I understood the husband's logic, I could foresee conflict over the distribution with his present wife.

I agreed that the husband should include such a distribution in the Trust, but I also suggested to the husband that he should take out $50,000 worth of life insurance on his life payable to the Trust, in order to offset the loss of the asset to his present wife. Buying the insurance policy would leave his current wife in the same financial position (that is, she would not be denied $50,000). The wife accepted the insurance alternative, but it was obvious that, without such a compromise, there would have been much future conflict at home.

If you still feel unsure about how you want to allocate and distribute your assets, please take some time to review the material in Chapter 7. That chapter explains some of the many possibilities and answers some frequently asked questions.

Selection of Desirable Provisions

The next step is to select which of the desirable provisions to include with your Living Trust. These provisions are described in Chapter 9. The following provisions should be considered:

- Living Will (Right-to-Die Clause)
- Durable Power of Attorney
- Competency Clause
- Catastrophic Illness Provision
- Transfer of Personal Property
- Appointment of Guardian
- Appointment of Conservator
- Anatomical Gift
- Separate Property Agreements

Three provisions I feel should be included with every Trust are the Living Will, the Durable Power of Attorney, and the Competency Clause. However, each provision requires your *personal* decision and may require reflection and thought before you arrive at the decision that is right for you. Not everyone decides to include all of the provisions, but each provision offers desirable legal protections. For guidance in selecting these provisions, refer to the discussion in Chapter 9.

YOUR FIRST VISIT TO THE ATTORNEY

Now that you have reviewed the critical questions that need to be answered and have made the decisions you believe are best for your particular situation, you are ready to seek out a qualified attorney who is well versed in drawing up Living Trusts. Chapter 8 provides some guidelines for identifying a qualified attorney. If you would like some help with this difficult task, you may want to use the referral number given in Chapter 17.

When you make your first visit to the attorney, you should take with you the necessary items of personal data (such as your parents' dates and places of birth); the names of the individuals whom you have chosen as trustees, executor, and guardian; and notes outlining the allocation and distribution of assets you desire for your heirs. In addition, take any real estate deeds, trust deeds, Separate Property Agreements, and business interest papers you have.

Real Estate Deeds

You need to bring the attorney a copy of the grant deeds to real estate you own, because these deeds need to be transferred into the name of your Living Trust. Unless you are particularly knowledgeable in this area, you should have legal counsel prepare and file these documents. If you take copies of these documents with you, the attorney can draw the new deeds at the same time that your Living Trust is being drawn. The final documents will be prepared and awaiting your signature and notarization when you return to the attorney's office to sign the necessary Trust documents.

As a precautionary measure, you should include with each deed the Assessor Parcel Number (which you will find on your tax bill) and the address of the property. In addition, be sure to read the property description on the deed. If the description says "See Exhibit A attached," be sure that Exhibit A *is* attached to the deed.

Be sure to bring deeds for each of your real estate properties, including any time-share properties in which you have an economic interest.

Trust Deeds

If you hold any first or second trust deeds on other people's property, these trust deeds are an asset to you and must also be transferred into the name of your Living Trust. Therefore, take them with you on your first meeting with the attorney.

Separate Property Agreements

You should also take along a list of any assets that are to be designated as separate property. To refresh your memory about the formal and specific information required for each asset, review the section on Separate Property Agreements in Chapter 9.

Business Interest Papers

If you have any business interest in a partnership or sole proprietorship, take your business documents representing this interest to the attorney. Ask for a Bill of Sale/Letter of Transfer, so that your interest in the business can be transferred into the name of the Trust.

WISE ESTATE PLANNING

The most important thing you can do now is to gather together as much information as possible on potential trustees, executor, and guardians, and your desires for allocation and distribution of your assets and then jot down your thoughts. Then find a professional who has in-depth experience in working with people and creating Living Trusts. Such an individual can bring priceless experience to bear upon your particular problem.

You need not have *all* the answers before you take that most important first step—the creation of your Living Trust. You should begin now to lay out your agenda for wise estate planning. Remember, any plan is better than no plan at all. Once you have a plan, you have the ability to adjust it to meet your changing needs or circumstances. As you do so, you will eventually create the perfect plan for your individual situation.

Once you have executed your Living Trust, I must say, "Congratulations! You have now taken a giant step in the direction of wise estate planning."

16

Appropriate Costs of the Living Trust and Accompanying Documents

A well-drawn Living Trust, with its accompanying documents and program services, has an almost unlimited market—if priced appropriately. There is a very definite price/demand curve for Living Trusts (as there is for most things). When the price is right, the potential of drawing Living Trusts for those people who are acquainted with the advantages is unlimited.

This chapter presents appropriate costs for a typical estate. Most of our clients have estates ranging in value from $200,000 to $1.5 million. For large estates, an exceptionally good estate-planning specialist has every right to charge fees far in excess of the fees mentioned here. The reason is that the estate-planning expert is bringing all of his or her skills to bear in an effort to preserve the client's estate. The estate-planning professional with extensive experience has developed skills that are well earned, and this person should be rightfully paid for his or her expertise.

On the other hand, I must warn you about the "inexpensive" Trust. Occasionally a client says, "I know of an attorney who will prepare a Trust for $250 or $350." Be careful; you get exactly what you pay for. Remember, a poorly written

Living Trust can be just as disastrous as not having a Trust at all!

PRICE STRUCTURE

Keep these comments in mind as you review the price structure for the Living Trust and its accompanying documents. Table 16-1 suggests appropriate costs for the basic forms of the Living Trust and the additional desirable provisions.

Amendments

With the sophisticated computer equipment, programs, and techniques used in our office, a typical simple amendment—such as a change of beneficiary, a change of successor trustee, or a change in the method of distribution—can be made for a cost of $50 to $100. Such a fee structure assumes that the firm making the amendment is the same as the firm that drew the original Trust document.

For each Living Trust created for our clients, all of the client information and Trust data are computerized. Therefore, it is a simple task to call up the client data and, by asking for an amendment, immediately have everything on

TABLE 16-1
APPROPRIATE COSTS FOR THE LIVING TRUST AND ACCOMPANYING DOCUMENTS

Basic Trust Forms	Cost
A Trust for single person	$775
A Trust for married couple	$850
A-B Trust for married couple	$950

Desirable Provisions	
Pour-Over Will	No extra charge
Living Will (Right-to-Die Clause)	No extra charge
Durable Power of Attorney	No extra charge
Competency Clause	No extra charge
Catastrophic Illness Provision (provided only in an A-B Trust)	No extra charge
Transfer of personal property	No extra charge
Appointment of Conservator	No extra charge
Appointment of Guardian	No extra charge

Supplementary Documents	
Anatomical Gift Provision (Gift of Vital Organs)	$50
Separate Property Agreements	$50

Tax-Saving Provisions or Trusts	
C (Q-Tip) Trust	$200
Gift to spouse	$100
Insurance Trust	$400
Children's Trust	$400

Changes to the Trust	
Standard changes	$50–$100*
Tax-change amendment	$50–$100*

Transfer of Deeds	
Deed located in state of residence	$50 per deed*
Deed located outside state of residence	$100 per deed*

Annual Upkeep	Fee only for special services*

Settlement Fee	Varies*

* For more details, see comments in text.

the computer screen, except the appropriate paragraph that needs to be added to or changed in the client's Living Trust. Since almost all of the clauses and provisions have been standardized in our Living Trusts, the proper paragraph formats are already contained in our computer library.

You should review your Trust at least once every five years to make sure that it is continuing to meet your personal desires. With such a small fee to make a standard change, clients rarely hesitate to make necessary changes to their Trusts, so their Trusts continue to work for them. Many years of experience have proven that, if the cost of amendments is excessive, clients will not keep their Trusts up to date with their personal desires.

Tax-Change Updates

Congress seems to change the estate tax laws about every five years. Depending upon the extent to which each tax change affects the Trust, our clients are charged only $50 to $100 for such an amendment—such a fee is quite reasonable. Providing notice of tax changes is a special service that is necessary to ensure that all clients' Trusts will continue to work for them regardless of the whims of Congress.

The Estate Plan codifies your Trust and will notify you of any tax change that affects your Trust. When there is a major tax change, the computer in our office searches all of the Trusts and associated provisions drawn up for our clients. The computer identifies which Trusts will be subject to a particular tax change and prints out the name and address of each client who is affected. The clients are then informed that they should have their Trusts amended to take advantage of the particular tax change. Thus, because The Estate Plan's Living Trusts have been logically organized, it is relatively easy to print a standard tax-change amendment, which simply needs to be signed and notarized by each client who needs the change.

Transfer of Deeds

Since legal accuracy is crucial in transferring grant deeds and trust deeds into the name of a Living Trust, any firm offering to create your Living Trust should, as a service, rewrite your deeds. An appropriate fee would be charged for each deed, depending on whether the property is located inside or outside your state of residence, and would pertain to grant deeds, first and second trust deeds, and time-share deeds.

A deed is a formal, legal document. Therefore, transferring a deed into the name of your Living Trust is *not* a do-it-yourself project. Before a deed can be recorded, it must meet *all* of the legal requirements, which vary from county to county and from state to state. Of even greater importance, however, is that, if the deed is not drawn properly, filing the deed may trigger reappraisal of your property in certain states, which will ultimately result in higher taxes! Over the years, I have seen too many do-it-yourself deed transfers go awry—with disastrous results—to be able to recommend such an approach to clients. The few dollars saved are usually spent many times over in time and anguish—and often at the additional expense of an unnecessary tax increase on the property involved.

Annual Upkeep

If you have a well-written Trust, which covers every contingency, and if all of your assets are placed in the Trust, an annual upkeep fee is unnecessary. Many clients seem to be concerned about continued upkeep fees, possibly because they have heard of firms that make such an annual charge. Since no annual accounting or administration needs to be performed, there is simply no ethical reason for charging an annual fee.

If you have a well-written Living Trust, a fee for annual upkeep should be unnecessary.

Our clients are encouraged to call on us for answers to any Trust-related or estate-planning questions or for help in resolving any problems that might arise. Such a service is provided to our clients without charge, since most questions are easily answered and most problems easily resolved. Every once in a while, a client tells me that, for every telephone call made to an attorney, he or she was billed $200! Such charges for Living Trust questions are entirely unnecessary. Years of experience and modern computer technology have shown us that a new era is dawning—offering outstanding Living Trusts and related appropriate services to clients at reasonable rates.

On the other hand, occasionally a client does abuse his or her privilege related to this service. One client brought *twelve pages* of bequests to our office to be included in his Living Trust! Courtesy and consideration should be a two-way street. Under such circumstances, a client should understand that extra services, above and beyond the ordinary, can willingly be accommodated—but for an appropriate additional fee.

Settlement Fee

Many different approaches can be taken in regard to charging clients for settling an estate with a Living Trust. The Estate Plan has not yet charged a client to settle an estate. Because of the extensiveness of our Living Trust and the organizational powers of the Estate Plan Book, it takes our firm less than an hour to settle an estate.

On the other hand, in that one hour, our staff brings to bear a great wealth of experience, and therefore our firm does have a right to be compensated. Some months ago, my wife asked me why I did not charge clients to settle their estates. I responded that being able to settle an estate in only an hour was a continuous testimonial that our Living Trust works in every situation imaginable. Whether our firm will continue to settle an estate for no charge, I do not know.

In contrast, there are several firms that readily charge hefty fees to settle a client's estate, even though the estate is in a Living Trust. I know of one law firm that charges 1 percent of your *total* estate to settle an estate in a Living Trust; another law firm charges one-third of what it would otherwise cost to take the same estate through probate! These fees seem unjustly high.

However, where estate tax needs to be paid (and the Federal Estate Tax Form 706 needs to be filed), the client will likely need assistance. In such a situation, the client should pay an appropriate fee for the assistance needed to comply with the tax-filing requirements.

HIDDEN COSTS

There should be *no* hidden costs, fees, charges, or administrative expenses related to creating a Living Trust!

I am appalled by one particular law firm that advertises extensively and presents seminars to generate clients. The firm tells its clients how much the Trust will cost (not too different from the costs listed in Table 16-1). However, as the firm progresses with the client's new Trust, "hidden" fees start to appear. For example, the firm suddenly advises its client that all property needs to be appraised before it can be placed in the Trust—and the firm "just happens" to have an appraiser whom it recommends. The appraisal fee is $250 per property!

For the life of me, I cannot figure out why, with a properly written Living Trust, you would need to appraise property to place it into the Trust—for any other reason than to generate additional (unjustified) fees.

CLIENT COOPERATION

The prices mentioned in this chapter are realistic only if each client cooperates. Working with most clients is absolutely delightful, but a few people unfortunately take advantage of the relaxed, friendly, low-key approach our firm endeavors to use with them. Abuses, although usually caused by only a very few individuals, can eventually make the Living Trust more expensive for everyone. Consequently, in an effort to keep the cost within reach of everyone, the following suggestions are offered:

Read this book—and understand the Living Trust and its desirable provisions.

Determine the size of your estate—and decide whether you should have an A Trust, an A-B Trust, or an A-B-C Trust. In addition, try to anticipate beforehand whether you should include any tax-saving provisions.

Make your key decisions. Before meeting with the attorney to draw up your Living Trust, give some serious thought to those difficult-to-make decisions:

- Selection of successor trustee(s)
- Selection of executor
- Selection of guardian (where appropriate)
- Selection of beneficiaries
- Desired allocation of Trust assets
- Desired distribution of Trust assets

Keep your appointments—particularly the appointment at which you will sign your Trust documents (referred to as the execution of your Trust), when the Trust becomes a legal entity. Occasionally, a client will call at the last moment to reschedule an appointment to execute the Trust. Since the Trust documents must be specifically dated, the documents must then be reprinted if you change your Trust execution appointment at the last minute. It costs our firm $60 to replace those documents. After too many abuses related to last-minute rescheduling, our firm has finally found it necessary to pass the added cost on to the client who reschedules his or her appointment at the last minute.

Photocopy your personal documents—ahead of time, whenever possible. You should bring copies of such documents as your checkbook and savings account passbooks; stocks, bonds, and mutual funds; life insurance policies; grant deeds for real estate; first and second trust deeds; and titles to other such valuable assets. If you are unable to photocopy your own documents, you should come into the office at least a half-hour ahead of your scheduled appointment, so that the documents can be copied before your appointment. The process of executing your Living Trust typically takes about one hour, but that time does not include the time needed to copy your personal documents.

If you bring copies of your documents at the time you execute your Trust, the job is finished. Too many people execute their Trusts and then never get around to organizing their estates with the Estate Plan Book or transferring all of their assets into their Trusts. By bringing copies of your documents with you, you ensure that everything can be handled at once. Nothing is overlooked or put off until tomorrow, when it is often forgotten.

If you will follow these simple courtesies, then the cost of the Living Trust can be kept reasonably low—ideally within reach of everyone.

IT CAN BE DONE

Admittedly, the comments made in this chapter have entered areas where angels fear to tread. On the other hand, thousands of happy and satisfied clients are proof that a well-written Living Trust, accompanied by the Estate Plan Book (for organizing your estate) and a highly experienced organization (readily available and willing to answer questions, as well as to help settle your estate), produces the right formula for enlightening people about the superiority of the Living Trust.

17

Conclusion

Now that you have read *The Living Trust*, you have become acquainted with the many advantages of a Living Trust, and you have begun to think about how a Living Trust fits into your own situation. You should now be able to determine what type of Trust will best suit your needs and the Trust provisions that are most appropriate for you. You should have some ideas about who should be the successor trustee and how to allocate and distribute your assets upon your death, or upon the death of you and your spouse. Finally, you should be able to differentiate between a good Trust and a poor one.

YOUR CHOICE
Now that you have become familiar with the Living Trust, the next step is up to you. You have three choices to make in establishing your estate plan:

- Do nothing.
- Find a competent attorney on your own.
- Use an attorney referral service.

If, after reading this book, you still think that probate is the better approach to settling your estate, the decision is certainly your prerogative. Everyone should be given the opportunity to go through the agonizing and frustrating process of probate—at least once.

Doing Nothing
Remember that, if you take the do-nothing approach (and such lack of action is an actual decision), you can at least take comfort in knowing that you will be doing the same thing as almost 80 percent of the adult population in the United States. If you do nothing, your state government already has a Will for you, and it is a very complicated legal document that may be very much to your detriment.

I hope, however, that you have wisely elected to preserve your estate. If you are like most people, your attitude may now be that "I have worked hard to build my estate, as meager or as large as it may be, and I would like to have a say in where it goes."

The choice is now yours. This book has shown you the good and the bad sides of passing on your estate to your heirs. Think a moment about what you would leave behind if—God forbid—you were to suddenly die tomorrow.

219

Remember the many benefits that accrue to you, your family, and your heirs when you have a well-written Living Trust and the accompanying documents *and* you have placed all your assets in the Trust.

Searching for a Competent Attorney

If you have decided that the best solution for your estate plan is a Living Trust, then you may go in search of a qualified, experienced, and competent estate-planning attorney. With this book in hand (in particular, the outline in Chapter 8), you are armed with the information that should enable you to identify a qualified attorney who can draw up your Living Trust document.

In today's world, there is a proliferation of inexperienced attorneys who are drawing up poorly written Living Trusts and trying to meet the rapidly increasing demand for this simple solution to the agony of probate. Reputable, experienced attorneys will quickly acknowledge that their Living Trust documents include all of the appropriate and necessary provisions discussed in this book. Inexperienced attorneys will either offer excuses or charge exorbitant fees to cover the time that will be required for research.

Unfortunately, because so few attorneys are knowledgeable enough to create an adequate Living Trust, your search may be long and arduous. It may well be similar to looking for a needle in a haystack.

Using an Attorney Referral Service

If you have difficulty in identifying a qualified attorney, you may wish to contact The Estate Plan's referral service. This service can give you the name of an ethical and competent attorney in your part of the country. These attorneys have been licensed to offer at a reasonable cost the same documents and services described throughout the book. The toll-free numbers for The Estate Plan's referral service are (800) 552-9969 and (800) 292-0223.

As I have said many times and will continue to say, I am an ardent believer that one of the finest gifts one spouse can give another, or that parents can give their children, is a Living Trust.

Appendix A

Comparison of Death Costs: Loving Will vs. Living Trust for Single Person with A Trust

This appendix consists of illustrations that compare death costs for a single person who has a Loving Will to the costs for a single person who has a Living A Trust. The comparisons use the following sizes of estates:

- $100,000
- $200,000
- $300,000
- $400,000
- $500,000
- $600,000
- $800,000
- $1.0 million
- $1.2 million
- $1.5 million
- $2.0 million

Each illustration shows that having a Living Trust rather than a Loving Will provides benefits in the areas of probate, estate taxes, and gain for the heirs.

To use this appendix, find the illustration that most closely corresponds to the size of your own estate, and study the comparison of the two methods of holding assets. For a further explanation of the computations used in the illustrations, please refer to Chapter 4.

Note that all examples assume a probate cost of 8 percent and a federal estate tax equivalent exemption of $600,000.

$100,000 ESTATE

Will	Living Trust
$100,000	$100,000

$8,000   Estimated Death Costs

$92,000 for Heirs $100,000 for Heirs

Gain for Heirs: $8,000

$200,000 ESTATE

Will

Living Trust

$200,000

$200,000

$16,000

Estimated Death Costs

$184,000 for Heirs

$200,000 for Heirs

Gain for Heirs: $16,000

$300,000 ESTATE

Will **Living Trust**

$300,000 $300,000

$24,000   Estimated Death Costs

$276,000 for Heirs $300,000 for Heirs

Gain for Heirs: $24,000

$400,000 ESTATE

Will	**Living Trust**
$400,000	$400,000

$32,000   Estimated Death Costs

$368,000 for Heirs	$400,000 for Heirs

Gain for Heirs: $32,000

$500,000 ESTATE

Will   **Living Trust**

$500,000 $500,000

$40,000   Estimated Death Costs

$460,000 for Heirs $500,000 for Heirs

Gain for Heirs: $40,000

$600,000 ESTATE

Will	Living Trust
$600,000	$600,000

$48,000   Estimated Death Costs

| $552,000 for Heirs | $600,000 for Heirs |

Gain for Heirs: $48,000

$800,000 ESTATE

Will	**Living Trust**
$800,000	$800,000

$115,000   Estimated Death Costs $75,000   Estimated Death Costs

$685,000 for Heirs $725,000 for Heirs

Gain for Heirs: $40,000

$1.0 MILLION ESTATE

Will	Living Trust
$1,000,000	$1,000,000

$200,000   Estimated Death Costs $155,000   Estimated Death Costs

$800,000 for Heirs $845,000 for Heirs

Gain for Heirs: $45,000

$1.2 MILLION ESTATE

Will   Living Trust

$1,200,000 $1,200,000

$290,000   Estimated Death Costs $235,000   Estimated Death Costs

$910,000 for Heirs $965,000 for Heirs

Gain for Heirs: $55,000

$1.5 MILLION ESTATE

Will	Living Trust
$1,500,000	$1,500,000

$430,000   Estimated Death Costs

$360,000   Estimated Death Costs

$1,070,000 for Heirs

$1,140,000 for Heirs

Gain for Heirs: $70,000

$2.0 MILLION ESTATE

Will	Living Trust
$2,000,000	$2,000,000

$680,000   Estimated Death Costs $590,000   Estimated Death Costs

$1,320,000 for Heirs $1,410,000 for Heirs

Gain for Heirs: $90,000

Appendix B

Comparison of Death Costs: Loving Will vs. Living Trust for Married Couple with A Trust

This appendix consists of illustrations that compare death costs for a married couple who have a Loving Will to the costs for a couple who have a Living A Trust. The comparisons use the following sizes of estates:

- $100,000
- $200,000
- $300,000
- $400,000
- $500,000
- $600,000

Each illustration shows that having a Living Trust rather than a Loving Will provides benefits in the areas of probate, estate taxes, and gain for the heirs.

To use this appendix, find the illustration that most closely corresponds to the size of your own estate, and study the comparison of the two methods of holding assets. For a further explanation of the computations used in the illustrations, please refer to Chapter 4.

Note that all examples assume a probate cost of 8 percent and a federal estate tax equivalent exemption of $600,000 per person.

$100,000 ESTATE

Loving Will   **Living Trust**

| $50,000 | $50,000 | $50,000 | $50,000 |

$4,000   Estimated Death Costs

$96,000
Surviving Spouse

$100,000
Surviving Spouse
(Trust A)

Estimated Death Costs $8,000

$88,000 for Heirs

$100,000 for Heirs

Gain for Heirs: $12,000

$200,000 ESTATE

Loving Will   **Living Trust**

$100,000 $100,000 $100,000 $100,000

$8,000   Estimated Death Costs

$192,000
Surviving Spouse

$200,000
Surviving Spouse
(Trust A)

Estimated Death Costs $15,000

$177,000 for Heirs

$200,000 for Heirs

Gain for Heirs: $23,000

$300,000 ESTATE

Loving Will   **Living Trust**

| $150,000 | $150,000 | $150,000 | $150,000 |

$12,000   Estimated Death Costs

| $288,000
Surviving Spouse | $300,000
Surviving Spouse
(Trust A) |

Estimated Death Costs $23,000

| $265,000 for Heirs | $300,000 for Heirs |

Gain for Heirs: $35,000

$400,000 ESTATE

Loving Will   **Living Trust**

$200,000 $200,000 $200,000 $200,000

$16,000   Estimated Death Costs

$384,000
Surviving Spouse

$400,000
Surviving Spouse
(Trust A)

Estimated Death Costs $31,000

$353,000 for Heirs $400,000 for Heirs

Gain for Heirs: $47,000

$500,000 ESTATE

Loving Will   **Living Trust**

$250,000 $250,000 $250,000 $250,000

$20,000   Estimated Death Costs

$480,000
Surviving Spouse

$500,000
Surviving Spouse
(Trust A)

Estimated Death Costs $38,000

$442,000 for Heirs

$500,000 for Heirs

Gain for Heirs: $58,000

$600,000 ESTATE

Loving Will   **Living Trust**

$300,000 $300,000 $300,000 $300,000

$24,000   Estimated Death Costs

$576,000
Surviving Spouse

$600,000
Surviving Spouse
(Trust A)

Estimated Death Costs $46,000

$530,000 for Heirs $600,000 for Heirs

Gain for Heirs: $70,000

Appendix C

Comparison of Death Costs: Loving Will vs. Living Trust for Married Couple with A-B Trust

This appendix consists of illustrations that compare death costs for a married couple who have a Loving Will to the costs for a couple who have a Living A-B Trust. The comparisons use the following sizes of estates:

- $100,000
- $200,000
- $300,000
- $400,000
- $500,000
- $600,000
- $800,000
- $1.0 million
- $1.2 million

Each illustration shows that having a Living Trust rather than a Loving Will provides benefits in the areas of probate, estate taxes, and gain for the heirs.

To use this appendix, find the illustration that most closely corresponds to the size of your own estate, and study the comparison of the two methods of holding assets. For a further explanation of the computations used in the illustrations, please refer to Chapter 4.

Note that all examples assume a probate cost of 8 percent and a federal estate tax equivalent exemption of $600,000 per person.

$100,000 ESTATE

Loving Will		**Living Trust**	
$50,000	$50,000	$50,000	$50,000

$4,000   Estimated Death Costs

$96,000 Surviving Spouse	$50,000 Decedent Spouse (Trust B)	$50,000 Surviving Spouse (Trust A)

Estimated Death Costs $8,000

$88,000 for Heirs	$100,000 for Heirs

Gain for Heirs: $12,000

$200,000 ESTATE

Loving Will   **Living Trust**

| $100,000 | $100,000 | $100,000 | $100,000 |

| $8,000 | Estimated Death Costs

| $192,000 Surviving Spouse | $100,000 Decedent Spouse (Trust B) | $100,000 Surviving Spouse (Trust A) |

Estimated Death Costs | $15,000 |

| $177,000 for Heirs | $200,000 for Heirs |

Gain for Heirs: $23,000

$300,000 ESTATE

Loving Will		**Living Trust**	
$150,000	$150,000	$150,000	$150,000

$12,000   Estimated Death Costs

$288,000 Surviving Spouse	$150,000 Decedent Spouse (Trust B)	$150,000 Surviving Spouse (Trust A)

Estimated Death Costs $23,000

$265,000 for Heirs	$300,000 for Heirs

Gain for Heirs: $35,000

$400,000 ESTATE

Loving Will   **Living Trust**

| $200,000 | $200,000 | $200,000 | $200,000 |

$16,000   Estimated Death Costs

| $384,000 Surviving Spouse | $200,000 Decedent Spouse (Trust B) | $200,000 Surviving Spouse (Trust A) |

Estimated Death Costs $31,000

$353,000 for Heirs $400,000 for Heirs

Gain for Heirs: $47,000

$500,000 ESTATE

Loving Will   **Living Trust**

| $250,000 | $250,000 | $250,000 | $250,000 |

$20,000   Estimated Death Costs

| $480,000
Surviving Spouse | $250,000
Decedent Spouse
(Trust B) | $250,000
Surviving Spouse
(Trust A) |

Estimated Death Costs $38,000

| $442,000 for Heirs | $500,000 for Heirs |

Gain for Heirs: $58,000

$600,000 ESTATE

Loving Will

Living Trust

$300,000

$300,000

$300,000

$300,000

$24,000   Estimated Death Costs

$576,000
Surviving Spouse

$300,000
Decedent Spouse
(Trust B)

$300,000
Surviving Spouse
(Trust A)

Estimated Death Costs $46,000

$530,000 for Heirs

$600,000 for Heirs

Gain for Heirs: $70,000

$800,000 ESTATE

Loving Will   **Living Trust**

$400,000 $400,000 $400,000 $400,000

$32,000   Estimated Death Costs

$768,000
Surviving Spouse

$400,000
Decedent Spouse
(Trust B)

$400,000
Surviving Spouse
(Trust A)

Estimated Death Costs $101,000

$667,000 for Heirs

$800,000 for Heirs

Gain for Heirs: $133,000

$1.0 MILLION ESTATE

Loving Will   **Living Trust**

| $500,000 | $500,000 | | $500,000 | $500,000 |

$40,000   Estimated Death Costs

$960,000
Surviving Spouse

$500,000
Decedent Spouse
(Trust B)

$500,000
Surviving Spouse
(Trust A)

Estimated Death Costs $184,000

$776,000 for Heirs

$1,000,000 for Heirs

Gain for Heirs: $224,000

$1.2 MILLION ESTATE

Loving Will   **Living Trust**

$600,000	$600,000

$600,000	$600,000

$48,000   Estimated Death Costs

$1,152,000
Surviving Spouse

$600,000
Decedent Spouse
(Trust B)

$600,000
Surviving Spouse
(Trust A)

Estimated Death Costs $270,000

$882,000 for Heirs

$1,200,000 for Heirs

Gain for Heirs: $318,000

Appendix D

Comparison of Death Costs: Loving Will vs. Living Trust for Married Couple with A-B-C Trust

This appendix consists of illustrations that compare death costs for a married couple who have a Loving Will to the costs for a couple who have a Living A-B-C Trust. The comparisons use the following sizes of estates:

- $1.5 million
- $2.0 million
- $2.5 million
- $3.0 million
- $4.0 million
- $5.0 million

Each illustration shows that having a Living Trust rather than a Loving Will provides benefits in the areas of probate, estate taxes, and gain for the heirs.

To use this appendix, find the illustration that most closely corresponds to the size of your own estate, and study the comparison of the two methods of holding assets. For a further explanation of the computations used in the illustrations, please refer to Chapter 4.

Note that all examples assume a probate cost of 8 percent and a federal estate tax equivalent exemption of $600,000 per person.

$1.5 MILLION ESTATE

Loving Will	Living Trust

$750,000	$750,000		$750,000	$750,000

$60,000   Estimated Death Costs

Insurance Trust

$1,440,000 Surviving Spouse	$150,000 Q-TIP (Trust C)	$600,000 Decedent Spouse (Trust B)	$750,000 Surviving Spouse (Trust A)

Estimated Death Costs $400,000

Estimated Death Costs $115,000

$1,040,000 for Heirs

$1,385,000 for Heirs

Gain for Heirs: $345,000

$2.0 MILLION ESTATE

Loving Will   **Living Trust**

| $1,000,000 | $1,000,000 | | $1,000,000 | $1,000,000 |

$8,000   Estimated Death Costs

Insurance Trust

$1,920,000
Surviving Spouse

| $400,000 Q-TIP (Trust C) | $600,000 Decedent Spouse (Trust B) | $1,000,000 Surviving Spouse (Trust A) |

Estimated Death Costs $640,000

Estimated Death Costs $320,000

$1,280,000 for Heirs

$1,680,000 for Heirs

Gain for Heirs: $400,000

$2.5 MILLION ESTATE

Loving Will	**Living Trust**

$1,250,000	$1,250,000	$1,250,000	$1,250,000

$100,000	Estimated Death Costs	Insurance Trust

$2,400,000 Surviving Spouse	$650,000 Q-TIP (Trust C)	$600,000 Decedent Spouse (Trust B)	$1,250,000 Surviving Spouse (Trust A)

Estimated Death Costs	$880,000	Estimated Death Costs	$540,000

$1,520,000 for Heirs	$1,960,000 for Heirs

Gain for Heirs: $440,000

$3.0 MILLION ESTATE

Loving Will	**Living Trust**

$1,500,000	$1,500,000	$1,500,000	$1,500,000

$120,000   Estimated Death Costs

Insurance Trust

$2,880,000 Surviving Spouse

$900,000 Q-TIP (Trust C)	$600,000 Decedent Spouse (Trust B)	$1,500,000 Surviving Spouse (Trust A)

Estimated Death Costs $1,140,000

Estimated Death Costs $785,000

$1,740,000 for Heirs

$2,215,000 for Heirs

Gain for Heirs: $475,000

$4.0 MILLION ESTATE

Loving Will   **Living Trust**

| $2,000,000 | $2,000,000 | $2,000,000 | $2,000,000 |

$160,000   Estimated Death Costs

Insurance Trust

$3,840,000
Surviving Spouse

| $1,140,000 Q-TIP (Trust C) | $600,000 Decedent Spouse (Trust B) | $2,000,000 Surviving Spouse (Trust A) |

Estimated Death Costs $1,700,000

Estimated Death Costs $1,320,000

$2,140,000 for Heirs

$2,680,000 for Heirs

Gain for Heirs: $540,000

$5.0 MILLION ESTATE

Loving Will

Living Trust

| $2,500,000 | $2,500,000 | $2,500,000 | $2,500,000 |

$200,000   Estimated Death Costs

Insurance
Trust

$4,800,000
Surviving Spouse

$1,900,000
Q-TIP
(Trust C)

$600,000
Decedent Spouse
(Trust B)

$2,500,000
Surviving Spouse
(Trust A)

Estimated Death Costs $2,260,000

Estimated Death Costs $1,870,000

$2,540,000 for Heirs

$3,130,000 for Heirs

Gain for Heirs: $590,000

Appendix E

Comparison of Death Costs: Testamentary Trust vs. Living Trust for Married Couple with A-B Trust

This appendix consists of illustrations that compare death costs for a married couple who have a Testamentary Trust to the costs for a couple who have a Living A-B Trust. The comparisons use the following sizes of estates:

- $400,000
- $500,000
- $600,000
- $800,000
- $1.0 million
- $1.2 million

Each illustration shows that having a Living Trust rather than a Testamentary Trust provides benefits in the areas of probate, estate taxes, and gain for the heirs.

To use this appendix, find the illustration that most closely corresponds to the size of your own estate, and study the comparison of the two methods of holding assets. For a further explanation of the computations used in the illustrations, please refer to Chapter 4.

Note that all examples assume a probate cost of 8 percent and a federal estate tax equivalent exemption of $600,000 per person.

$400,000 ESTATE

Testamentary Trust   **Living Trust**

| $200,000 | $200,000 | $200,000 | $200,000 |

$16,000   Estimated Death Costs

| $184,000 Decedent Trust | $200,000 Surviving Spouse | $200,000 Decedent Spouse (Trust B) | $200,000 Surviving Spouse (Trust A) |

Estimated Death Costs $16,000

$368,000 for Heirs

$400,000 for Heirs

Gain for Heirs: $32,000

$500,000 ESTATE

Testamentary Trust

Living Trust

$250,000

$250,000

$250,000

$250,000

$20,000   Estimated Death Costs

$230,000
Decedent Trust

$250,000
Surviving Spouse

$250,000
Decedent Spouse
(Trust B)

$250,000
Surviving Spouse
(Trust A)

Estimated Death Costs $20,000

$460,000 for Heirs

$500,000 for Heirs

Gain for Heirs: $40,000

$600,000 ESTATE

Testamentary Trust   **Living Trust**

$300,000	$300,000

$300,000	$300,000

$24,000   Estimated Death Costs

$276,000 Decedent Trust	$300,000 Surviving Spouse

$300,000 Decedent Spouse (Trust B)	$300,000 Surviving Spouse (Trust A)

Estimated Death Costs $24,000

$552,000 for Heirs

$600,000 for Heirs

Gain for Heirs: $48,000

$800,000 ESTATE

Testamentary Trust

Living Trust

| $400,000 | $400,000 | $400,000 | $400,000 |

$32,000   Estimated Death Costs

| $368,000 Decedent Trust | $400,000 Surviving Spouse | $400,000 Decedent Spouse (Trust B) | $400,000 Surviving Spouse (Trust A) |

Estimated Death Costs $32,000

$736,000 for Heirs

$800,000 for Heirs

Gain for Heirs: $64,000

$1.0 MILLION ESTATE

Testamentary Trust   **Living Trust**

| $500,000 | $500,000 | $500,000 | $500,000 |

$40,000   Estimated Death Costs

| $460,000 Decedent Trust | $500,000 Surviving Spouse | $500,000 Decedent Spouse (Trust B) | $500,000 Surviving Spouse (Trust A) |

Estimated Death Costs $40,000

| $920,000 for Heirs | $1,000,000 for Heirs |

Gain for Heirs: $80,000

$1.2 MILLION ESTATE

| **Testamentary Trust** | **Living Trust** |

| $600,000 | $600,000 | $600,000 | $600,000 |

$48,000   Estimated Death Costs

| $552,000 Decedent Trust | $600,000 Surviving Spouse | $600,000 Decedent Spouse (Trust B) | $600,000 Surviving Spouse (Trust A) |

Estimated Death Costs $48,000

$1,104,000 for Heirs

$1,200,000 for Heirs

Gain for Heirs: $96,000

Appendix F

Comparison of Death Costs: Testamentary Trust vs. Living Trust for Married Couple with A-B-C Trust

This appendix consists of illustrations that compare death costs for a married couple who have a Testamentary Trust to the costs for a couple who have a Living A-B-C Trust. The comparisons use the following sizes of estates:

- $1.5 million
- $2.0 million

Each illustration shows that having a Living Trust rather than a Testamentary Trust provides benefits in the areas of probate, estate taxes, and gain for the heirs.

To use this appendix, find the illustration that most closely corresponds to the size of your own estate, and study the comparison of the two methods of holding assets. For a further explanation of the computations used in the illustrations, please refer to Chapter 4.

Note that all examples assume a probate cost of 8 percent and a federal estate tax equivalent exemption of $600,000 per person.

$1.5 MILLION ESTATE

Testamentary Trust

Living Trust

$750,000	$750,000

$750,000	$750,000

$95,000   Estimated Death Costs

$655,000 Decedent Trust	$750,000 Surviving Spouse

$150,000 Q-TIP (Trust C)	$600,000 Decedent Spouse (Trust B)	$750,000 Surviving Spouse (Trust A)

Estimated Death Costs $95,000

Estimated Death Costs $115,000

$1,310,000 for Heirs

$1,385,000 for Heirs

Gain for Heirs: $75,000

$2.0 MILLION ESTATE

Testamentary Trust	Living Trust

$1,000,000	$1,000,000	$1,000,000	$1,000,000

$200,000   Estimated Death Costs

$800,000 Decedent Trust	$1,000,000 Surviving Spouse	$400,000 Q-TIP (Trust C)	$600,000 Decedent Spouse (Trust B)	$1,000,000 Surviving Spouse (Trust A)

Estimated Death Costs $200,000   Estimated Death Costs $320,000

$1,600,000 for Heirs $1,680,000 for Heirs

Gain for Heirs: $80,000

Appendix G

Everything You Always Wanted to Know About the Living Trust—but Were Afraid to Ask

Today, more and more people are beginning to know a little bit about the Living Trust; however, an enormous amount of misinformation about the Living Trust is being disseminated. The American Bar Association says that less than 1 percent of the legal profession understands the Living Trust—and I heartily concur! As more and more people become aware of the agony of probate—and of the much better alternative of the Living Trust—the proliferation of Living Trusts has dramatically reduced the quality of the Trust documents being produced.

To correct the misperceptions and fears caused by misinformation, this chapter answers the questions that people most commonly ask about the Living Trust. The questions, along with their answers, are grouped into the following categories:

- Wills
- Probate
- Joint tenancy
- The Living Trust
- Beneficiaries
- Rights of the surviving spouse
- Amendments to the Living Trust

- Successor trustee
- Requirements
- Taxes
- Assets
- Perceived disadvantages

Although these questions have been answered in more detail in various parts of the book, they are presented here to provide a quick overview of the Living Trust. This compilation of questions and answers is not designed to be a summary of the book, but rather it is structured to go directly to the heart of the most common areas of misinformation and fear.

WILLS

Almost half of the people attending our seminars have been told by some misinformed person that, if they have a Will, their estates will avoid probate. Unfortunately, too many people are unaware of the agony that awaits them. To paraphrase the instructions of a popular board game, "If you have a Will, you must go through probate, you shall not pass Go, and you shall not collect $200."

Q: *What happens if I don't have a Will?*

A: If you die without a Will, then the state automatically provides one for you; it is much more complex for your survivors, and the distribution of your assets may not be as you desired. (See Chapter 4.)

Q: *How is distribution different if I have a Living Trust rather than a Will?*

A: Most people have the "Will syndrome," which means that they believe that all of their assets must be distributed upon their death. Such a belief is correct for a Will, but not for a Living Trust. When you have a Will, once probate is completed, your assets must be immediately distributed outright, since there is no legal entity to hold your assets. However, with a Living Trust, the assets may remain in the Trust almost indefinitely, since the Trust is a legal entity and "lives on" after a person's death. (See Chapter 7.)

Q: *Why didn't my attorney tell me about the Living Trust?*

A: The best answer to this question is to repeat the words of an attorney (previously quoted in this book): "In most states, the only justification for not having a Trust is that the attorney will not get his probate fee." Remember that 8 percent to 10 percent of the gross estate is charged *each time* an individual dies—which is a lot of money! Many practicing attorneys today are not aware of the alternative to probate offered by the Living Trust. (See Chapter 5.)

Q: *Do I need to notify my attorney that I replaced my Will?*

A: There is no need to notify your attorney. When you execute your Trust (and specifically your Pour-Over Will), you revoke any former Wills. (See Chapter 5.)

PROBATE

Frequently, an individual will say, "My spouse died, and I never went through probate." Upon the death of a spouse, no one directs that you must go through probate. You do not *have* to go through probate—until you want to sell an asset that is held in the name of the deceased person. As long as you do not desire to sell anything, you do not need to go through probate. The purpose of probate is to establish clear title, and you must have clear title in order to sell an asset.

For example, assume that, seven years after the death of your spouse, you decide to sell your house. You list the house with a real estate broker, who finds a buyer, and you enter escrow. When escrow is ready to close, you are invited to come into the escrow office to sign over the deed. After you sign your name, the escrow officer says, "We also need to have the signature of your spouse." When you say, "My spouse died seven years ago," the words fall on deaf ears. Escrow immediately stops, the buyer for your home is gone—and you now have to go through probate. The same situation would be true with your stocks, bonds, and other assets.

Q: *My accountant tells me that, since my estate is worth less than $600,000, I don't need a Living Trust. Is this statement really true?*

A: The $600,000 amount has *nothing* to do with probate. The $600,000 amount is your federal estate tax equivalent exemption. This means that, as long as your total estate is valued at less than $600,000, it will not be subject to federal estate tax.

In most states, if the value of your real estate exceeds $10,000 *or* if the amount of your total assets, including personal effects, exceeds $30,000 (in some states the figure is $60,000), your estate must go through probate—unless your estate is in a Living Trust. The greatest advantage of a Living Trust is that it avoids the agony of probate—as well as the unnecessary costs, frustration, and mental anguish that automatically accompany the probate process. (See Chapter 1.)

Q: *Is an attorney required to charge statutory fees for probate?*

A: Statutory fees are those fees established by the state legislature as the theoretical maximum. In most instances (even for the simplest of estates), it is commonplace to begin by charging the statutory fee as the standard fee. Thereafter, "extraordinary fees" are usually added on to the standard fee. Extraordinary fees are simply additional costs submitted by the attorney and approved by the court, usually without any discussion or examination for reasonableness. (See Chapter 1.)

Q: *How can attorneys justify their exorbitant probate fees?*

A: The fees charged by attorneys to take an estate through the probate process often cannot be justified. Many people call the practice just plain greed. The American Bar Association has strongly urged all fifty states to substantially revise their probate codes. However, all fifty states rejected this recommendation—and made virtually no changes to their probate codes. A few states made some modest adjustments and called the changes the "Revised Probate Code."

Today's probate system is unjustifiable. The entire process is running along unchecked, and it has become far too costly and bureaucratic. Eventually, enough people will adopt the Living Trust, and the state legislatures will be forced someday to revise the probate code to a reasonable procedure and a justifiable cost. Until then, your only solution is the Living Trust. (See Chapters 1 and 4.)

Q: *What happens to assets that are outside my Living Trust? Since they pour over into the Trust, must they go through probate?*

A: Any assets that are inadvertently (or intentionally) left outside your Living Trust—and whose value exceeds the probate limits of your particular state—must go through probate. The Pour-Over Will, which is provided for just such a contingency, identifies the executor and gives him or her the necessary power to take the assets through probate. Once the assets have gone through the long, onerous probate process, the assets can then be "poured over" into the Trust. (See Chapter 5.)

JOINT TENANCY

Q: *Can probate be avoided by the use of joint tenancy?*

A: Yes—and no. Joint tenancy can *delay* probate, but it cannot avoid probate altogether. The probate process (but not necessarily the cost)

can be avoided only on the first to die, if you hold your assets in joint tenancy (for example, between husband and wife). However, when the second spouse finally dies, *all* of the assets in the estate must go through the probate process. Consequently, all that you have really accomplished with joint tenancy is to delay the inevitable—ultimately causing your heirs to go through the agonizing probate process. In addition, by holding assets in joint tenancy, you lose half of the stepped-up valuation when the first spouse dies.

If you decide that the way to avoid probate is to go into joint tenancy with your children, any such assets in joint tenancy are subject to any lawsuits to which your children might be a party. The problems with holding property in joint tenancy are covered in detail in Chapter 2.

Q: *In a community property state, why isn't property that is held in joint tenancy treated as community property?*

A: In a community property state, husband and wife each have an *equal* interest in the assets acquired during their marriage. However, everyone has the right of free agency (that is, the right to take his or her assets from community property and place them into joint tenancy). In effect, such an action simply deprives those misinformed individuals of the right to get full stepped-up valuation upon the death of the first spouse. (See Chapter 2.)

Q: *Is there any problem with transferring assets held in joint tenancy into the Living Trust?*

A: Transferring assets held in joint tenancy into a Living Trust causes no problems. Once an asset held in joint tenancy is transferred into the Trust, it is automatically transferred from joint tenancy. (See Chapter 2.)

Q: *What would happen if I owned stock or real estate in joint tenancy with my children?*

A: The answer depends upon how your children acquired their interest in the asset. If the children received the asset by your gift, you should, in effect, take the gift back—and transfer the asset into the Living Trust in *your* name, so that, when that asset passes on to your children upon your death, the asset will receive full stepped-up valuation.

On the other hand, if the children paid for their share of the asset, then only *your* share should be transferred into the Living Trust. However, be aware of a pitfall of such an arrangement with your children. If your children were to die, their share of *your* assets (passed to your children) would then be subjected to the probate process—unless your children have their own Living Trusts. (See Chapter 2.)

THE LIVING TRUST

Q: *Where did this "new idea" of the Living Trust come from, and how long has the Living Trust been in existence?*

A: The Living Trust has been around for 1,200 years! The Living Trust dates back to A.D. 800 as Roman law, and was adopted by the English. The king and the nobles challenged the Living Trust in 1535 in the highest court (the Chancery Court)—and lost! The Living Trust was adopted by the United States when this nation was formed, using English law as the basis of the legal system. The first known Living Trust drawn in the United States was written by Patrick Henry. A more detailed discussion of the Living Trust is presented in Chapter 5.

Q: *When will Congress take away the Living Trust?*

A: Nearly half of my clients are concerned about whether Congress might take away the Living Trust and when that might happen. Almost every one of my clients feels that "Congress is out to get me." (If I were a congressman or a senator, I would be deeply concerned about this lack of confidence on the part of my constituents.)

Basically, Congress has little chance of ever taking away the Living Trust. Two hundred years ago, thirteen states met to form a federal government and, in so doing, created one of the finest documents in existence—the Constitution of the United States of America. In the process of creating this nation, the states relinquished to the federal government certain "states' rights," which are spelled out in the Constitution.

One of these states' rights that was *not* granted to the federal government and that is sacrosanct to the states is the right to create a "legal entity," such as a corporation or Trust. A corporation or a Trust created in one state is recognized by the other states. Congress has little chance of invading this area of states' rights. (See Chapter 5.)

Q: *Is the Living Trust valid in all fifty states?*

A: Yes, the Living Trust is valid in each state and in all commonwealth nations—since the Trust came specifically from English law. The Living Trust should also be valid in most nations that have a civil code. With clients all over the world today, we have found that, by and large, most nations recognize the Living Trust. (See Chapter 5.)

Q: *Is a Living Trust that has been notarized in the United States recognized as a legal document in a foreign country?*

A: The 1961 Hague Convention (which went into effect for the United States in October 1981) abolished the requirements of having to have foreign governments legalize public documents of other nations. In effect, the convention decreed that documents notarized as public documents in a particular country would be recognized as valid documents by the other countries, where both countries are signatories to the Hague Convention. (See Chapter 5.)

Q: *How is a Living Trust named?*

A: The most appropriate way to name a Living Trust is as follows:

The Smith Family Trust, dated August 18, 1988, John J. Smith and Mary Ann Smith, Trustor(s) and/or Trustee(s).

Q: *Is the Living Trust formed by a state in the same manner as a corporation is formed?*

A: Each state has the right to create a legal entity—whether it is a corporation or a Trust. The difference between a corporation and a Trust is that a Trust has neither the red tape nor the taxation of a corporation. The Trust is a very simple legal entity to handle. (See Chapter 5.)

Q: *Where do I register my Living Trust document?*

A: The Living Trust document does not have to be registered anywhere. In fact, on the death of the trustor (or trustors), the only person who has a right to see the Trust document is the successor trustee; no one else has a right to view the document—not even by court subpoena.

The name of the Living Trust is submitted only to the Internal Revenue Service, in order to request a Tax Identification Number for the Trust. Even this step is unnecessary when you first draw up your Trust; however, the number *will* be needed upon the death of a settlor. (See Chapter 5.)

Q: *How long does it take to establish a Living Trust?*

A: With the sophisticated technology available today, the time needed to establish a Living Trust is based upon the client, not the actual time required to create the document itself.

Usually, a client's first visit lasts for about an hour, during which time the advantages of the Living Trust are discussed, as well as the type of Trust the client should have and the provisions that should be included in the Trust. During the first visit, the many options available to the client are also discussed and reviewed, and the important decisions that must be made are identified. Presumably, if you have read this book, you have already made those critical decisions and are ready to proceed. A workbook will be completed in order to prepare the draft documents.

A client usually needs anywhere from two to three weeks to pull together copies of all of his or her assets—to be included in the Estate Plan Book. During this same time period, draft documents of the Trust and the various associated legal documents are printed and then sent to the client—with summaries in plain English—so that the client has the opportunity to review the documents and to understand them.

The client then returns to sign the documents—which legally puts the new Living Trust into effect. From beginning to end, the process typically takes from two to three weeks. However, in urgent situations, the entire process—making the decisions and creating and signing all of the documents—has been completed in less than two hours. (See Chapters 11 and 15.)

Q: *Can a Living Trust be contested in the same manner as a Will?*

A: Yes, anybody can sue a Trust. However, I have yet to learn of any properly drawn Living Trust that has been *successfully* contested. Because a Trust is a "living" document that can be changed as often as desired by the trustors, it is much more difficult for dissident heirs to successfully challenge than is a Will, which is usually written and then placed in a safe-deposit box and forgotten. With a Living Trust, you should have the Trust readily available to you, and you have the right to alter your Trust, right up to the date of your death—and the change will be upheld in court. In contrast, about one-third of the Wills that are contested are successfully challenged—and the Wills are overturned. (See Chapter 4.)

Q: *Can I have a Living Trust if I am unmarried?*

A: Most definitely. If you want to avoid probate, you should have a Living Trust whether you are married or not. (See Chapter 4.)

Q: *Can two unmarried people who are living together create a Living Trust?*

A: It is quite common to create an A-B Trust for an unmarried couple and to identify the individuals' Separate Property Agreements. A Living Trust, with Separate Property Agreements, is particularly appropriate for an unmarried couple when the two individuals have purchased a house together. If the two parties were John Jones and Mary Brown, the Trust would typically be known as the "Jones/Brown Trust Agreement." (See Chapter 5.)

Q: *Can parents create a Living Trust with their children?*

A: Yes, such a Living Trust could be created, but such a situation is most unusual. Parents have their particular goals and objectives, and the children eventually have their own goals and objectives. Since parents and children who are establishing a Trust together must be co-trustees, parents and children both must have common objectives. Such Trusts have been done successfully on a few occasions, but this arrangement is not recommended. (See Chapter 2.)

Q: *Can a Living Trust continue on, generation after generation?*

A: A Living Trust can go on for several generations, but there *is* a time when the Trust must cease to exist. A Living Trust *must* dissolve at some point—but, with the law of perpetuity, the time can be decades away! Typically, the Trust will simply dissolve when all of the assets have been distributed from the Trust.

The law of perpetuity, on the other hand, states that, upon the death of the trustors, every potential heir then living is identified—including children and grandchildren as well as aunts, uncles, nieces, and nephews. Under the law of perpetuity, the Living Trust must cease twenty-one years after the death of the *last* of the potential heirs! I have yet to discover a client who finds the law of perpetuity to be of any concern. (See Chapter 7.)

Q: *Is an A-B Trust actually two different Trusts?*

A: An A-B Trust is one Trust while both spouses are living and even after a spouse dies. The terms *Trust A* and *Trust B* are used to differentiate between the decedent's share of the assets (Trust B) and the survivor's share of the assets (Trust A). Only upon the death of the first spouse does the distinction between the A part of the A-B Trust and the B part have any significance. Other than the A and B parts, which are used to apportion assets, the Living Trust is a single entity. Assets identified as being in the B Trust are thereafter insulated from further estate taxes. (See Chapter 5.)

Q: *What is involved in "settling" an estate in a Living Trust?*

A: The word *settle* is used rather loosely, simply to mean that certain things need to be done upon the death of one or both settlors (creators of the Trust). These steps are identified in the Estate Plan Book under "Final Instructions" and are also covered in more detail in Chapters 11 and 13.

With all of an estate's assets in a Living Trust, the survivor and/or heirs can best perform the tasks required to "settle" the estate themselves—when they fully understand the specific requirements that need to be satisfied.

BENEFICIARIES

It is extremely important for anyone creating a Living Trust to understand that the creator of the Trust, along with all of his or her other rights, is also the beneficiary of that Trust. If a husband and wife create a Living Trust, they are also the beneficiaries of that Trust. Upon the death of the first spouse, the surviving spouse is the beneficiary of the Trust. The primary purpose of the Trust is to do whatever is necessary to provide for the surviving spouse—even if that means exhausting the entire estate in order to adequately provide and care for the surviving spouse.

Most people tend to think of their children as the beneficiaries. However, with a Living Trust, the children are *contingent* beneficiaries. Being a contingent beneficiary means that the children must fulfill two conditions in order to ultimately become beneficiaries. First, the children must be living upon the death of the trustors (the creators of the Trust). Second, there must be assets remaining in the Trust to be distributed to the beneficiaries. If either of these requirements is not met, the children are not considered to be beneficiaries. A more complete discussion of beneficiaries can be found in Chapter 6.

Q: *Can I leave all or part of my estate to an as-yet-unconceived child or grandchild?*

A: Yes, with a Living Trust, it is possible to leave assets to an individual who has not yet been conceived. For instance, a young couple get married and then desire to create a Living Trust. The couple have no children, but husband and wife do have separate property. In anticipation of future children, the husband and wife name their yet-to-be-conceived children as the primary beneficiaries. The language of the Trust states that, if there are no children living upon the death of the settlors, the assets of the estate will thereupon go to the contingent beneficiaries designated—typically to the settlors' brothers and sisters or parents.

In a similar manner, it is quite common to leave a specific amount or a specific percentage of your estate to each of your grandchildren. When you first draw up your Living Trust, you may have only one grandchild; however, as the years pass, you may eventually have many grandchildren. The language of the Trust provides for such a change in the number of grandchildren. (See Chapter 7.)

Q: *If my child dies before me, does his or her spouse become a beneficiary of that child's share of the estate?*

A: The answer is almost always a sound *no*. The deceased child's share of the estate passes on to the children of that child (your grandchildren), whether the children are by blood or adoption. If the deceased child has no children, then the deceased child's share of the estate would be redivided among your other remaining children.

However, your assets do *not* have to be distributed that way. You may leave all or part of your child's share (or whatever portion you desire) to your child's spouse. Most clients desire to pass their assets to those individuals who are related by blood or adoption but seldom by marriage. (See Chapter 7.)

Q: *How do I prevent my assets, destined for my son, from being acquired by his wife if they get divorced?*

A: There are several ways to avoid such an outcome. First of all, recognize that, if you distribute your assets to your son outright, the assets may well become commingled with the community assets of your son and his wife. Thereafter, the assets would be considered community assets in the event of a divorce. Several alternatives could be used to ensure that the assets distributed to your son *remain* as his assets.

First, you could leave all of your assets in trust, with only the income from the assets going to your son; the assets themselves would then pass on to your grandchildren upon your son's eventual death. Such assets in your Trust would never be subject to divorce claims of your son's wife.

Second, you could distribute the assets to your son as a deferred distribution—one-third outright, one-third in five years, and one-third in ten years. This practice assumes that the longer your son and his wife are married, the greater the possibility is that they will remain married.

The third, and most logical, approach would be for your son to have a Living Trust of his own. Then, upon receipt of those assets being distributed to him, he would establish them as separate property, under Separate Property Agreements within his own Trust. If there should eventually be a divorce, in most circumstances, the court would recognize these separate assets as distinctly belonging to the son. (See Chapter 9.)

Q: *What happens if my daughter divorces or remarries and changes her name?*

A: One of the nice aspects of a properly written Living Trust is that your daughter's name does not make any difference. In your Trust, you have identified your children in your Pour-Over Will as your children. No matter what name the children may go by in the future, they are still your children. You need not change any of the children's names in your Living Trust. (See Chapter 5.)

Q: *Can I make a gift to charity through my Living Trust?*

A: Yes, you may designate a charity to be the recipient of assets in your estate. The Living Trust that is drawn up for our clients includes a "Schedule B" where the client can simply indicate each charity and the percentage of distribution that is desired. (See Chapter 7.)

Q: *Can I use a Living Trust for my handicapped child?*

A: I believe that the *only* way by which you can adequately provide for your handicapped child is with a Living Trust! This special situation is provided in all Living Trusts drawn up for our clients. Specific language is used to ensure that the well-being of the handicapped individual is protected. The language of the provision will protect your handicapped child's share of the estate from being acquired by a federal agency and will also prevent jeopardizing the ability to receive government benefits that would otherwise be available to that handicapped child. (See Chapter 7.)

Q: *How do I exclude children as beneficiaries of my Living Trust?*

A: All of your children are identified in your Pour-Over Will—which clearly establishes, from a legal standpoint, that you have not overlooked anyone. Since the Living Trust is a contract, you simply exclude (in the allocation and distribution sections of the Trust) those children whom you do not want to be included as beneficiaries. You do *not* have to state in writing, "I leave this child one dollar and no more." (See Chapter 7.)

Q: *Can I provide for my pets in my Living Trust?*

A: Yes, a well-written Trust can provide for the continued care of your beloved pets after you are gone. It is suggested that you find someone whom you trust and then leave an incentive, whether it is money, the right to live in your home, or something to that effect, for that person to provide for your pets. However, I do not recommend that you select your favorite veterinarian and then leave him or her $20,000 to provide for your pet. All too often, when family or friends later inquire as to the whereabouts of the pet or pets, they are rebuffed. Where are the pets? Are they still alive?

One couple solved the problem of caring for their pet by suggesting that a young man down the street would be more than happy to take care of the dog for the rest of its life, giving this young neighbor a gift of $10,000 toward his education. (See Chapter 7.)

RIGHTS OF THE SURVIVING SPOUSE

A well-written Living Trust ensures that the surviving spouse continues to have almost all of the same rights as when both spouses were alive. Special provisions in the Trust assure that the surviving spouse cannot be deprived of the

right to remain in the family home as long as he or she is still living.

However, clients often have the misperception that, when one of the spouses dies, the rights of the surviving spouse are drastically reduced. Remember that, even when both spouses are alive, the Living Trust allows either of the trustees to act independently on behalf of the Trust. Therefore, when one spouse dies, the other trustee can continue to act on behalf of the Trust.

Q: *What are the rights of the surviving spouse as trustee?*

A: As the surviving trustee, the surviving spouse continues to retain the same rights as before—the power (without restriction) to buy, sell, and transfer any or all of the assets in the Trust. However, the rights of the surviving trustee may be restricted by the settlors when they create their Living Trust or, thereafter, by amending the Trust while both settlors are still living. (See Chapters 5 and 6.)

Q: *What are the beneficial rights of the surviving spouse to the Decedent's Trust B?*

A: At every seminar, at least one attendee wants to know why the surviving spouse is entitled to only 5 percent or $5,000 of the Decedent's B Trust each year. All too often, people only seem to hear this particular right of the surviving spouse, while entirely missing the other rights—which are, by far, the most important!

The surviving spouse is the beneficiary of the Decedent's B Trust (and the Decedent's C Trust, where appropriate). The tax code specifically provides that the surviving spouse has three rights:

- The right to *all* of the income (from the B Trust)
- The right to all of the principal (in the B Trust) that is necessary to maintain the *same* standard of living as before the decedent passed away
- The right to $5,000 or 5 percent of the assets in the B Trust, whichever is greater, once a year—for any reason, regardless of how frivolous

These three rights in effect give the surviving spouse the right to use the funds in the Decedent's B Trust without restriction. In fact, the only real restriction is "the right to use the principal to maintain the same standard of living." Who is responsible for determining the standard of living? Why, of course, the trustee is responsible for making that determination. Who is the trustee? Usually, the surviving spouse is the trustee. Therefore, there really is no restriction!

However, the one thing that the surviving spouse *cannot* do is to change the beneficiaries designated in the Decedent's B Trust or to jeopardize the beneficiaries' rights to the assets in the Decedent's B Trust. Such a restriction is very appropriate when a husband and wife have been married before and each have children from former marriages. Specifically, the surviving spouse may not reach into the B Trust, take out $200,000, go to Las Vegas, and then gamble away the money. The decedent's children have a right to say, "Mother, you effectively took that $200,000 from *your* side—the Survivor's A Trust." The surviving spouse also does not have the right to reach into the Decedent's B Trust, take out funds, and move them to the A Trust—so that, upon the death of the surviving spouse, a greater share of the estate will go to the heirs of the surviving spouse. (See Chapter 5.)

Q: *What are the rights of the surviving spouse to the assets in Trust A?*

A: Since the assets in the Survivor's Trust A are the assets of the surviving spouse, the surviving spouse may do anything desired with these assets—including being able to remove the assets from the Trust entirely. (See Chapter 5.)

Q: *If the surviving spouse relinquishes the position of trustee, can he or she regain the position at a later time?*

A: The surviving spouse is always given the right to relinquish trusteeship; however, the surviving spouse retains the right to take back (reassume) the trusteeship, as well as to name a different successor trustee. (See Chapter 6.)

Q: *Can the surviving spouse change the successor trustee(s)?*

A: Unless the wording of the Trust is modified to exclude such a right, the surviving spouse may change the successor trustee or successor trustees at any time. (See Chapter 6.)

AMENDMENTS TO THE LIVING TRUST

A Living Trust is a *revocable* Trust, which means that the Trust may be changed whenever the clients desire. A change to the Trust is legally called an amendment. Typical changes to a Living Trust would be a change of a beneficiary, a change of a successor trustee, or a change to a method of allocation and/or distribution. Those items are changes to your *plan*.

On the other hand, changes of assets—to buy, sell, or transfer an asset—are not "changes" to your Living Trust; these changes are actually the process of managing your assets. Simply tell your stockbroker that you want to sell a particular stock or that you want to buy some stock (and, by the way, put ownership in the name of the Trust). In a similar manner, if you buy a piece of real estate, simply have the deed recorded in the name of your Trust. Such changes of assets are *not* changes to your plan.

You may change your Living Trust as often as you want—even every day or every week. However, it is a good idea to review your Trust at least every five years and to formally amend your Trust for any changes you might have made in the interim.

A more detailed discussion of making changes to the Living Trust is presented in Chapter 5.

Q: *Is it difficult to change my Living Trust, and when would I want to make a change to my Living Trust?*

A: It is a simple matter to make an amendment to your Living Trust. Typically, there are two types of changes you would want to make to your Trust. One type of change involves making a change to your plan, such as a change of a beneficiary, a change of method of distribution, or a change of successor trustee. You should review your Trust every five years to see whether it needs this type of modification.

The second type of change involves amending your Trust to keep it current with estate tax laws authorized by Congress. If a particular tax change would benefit your estate, you would obviously want to incorporate such a change into your Trust. (See Chapter 16.)

Q: *Do I ever need to update my Living Trust?*

A: You should periodically review and update your Living Trust. As mentioned previously, you should review your Trust every five years. Circumstances change, and no one can really look ahead clearly for a time span of five years or more. (See Chapters 5 and 7.)

Q: *Can my successor trustee make changes to my Living Trust?*

A: Upon your death (if you are single), or upon the death of both husband and wife (if you are married), the right to change *any* part of that Living Trust ceases. The successor trustee may not make any changes whatsoever in the Trust document. Instead, the successor trustee is under a fiduciary responsibility to fulfill every requirement spelled out in that Trust. (See Chapter 6.)

Q: *What happens to my Living Trust if I get divorced?*

A: Unfortunately, a Living Trust cannot, in all practicality, be cut in half. Therefore, one individual usually retains the Trust, and the other individual must revoke his or her interest in the Trust. The party who retains the Trust will retain his or her assets in the name of the Trust, and the other party will remove his or her assets from the Trust and revoke his or her interest in the Trust. Such an action is accomplished by executing a Disclaimer of Trust Interest form. (See Chapter 5.)

Q: *What happens to my Living Trust if I remarry?*

A: The answer to this question depends somewhat on the age of the individuals. If you are young and still building your estate, it would be most appropriate to include your new spouse in the existing Living Trust. It would also be appropriate to identify each individual's separate property, by including Separate Property Agreements in the Trust. Using this approach, your new spouse would become trustor, settlor, trustee, and beneficiary.

If you are older and have, in essence, finished building your estate, it may be more appropriate to simply retain the Trust in its existing form and not to include your new spouse in the Trust. Such occurrences are quite common when an individual is in his or her seventies or eighties, is retired, and is a widow or widower. Since the original spouse has died, the B Trust is now irrevocable. Although the new spouse could be included within the Survivor's A Trust, it is much simpler just to retain the assets in the Trust, as is. In this situation, the new spouse should then have a separate Trust for his or her own assets.

When two older individuals have remarried and are living in the home previously occupied by one of them, another important aspect of the Trust comes to light. It is most important that the owner of the home in which both parties are residing make an appropriate amendment to his or her Trust to ensure that the surviving spouse is allowed to remain in that home during his or her lifetime. (See Chapter 9.)

Q: *How does the Living Trust dissolve, and is there any probate at that time?*

A: Once all of the assets are distributed from the Living Trust, the Trust is effectively dissolved. There will be no probate if all of the assets had been in the Living Trust. Once all the assets are removed from the Trust, you may take the Trust document and put it up on a shelf or dispose of it in any manner. (See Chapter 5.)

Q: *Can I revoke my Living Trust?*

A: The creators of the Living Trust always reserve the right to revoke the Trust at any time. However, I have yet to learn of a valid reason to revoke a Trust. The easiest way to revoke an entire Living Trust, although such action is discouraged, is simply to transfer *all* of the assets from the Trust. (See Chapter 5.)

SUCCESSOR TRUSTEE

The successor trustee is the individual (or individuals) who assumes management of the Living Trust upon the death, incompetence, or resignation of the trustors (creators of the Trust).

The most logical parties for consideration as successor trustee or successor trustees are one or more of your adult children, close family members, or close friends. Only under the most unusual circumstances should a financial institution be considered as successor trustee.

Q: *Should my children read my Living Trust?*

A: It is not necessary for your children to read your Living Trust, and in many cases they would most likely be confused by it. However, it would certainly make sense to advise your children that you have a Living Trust. Depending upon how close you are to your children, you may want to apprise them of what you want to accomplish with your Living Trust, particularly where special circumstances are involved (such as caring for a handicapped individual).

In most instances, however, I do not recommend to clients that they share the contents of their Living Trust with their children. Although such a recommendation may sound strange, there is valid logic behind it. When the contents of the Living Trust document are not shared with future heirs, the settlors feel much more at ease in altering the document at any time and for any reason—without feeling guilty or feeling a compunction to explain the reasons behind the changes to their Trust. A Living Trust is a document created to meet the needs of the *settlors*; the document belongs to them, to do with it as they see fit, and no one else really needs to know its contents.

However, always be sure to tell your successor trustee or successor trustees where your Estate Plan Book and Living Trust documents are located, in the event that something happens to you. It would also be appropriate to inform the successor trustee of the name and address (or telephone number) of the firm that drew up your Trust documents, so that, if there were a fire or for some reason the Trust documents could not be located, the successor trustees would know where to get a duplicate copy of the Trust documents. (See Chapter 11.)

Q: *How old must a child be in order to be a successor trustee?*

A: The minimum age for a successor trustee is eighteen years. (See Chapter 6.)

Q: *How is the successor trustee forced to abide by the wishes of the creators of the Living Trust?*

A: To me, the greater part of the word *trustee* is *trust*. Consequently, a trustee should be someone whom you trust. Two or three children acting together as successor co-trustees can often be better than only one child, particularly when there is a question about the proper way to handle various aspects of the estate. Successor co-trustees tend to monitor each other. Every parent should have his or her children read the section of this book titled "Successor Trustee" in Chapter 6, so that each of them understands his or her fiduciary responsibility as successor trustee.

Q: *Are the successor trustees personally liable for the debts of the Living Trust?*

A: The successor trustees are *not* responsible (liable) for debts attributable to the Living Trust. A creditor has a claim solely against the assets of the *Trust*—not against the trustees (assuming, of course, that the successor trustees have acted in good faith and have not abused their capacity as successor trustees). If, on the other hand, a successor trustee has illegally appropriated funds from the Trust, then a creditor would obviously have a right to those funds.

If the liabilities in the Living Trust exceed the value of the assets in the Trust, the successor trustees are *not* responsible for making good on those debts. (See Chapter 6.)

REQUIREMENTS

A frequent fear of many people concerns the "requirements" of the Living Trust; in other words, what restrictions would be placed on an individual or on the control of his or her assets if the assets were in a Living Trust? Frankly, your control over your assets does not change one iota, whether you have your assets inside or outside a Living Trust.

Q: *Is there a federal or state agency that watches over Living Trusts?*

A: No federal or state agency "watches over" the trustees of a Living Trust (either surviving trustees or successor trustees). In other words, Big Brother is *not* watching over you.

Q: *Are there any restrictions on how the surviving spouse can use the estate?*

A: Remember that a surviving spouse has the right to do anything he or she desires with the Survivor's A Trust, because that part of the Trust is solely under his or her personal direction. In addition, in an A-B Trust, the surviving spouse typically has the right to *all* of the income from the Decedent's B Trust, the right to the principal of the B Trust (as necessary to maintain the same standard of living), and also the right of 5 percent of the assets in the B Trust or $5,000 (whichever is greater) once a year for any reason, regardless of how frivolous. The children, on the other hand, are specifically restricted to the provisions of the Trust, and they must adhere to the provisions without any alteration whatsoever. (See Chapter 5.)

TAXES

When an individual dies, two types of taxes suddenly make an appearance. The first type is the combination of federal estate tax and state inheritance tax. The second type, the yearly income tax, will also take its bite one more time. Under the concept of the federal estate tax, Uncle Sam says that he is in business with you; however, upon your death, he wants out, and he wants his interest right now. Congress has decreed, to everyone's benefit (at least at the present), that each person has a federal estate tax equivalent exemption of $600,000.

As long as the total value of an estate is under $600,000, Uncle Sam will not get any estate taxes at all. If you are married and have done *proper* estate planning (have a Living Trust), Uncle Sam will not get any estate taxes upon the first spouse to die. However, once the federal estate tax equivalent exemptions have been exhausted ($600,000 for a single person and $1.2 million for a married couple), Uncle Sam will eventually get his share. If you are single, the tax rate begins at 37 percent of every dollar beyond $600,000. If you are married, the tax rate begins at 40 percent of every dollar beyond

$1.2 million. The tax rate rises to 50 percent at $2.5 million and then to 55 percent at $3 million! For estates valued above $3 million, a surtax is also imposed.

What is most important to emphasize, though, is that the tax is on the estate—not on the heirs. Strangely, although the states justify their inheritance tax based on the right of the asset to pass to the heirs, in fact, the tax is imposed upon the estate (and paid by the estate) *before* any distribution is made to the heirs. Once the taxes are paid, the assets pass to the heirs and are thereafter free of any estate taxes.

Income will continue to be paid, as earned, on investments. The Living Trust may pay the income to the heirs, and the heirs must include such income on their personal income tax returns. If the Trust is irrevocable, the Trust may retain the income in trust, and the trustee must then file a Trust income tax return, including any Trust income in the Trust tax return.

Q: *What is a Q-TIP Trust?*

A: The term *Q-TIP Trust* stands for "Qualified Terminal Interest Property" Trust, which is simply an extension of the Living Trust created to hold any part of the decedent's assets that exceed the $600,000 limit (one federal estate tax equivalent exemption) usually placed in the Decedent's Trust B.

Even though such a long name sounds imposing, the Q-TIP Trust (also referred to as a C Trust) allows taxes on a large estate to be deferred until both spouses have died. For example, if you are married, have an A-B-C Trust, have an estate that exceeds $1.2 million, and if the surviving spouse has the right to the income of the assets in the Q-TIP Trust, then the surviving spouse has the right to elect to defer paying any taxes upon the death of the first spouse. (See Chapter 4.)

Q: *What is the Unlimited Marital Deduction, and how does it differ from the federal estate tax equivalent exemption?*

A: In 1981, Congress created what is called the Unlimited Marital Deduction, which gives a spouse the right to gift all of his or her assets to his or her surviving spouse without any gift or estate tax impact.

Generally speaking, the Unlimited Marital Deduction applies to a husband and wife who do not have a Living Trust. One spouse can, in effect, gift all of his or her assets to the other spouse.

On the other hand, if a husband and wife are astute enough to have a Living Trust, the Unlimited Marital Deduction does not apply—but the provisions of a well-written Trust provide essentially the same advantages with the Decedent's B Trust and, where appropriate, the C Trust.

The Decedent's Trust B and the C Trust allow people to put their assets in trust and gift the income from those assets to the surviving spouse (as well as the rights to those assets for life, as described in Chapters 4 and 5), and no federal estate tax will be computed until the death of the second spouse.

The Unlimited Marital Deduction can be both a blessing and a disadvantage. For example, if you have a Loving Will (instead of a Living Trust) and an estate whose value exceeds $600,000, by passing all of your assets to the surviving spouse with the Unlimited Marital Deduction, you effectively throw away one of the federal estate tax equivalent exemptions. (This subject is more fully discussed in Chapter 4.)

The federal estate tax equivalent exemption is comparable to exempting $600,000 for *each* spouse from federal estate taxes. Thus, if you have a Loving Will and an estate that exceeds $600,000 and if you pass the entire estate to your surviving spouse, you throw away one of your federal estate tax equivalent exemptions.

If, on the other hand, you have an A-B Trust, you preserve the federal estate tax equivalent exemptions of *both* spouses and, therefore, can have an estate valued at up to $1.2 million before any federal estate taxes must be paid. (See Chapter 4.)

Q: *How do I file an income tax return with a Living Trust?*

A: In 1981, Congress specifically mandated that a Trust tax return (Form 1041) should *not* be filed for a revocable Trust (that is, a Living Trust). However, upon the death of a spouse, one-half of an A-B Trust becomes irrevocable, and the surviving spouse must then file a Trust tax return.

With a Living Trust, the Trust tax return should be nothing more than an information return, because all of the income is usually paid out from the Trust. (See Chapter 5 for a more in-depth discussion of this subject.)

If you are single, your Living Trust becomes irrevocable upon your death. In the same manner, if you are married, the Trust becomes irrevocable upon the death of both husband and wife. If any assets are retained in trust, a Trust tax return must be filed each year. The tax return shows the income of the Trust and the income paid out. Any income that is retained in the Trust is taxable to the Trust. Therefore, you compute the taxes on the income and pay the taxes due, since the Trust is treated as a separate tax entity. (See Chapter 5.)

Q: *Can a Living Trust shelter my income from income taxes?*

A: A Living Trust does not in any way act as a tax shelter for income taxes. A revocable Trust is transparent, because the Internal Revenue Service says that, as long as the Trust is revocable, there is no impact upon income tax. You must continue to file your income tax return (the normal Form 1040 individual tax return) as you have in the past.

Upon the death of a spouse, the decedent's half of an A-B Trust becomes irrevocable and is thereafter treated as a special tax entity. Under current tax laws, filing a Trust tax return for the Decedent's B Trust provides no income tax advantage. (See Chapter 5.)

Q: *Will I lose any of my income tax deductions by placing my assets in a revocable Living Trust?*

A: No, tax deductions are *not* lost by placing your assets in a Living Trust. A Living Trust is transparent as far as income is concerned. A revocable Trust has absolutely no impact upon income taxes from either an income or expense viewpoint. With a Living Trust, you will continue to file your Form 1040 Individual Income Tax Return, as you have in the past. (See Chapter 5.)

Q: *Is the cost of a Living Trust tax deductible?*

A: Yes, the cost of creating a Living Trust is tax deductible. However, you must first subtract the cost of the Pour-Over Wills, which, though minimally priced, are *not* tax deductible. Innumerable tax cases have clearly established that the cost of a Living Trust for "estate tax planning" purposes is tax deductible. However, such a tax deduction comes under "Miscellaneous Expenses," and, because of the 1986 tax code, miscellaneous expenses must exceed 2 percent of your adjusted gross income in order to have any effect.

Q: *If I put my home in a Living Trust, can I still deduct my mortgage interest?*

A: Since a revocable Living Trust has no impact upon income taxes and since you are still in control of your assets, you will continue to file your income and expenses—including your mortgage interest—on your Form 1040 income tax return, as you have done in the past. (See Chapter 5.)

Q: *Do I place rental properties in my Living Trust, and, if so, how is the rent treated?*

A: Yes, you should put your rental properties into your Living Trust. The rental income will be recorded on your Form 1040, just as before, as will the depreciation expense on your rental real estate. (See Chapter 5.)

Q: *Will having a Living Trust affect my social security benefits?*

A: A Living Trust will have no impact on your social security benefits. Social security benefits are considered income, and the Living Trust has no effect upon income received. (See Chapter 5.)

ASSETS

When assets are transferred from an individual or individuals and placed in the name of the Living Trust, the process involves simply changing the title (ownership) of the asset to the name of the Trust. The individual who *controls* those assets has not changed at all. In other words, you retain the same control over your assets once they are in the Trust, in exactly the same manner as before you had placed the assets in the Trust.

Q: *Is it costly to transfer assets into the Living Trust?*

A: Except for real estate deeds, transferring assets into a Living Trust should have no cost. Legal counsel should transfer real estate deeds, unless you specialize in this particular area. The cost of transferring deeds should be nominal (less than $100). All other assets can be transferred by letter of transfer, and no fee should be charged. Stocks and bonds typically should be transferred by your stockbroker, as a service to you, without fee. In some instances, there may be a small charge to transfer stocks and bonds into the name of your Trust. Overall, the cost of transferring your assets into the Trust should be minimal. (See Chapter 12.)

Q: *Who transfers the assets into the Living Trust?*

A: With the exception of your grant deeds and trust deeds (which should be transferred by legal counsel), you can easily transfer the assets into the Trust yourself by using the appropriate transfer letters. (See Chapter 12.)

Q: *Can I transfer my assets from my Living Trust?*

A: The settlor is the individual who places the assets into the Trust, and this same individual (or individuals) has the absolute right to also transfer those assets from the Trust or do whatever is desired with those assets. (See Chapter 12.)

Q: *Can I sell my assets once they are in a Living Trust?*

A: You have exactly the same control over your assets—the right to buy, sell, or transfer the assets—when they are in the Trust as you did when the assets were outside the Trust. (See Chapter 6.)

Q: *What do I do with the cash I receive from the sale of my home, which is in my Living Trust?*

A: Until you are ready to make another investment, you should place the proceeds from the sale of your home in a savings account that is already in the name of the Living Trust. It is extremely important that you do *not* place such a large amount of money in your checking account—which is usually outside your Living Trust. If you do so and you or your spouse dies, those funds in your checking account outside your Trust *must* go through probate! (See Chapter 12.)

Q: *How are assets acquired after my Living Trust is created?*

A: Acquiring assets after you have a Living Trust is done just as easily as before. Simply tell your real estate broker, stockbroker, or bank officer to record title to the asset in the name of your Living Trust. It really *is* that simple! (See Chapter 12.)

Q: *What should be inside my Living Trust?*

A: For your Living Trust to be effective, *every* asset must be inside your Trust, with two minor exceptions. For convenience, it is suggested that your checking accounts be kept outside the Trust, as long as the accounts collectively remain under $30,000. As a general rule, your average-priced automobile can also be left outside the Trust, because automobiles are usually exempted from probate, since they are under the jurisdiction of the motor vehicle code. (See Chapter 12.)

Q: *Do I need to change ownership of my stocks and bonds?*

A: Absolutely! *All* of your assets, with two exceptions—checking accounts (as long as they collectively remain under $30,000) and automobiles—must be recorded in the name of your Living Trust, in order to avoid probate. (See Chapter 12.)

Q: *Do I need to transfer ownership of stocks and bonds that are held in street name?*

A: Yes, stocks held in street name also should be transferred. Simply have your brokerage account changed to the name of your Living Trust. (See Chapter 12.)

Q: *Will my homeowners policy be affected by the Living Trust, and do I need to notify my insurance company?*

A: Your homeowners insurance policy will automatically follow the asset. Thus, your homeowners insurance policy need not be placed in the name of your Living Trust, nor do you need to advise your insurance company of the change in ownership (that is, putting the house into the Trust). (See Chapter 5.)

Q: *Will I lose my $125,000 exemption on my home if it is in a revocable Living Trust?*

A: No, you will not lose your homeowners exemption by placing your home in the name of the Living Trust. However, if you have an A-B Trust and a spouse dies—and you are planning to utilize this $125,000 once-in-a-lifetime exemption—it is recommended that you retain the house in the Survivor's A Trust rather than putting the home in the irrevocable Decedent's Trust B. (See Chapter 5.)

Q: *Should I transfer my mortgage into the Living Trust?*

A: Transferring your mortgage into the Living Trust is not necessary, because liabilities follow assets. You are transferring your assets, not the liabilities associated with those assets. (See Chapter 5.)

Q: *If I place my home in the Living Trust, will it affect my mortgage? Can the mortgage company "call" my mortgage?*

A: There is no effect on your mortgage when you place your home inside the Living Trust. Many clients are concerned about the change of ownership in their property when it is placed in the name of the Trust. Such a change of ownership does *not* trigger the "entire balance due and payable" clause in many mortgages—because the same individuals continue to maintain control of the real estate. (See Chapters 5 and 12.)

Q: *By placing my home inside the Living Trust, will I cause my home to be reappraised under California's Proposition 13 or similar property tax rollback provisions in other states?*

A: No, your home will not be reappraised by placing it in your Living Trust. Four months after Proposition 13 was passed, for example, the California state legislature specifically addressed the issue of reappraisal and legislated (by Constitutional article) that your real estate would not be reappraised under Proposition 13 if you place your home or other real estate into a revocable Living Trust. You also avoid reappraisal in other states that have similar property tax rollback provisions. (See Chapter 12.)

Q: *Do I have to value my assets as they go into the Living Trust?*

A: Valuation of your assets before putting them into a Living Trust is totally unnecessary. Such an action would accomplish nothing useful or legally required. The only time you need to value your assets would be upon the death of one of the settlors, at which time the new valuation would be needed to substantiate stepped-up valuation. Obtaining a current valuation when a settlor dies is extremely important. (See Chapter 12.)

Q: *Should my personal effects be placed inside the Living Trust?*

A: Years of experience have shown that it is better to transfer your personal effects into the Living Trust. A document entitled "Assignment of Furniture, Furnishings, and Personal Effects," which is provided to all of our clients, is used to transfer all untitled assets (such as furniture, appliances, furnishings, antiques, artworks, china, silverware, glass, jewelry, books, wearing apparel, and so on) into the Trust. By transferring all of the personal effects into the Trust, you eliminate any future conflict among the heirs. (See Chapter 9.)

Q: *Should I put my safe-deposit box in the name of my Living Trust?*

A: It is not necessary to put your safe-deposit box in the name of the Living Trust. However, such an action is good preventive medicine. Therefore, to be on the conservative side, you may wish to put your safe-deposit box in the name of the Trust. (See Chapter 12.)

Q: *Is there anything that I should* not *put into the Living Trust?*

A: As mentioned earlier, you may wish to keep your checking accounts (as long as they remain collectively under $30,000) and your automobiles of moderate value outside your Living Trust. Everything else must go into the Trust, in order to avoid probate. (See Chapter 12.)

Q: *Should an expensive car go into the Living Trust?*

A: Any automobile of unusually high value should, as a matter of prudence, be recorded in the name of the Living Trust. The motor vehicle department will make such a transfer for you. All you need to do is fill out a simple form. As a precautionary measure, you should record in the name of the Trust any vehicle that exceeds $20,000 in value. (See Chapter 12.)

Q: *Do I put recreational vehicles and boats into the Living Trust?*

A: Yes, such items should be put into the Living Trust, because they are usually of substantial value. Putting such items into the Trust acts as a precautionary measure against the possibility of probate. (See Chapter 12.)

Q: *Can I borrow against my assets in my Living Trust?*

A: Whether your assets are inside or outside your Trust, your ability to borrow money against them (that is, use the assets as collateral for a loan) has not been affected in any way. (See Chapter 7.)

Q: *Can I pledge my Living Trust as collateral for a loan?*

A: Pledging your Living Trust as collateral for a loan does not satisfy lenders. You may pledge your assets, but not your Trust. Think about the question from the viewpoint of the lender: If you have control over your Living Trust and pledge your Living Trust as collateral, the lending institution has no assurance that you would not withdraw those assets from the Living

Trust, leaving the lending institution with a Living Trust that contains no assets. (See Chapter 6.)

Q: *Should my life insurance policies be placed inside the Living Trust?*

A: Your Living Trust should be the beneficiary of all of your life insurance policies. By making your Trust the beneficiary of all policies, you will avoid probate, regardless of who may die simultaneously with the insured person. If your Trust is *not* the beneficiary of your life insurance policies (and you and the beneficiary die simultaneously), the insurance money must go through probate before the money can pass from the now-deceased beneficiary to any heirs.

It always makes good sense to name your Living Trust as the recipient of all of your beneficial assets. Then, in the future, when you want to make any type of change, you need only change the Trust instrument, and not each of the policies. (See Chapter 12.)

Q: *Should I put IRAs and Keoghs inside the Living Trust?*

A: The Living Trust should be the *contingent beneficiary* of IRAs and Keoghs. The Living Trust should never be the *owner* of your IRAs or Keoghs, because that is comparable to an outright distribution. (See Chapter 12.)

Q: *What happens if one or both spouses have separate property?*

A: In the case where husband and/or wife have separate property, the spouses should use Separate Property Agreements when their assets are placed in the Living Trust. The separate property will go into the Trust in the Trust name, but the assets will retain the characteristics of separate property. (See Chapter 9.)

Q: *Is there any circumstance where I should keep any assets outside the Living Trust, so they can be probated?*

A: Only in a rare situation would it be necessary to keep assets outside the Living Trust in order that they can be probated. If you think that your estate might ultimately be subject to a

liability suit, then it might well be appropriate to leave certain assets outside the estate, which can then be probated. Although such situations are infrequent, this approach is appropriate for successful real estate developers, some doctors, and some very well-known people of high public exposure.

Even though the probate process may be long and arduous, the probate court looks at civil suits in a very different manner. The objective of the probate court is to dispatch any civil claim as swiftly as possible; settlement is typically completed within a four-month period and without a jury. In contrast, civil suits can be dragged through the courts for as long as five years. The one advantage of the probate courts in such situations is that it effectively shortstops a potentially long civil suit. (See Chapter 5.)

Q: *Do I need to liquidate the Living Trust assets in order to distribute the assets?*

A: No, liquidation of the Living Trust assets is not required. Preferably, the assets will be distributed directly to the heirs, rather than selling the assets and then distributing the resultant cash. For example, a real estate deed may be simply recorded in the name of one or more of the heirs (without their having to first sell the home or property). (See Chapter 7.)

PERCEIVED DISADVANTAGES

Q: *What are the disadvantages of a Living Trust?*

A: After more than eighteen years of working with the Living Trust, I have yet to find a disadvantage to a *well-drawn* Living Trust that is accompanied by a well-designed estate-planning program. All too frequently, however, I see Trusts that ultimately become nightmares. In fact, one of the primary objectives of writing this book is to help people identify the characteristics of a good Living Trust.

The following statements address what some people *perceive* to be disadvantages of a Living Trust. Bear in mind that a well-written Trust (along with a good estate-planning program) should overcome or prevent the perceived disadvantages from becoming real.

The Living Trust document may be poorly written. This book should help you to identify the difference between a poorly drawn Trust and a well-written Trust. A poorly drawn Trust can be particularly disastrous upon the death of a trustor (settlor). In contrast, a well-drawn Trust, which includes the provisions outlined in Chapter 7, has absolutely no disadvantages. Indeed, such a Trust literally identifies and provides for every possible contingency.

The client does not understand the Living Trust. Unfortunately, attorneys are not necessarily good communicators. Thus, even the best estate-planning attorney may create an outstanding document but fail to convey an adequate understanding of the Trust to a client.

The assets are not placed in the Living Trust. All too often, Trusts are well written, but the assets have not been recorded in the name of the Trust. Recognize that a Living Trust that is not funded by having assets placed in the name of the Trust is nothing more than a Testamentary Trust—which does not avoid the probate process. For a Living Trust to be truly effective, all of the assets must be recorded in the Trust. Any grant deeds or trust deeds should be redrawn and recorded in the name of your Trust. Letters of transfer should be provided to enable you to transfer all of your assets into your Trust. (See Chapter 12.)

The Living Trust failed to meet the client's needs. Even the best estate-planning attorney often fails to do an in-depth client financial analysis; therefore, even though the attorney may draw an outstanding Living Trust, the Trust may lack adequate provisions to cover the individual circumstances of the client. For example, a Trust drawn for an estate that exceeds $1.2 million might not include a C Trust, or a Trust drawn for a client who has substantial amounts of insurance might not provide an Insurance Trust (in addition to the basic Living Trust).

If you have read this book, particularly Chapter 14, you should be able to identify for yourself the type of Trust and provisions that *you* should have. You need not rely on the judgment of others; you are now the master of your own destiny.

It costs $500 to $1,000 to update the Living Trust. Death and taxes are inevitable—and just as inevitable is the knowledge that Congress will change the estate tax laws about every five years. It should be the responsibility of the person or firm who drew up your Living Trust to notify you of any appropriate tax changes that would benefit your situation. Further, it is the responsibility of the same individual or firm to organize the Trust in such a manner that the Trust can be quickly reviewed and economically updated when the need arises.

When you have a Living Trust drawn up, you have the right to be assured that you will be notified of any necessary updates to your Trust, that such updates will be reasonably priced, and to know, ahead of time, the cost of such updates. (See Chapter 16.)

A Living Trust can be expensive, ranging from $750 to $3,500 or more. With the sophisticated computer equipment now available, a good Living Trust can be made available to everyone and can be priced within a reasonable range. This area has been addressed directly in Chapter 16, which specifically identifies what a good Trust should cost when you utilize today's sophisticated computers.

Even though the Living Trust avoids probate, it is still quite costly to settle the estate. Most Living Trusts can be settled by the surviving spouse and/or heirs—without requiring the services of an attorney. Settling large estates may well require the services of an estate-planning attorney, but settling the average estate does *not* require the services of legal counsel. In fact, all too often, I either see attorneys charging unnecessary fees to "settle" an estate in a Living Trust or trying to settle an estate in a Living Trust when they do not have the slightest idea of what they are doing. (See Chapter 13.)

Financial institutions charge excessive fees for managing the assets in a Living Trust and generate very little return on investments. Although this situation is not always the case, it is certainly true that selecting a financial institution as your successor trustee is seldom a wise move. The ideal successor trustee(s) for your Living Trust should be your adult children, close family members, or close friends. For a more detailed description of who would best serve as the successor trustee, refer to Chapter 6.

Index

289